HOMOSEXUALITY:

A Selective Bibliography
of over 3,000 Items

by
WILLIAM PARKER

The Scarecrow Press, Inc.
Metuchen, N.J.   1971

HQ
76
.P37

ISBN 0-8108-0425-5

ongress Catalog Card Number 71-163430

72-5126

Femininity, Collier 07684; Parts III-V: Society and the
Sex Variant, Collier 09590.)

54)   Henry, George W.   Sex Variants: A Study of Homo-
      sexual Patterns.   New York: Hoeber, 1948.   1130 pp.

55)   Hesnard, Angelo.   Strange Lust: The Psychology of
      Homosexuality.   Translation by J.C. Summers.   New
      York: Amethnol Press, 1933.   256 pp.

56)   Hoffman, Martin.   The Gay World: Male Homosexuality
      and the Social Creation of Evil.   New York: Basic
      Books, 1968.   212 pp.   (Paperback--Bantam--Q4492)

57)   Holliday, Don.   Sex and the Single Gay.   San Diego:
      Corinth Publications, 1967.   (Paperback: Leisure Book
      LB1196.)   160 pp.

58)   Humphreys, Laud.   Tearoom Trade: Impersonal Sex in
      Public Places.   Chicago: Aldine Press, 1970.   180 pp.

59)   Hutton, Robert.   Of Those Alone.   London: Sidgwick
      and Jackson, 1958.   235 pp.   (An autobiography.)

59a) Hyde, H. Montgomery.   The Love that Dared Not
      Speak its Name: A Candid History of Homosexuality in
      Britain.   Boston: Little, Brown and Co., 1970. 323 pp.

60)   Hyde, H. Montgomery (ed.).   The Trials of Oscar
      Wilde.   London: W. Hodge, 1948.   Foreword by
      Travers Humphreys.   (American edition: The Three
      Trials of Oscar Wilde.   New York: University Books,
      1956.   384 pp.)

61)   James, Anthony.   America's Homosexual Underground.
      New York: L.S. Publications, 1965.   (Paperback:
      Imperial IMP 714.)   192 pp.

62)   Jersild, Jens.   Boy Prostitution.   Translation by
      Oscar Bojesen.   Copenhagen: G.E.C. Gad, 1956. 101 pp.

63)   Jersild, Jens.   The Normal Homosexual Male Versus
      the Boy Molester.   Copenhagen: Nyt Nordisk Forlag,
      1967.   112 pp.

64)   Jones, H. Kimball.   Toward a Christian Understanding
      of the Homosexual.   New York: Association Press, 1966.

45) Gerber, Israel J. Man on a Pendulum: A Case His-
     tory of an Invert. New York: American Press, 1955.
     320 pp.

46) Gide, André. Corydon. New York: Farrar, Straus,
     1950. Translation by Hugh Gibb. Commentary by
     Frank A. Beach. 220 pp. (Paperback--Noonday N211.)

46a) Gigeroff, Alex K. Sexual Deviations in the Criminal
     Law: Homosexual, Exhibitionistic, and Pedophilic Of-
     fenses in Canada. Toronto: University of Toronto
     Press, 1968. (218 pp.)

47) Goodman, Alexander. A Summer on Fire Island.
     Washington, D.C.: Guild Press, 1966. Paperback.
     119 pp.

48) Graham, James. The Homosexual Kings of England.
     London: Tandem, 1968. (Paperback: Tandem T177.)
     92 pp.

49) Gross, Alfred A. Strangers in our Midst: Problems
     of the Homosexual in American Society. Washington,
     D.C.: Public Affairs Press, 1962. 182 pp.

50) Hanson, Doris. Homosexuality: The International
     Disease. New York: L.S. Publications, 1965. (Paper-
     back: Imperial IMP 728.) 192 pp.

50a) Harper, James. Homo Laws in all 50 States. San
     Diego: Publishers Export Co., 1968. (Paperback:
     PEC Sp 22.) 208 pp.

51) Harris, Frank. Oscar Wilde, His Life and Confes-
     sions. Garden City, N.Y.: Garden City Publishing
     Co., 1930. 470 pp. (Paperback--Dell LX130.)

51a) Hatterer, Lawrence J. Changing Homosexuality in the
     Male: Treatment for Men Troubled by Homosexuality.
     New York: McGraw-Hill, 1970. 492 pp.

52) Hauser, Richard. The Homosexual Society. London:
     Bodley Head, 1962. 167 pp.

53) Henry, George W. All the Sexes: A Study of
     Masculinity and Femininity. New York: Rinehart, 1955.
     599 pp. (Paperback--Parts I-II: Masculinity and

Contents

Page

Foreword

In increasing numbers, distinguished as well as
ordinary homosexuals in every walk of life are openly de-
claring their sexual orientation and demanding that the cen-
turies old persecution and discrimination against them cease.
In the theatre, in the mass media, as well as in college
courses and demonstrations, homosexuality is being presented
in all of its diversified aspects as a social, scientific, legal,
moral and religious issue affecting the lives of millions of
citizens. In the courts and legislatures, antiquated laws are
being challenged and legislation is under discussion or al-
ready in effect which will, it is hoped, remove the legal
penalties for homosexual behavior which does not offend public decency or involve minors or the use of force.

The demand for knowledge concerning homosexuality
by mental health professionals, teachers, parents, legis-
lators, jurists, prison officials, the armed services and the
church (among others) is expressed in urgent terms. To
meet this demand, sociologists, psychologists, psychiatrists,
anthropologists, psychobiologists, lawyers, criminologists
and theologians are conducting research resulting in an increasing volume of publications. To keep abreast of the
literature on homosexuality in these diversified fields is im-
possible even for the researcher. It is, therefore, a very
timely and valuable project that Parker has undertaken in
bringing together this comprehensive bibliography on every
facet of homosexuality. It fills a long-felt need not only for
the research specialist but for interested laymen and professionals as well.

Dr. Evelyn Hooker
Former Research Psychologist,
Department of Psychology, UCLA
and Chairman (National Institutes of Mental
Health) Task Force on Homosexuality

Preface

Several years ago, in response to the question "What can I read on the subject of homosexuality?" I drew up a list of 50 books and articles and suggested, quite naively as it turned out, that a comprehensive bibliography would include as many as 500 titles. My original list of 50 items has grown to nearly 5,000--over 3,000 of which are included here. Though selective rather than all-inclusive, this bibliography on homosexuality is the most comprehensive yet assembled. Since homosexuality has now become a subject of wide public as well as professional interest and since the amount of material published has greatly increased in recent years, this bibliography should prove timely and useful for both the research specialist and the general reader.

All the significant writings on homosexuality which have appeared in English through 1969 are included. However, except where translated, materials written in foreign languages have been omitted. The researcher knows or can find them without much difficulty; others have little need for them. Until World War II most of the material on homosexuality was written in foreign languages. Since then, books and articles in English have far outnumbered the foreign language material. But in the last few years, foreign writers have sharply increased their publications on the subject.

As indicated in the Table of Contents, the items listed in this bibliography are arranged under fourteen different headings, depending upon the type of publication in which they appear. All important books and pamphlets on the subject, plus a few marginal ones, have been included. The lists of articles in religious, legal, medical, scientific, and other specialized journals are nearly complete. But because the standard and specialized guides to periodical literature do not index all published materials and are sometimes a year or more behind in some of their listings, a few articles, especially for 1968-69, have no doubt been missed. Only enough articles in popular magazines, newspapers, and homophile publications have been included to provide a sampling and to suggest that serious research on homosexuality must include some familiarity with them. Similarly, the section on literature is incomplete. In addition, such materials as letters to the editor, book reviews, and articles in pulp magazines have largely been omitted.

The titles of many items reveal the attitudes and methodology of their authors as well as the specific subject matter. When the dates of publication are also noted, one may in general observe not only an increasing particularization of subject matter and refinement of methodology but also an increasing degree of impartiality. Long regarded as a sickness, sin, or crime, homosexuality is now being approached more and more in terms of sexual preference, minority status, and personal rights. Where once only the works of medical specialists, criminologists, and moralists found their way into print, we now see sociologists, religious leaders, journalists, and homosexuals themselves writing on the subject. But unfortunately many writers are still careless in defining terms and examining premises, in researching their subject, and in drawing their conclusions.* Too many writings, even those of some "experts," are marred by ignorance, fear, bias, special pleading, sensationalism, conclusions not supported by the evidence, and a passion for passing judgment. In short, the reader must be most careful in evaluating what he reads on the subject of homosexuality.

Most of the research for this bibliography was done in the San Francisco area. In addition to the public library of San Francisco and the various libraries of the University of California in the Bay area, I found the special resources of the Mattachine Society, the Society for Individual Rights, and the Council on Religion and the Homosexual of great value.

W. P.

---

*I consider the following 135 entries, even though they are of unequal merit, the most significant or influential writings on the subject: 5, 6, 8, 9, 12, 14, 18, 24, 26-29, 32, 39, 43, 44, 49, 52-54, 56, 58, 64, 69, 72, 75, 77, 89, 96, 98, 101, 116, 118, 120, 122, 124, 127, 128, 147, 150-52, 157-59, 170, 171, 174, 181, 185, 187, 195, 197, 202, 204, 207, 208, 221, 266, 351, 367a, 376, 383, 385, 400, 422, 427, 440, 441, 467, 509, 534, 540, 563, 579, 595, 656, 657, 684, 710, 712, 830, 841, 844, 977, 1055, 1100, 1112, 1160, 1259, 1263, 1303, 1310, 1315, 1316, 1330, 1436, 1447, 1486, 1492, 1496, 1499, 1500, 1502, 1509, 1513, 1521, 1529, 1688, 1742, 1751, 1753, 1813, 1967, 2017, 2019, 2021, 2064, 2065, 2088, 2148, 2164, 2268, 2542, 2664, 2700, 2744, 2997, 3001, 3003, 3025, 3046 3060, 3077, and 3081.

Books

1) Ackerley, J. R. My Father and Myself. New York: Coward-McCann, 1968. 219 pp. (An autobiography.)

2) Allen, Clifford. Homosexuality: Its Nature, Causation and Treatment. London: Staples, 1958. 142 pp.

3) Anomaly. The Invert and his Social Adjustment. London: Balliere, Tindall and Cox, 1927. 160 pp. Enlarged edition--Baltimore: Williams and Wilkins, 1948. 289 pp.

4) Anonymous. The White Paper. New York: Macauley, 1958. Preface and illustrations by Jean Cocteau. 88 pp.

5) Asprey, Robert. The Panther's Feast. New York: Putnam, 1959. 317 pp. (Paperback--Bantam N4473) (A biography of Colonel Alfred V. Redl.)

6) Bailey, Derrick Sherwin. Homosexuality and the Western Christian Tradition. London: Longmans, Green, 1955. 181 pp.

7) Bailey, Derrick Sherwin (compiler and editor). Sexual Offenders and Social Punishment. Westminster: Church Information Board, 1956. 120 pp. (Report of the Moral Welfare Council of the Church of England.)

8) Becker, Raymond de. The Other Face of Love. Translation by Margaret Crosland and Alan Daventry. New York: Grove Press, 1969. 209 pp. (Paperback-- Sphere 28770.)

9) Benson, R. O. D. In Defense of Homosexuality. New York: Julian Press, 1965. 239 pp. (Reprinted in paperback--Ace Star 88055--as: What Every Homosexual Knows.)

10) Berg, Charles and Allen, Clifford. The Problem of

1

Homosexuality. New York: Citadel Press, 1958.
221 pp. (Paperback--Citadel C87.)

11)   Berg, Charles and Krich, Aaron M. (eds.). Homosexuality: A Subjective and Objective Investigation.
London: Allen and Unwin, 1958. 415 pp.

12)   Bergler, Edmund. Homosexuality: Disease or Way of
Life? New York: Hill and Wang, 1956. 302 pp.
(Paperback--Collier AS199X)

13)   Bergler, Edmund. One Thousand Homosexuals: Con-
spiracy of Silence or Curing and Deglamorizing Homosexuals? Patterson, N.J.: Pageant Books, 1959.
249 pp.

14)   Bieber, Irving and Associates. Homosexuality: A
Psychoanalytic Study of Male Homosexuals. New York:
Basic Books, 1962. 358 pp. (Paperback--Vintage
V291)

15)   Blake, Roger. The Homosexual Explosion. North
Hollywood, Calif.: Brandon House, 1966. (Paperback:
Brandon House 1959.) 188 pp.

16)   Branson, Helen P. Gay Bar. San Francisco: Pan-
Graphic Press, 1957. (Paperback.) 89 pp. Introduction by Blanche Baker.

17)   Buckley, Michael J. Morality and the Homosexual:
A Catholic Approach to a Moral Problem. Westminster,
Md.: Newman Press, 1959. 214 pp.

18)   Cappon, Daniel. Toward an Understanding of Homosexuality Englewood Cliffs, N.J.: Prentice-Hall, 1965.
302 pp.

19)   Caprio, Frank S. Female Homosexuality. New York:
Citadel Press, 1954. 334 pp. (Paperback--Black Cat
BC27.)

20)   Carpenter, Edward. The Intermediate Sex: A Study of
Some Transitional Types of Men and Women. London:
Allen and Unwin, 1908. 175 pp. (Reprinted in Cory,
no. 27 below, pp. 139-204.)

21)   Cavanagh, John. Counseling the Invert. Milwaukee:
Bruce, 1965. 306 pp.

22) Chesser, Eustace. Odd Man Out: Homosexuality in
Men and Women. London: Gallancz, 1959. 192 pp.
Foreword by Kenneth Walker.

23) Chideckel, Maurice. Female Sex Perversions: The
Sexually Aberrated Woman as She Is. New York:
Eugenics Publishing Co., 1938. 331 pp.

24) Churchill, Wainwright. Homosexual Behavior Among
Males: A Cross-Cultural and Cross-Species Investigation. New York: Hawthorn, 1967. 349 pp.

25) Cleckley, Hervey. The Caricature of Love: A Discussion of Social, Psychiatric, and Literary Manifestations of Pathologic Sexuality. New York: Ronald, 1957.
319 pp.

26) Cory, Donald W. The Homosexual in America: A Subjective Approach. New York: Greenberg, 1951. 326
pp. Introduction by Albert Ellis. (Paperback--Paper-
back Library 54-207) 2d edition--New York: Castle
Books, 1960. 334 pp. (Printed in England as The
Homosexual Outlook--London: Peter Nevill, 1953.)

27) Cory, Donald W. Homosexuality: A Cross-Cultural
Approach. New York: Julian Press, 1956. 440 pp.
(See nos. 20, 110, 318, 332, 404, 465, 476, 509, 570,
580, 1180, 1730, 1793, 2092, and 2809.)

28) Cory, Donald W. The Lesbian in America. New York:
Citadel Press, 1964. 288 pp. Introduction by Albert
Ellis. (Paperback--Macfadden 75-160.)

29) Cory, Donald W. and LeRoy, John P. The Homosexual and his Society: A View from Within. New
York: Citadel Press, 1963. 276 pp.

30) Crisp, Quentin. The Naked Civil Servant. London:
Jonathan Cape, 1968. 217 pp. (An autobiography.)

31) Croft-Cooke, Rupert. Bosie: The Story of Lord Alfred
Douglas, His Friends and His Enemies. London:
W.H. Allen, 1963. 414 pp.

32) Croft-Cooke, Rupert. The Verdict of You All. London:
Warburg, 1955. 254 pp. (An autobiography.)

33) Cutler, Marvin (compiler and editor). Homosexuals
    Today: A Handbook of Organizations and Publications.
    Los Angeles: One, Inc., 1956. 188 pp.

34) Davidson, David. Male Deviates and Their Partners.
    New York: Dalhousie Press, 1967. (Paperback.)
    127 pp.

34a) Davidson, Michael. The World, the Flesh, and
    Myself. London: Arthur Barker, Ltd. 1962. 354 pp.
    (An autobiography.)

35) DeSavitsch, Eugene. Homosexuality, Transvestism,
    and Change of Sex. London: Heinemann, 1958. 120
    pp.

36) Dorian, Lee. The Anatomy of a Homosexual. New
    York: L.S. Publications, 1965. (Paperback: Imperial
    IMP 718.) 192 pp.

37) Dorian, Lee. The Young Homosexual. New York:
    L.S. Publications, 1965. (Paperback: Imperial IMP
    730.) 191 pp.

38) Eglinton, J.Z. Greek Love. New York: Layton Press,
    1964. 504 pp.

39) Ellis, Albert. Homosexuality: Its Causes and Cure.
    New York: Lyle Stuart, 1965. 288 pp.

40) Ellis, Havelock. Sexual Inversion (part IV of Volume
    I of Studies in the Psychology of Sex). New York:
    Random House, 1936. 391 pp.

41) Foster, Jeanette H. Sex Variant Women in Literature:
    A Historical and Quantitative Survey. London:
    Frederick Muller, 1958. 412 pp.

42) Freud, Sigmund. Leonardo da Vinci: A Psychological
    Study of an Infantile Reminiscence. New York: Dodd
    Mead, 1932. 130 pp. (Paperback--Vintage V132.)

43) Garde, Noel I. Jonathan to Gide: The Homosexual in
    History. New York: Vantage Press, 1964. 751 pp.

44) Gerassi, John. The Boys of Boise: Furor, Vice, and
    Folly in an American City. New York: Macmillan,
    1966. 328 pp. (Paperback--Collier 07341.)

Introduction by William H. Genne. (Paperback--SCM
Press.) 160 pp.

65) Kahn, Samuel. Mentality and Homosexuality. Boston:
     Meador, 1937. 249 pp.

66) Karlson, Eric. The Homosexual Uprising. Book I:
     Man, Book II: Women. 2 vols. San Diego: Green-
     leaf Classics, 1967. (Paperback: Adult Book AB 401
     and 402.) 159 and 160 pp.

67) Kayy, W. H. The Gay Geniuses: Psychiatric and
     Literary Studies of Famous Homosexuals. Glendale,
     Calif.: Marvin Miller, 1965. (Paperback.) 223 pp.

68) Konraad, William. Someone You May Know: A
     Heterosexual Looks at Homosexuality. Beverly Hills,
     Calif.: Book Company of America, 1965. (Paper-
     back: 13-011.) 256 pp.

69) Krich, Aaron M. (ed.). The Homosexuals: As Seen
     by Themselves and Thirty Authorities. New York:
     Citadel Press, 1954. (Paperback.) 346 pp. (See
     below, nos. 357, 367, 373, 374, 379, 404, 419, 431,
     437, 466, 471, 555, 580, 1617, 1664, 1887, 1945, 1974,
     2418, 2498, 2542, and 2631.)

70) Leslie, Robert. Casebook Homophile. New York:
     Dalhousie Press, 1966. (Paperback.) 128 pp.

71) Lind, Earl (pseud.) Autobiography of an Androgyne.
     New York: Medico-Legal Journal Press, 1918. 265 pp.

72) Magee, Bryan. One in Twenty: A Study of Homo-
     sexuality in Men and Women. New York: Stein and
     Day, 1966. 192 pp.

73) Marlowe, Kenneth. The Male Homosexual. Los
     Angeles: Sherbourne Press, 1965. 158 pp.

74) Marlowe, Kenneth. Mr. Madam: Confessions of a
     Male Madam. Los Angeles: Sherbourne Press, 1964.
     Introduction by Leonard A. Lowag. 246 pp. (Paper-
     back--Paperback Library 55-857.)

75) Marmor, Judd (ed.). Sexual Inversion: The Multiple
     Roots of Homosexuality. New York: Basic Books,

1965.   358 pp.   (See below, nos. 300, 345, 370, 426,
478, 485, 502, 504, 505, 508, 525, 536, 557, 561, 562, 583,
and 2359.)

76)   Martin, Harold.   Men and Cupid: A Reassessment of
Homosexuality and of Man's Sexual Life in General.
London: Fortune Press, 1965.   159 pp.

77)   Masters, R. E. L.   The Homosexual Revolution: A
Challenging Exposé of the Social and Political Directions of a Minority Group.   New York: Julian Press,
1962.   230 pp.   (Paperback--Belmont 95-102.)

78)   Matthews, Arthur G.   Is Homosexuality A Menace?
New York: McBride, 1957.   302 pp.

79)   Mercer, Jessie D.   They Walk in Shadow: A Study of
Sexual Variation with Emphasis on the Ambisexual and
Homosexual Components and Our Contemporary Sex
Laws.   New York: Comet Press, 1959.   573 pp.

80)   Mitchell, Roger S.   The Homosexual and the Law:
The Special Legal Problems Facing the Homosexual
in Our Society.   New York: Arco Publishing Co. ,
1969.   96 pp.

81)   Moll, Albert.   Perversions of the Sex Instinct: A
Study of Sexual Inversion.   Translation by Maurice
Popkin.   Newark: Julian Press, 1931.   237 pp.

82)   Morse, Benjamin.   The Homosexual.   Derby, Conn.:
Monarch Books, 1962.   (Paperback: MB527.)   158 pp.

83)   Morse, Benjamin.   The Lesbian.   Derby, Conn.:
Monarch Books, 1961.   (Paperback: MB513.)   142 pp.

84)   Ollendorf, Robert H. V.   The Juvenile Homosexual
Experience and Its Effect on Adult Sexuality.   New
York: Julian Press, 1966.   245 pp.

84a)   Ovesey, Lionel.   Homosexuality and Pseudo-Homosexuality.   New York: Science House, 1969.   157 pp.

85)   Parke, Joseph R.   Human Sexuality: A Medico-Legal
Treatise... with Especial Reference to Contrary Sexual
Desire.   Philadelphia: Professional Publishing Co. ,
1906.   476 pp.

85a) Pittenger, Norman. Time for Consent. London: Stu-
     dent Christian Movement Press, 1970. 124 pp. (See
     no. 196 below.)

86) Plummer, Douglas. Queer People: The Truth about
     Homosexuals. London: W. H. Allen, 1963. 122 pp.
     American edition--New York: Citadel Press, 1965,
     with introduction by Donald W. Cory. (Paperback--
     Compact C8.)

87) Potter, LaForest. Strange Loves: A Study in Sexual
     Abnormalities. New York: Padell Book Co., 1933.
     227 pp.

88) Quill, Zachary. Homosexuality Through the Ages.
     Los Angeles: Wiz Books, 1969. (Paperback: Wiz
     102.) 241 pp.

89) Rees, J. Tudor and Usill, Harley V. (eds.). They
     Stand Apart: A Critical Survey of the Problems of
     Homosexuality. London: Heinemann, 1955. 220 pp.
     (See below, nos. 265, 275, 284, 364, 401, 405, 501, and
     518.)

90) Robertiello, Richard C. Voyage From Lesbos: The
     Psychoanalysis of a Female Homosexual. New York:
     Citadel Press, 1959. 233 pp.

91) Roberts, Aymer. Forbidden Freedom. London:
     Linden Press, 1960. 112 pp.

92) Roberts, Aymer. Judge Not: The Problem of Man's
     Nature and the Law. London: Linden Press, 1957.
     195 pp. (An Autobiography.)

93) Rubin Isadore (ed.). Homosexuals Today. New York:
     Health Publications, 1965. (Paperback.) 112 pp.
     (Reprint of 21 articles and 8 notes from Sexology,
     slightly revised from the 1961 edition listed next be-
     low.)

94) Rubin, Isadore (ed.). The Third Sex. New York:
     New Book Co., 1961. (Paperback.) 112 pp. (See
     preceding entry.)

95) Ruitenbeek, Hendrik M. (ed.). Homosexuality and
     Creative Genius. New York: Obolensky, 1967. 349 pp.

(Reprint of 16 articles, see below, nos. 270, 272, 309, 342, 383, 491, 560, 1691, 1744, 1807, 1940, 2338, 2339, 2704, and 2765.)

96)   Ruitenbeek, Hendrik M. (ed.). The Problem of Homosexuality in Modern Society. New York: Dutton, 1963. 304 pp. (Paperback--Dutton D127) (See below, nos. 227, 291, 367, 434, 467, 516, 531, 532, 992, 1762, 1789, 1856, 2017, 2297, 2542, 2707, and 2728.)

97)   Sartre, Jean-Paul. Saint Genet: Actor and Martyr. Translation by Bernard Frechtman. New York: George Braziller, 1963. 625 pp. (Paperback--Mentor MY595.)

98)   Schofield, Michael. Sociological Aspects of Homosexuality. London: Longmans, 1965. 244 pp.

99)   Schrenk-Notzing, Albert P. F. von. Therapeutic Suggestion in Psychopathia Sexualis with Especial Reference to Contrary Sexual Instincts. Philadelphia: Davis, 1895.

100) Sinistrari, Friar Ludovico M. Peccatum Mutum (The Mute Sin) Alias Sodomy. New York: Collection "Le Ballet des Muses," 1958. Introduction by Montague Sommers. (Paperback.)   89 pp.

101) Socarides, Charles W. The Overt Homosexual. New York: Grune and Stratton, 1968. 245 pp.

102) Sprague, W. D. The Lesbian in Our Society. New York: Midwood, 1962.

103) Stearn, Jess. The Grapevine. Garden City, N. Y.: Doubleday, 1964. 372 pp. (Paperback--Macfadden MB95-107.)

104) Stearn, Jess. The Sixth Man. Garden City, N. Y.: Doubleday, 1961. 281 pp. (Paperback--Macfadden MB60-106.)

105) Steiner, Lucius B. Sex Behavior of the Homosexual. Hollywood, Cal.: Genell Corp., 1964. (Paperback: Viceroy VP114.)   160 pp.

106) Stekel, Wilhelm. Bisexual Love. Translation by

James S. VanTeslaar. New York: Emerson Books,
1946. 359 pp.

107) Stekel, Wilhelm. The Homosexual Neurosis. Translation by James S. VanTeslaar. New York: Emerson Books, 1950. 322 pp.

108) Sterling, D. L. Sex in Basic Personality. Wichita,
Kans.: Hubbard Dianetic Foundation, 1952. 180 pp.

109) Sutherland, Alistair and Anderson, Patrick (eds.).
Eros: An Anthology of Male Friendship. New York:
Citadel Press, 1963. 433 pp.

110) Symonds, John A. Studies in Sexual Inversion Em-
bodying: "A Study of Greek Ethics" and "A Study
in Modern Ethics." New York: Medical Press,
1964. (Paperback.) 119 pp. (Originally privately
printed in 1896 and 1901.) ("A Study in Modern
Ethics" is reprinted in Cory, no. 27 above, pp. 3-
100.)

111) Tarnowsky, Benjamin. Anthropological, Legal and
Medical Studies on Pederasty in Europe. North
Hollywood, Calif.: Brandon House, 1967. (Paper-
back: Brandon 2015.) 233 pp.

112) Tobin, William J. Homosexuality and Marriage.
Rome: Catholic Book Agency, 1964. 378 pp.

113) Vedder, Clyde B. and King, Patricia G. Problems
of Homosexuality in Corrections. Springfield, Ill.:
Thomas, 1967. 63 pp.

114) Wade, Carlson. Male Homosexuality--Case Studies.
New York: L. S. Publications, 1965. (Paperback:
Imperial IMP 713.) 192 pp.

115) Wade, Carlson. The Twilight Sex. New York:
L. S. Publications, 1964. (Paperback: Gaslight
129.) 192 pp.

116) Weltge, Ralph W. (ed.). The Same Sex: An Ap-
praisal of Homosexuality. Philadelphia: Pilgrim
Press, 1969. (Paperback.) 164 pp. (See below,
nos. 322, 389, 397, 422, 433, 474, 512, 542, 546, 577, and
2744.)

117) West, Donald J. Homosexuality. London: Duck-
      worth, 1960. (Paperback: Pelican A477.) 200 pp.
      (Revision of no. 119 below.)

118) West, Donald J. Homosexuality. Chicago: Aldine
      Publishing Co., 1968. 304 pp. (Revision of the
      preceding entry.)

119) West, Donald J. The Other Man: A Study of the
      Social, Legal and Clinical Aspects of Homosexuality.
      New York: Whiteside and Morrow, 1955. Fore-
      word by Alfred A. Gross. 224 pp. (See no. 117
      above.)

120) Westwood, Gordon. A Minority: A Report on the
      Life of the Male Homosexual in Great Britain. Lon-
      don: Longmans, 1960. 216 pp.

121) Westwood, Gordon. Society and the Homosexual.
      New York: Dutton, 1953. 191 pp.

122) Wildeblood, Peter. Against the Law. London:
      Weidenfeld and Nicolson, 1955. (Paperback--Pen-
      guin 1188.) 189 pp. (An autobiography.)

123) Wildeblood, Peter. A Way of Life. London: Wei-
      denfeld and Nicolson, 1956. 191 pp.

124) Willis, Stanley E. Understanding and Counseling the
      Male Homosexual. Boston: Little, Brown and Co.,
      1967. Foreword by Charles W. Wahl. 225 pp.

125) Winski, Norman. The Homosexual Explosion. North
      Hollywood, Calif.: Challenge Publications, 1966.
      (Paperback: Viceroy VP201.) 160 pp.

126) Winski, Norman. The Homosexual Revolt. Canoga
      Park, Calif.: Viceroy Books, 1967. (Paperback:
      Viceroy VP267.) 160 pp.

127) Wolfenden, John and Others. Report of the Com-
      mittee on Homosexual Offenses and Prostitution.
      London: Her Majesty's Stationery Office, 1957.
      American edition--New York: Stein and Day, 1963.
      Introduction by Karl Menninger. 243 pp. (Paper-
      back--Lancer 74-849.)

128) Wood, Robert W. Christ and the Homosexual. New York: Vantage Press, 1960. Introduction by Albert Ellis. 221 pp.

129) Worthy, Ken. The Homosexual Generation. New York: L. S. Publications, 1965. (Paperback: Imperial IMP 735.) 192 pp.

130) Worthy, Ken. The "New" Homosexual Revolution. New York: L. S. Publications, 1965. (Paperback: Imperial IMP 727.) 192 pp.

131) Worthy, Ken. Sexual Deviation and the Law. New York: L. S. Publications, 1965. (Paperback: Imperial IMP 715.) 192 pp.

132) Wyden, Peter and Barbara. Growing Up Straight: What Every Thoughtful Parent Should Know About Homosexuality. New York: Stein and Day, 1968. Introduction by Stanley F. Yolles. 256 pp.

133) Yankowski, John S. and Wolff, Herman K. The Tortured Sex. Los Angeles: Holloway House, 1965. (Paperback: Holloway House HH113.) 224 pp.

Pamphlets and Documents

134) Albany Trust. Some Questions and Answers About Homosexuality. 2d ed. London: Albany Trust, 1965.

135) American Civil Liberties Union. Official Statement. Jan. 7, 1957.

136) American Civil Liberties Union. Official Statement. Aug. 31, 1967.

137) American Civil Liberties Union of Southern California. Official Statement. Dec. 4, 1965.

138) American Law Institute. Model Penal Code: Proposed Official Draft. Philadelphia: American Law Institute, 1962. Sections 213.2 and 251.3.

138a) American Psychiatric Association, Committee on Nomenclature and Statistics. Diagnostic and Statistical Manual on Mental Disorders. 2d ed. Washington, D.C.: American Psychiatric Association, 1968. Section 3: "Definition of Terms," sub-section V: "Personality Disorders and Certain Other Non-Psychotic Mental Disorders," paragraph 302.0: "Sexual Deviation: Homosexuality." (Classification of homosexuality as illness.)

139) Amicus Curiae Brief. Boutilier v. Immigration and Naturalization Service. Philadelphia: Homosexual Law Reform Society, 1967. 96 pp.

140) Anonymous. Guild Dictionary of Homosexual Terms. Washington, D.C.: Guild Press, 1965. Introduction by Albert Ellis. 51 pp.

141) Anonymous and Ayer, A.J. Every Tenth Man. San Francisco: Mattachine Society, 1960. 31 pp. (Reprint of nos. 726, 2009, and 2192 below.)

142)   Army Medical Library. Bibliography of Homo-
         sexuality. Washington, D. C.: U. S. Army, 1942.
         (Microfilm.)

143)   British Medical Association. Homosexuality and
         Prostitution: A Memorandum of Evidence ... For
         ... The Departmental Committee .... London: Brit-
         ish Medical Association, 1955. 94 pp. (Reprinted
         in British Medical Journal Supplement, 2:165-70,
         1955, see below, no. 2008.)

144)   Code of Justinian. Corpus Juris Civilis: Novellae.
         Berlin: Weidmann, 1954. Edited by Rudolf Schoell
         and William Kroll. (Novel no. 77.)

145)   Code of Theodosius. The Theodosian Code and
         Novels. Princeton: Princeton University, 1952.
         Translation by Clyde Pharr. (Sections 9. 7. 3 and
         9. 7. 6.)

146)   Council on Religion and the Homosexual. A Brief
         of Injustices: An Indictment of Our Society in its
         Treatment of the Homosexual. San Francisco:
         C. R. H., 1965. 12 pp.

147)   Council on Religion and the Homosexual. Church-
         men Speak Out on Homosexual Law Reform. San
         Francisco: C. R. H., 1967. 10 pp.

148)   Council on Religion and the Homosexual. Consulta-
         tion on Theology and the Homosexual. San Francis-
         co: C. R. H., 1967. (5 papers, mimeographed)
         107 pp.

149)   Council on Religion and the Homosexual. CRH:
         1964-68 The Council on Religion and the Homosexual.
         San Francisco: C. R. H., 1968. 16 pp.

150)   Council on Religion and the Homosexual and others.
         The Challenge and Progress of Homosexual Law Re-
         form. San Francisco: C. R. H. and others, 1968.
         72 pp.

151)   Council on Religion and the Homosexual and others.
         Homosexuals and Employment. San Francisco:
         C. R. H. and others, 1970. 32 pp.

152)   Crompton, Louis. Homosexuals and the Sickness
        Theory. London: Albany Trust, 1969. 12 pp.

153)   Dean, Roger. Gay. San Francisco: Teen Chal-
        lenge, 1966. 12 pp. (Reprinted in Mattachine Re-
        view, 12:22-26, July 1966.)

154)   Devlin, Patrick. The Enforcement of Morals. Lon-
        don: Oxford, 1959. 25 pp. (Reprinted in Pro-
        ceedings of the British Academy, 45:129-51, 1959.)

155)   Draft Help. Homosexuality: The Draft and the
        Armed Forces. San Francisco: Draft Help, 1969.
        6 pp. (Mimeographed.)

156)   East Coast Homophile Organizations. Homosexuality:
        Civil Liberties and Social Rights. New York:
        E. C. H. O., 1965. (Transcript of addresses de-
        livered at E. C. H. O. Conference in Washington, D. C.,
        Oct. 9-11, 1964.) 82 pp.

157)   Elliott, Richard H. Enforcement of Laws Directed
        at Homosexuals: A Typical Metropolitan Approach.
        (Research paper, University of Pennsylvania Law
        School Library, 1961.) (Reprinted in Drum, no. 26,
        pp. 10-13, 26-28, Sep. 1967.)

158)   Florida Legislative Investigation Committee. Homo-
        sexuality and Citizenship in Florida. Tallahassee:
        Florida Legislature, 1964. 48 pp.

159)   Fonzi, Gaeton J. The Furtive Fraternity. San
        Francisco: Pan-Graphic Press, 1963. 28 pp. (Re-
        print of article in The Greater Philadelphia Maga-
        zine, Dec. 1962.)

160)   Fritze, Herbert P. Toward an Understanding of
        Homosexuality. St. Louis, 1965. 44 pp. (Mimeo-
        graphed.)

161)   Fry, C. C. and Rostow, E. C. Interim Report.
        Washington, D. C.: National Research Council,
        O. E. M., cmr. 337, Apr. 1945.

162)   Fuller, Norman. The Use of Closed Circuit TV for
        the Study and Elimination of Homosexual Activity in
        the YMCA. Philadelphia: Y. M. C. A., 1961.

163)   Garde, Noel I.   The Homosexual in Literature: A
       Chronological Bibliography Circa 700 B.C. - 1958.
       New York: Village Press, 1959.   32 pp.

164)   Glover, Edward.   The Problem of Homosexuality.
       London: Institute for the Scientific Treatment of
       Delinquency, 1957.   40 pp.

165)   Glover, Edward.   Social and Legal Aspects of Sexual
       Abnormality.   London: Institute for the Scientific
       Treatment of Delinquency, 1946.   16 pp.

166)   Greater Philadelphia Council of Churches.   Consul-
       tation on the Church and Homosexuality.   Philadel-
       phia: G. P. C. C., 1965.   (6 papers, mimeographed.)
       34 pp.

167)   Grey, Antony.   Christian Society and the Homosexual.
       "Faith and Freedom" Pamphlet No. 56.   Oxford:
       Manchester College, 1966.

168)   Gross, Alfred A.   The Church's Mission to the
       Sexually Deviated.   New York: George W. Henry
       Foundation, 1966.   23 pp.   (Mimeographed.)

169)   Gross, Alfred A.   Is Homosexuality a Minority
       Problem?   New York: George W. Henry Founda-
       tion, 1963.

170)   Group for the Advancement of Psychiatry.   Report
       on Homosexuality with Particular Emphasis on this
       Problem in Governmental Agencies.   Report No. 30.
       Topeka, Kans.:   G. A. P., 1955.   7 pp.

171)   Gunnison, Foster.   An Introduction to the Homophile
       Movement.   Hartford, Conn.:   Institute of Social
       Ethics, 1967.   37 pp.

172)   Hamilton, Gilbert and Legman, Gershon.   On the
       Cause of Homosexuality: Two Essays ("Homosexuals
       and Their Mothers" and "Fathers and Sons").   New
       York: Friends of the Oscar Wilde Society, 1940.
       31 pp.

173)   Harding, Carl B.   Education Handbook: Individual
       and Group Projects and Organizational Techniques.
       San Francisco: Mattachine Society, 1954.   64 pp.

18   Homosexuality

174)   Heron, Alastair (ed.). Towards a Quaker View of
        Sex. London: Friends Home Service Committee,
        1963. 75 pp. Revised edition, 1964.

175)   Hooker, Evelyn. The Male Homosexual. Veneral
        Disease Control Informational Report No. 8. Sacra-
        mento: California State Health Department, 1964.
        6 pp.

176)   Hooker, Evelyn. Male Homosexual Life Styles and
        Venereal Disease. Washington, D. C.: Department
        of Health, Education, and Welfare, 1961.

177)   Humphreys, Laud. They Meet in Tearooms: A
        Preliminary Study of Participants in Homosexual
        Encounters. 18 pp. (Mimeographed paper, 1967.)

178)   Janus Society of America. Homosexuals and the
        Armed Forces--A Moral Dilemma. Philadelphia:
        J. S. A., n. d. 6 pp.

179)   Joint Committee on Homosexuality. Report of the
        Diocesan Committee on Homosexuality. San Fran-
        cisco: Episcopal Diocese of California, 1966.
        19 pp.

180)   Kane, John J. Understanding Homosexuality. Chi-
        cago: Claretian Publications, 1966. 30 pp. (Re-
        printed in U. S. Catholic, see no. 1189 below.)

181)   Katz, Sidney. The Homosexual Next Door. San
        Francisco: Pan-Graphic Press, 1964. 25 pp. (Re-
        print of two articles from MacLean's Magazine, see
        nos. 868 and 869 below.)

182)   KPFA-FM. The Homosexual in Our Society. San
        Francisco: Pan-Graphic Press, 1959. 40 pp.
        (Transcript of radio broadcast, Nov. 24, 1958.)

183)   Kuhn, Donald. The Church and the Homosexual: A
        Report on a Consultation. San Francisco: Council
        on Religion and the Homosexual, 1965. 38 pp.

184)   Los Angeles Police Department. Some Character-
        istics of the Homosexual. Los Angeles: L. A. Po-
        lice Department, 1963. 7 pp. (Typewritten paper.)

185)   Lucas, Donald S. (ed.). The Homosexual and
       the Church. San Francisco: Mattachine Society,
       1966. 50 pp.

186)   Mattachine Society of Washington. Discrimination
       Against the Employment of Homosexuals. Washing-
       ton, D.C.: Mattachine Society, 1963. 8 pp.
       (Mimeographed.)

187)   Mattachine Society of Washington. Federal Employ-
       ment of Homosexual American Citizens. Washington,
       D.C.: Mattachine Society, 1965. 17 pp. (Mimeo-
       graphed.)

188)   Meek, Oscar. A New Selected Bibliography of
       Homosexuality. Santa Fe, N. Mex.: New Mexico
       Research Library of the Southwest, 1969. 34 pp.

189)   Monroe, R. L. Male Transvestism and Male Homo-
       sexuality. Harvard: Laboratory of Human Develop-
       ment, 1961. (Mimeographed.)

190)   National Capital Area Civil Liberties Union. Offi-
       cial Statement. Aug. 7, 1964.

191)   National Educational Television. The Rejected.
       Written by John W. Reavis, Jr. San Francisco:
       Pan-Graphic Press, 1961. 26 pp. (Transcript of
       TV documentary.) (See below, no. 3185.)

192)   New Zealand Homosexual Law Reform Society.
       Fifty Questions and Answers About Homosexuality
       and the Law. Wellington, N. Z.: H. L. R. S., 1968.
       12 pp.

193)   Norton, H. The Third Sex. Portland, Ore.: Facts
       Publishing Co., 1949.

194)   Parker, William Homosexuality: Selected Abstracts
       and Bibliography. San Francisco: Society for In-
       dividual Rights, 1966. 107 pp. (Mimeographed.)

195)   Petitioner's Brief. Boutilier v. Immigration and
       Naturalization Service. Washington, D.C.: Homo-
       sexual Law Reform Society, 1966. 51 pp.

196)   Pittenger, Norman. Time for Consent? A Christian's

Approach to Homosexuality. London: S. C. M. Press, 1967. 64 pp. (For revised edition, see no. 85a above.)

197)   Roman Catholic Church in England. Report of the Roman Catholic Advisory Committee on Prostitution and Homosexual Offences and the Existing Law. London, 1956. 6 pp. (Reprinted in Dublin Review, no. 1187 below.)

198)   Ross, Kenneth H. Letter to a Homosexual. Cincinnati: Forward Movement, 1955. 12 pp.

199)   Rubin, Isadore. Homosexuality [A Study Guide]. New York: Sex Information and Education Council of the U.S., 1965. 8 pp.

199a) Selective Service Law Reporter. Practice Manual. October, 1968. Section 1052. (Exclusion of homosexuals from military service--Class I-Y.)

200)   Shackleton, Edward R. Religion and the Law. Ridbeugh, Kilbirnie, Ayreshire: E. R. Shackleton, 1966. 48 pp.

201)   Simon, C. Homosexuals and Sex Crimes. International Association of Chiefs of Police, 1947. 8 pp.

202)   Society for Individual Rights. The Armed Services and Homosexuality. San Francisco: S. I. R., 1968. 12 pp.

203)   Society for Individual Rights. If You are in the Service. San Francisco: S. I. R., 1969. 6 pp.

204)   Society for Individual Rights. The Military Discharge and Employment Experiences of 47 Homosexuals. San Francisco: S. I. R., 1969. 9 pp. (Mimeographed.)

205)   Society for Individual Rights. What Should I Do About the Draft? San Francisco: S. I. R., 1968. 6 pp.

205a) Thorp, Charles P. What It's Like to be a Teenage Homosexual. Hollywood, Calif.: The Prosperos, 1969. 9 pp.

206)   Treese, Robert L. Homosexuality: A Contemporary
       View of the Biblical Perspective. San Francisco:
       Council on Religion and the Homosexual, 1966. 37
       pp.

207)   United Church of Christ, Council for Social Action.
       Civil Liberties and Homosexuality: An Issue in
       Christian Responsibility. Lebanon, Pa.: U.C.C.,
       1967. 48 pp. (Dec. 1967 issue of Social Action--
       see below nos. 1197, 1199, and 1251.)

208)   United Presbyterian Church in the U.S.A. Office
       of Church and Society of the Board of Christian
       Education. What About Homosexuality? Lancaster,
       Pa.: U. P. C., 1967. 48 pp. (Nov.-Dec. 1967
       issue of Social Progress--see below, nos. 749, 1201,
       1215, 1219, 1246, and 2277.)

209)   U. S. Civil Service Commission. Letter of John C.
       Macy, Jr., Chairman of the Civil Service Commis-
       sion, to the Mattachine Society of Washington, dated
       Feb. 25, 1966. (Reprinted in Mattachine Review,
       12:27-30, July 1966.)

210)   U. S. Code. Title 8, Section 1182(a)(4)--Public
       Law 89-236, Sections 10 and 15 (79 Statutes 917,
       919), Oct. 3, 1965. (Exclusion of aliens suffering
       from psychopathic personality, sexual deviation, or
       mental defect.)

211)   U. S. Code of Federal Regulations. Title 5, Ad-
       ministrative Personnel, section 731.201. 1968.
       (Exclusion of persons involved in "criminal, in-
       famous, dishonest, immoral, or notoriously disgrace-
       ful conduct.")

212)   U. S. Code of Federal Regulations. Title 38, Veter-
       ans' Benefits, section 3.12(d)(5). 1969. (Exclusion
       of homosexuals from veterans' benefits.)

213)   U. S. Congress: House of Representatives. Hearings
       Before Subcommittee No. 4 of the Committee on the
       District of Columbia on H. R. 5990. Aug. 8-9,
       1963 and Jan. 10, 1964. 147 pp. (A bill to revoke
       a permit to solicit funds issued to the Mattachine
       Society of Washington.)

214)   U. S. Congress: Senate. Committee on Expenditures
       in the Executive Departments--Subcommittee on In-
       vestigations. Interim Report: Employment of Homo-
       sexuals and Other Sex Perverts in Government.
       Senate Document No. 241, Dec. 1950. 26 pp.

215)   U. S. Congress: Senate. Committee on the Judiciary--
       Subcommittee on Administrative Practice and Proce-
       dure. Hearings on Invasions of Privacy. Feb. 1965-
       Sep. 1966, at pp. 66, 68, 77, 108, 320, 332, 535-36, 544.

216)   U. S. Congress: Senate. Committee on the Judiciary--
       Subcommittee on Constitutional Rights. Hearings on
       Protecting Privacy and the Rights of Federal Employ-
       ees. Sep.-Oct. 1966, at pp. 120, 161, 203-04, 601,
       603, 712-16.

217)   U. S. Congress: Senate. Committee on Post Offices
       and the Civil Service--Subcommittee to Investigate
       the Administration of the Federal Employees' Security
       Program. Hearings on the Administration of the
       Federal Employees' Security Program. Nov. 1955-
       Jan. 1956, at pp. 657, 726-32.

218)   U. S. Department of the Air Force. Air Force
       Manual 39-12: Separation for Unsuitability, Mis-
       conduct, Resignation, or Request for Discharge for
       the Good of the Service. Sep. 1, 1966. (See pp.
       2-3, 9-32, 52, 54-64, and 57-100 for discharge of
       homosexuals.)

219)   U. S. Department of the Air Force. Air Force
       Regulation 35-66: Discharge Processing Where
       Homosexual Acts or Tendencies are Involved. Mar.
       17, 1959. Changes dated Nov. 17, 1960 and July
       19, 1963. 21 pp.

219a) U. S. Department of the Army. Army Regulation
       40-501: Medical Service, Standards of Fitness.
       Dec. 1960. Chap. 2, sec. 16, sub-sec. 34a(2) and
       Chap. 6, sec. 16, sub-sec. 32a(2). (Exclusion of
       homosexuals from military service.)

220)   U. S. Department of the Army. Army Regulation
       635-89; Personnel Separations--Homosexuality,
       July 15, 1966. 16 pp.

220a)   U. S. Department of the Army.   Army Regulation
        635-100:   Personnel Separations: Officer Personnel.
        19 Feb. 1966.   Change 4 dated 21 Jan. 1970.   21 pp.

220b)   U. S. Department of the Army.   Army Regulation
        635-212:   Personnel Separations: Discharge: Unfit-
        ness and Unsuitability.   15 July 1966.   Change 8
        dated 21 Jan. 1970.   18 pp.

220c)   U. S. Department of Defense.   Directive No. 5220. 6:
        Industrial Personnel Access Authorization and Review
        Program.   Dec. 7, 1966.   Sections V, E and VI, N,
        P, and S.

221)   U. S. Department of Health, Education, and Welfare.
        National Institute of Mental Health.   Final Report of
        the Task Force on Homosexuality ("The Hooker Re-
        port").   Oct. 1969.   21 pp.

222)   U. S. Department of the Navy.   Bureau of Naval
        Personnel Manual--Part C-10311:   Discharge of En-
        listed Personnel by Reason of Unfitness.   3 pp.

223)   U. S. Department of the Navy.   Secretary of Navy
        Instruction 1900. 9:   Policies and Procedures for the
        Separation of Members of the Naval Service by
        Reason of Homosexuality.   Apr. 20, 1964.   5 pp.

224)   U. S. Equal Employment Opportunity Commission.
        Digest of Legal Interpretations Issued or Adopted by
        the Commission.   1967.   (See General Counsel
        Opinion M-108,   Feb. 10, 1966 for exclusion of
        homosexuals.)

225)   U. S. Office of the President.   Executive Order
        10450:   The Federal Security System.   Apr. 27,
        1953.   18 Federal Register 2489.   (Reprinted in
        Bulletin of Atomic Scientists, 11:156-58, 1955.)

225a)   U. S. Office of the President.   Executive Order
        10865:   Safeguarding Classified Information Within
        Industry.   Feb. 20, 1960.   3 Code of Federal
        Regulations 398.

226)   Utley, Thomas E.   What Laws May Cure: A New
        Examination of Morals and the Law.   London: Con-
        servative Political Center, 1968.   15 pp.

227)   Van den Haag, Ernest.   The Social Setting of Homo-
       sexuality.   San Francisco: Pan-Graphic Press, 1963.
       16 pp.

228)   Waring, Paul and Bryce, Dean T.   Homosexual Free-
       dom.   1961.   26 pp.

229)   White, Ernest.   The Homosexual Condition: A Study
       of 50 Cases.   Derby, Eng.:   Peter Smith, 1963.
       41 pp.

230)   White, H. D. Jennings.   Psychological Causes of
       Homoeroticism and Inversion.   London: British
       Society for the Study of Sex Psychology, 1925.   16
       pp.

231)   Wilkerson, David.   New Hope for Homosexuals.
       New York: Teen Challenge, 1964.   43 pp.

Theses and Dissertations

232) Achilles, Nancy. The Homosexual Bar. Master's
      Thesis, Human Development, University of Chicago,
      1964. 120 pp.

233) Austin, Sean H. Analysis and Prediction of Male
      Homosexual Case History Material: A Replication
      and Extension. Master's Thesis, Psychology, San
      Francisco State College, 1967. 125 pp.

234) Austin, Sean H. An Experimental Multivariate
      Analysis of Male Homosexual Case History Material.
      Bachelor's Honors Thesis, Lawrence University,
      1965.

234a) Beggs, Keith S. Some Legal, Social, and Psychiatric
       Aspects of Homosexual Behavior--A Guide for the
       Social Worker in the Sex Clinic. Master's Thesis,
       Social Work, University of Wisconsin, 1950. 298 pp.

235) Bills, Norman. The Personality Structure of Alco-
      holics, Homosexuals, and Paranoids as Revealed by
      Their Responses to the Thematic Apperception Test.
      Doctoral Dissertation, Psychology, Western Reserve
      University, 1953.

235a) Dank, Barry M. A Social Psychological Theory of
       Homosexuality and Sex-Role Learning. Master's
       Thesis, Sociology, University of Wisconsin, 1966.
       211 pp.

236) Dashon, Paul G. Perception of Homosexual Words
      in Paranoid Schizophrenia. Doctoral Dissertation,
      Psychology, Michigan State College, 1952. 102 pp.

237) David, Henry P. Relationship of Szondi Picture
      Preferences to Personality. Doctoral Dissertation,
      Psychology, Columbia University, 1951. University
      Microfilm no. 2805. (Summary in Microfilm Ab-
      stracts, 11:1091-92, 1951.)

25

238)   Dean, Dawson F.   Significant Characteristics of the
       Homosexual Personality.   Doctoral Dissertation,
       Psychology, New York University, 1936.

239)   Dean, P.   The Body Image and Sexual Preferences
       of Alcoholic, Homosexual, and Heterosexual Males.
       Master's Thesis, Adelphi College, 1960.

240)   Dean, Robert B.   Some MMPI and Biographical
       Questionnaire Correlates of Non-Institutionalized
       Male Homosexuals.   Master's Thesis, Psychology,
       San Jose State College, 1967.   113 pp.

241)   Edwards, Harold E.   The Relationship Between Re-
       ported Early Life Experiences with Parents and
       Adult Male Homosexuality.   Doctoral Dissertation,
       Psychology, University of Tennessee, 1963.   Uni-
       versity Microfilm no. 64-4876.   (Summary in Dis-
       sertation Abstracts, 24:4793, 1964.)

242)   Freedman, Mark J.   Homosexuality Among Women
       and Psychological Adjustment.   Doctoral Disserta-
       tion, Psychology, Case Western Reserve University,
       1967.   124 pp.   University Microfilm no. 68-3308.
       (Summary in Dissertation Abstracts, 28:4294-95B,
       1968.)

243)   Friberg, Richard R.   A Study of Homosexuality and
       Related Characteristics in Paranoid Schizophrenia.
       Doctoral Dissertation, Psychology, University of
       Minnesota, 1965.   153 pp.   University Microfilm no.
       65-7880.   (Summary in Dissertation Abstracts, 26:
       491, 1965.)

244)   Goldfarb, Jack H.   The Concept of Sexual Identity in
       Normals and Transvestites: Its Relationship to the
       Body-Image, Self-Concept, and Parental Identification.
       Doctoral Dissertation, Psychology, University of
       Southern California, 1963.   216 pp.   University
       Microfilm no. 64-3098.   (Summary in Dissertation
       Abstracts, 24:3835-36, 1964.)

245)   Greenblatt, D. R. Semantic Differential Analysis of
       the "Triangular System" Hypothesis in "Adjusted"
       Overt Male Homosexuals.   Doctoral Dissertation,
       Psychology, University of California at Los Angeles,
       1968.   273 pp.   University Microfilm no. 67-6178.

(Summary in <u>Dissertation Abstracts,</u> 27B:4123-25, 1968.)

246)   Haselkorn, Harry.   <u>The Vocational Interests of a</u>
       <u>Group of Homosexuals.</u>   Doctoral Dissertation,
       Psychology, New York University, 1953.   119 pp.
       University Microfilm no. 5418.   (Summary in <u>Dis-</u>
       <u>sertation Abstracts,</u> 13:582-83, 1953.)   (See no.
       1959 below.)

247)   Houston, Lawrence N.   <u>An Investigation of the Rela-</u>
       <u>tionship Between the Vocational Interests and Homo-</u>
       <u>sexual Behavior of Institutionalized Youthful Offenders.</u>
       Doctoral Dissertation, Education, Temple University,
       1963.   107 pp.   University Microfilm no. 64-1115.
       (Summary in <u>Dissertation Abstracts,</u> 24:2984-85,
       1964.)   (See no. 2028 below.)

248)   Howard, Stephen J.   <u>Determinants of Sex-Role Identi-</u>
       <u>fications of Homosexual Female Delinquents.</u>   Doc-
       toral Dissertation, Psychology, University of Southern
       California, 1962.   80 pp.   University Microfilm no.
       62-6673.   (Summary in <u>Dissertation Abstracts,</u> 22:
       2588, 1962.)

249)   Humphreys, R. A. L.   <u>The Tearoom Trade: Imper-</u>
       <u>sonal Sex in Public Places.</u>   Doctoral Dissertation,
       Sociology, Washington University, 1968.   282 pp.
       University Microfilm no. 69-19905.   (See no. 58
       above.)

250)   Kopp, M. A.   <u>A Study of Anomia and Homosexuality in</u>
       <u>Delinquent Adolescent Girls.</u>   Doctoral Dissertation,
       St. Louis University, 1960.

251)   Liddicoat, Renee.   <u>Homosexuality: Results of a</u>
       <u>Survey as Related to Various Theories.</u>   Doctoral
       Dissertation, University of Witwatersrand, South
       Africa, 1956.   (See below, nos. 2148 and 2709.)

251a) Loeffler, Donald L.   <u>An Analysis of the Treatment</u>
       <u>of the Homosexual Character in Dramas Produced in</u>
       <u>the New York Theater from 1950 to 1968.</u>   Doctoral
       Dissertation, Theater, Bowling Green State University,
       1969.   212 pp.   University Microfilm no. 70-5518.
       (Summary in <u>Dissertation Abstracts,</u> 29:4599A,
       1970.)

252) MacVicar, Joan A. Homosexual Delinquent Girls:
      Identification with Mother and Perception of Parents.
      Doctoral Dissertation, Psychology, Boston University,
      1967. 155 pp. University Microfilm no. 67-13291.
      (Summary in Dissertation Abstracts, 28:2144B, 1967.)

253) Mathes, Irma D. B. Adult Male Homosexuality and
      Perception of Instrumentality, Expression, and Coa-
      lition in Parental Role Structure. Doctoral Disserta-
      tion, Sociology, University of Missouri, 1966. 256
      pp. University Microfilm no. 67-2897. (Summary
      in Dissertation Abstracts, 28:811A, 1967.)

254) McGuire, Ruth M. An Inquiry into Attitudes and
      Value Systems of a Minority Group: A Comparative
      Study of Attitudes and Value Systems of Adult Male
      Homosexuals with Adult Male Heterosexuals. Doc-
      toral Dissertation, Social Psychology, New York
      University, 1966. 194 pp. University Microfilm no.
      66-9465. (Summary in Dissertation Abstracts, 24:
      1110-11, 1966.)

255) Musiker, H. R. Sex Identification and Other Aspects
      of the Personality of the Male Paranoid Schizophrenic.
      Doctoral Dissertation, Psychology, Boston University,
      1952.

256) Paitich, Daniel. Attitudes Toward Parents in Male
      Homosexuals and Exhibitionists. Doctoral Disserta-
      tion, Psychology, University of Toronto, 1964. 138
      pp. University Microfilm no. 64-11275. (Summary
      in Dissertation Abstracts, 25:4260, 1965.)

256a) Porter, Howard K. Prison Homosexuality: Locus of
      Control and Femininity. Doctoral Dissertation, Psy-
      chology, Michigan State University, 1969. (79 pp.)
      University Microfilm No. 70-15,113D.

257) Pritchard, Michael J. A Study of Chromosomal Sex
      in Six Male Homosexuals. Dissertation for Diploma
      in Psychological Medicine, University of London, 1961.

258) Reitzell, Jeanne M. A Comparative Study of Hysterics,
      Homosexuals, and Alcoholics Using Content Analysis
      of Rorschach Responses. Master's Thesis, Clare-
      mont Graduate School, 1949. (See no. 2376 below.)

259)   Sagarin, Edward. Structure and Ideology in an
       Association of Deviants.   Doctoral Dissertation,
       Sociology, New York University, 1966.   463 pp.
       University Microfilm no. 68-10123.   (Summary in
       Dissertation Abstracts, 29A:1305-06, 1968.)

260)   Spencer, S. J. G.   Comparative Study of Psychological
       Illnesses among Oxford Undergraduates.   Doctoral
       Dissertation, Medicine, Oxford University, 1957.

261)   Sweet, Roxanna B. T.   Political and Social Action in
       Homophile Organizations.   Doctoral Dissertation,
       Sociology, University of California, Berkeley, 1968.
       256 pp.   University Microfilm no. 69-4283.   (Sum-
       mary in Dissertation Abstracts, 29A:3239-40, 1969.)

262)   Thomas, Richard W.   An Investigation of the Psy-
       choanalytic Theory of Homosexuality.   Doctoral Dis-
       sertation, University of Kentucky 1951.   167 pp.
       University Microfilm no. 60-712.   (Summary in Dis-
       sertation Abstracts, 20:3847, 1960.)

263)   Wheeler, William M.   An Analysis of Rorschach
       Indices of Male Homosexuality.   Doctoral Disserta-
       tion, Psychology, University of California at Los
       Angeles, 1948.   60 pp.   (See no. 2591 below.)

264)   Wolowitz, Howard M.   Attraction and Aversion to
       Power: A Conflict Theory of Homosexuality in Male
       Paranoids.   Doctoral Dissertation, Psychology, Uni-
       versity of Michigan, 1963.   91 pp.   University
       Microfilm no. 64-2535.   (Summary in Dissertation
       Abstracts, 24:3429-30, 1964.)   (See no. 2621 below.)

Articles in Books

265) "Abstracts from the House of Lords Debate" and "Abstracts from the House of Commons Debate," in Rees and Usill, no. 89 above, pp. 198-208.

266) Achilles, Nancy. "Development of the Homosexual Bar as an Institution," in John H. Gagnon and William Simon (eds.), Sexual Deviance (New York: Harper and Row, 1967), pp. 247-82. (Paperback) (See no. 232 above.)

267) Adams, Mark E. "The Sexual Criminal in Prison," in J. Paul DeRiver, The Sexual Criminal: A Psychoanalytical Study (2d ed.; Springfield, Ill.: Thomas, 1956), pp. 287-307. (chap. 25).

268) Adler, Alfred. "Homosexuality," in The Practice and Theory of Individual Psychology, translation by P. Radin (London: Kegan Paul, Trench, Trubner, 1925), pp. 184-96 (chap. 14).

269) Allen, Clifford. "The Heterosexual and Homosexual Perversions," in A Treatment of Psychosexual Disorders (London: Oxford, 1962), pp. 165-204 (chap. 9).

270) Allen, Clifford. "Homosexuality and Oscar Wilde: A Psychological Study," in Ruitenbeek, no. 95 above, pp. 60-83.

271) Allen, Clifford. "The Nature and Causation of the Sexual Perversions or Paraphilias," in The Sexual Perversions and Anomalies (London: Oxford, 1949), pp. 57-72 and 116-44.

272) Allen, Clifford. "The Personality of Radclyffe Hall," in Ruitenbeek, no. 95 above, pp. 183-88.

273) Allen, Clifford. "Sexual Perversions," in Albert Ellis and Albert Abarbanel (eds.), The Encyclopedia

of Sexual Behavior (2d ed.; New York: Hawthorn, 1967), pp. 802-11.

274) American Law Institute. "Commentary," in Model Penal Code--Tentative Draft No. 4 (Philadelphia: A.L.I., 1955), pp. 276-81. (Reprinted in Matta-chine Review, 2:10-14, Sep. 1956.)

275) Anonymous. "A Critical Survey of Statistics," in Rees and Usill, no. 89 above, pp. 187-97.

276) Anonymous. "Homosexuality," in Encyclopedia Britannica, 11:648-49 (1967).

277) Anonymous. "Sodomy," in Corpus Juris Secundum, 81:367-85 (1953).

278) Aronson, Marvin L. "A Study of the Freudian Theory of Paranoia by Means of the Rorschach Test," in Charles F. Reed, Irving E. Alexander, and Sil-van S. Tomkins (eds.), Psychopathology: A Source Book (Cambridge, Mass.: Harvard, 1958), pp. 370-87 (chap. 24).

279) Arthur, Gavin. "The Dorian Type," "The Finocchio Type," "The Lesbian Type," and "The Dyke Type," in The Circle of Sex (New Hyde Park, N.Y.: Uni-versity Books, 1966), pp. 49-62 (chaps. 3-4) and 89-100 (chaps. 9-10).

280) Atkinson, Ronald. "Homosexuality," in Sexual Morality (New York: Harcourt, Brace, and World, 1965), pp. 132-51.

281) Auchinloss, Douglas. "The Gay Crowd," in Joe D. Brown (ed.), Sex in the '60s (New York: Time-Life Books, 1968), pp. 65-75 (chap. 5). (Paperback.)

282) Baab, O.J. "Homosexuality," in The Interpreter's Dictionary of the Bible (Nashville, Tenn.: Abing-don Press, 1962), 2:639.

283) Bacon, Catherine L. "A Developmental Theory of Female Homosexuality," in Sandor Lorand and Michael Balint (eds.), Perversions: Psychodynamics and Therapy (New York: Random House, 1956), pp. 131-59.

284)   Bailey, Derrick Sherwin. "Homosexuality and Chris-
       tian Morals," in Rees and Usill, no. 89 above, pp.
       36-63.

285)   Bailey, Derrick Sherwin. "Homosexuality and Homo-
       sexualism," in John Macquarrie (ed.), Dictionary of
       Christian Ethics (Philadelphia: Westminster Press,
       1967), pp. 152-53.

286)   Barber, Bernard. "The Three Human Females," in
       Donald P. Geddes (ed.), An Analysis of the Kinsey
       Reports on Sexual Behavior in the Human Male and
       Female (New York: New American Library, 1954),
       pp. 50-61 at 58-59. (Paperback--Mentor MP391)

287)   Barnouw, Victor and Stern, John A. "Some Sug-
       gestions concerning Social and Cultural Determinants
       of Human Sexual Behavior," in George Winokur (ed.),
       Determinants of Human Sexual Behavior (Springfield,
       Ill.: Thomas, 1963), pp. 206-09 (chap. 13).

288)   Barth, Karl. "Freedom in Fellowship," in Church
       Dogmatics (Edinburgh: Clark, 1961), vol. 3, part
       4, p. 166.

289)   Barton, George A. "Sodomy," in James Hastings
       (ed.), Encyclopedia of Religion and Ethics (Edin-
       burgh: Clark, 1920), 11:672-74.

290)   Beach, Frank A. "A Cross-Species Survey of Mam-
       malian Sexual Behavior," in Paul H. Hoch and
       Joseph Zubin (eds.), Psychosexual Development in
       Health and Disease (New York: Grune and Stratton,
       1949), pp. 52-78 at 63-65. (Rev. ed., 1955)

291)   Beauvoir, Simone de. "The Lesbian," in The Second
       Sex, translation by H. M. Parshley (New York:
       Knopf, 1957), pp. 404-24 (chap. 15). (Paperback--
       Bantam 03192.) (Reprinted in Ruitenbeek, no. 96
       above, pp. 227-48.)

292)   Benjamin Harry and Masters, R. E. L. "Homosexual
       Prostitution," in Prostitution and Morality (New
       York: Julian Press, 1961), pp. 286-337 (chap. 10).

293)   Berg, Charles. "The Wolfenden Report on Homo-
       sexual Offences," in Fear, Punishment, Anxiety and

the Wolfenden Report (London: Allen and Unwin, 1959), pp. 11-50 (chap. 1).

294)   Bergler, Edmund. Interview, in Lucy Freeman and Martin Theodores (eds.), The Why Report (New York: Pocket Books, 1965), pp. 208-15. (Paperback--Cardinal 95017.)

295)   Bergler, Edmund. "Male Homosexuality and Lesbianism," in The Basic Neurosis: Oral Regression and Psychic Masochism (New York: Grune and Stratton, 1949), pp. 213-42.

296)   Bergler, Edmund. "Male Homosexuality" and "Lesbianism," in Counterfeit Sex: Homosexuality, Impotence, and Frigidity (2d ed.; New York: Grune and Stratton, 1958), pp. 184-222 (chap. 4) and 337-62 (chap. 9).

297)   Berne, Eric. "What is Homosexuality?" in A Layman's Guide to Psychiatry and Psychoanalysis (New York: Grove Press, 1957), pp. 202-05. (Paperback-Black Cat BC130.) (Revision of The Mind in Action.)

298)   The Bible: New Testament. Romans 1:24-32; I Corinthians 6:9-10; Galatians 5:19-21; I Timothy 1:9-10; II Peter 2:6; Jude 1:7; Revelation 21:8, 22:15.

299)   The Bible: Old Testament. Genesis 13:13, 18:20-22, 19:4-8, 19:13, 19:24-25; Leviticus 18:22, 20:13; Deuteronomy 23:17-18; Judges 19:22-24; Ruth 1:16-17; II Samuel 1:26; I Kings 14:24, 15:12, 22:46; II Kings 23:7; Proverbs 10:9.

300)   Bieber, Irving. "Clinical Aspects of Male Homosexuality," in Marmor, no. 75 above, pp. 248-67 (chap. 14).

301)   Bieber, Irving. "Sexual Deviations: Homosexuality," in Alfred M. Freedman and Harold D. Kaplan (eds.), Comprehensive Textbook of Psychiatry (Baltimore: Williams and Wilkins, 1967), pp. 963-76.

302)   Blackman, Nathan. "Homosexuality," in Edward Podolsky (ed.), Encyclopedia of Sexual Aberrations (New York: Philosophical Library, 1953), pp. 271-75.

303)   Blaine, Graham B. Jr. and McArthur, Charles C.
       "Basic Character Disorders and Homosexuality," in
       Emotional Problems of the Student (New York:
       Appleton-Century-Croft, 1961), pp. 110-27. (Paper-
       back--Anchor A527.)

304)   Bloch, Herbert A. and Geis, Gilbert. "The Sexual
       Offender: ... Sodomy Offenses," in Man, Crime, and
       Society: The Forms of Criminal Behavior (New
       York: Random House, 1962), pp. 300-08 (chap. 11).

305)   Bloch, Iwan. "Venereal Diseases in the Homosexual,"
       "The Riddle of Homosexuality," and "Pseudo-Homo-
       sexuality," in The Sexual Life of our Time in its
       Relation to Modern Civilization, translation by M. E.
       Paul (London: Rebnam, 1910), pp. 368-69, 487-
       535 (chap. 19), and 537-54 (chap. 20).

306)   Boss, Medard. "Three Homosexuals," in Meaning
       and Content of Sexual Perversions, translation by
       Liese L. Abell (2d ed.; New York: Grune and
       Stratton, 1949), pp. 114-42.

307)   Bowman, Karl M. and Engle, Bernice. "Sexual
       Psychopath Laws," in Ralph Slovenko (ed.), Sexual
       Behavior and the Law (Springfield, Ill.: Thomas,
       1965), pp. 757-78 at 762-63 and 770-71.

308)   Boyd, Malcolm. "This is a Homosexual Bar, Jesus,"
       in Are You Running with Me, Jesus? (New York:
       Holt, Rinehart, and Winston, 1965), p. 106. (Paper-
       back--Avon VS17.)

309)   Bragman, Louis J. "The Case of John Addington
       Symonds: A Study in Aesthetic Homosexuality," in
       Ruitenbeek, no. 95 above, pp. 86-111.

310)   Brancale, Ralph. "The Sex Offense Problem," in
       New York State Association of Magistrates, Pro-
       ceedings of the 29th Annual Conference (Albany,
       N. Y.: State Department of Corrections, 1939), pp.
       23-32.

311)   Brill, A. A. "Paranoia and Its Relation to Homo-
       sexuality," in Freud's Contribution to Psychiatry
       (New York: Norton, 1944), pp. 104-24 (chap. 6).

312)   Bromberg, Walter. "Homosexuality," in Albert
         Deutsch and Helen Fishman (eds.), Encyclopedia of
         Mental Health (New York: Franklin Watts, Inc.,
         1963), 3:747-64.

313)   Bromley, Dorothy D. and Britten, F. H. "The Homo-
         sexually Inclined" and "The Homosexual Variants," in
         Youth and Sex: A Study of 1300 College Students
         (New York: Harper, 1938), pp. 117-30 (chap. 9) and
         209-22 (chap. 15).

314)   Brown, Daniel G. "Transvestism and Sex-Role In-
         version," in Ellis and Abarbanel, no. 273 above,
         pp. 1012-22.

315)   Brown, Fred and Kempton, Rudolf. "Homosexuality"
         in Sex Questions and Answers (New York: McGraw
         Hill, 1950), pp. 226-39. (Paperback.)

316)   Brown, W. Paterson. "The Homosexual Male:
         Treatment in an Out-Patient Clinic," in Ismond
         Rosen (ed.), The Pathology and Treatment of Sexual
         Deviation: A Methodological Approach (London:
         Oxford, 1964), pp. 196-220 (chap. 8).

317)   Burgess, Ernest W. "The Sociological Theory of
         Psychosexual Behavior," in Hoch and Zubin, no. 290
         above. (Reprinted in Jerome Himmelhoch and
         Sylvia F. Fava (eds.), Sexual Behavior in American
         Society: An Appraisal of the First Two Kinsey Re-
         ports (New York: Norton, 1955), pp. 12-28 at
         18-20.

318)   Burton, Richard F. "Terminal Essay," in The
         Book of the Thousand Nights and a Night (London:
         Printed for the Burton Club, 1886), 10:178-220.
         (Reprinted in Cory, no. 27 above, pp. 204-47 and in
         The Vice [Atlanta: E. Theris, 1967], pp. 7-73
         [Paperback--Pendulum 212].)

319)   Bychowski, Gustav. "Homosexuality and Psychosis,"
         in Lorand and Balint, no. 283 above, pp. 97-130.

320)   Cambridge Department of Criminal Science. "The
         State of the Law: ... Homosexual Offenses" and "A
         Summary of Certain Data relating to Homosexual
         Offenses," in Sexual Offenses: A Report ... (London:

Macmillan, 1957), pp. 344-52 and 528-31. Edited
by Leon Radzinowicz.

321)   Cameron, Norman. "Sexual Deviations," in Personality Development and Psychopathology (Boston:
Houghton Mifflin, 1963), pp. 659-71 at 661-66.

322)   Cantor, Gilbert M. "The Need for Homosexual Law
Reform," in Weltge, no. 116 above, pp. 83-94 (chap.
7).

323)   Caprio, Frank S. "Female Homosexuality," in The
Sexually Adequate Female (New York: Citadel Press,
1953), pp. 188-210 (chap. 9). (Paperback--Citadel
C91.)

324)   Caprio, Frank S. "Male Homosexuality" and "Female Homosexuality," in Variations in Sexual Behavior (New York: Citadel Press, 1955), pp. 85-
158 (chap. 3) and 159-88 (chap. 4). (Paperback--
Black Cat BC45 and Citadel C257.)

325)   Caprio, Frank S. "Sexual Aberrations: Homo-
sexuality," in The Sexually Adequate Male (New
York: Citadel Press, 1952), pp. 172-91 (chap. 8).
(Paperback--Citadel C92.)

326)   Caprio, Frank S. and Brenner, Donald R. "The
Homosexual Problem" and "Psycho-legal Manage-
ment," in Sexual Behavior: Psycho-Sexual Aspects
(New York: Citadel Press, 1961), pp. 99-172
(chap. 4) and 307-58 (chap. 13). (Paperback--
Paperback Library 55-900.)

327)   Carstairs, G. Morris. "Cultural Differences in
Sexual Behavior," in Rosen, no. 316 above, pp.
419-34 (chap. 13).

328)   Chesser, Eustace. "The Facts about Homosexuality"
and "Homosexuality: the Law and Treatment," in
Live and Let Live: The Moral of the Wolfenden
Report (London: Heinemann, 1958), pp. 29-63
(chaps. 2-3). Foreword by Sir John Wolfenden.

329)   Cole, William G. "Homosexuality in the Bible," in
Sex and Love in the Bible (London: Hodder and
Stoughton, 1960), pp. 342-72 (chap. 10).

330)   Conwell, Chic. "The Shake," in The Professional
        Thief: By a Professional Thief (Chicago: Uni-
        versity of Chicago Press, 1937), annotated and
        interpreted by Edwin H. Sutherland, pp. 78-80.
        (Paperback--Phoenix P10.)

331)   Cormier, Bruno M., Kennedy, Miriam, and Sango-
        wicz, Jadwiga M. "Sexual Offenses, Episodic
        Recidivism, and the Psychopathological State," in
        Slovenko, no. 307 above, pp. 707-41 at 721-26.

332)   Cory, Donald W. "Changing Attitudes toward Homo-
        sexuals," in Cory, no. 27 above, pp. 427-40.

333)   Cory, Donald W. "Homosexual Incest," in R. E. L.
        Masters (ed.), Patterns of Incest (New York:
        Basic Books, 1963), pp. 265-73. (Paperback--
        Ace Star 65380.)

334)   Cory, Donald W. "Homosexuality," in Ellis and
        Abarbanel, no. 273 above, pp. 485-93.

335)   Cory, Donald W. "Homosexuality and the Mystique
        of the Gigantic Penis," in Ellis, no. 39 above, pp.
        271-79.

336)   Crane, H. W. "Environmental Factor in Sexual
        Inversion," in William C. Coker (ed.), Studies in
        Science (Chapel Hill: University of North Carolina
        Press, 1946), pp. 243-48.

337)   Crespi, Leo P. "Are Kinsey's Methods Valid?" in
        Albert Deutsch (ed.), Sex Habits of American Men:
        A Symposium on the Kinsey Report (New York:
        Prentice-Hall, 1948), pp. 105-24.

338)   Cross, Harold H. U. "The Third Sex" and "More
        about Inverts," in The Cross Report on Perversion
        (New York: Softcover Library, 1964), pp. 20-55
        (chaps. 3-4). (Paperback--B794X.)

339)   Davenport, William. "Sexual Patterns and their
        Regulation in a Society of the Southwest Pacific,"
        in Frank A. Beach (ed.), Sex and Behavior (New
        York: Wiley and Sons, 1965), pp. 164-207 at 199-
        201 (chap. 7).

340)   Davis, Katherine B. and Kopp, Mario E. "Homo-
        sexuality: the Unmarried College Woman" and
        "Homosexuality: the Married Woman," in Katherine
        B. Davis, Factors in the Sex Life of 2200 Women
        (New York: Harper, 1929), pp. 238-96 (chap. 10)
        and 297-328 (chap. 11).

341)   Davis, Maxine. "Homosexuality--What It is and is
        not," in Sex and the Adolescent (New York: Dial
        Press, 1958), pp. 58-64 (chap. 6) and 224-28 (chap.
        21.) (Paperback--Permabook M5028.)

342)   Delay, Jean. "Meeting with Oscar Wilde" and "Urien,
        or Le Voyage d'Urien (1898)," in Ruitenbeek, no. 95
        above, pp. 239-48 and 248-59.

343)   DeMott, Benjamin. "But He's a Homosexual...,"
        in New American Review (New York: New Ameri-
        can Library, 1967), 1:166-82. (Paperback.)

344)   Dennison, George. "The Moral Effect of the Legend
        of Genet," in no. 343 above, pp. 183-98.

345)   Denniston, Rollin H. "Ambisexuality in Animals,"
        in Marmor, no. 75 above, pp. 27-43 (chap. 2).

346)   DeRiver, J. Paul. "Homosexual Sadism," in De-
        River, no. 267 above, pp. 87-96 (chap. 7).

347)   Dewey, Richard and Humber, W. J. "Personality
        Types...The Homosexual," in The Development of
        Human Behavior (New York: Macmillan, 1966),
        pp. 336-54.

348)   Dickinson, Robert L. "The Gynecology of Homo-
        sexuality," in Henry, no. 54 above, pp. 1069-1130.

349)   Dickinson, Robert L. and Beam, Lura. "Homo-
        sexuality," in The Single Woman: A Medical Study
        in Sex Education (Baltimore: Williams and Watkins,
        1934), pp. 203-22 (chap. 9).

350)   Dizazga, John. "Homosexuality," in Sex Crimes
        Springfield, Ill.: Thomas, 1960), pp. 205-16 (chap.
        32).

351)   Donnelly, Richard C., Goldstein, Joseph, and

Schwartz, Richard D. "Consensual Homosexual Acts between Adults in Private--A Crime: A Problem for the Legislature? in Criminal Law: Problems for Decision in the Promulgation, Invocation, and Administration of a Law of Crimes (New York: Free Press of Glencoe, 1962), pp. 123-202 (chap. 1, part 3).

352) Drummond, Isabel. "Sodomy, Exhibitionism, and Other Acts 'Contrary to Nature' " and "Table of Penalties--Sodomy," in The Sex Paradox (New York: Putnam, 1953), pp. 119-55 (chap. 4) and 350-52.

353) Duffy, Clinton T. and Hirshberg, Al. "The Homosexuals," in Sex and Crime (New York: Doubleday, 1965), pp. 28-39 (chap. 4). (Paperback--Pocket Book 75-213.)

354) East, Norwood. "Homosexuality or Sexual Inversion," in Sexual Offenders (London: Delisle, 1955), pp. 37-42.

355) Edwardes, Allen. "Sexual Perversion: Matter of Taste," in The Jewel in the Lotus (New York: Julian Press, 1959), sections 200-62. Introduction by Albert Ellis.

356) Eidelberg, Ludwig. "Analysis of a Case of a Male Homosexual," in Lorand and Balint, no. 283 above, pp. 279-89.

357) Eidelberg, Ludwig. "Better than the Love of Women," in Take Off Your Mask (New York: International Universities Press, 1948), pp. 47-65. (Paperback--Pyramid G558.) (Reprinted in Krich, no. 69 above, pp. 52-70.)

358) Ellis, Albert. "Constitutional Factors in Homosexuality: A Re-examination of the Evidence," in Hugo G. Beigel (ed.), Advances in Sex Research (New York: Harper and Row, 1963), pp. 161-86 (chap. 19).

359) Ellis, Albert. "Deviation, an Ever-increasing Social Problem," in J. E. Fairchild (ed.), Personal Problems and Psychological Frontiers (New York: Sheridan House, 1957), pp. 138-51.

360)   Ellis, Albert. "How American Women are Driving
        American Males into Homosexuality," in Sex Without
        Guilt (New York: Lyle Stuart, 1958), pp. 143-50
        (chap. 11). (Paperback--Black Cat BC94.)

361)   Enelow, Morton L. "Public Nuisance Offenses: Ex-
        hibitionism, Voyeurism, and Transvestism," in
        Slovenko, no. 307 above, pp. 478-86.

362)   English, O. Spurgeon and Finch, Stuart M. "Per-
        sonality Disorders," in Introduction to Psychiatry
        (New York: Norton, 1954), pp. 232-91 at 266-72.

363)   Evans, Joan. "Martin Beardson," in Three Men:
        An Experiment in the Biography of Emotion (New
        York: Knopf, 1954), pp. 183-295 (chap. 3). (Paper-
        back--Black Cat BC40.)

364)   "Extracts from a Report of the Joint Committee on
        Psychiatry and the Law appointed by the British
        Medical Association and Magistrates' Association," in
        Rees and Usill, no. 89 above, pp. 209-12.

365)   Feldman, M. P. "The Treatment of Homosexuality
        by Aversion Therapy," in Hugh L. Freeman (ed.),
        Progress in Behaviour Therapy (Bristol, England:
        J. Wright, 1968), pp. 59-72.

366)   Feldman, Sandor S. "On Homosexuality," in Lorand
        and Balint, no. 283 above, pp. 71-96.

367)   Ferenczi, Sandor. "More about Homosexuality," in
        Final Contributions to the Problem and Methods of
        Psychoanalysis (New York: Basic Books, 1955),
        pp. 168-74.

367a)   Ferenczi, Sandor. "On the Part Played by Homo-
        sexuality in the Pathogenesis of Paranoia" and "The
        Nosology of Male Homosexuality," in Contributions
        to Psychoanalysis, translation by Ernest Jones
        (New York: Brunner, 1950), pp. 154-84 (chap. 5)
        and 296-318 (chap. 12). ("Nosology" is reprinted
        in Krich, no. 69 above, pp. 188-201 and in Ruiten-
        beek, no. 96 above, pp. 3-16.)

368)   Fiedler, Leslie A. "Come Back to the Raft Ag'in,
        Huck, Honey," in An End to Innocence (Boston:

Beacon Press, 1955), pp. 142-51. (Reprinted in
Wilbur S. Scott [ed.], Five Approaches of Literary
Criticism [New York: Macmillan, 1962], pp. 303-12
and in Irving Malin [ed.], Psychoanalysis and American Fiction [New York: Dutton, 1965], pp. 121-29.)

369)   Field, Alice W.   "Significance [of the Kinsey Re-
         port] for American Women," in Deutsch, no. 337
         above, pp. 144-61.

370)   Fisher, Saul H.   "A Note on Male Homosexuality
         and the Role of Women in Ancient Greece," in
         Marmor, no. 75 above, pp. 165-72 (chap. 9).

371)   Fishman, Joseph F.   "Homosexuals Who Come to
         Prison" and "Homosexuals Who are Formed in
         Prison," in Sex in Prison (New York: National
         Library Press, 1934), pp. 57-107 (chaps. 3-4).

372)   Flaceliere, Robert.   "Homosexuality," in Love in
         Ancient Greece, translation by James Cleugh (New
         York: Crown Publishers, 1962), pp. 62-100 (chap.
         3). (Paperback--Macfadden MB60-170.)

373)   Flournoy, Henri.   "An Analytic Session in a Case
         of Male Homosexuality," in Rudolph M. Loewen-
         stein (ed.), Drives, Affects, Behavior, translation
         by Vera Damman (New York: International Univer-
         sities Press, 1953), pp. 229-40. (Reprinted in
         part in Krich, no. 69 above, pp. 308-12.)

374)   Fodor, Nandor.   "Dreams of Masculine Regret," in
         New Approaches to Dream Interpretation (New York:
         Citadel Press, 1951), pp. 28-31. (Reprinted in
         Krich, no. 69 above, pp. 25-28.)

375)   Ford, Clellan S.   "Toward a Better Understanding
         of Human Sex Behavior," in James Wortis (ed.),
         Recent Advances in Biological Psychiatry (New York:
         Grune and Stratton, 1960), pp. 226-34 (chap. 17).

376)   Ford, Clellan S. and Beach, Frank A.   "Homosexual
         Behavior," in Patterns of Sexual Behavior (New
         York: Harper, 1951), pp. 125-43 (chap. 7). (Paper-
         back--Ace Star K1285.)

377)   Fraiberg, Selma H.   "Homosexual Conflicts," in

Sandor Lorand and Henry I. Schneer (eds.), Adolescents: Psychoanalytic Approach to Problems and
Therapy (New York: Hoeber, 1961), pp. 78-112
(chap. 5).

378)   Freeman, William. "Wilde," in The Life of Lord
Alfred Douglas (London: Hubert Joseph Ltd., 1948),
pp. 66-158 (chap. 4).

379)   Freud, Sigmund. "Certain Neurotic Mechanisms in
Jealousy, Paranoia, and Homosexuality," in Ernest
Jones (ed.), Collected Papers of Sigmund Freud,
translation by Joan Riviere (London: Hogarth
Press, 1933 and New York: Basic Books, 1959),
2:232-43. (Reprinted in Complex, 1:3-13, 1950.)

379a) Freud Sigmund. "Contribution I: The Sexual
Aberrations," in Three Contributions to the Theory
of Sex, translation by A.A. Brill (New York: Dutton, 1962), pp. 1-34. Paperback: Dutton D-105.

380)   Freud, Sigmund. "The Psychogenesis of a Case of
Homosexuality in a Woman," in Jones, no. 378 above
2:202-31. (Reprinted in Krich, no. 69 above, pp.
262-85.)

381)   Freund, Kurth. "Some Problems in the Treatment
of Homosexuality," in Hans J. Eysenck (ed.), Behaviour Therapy and the Neuroses: Readings in
Modern Methods of Treatment (London: Pergamon
Press, 1960), pp. 312-26.

382)   Friedman, Paul. "Sexual Deviations," in Silvano
Arieti (ed.), American Handbook of Psychiatry
(New York: Basic Books, 1959), 1:589-613 at 590-
96.

383)   Gagnon, John H. "Sexual Behavior: Sexual Deviation: Social Aspects," in International Encyclopedia
of the Social Sciences (New York: Macmillan, 1968),
14:215-22.

384)   Garma, Angel. "A Psychoanalytic Study of Arthur
Rimbaud," translation by Richard McConchie, in
Ruitenbeek, no. 95 above, pp. 205-36. (Translated
and reprinted from Revue Française de Psycho-
analyse, vol. 10, 1938.)

385)   Gebhard, Paul H., Gagnon, John H., Pomeroy,
        Wardell B., and Christensen, Cornelia V. "Homo-
        sexual Offenders against Children, ... against
        Minors, ... against Adults, ... [and] Homosexual
        Activity," in Sex Offenders: An Analysis of Types
        (New York: Harper and Row, 1965), pp. 272-357
        (chaps. 13-15) and 623-53 (chap. 29). (Paperback--
        Bantam D3279.)

386)   Giedt, F. Harold. "Changes in Sexual Behavior and
        Attitudes following Class Study of the Kinsey Report,"
        in Himmelhoch and Fava, no. 317 above, pp. 405-16.

387)   Gillespie, W. H. "The Structure and Aetiology of
        Sexual Perversion," in Lorand and Balint, no. 283
        above, pp. 28-41.

388)   Ginsberg, Morris. "Morality, Law and the Climate
        of Opinion," in Rosen, no. 316 above, pp. 435-50
        (chap. 14).

389)   Gittings, Barbara B. "The Homosexual and the
        Church," in Weltge, no. 116 above, pp. 146-55
        (chap. 11).

390)   Glueck, Bernard C. Jr. "Pedophilia," in Slovenko,
        no. 307 above, pp. 539-62 at 542-45 and 549-54.

391)   Gonzales, John R. "Sexual Aberration and Problems
        of Identity in Schizophrenia," in Slovenko, no. 307
        above, pp. 578-90 at 579-80 and 584.

392)   Gray, Kenneth G. and Mohr, Johann W. "Follow-
        Up of Male Sexual Offenders," in Slovenko, no. 307
        above, pp. 742-56.

393)   Green, Richard. "Sissies and Tomboys," in Charles
        W. Wahl (ed.), Sexual Problems: Medical Diagnosis
        and Treatment (New York: Free Press of Glencoe,
        1966), pp. 93-111.

393a)   Grosskurth, Phyllis. "The Problem," in John
        Addington Symonds, A Biography (London: Long-
        mans, 1964), pp. 262-94 (chap. 11).

394)   Group for the Advancement of Psychiatry, Committee
        on the College Student. "Homosexual Behavior," in

Sex and the College Student (New York: Atheneum Press, 1966), pp. 66-75 and 126-27. Report no. 60. Edited by Harrison P. Eddy. (Paperback-- Fawcett Crest t968.)

395)   Grunewald, Henry A. (ed.) "The Invert's Problem," in Sex in America (New York: Bantam, 1964), pp. 256-82 (chap. 7). Paperback: Bantam S2895.

396)   Gundlach, R. H. and Riess, B. F. "Self and Sexual Identify in the Female: A Study of Female Homosexuals," in B. F. Riess (ed.), New Directions in Mental Health (2 vols.; New York: Grune and Stratton, 1968), I:205-31.

397)   Gunnison, Foster Jr. "The Homophile Movement in America" in Weltge, no. 116 above, pp. 113-28 (chap. 9).

398)   Guttmacher, Manfred S. and Weihofen, Henry. "Sex Offenders," in Psychiatry and The Law (New York: Norton, 1952), pp. 110-37 (chap. 6).

399)   Guyon, Rene. "The Psycho-Physiology of the So-called Sexual Aberrations," in The Ethics of Sexual Acts, translation by J. C. and Ingeborg Flugel (New York: Knopf, 1934), pp. 299-348 at 330-35 (chap. 10).

400)   Hagmeier, George and Gleason, Robert. "Homosexuality" and "Moral Aspects of Homosexuality," in Counselling the Catholic (New York: Sheed and Ward, 1959), pp. 94-112 (chap. 5) and 228-35 (chap. 11).

401)   Hailsham, Viscount. "Homosexuality and Society," in Rees and Usill, no. 89 above, pp. 21-35.

402)   Halleck, Seymour L. "Emotional Effects of Victimization," in Slovenko, no. 307 above, pp. 673-86 at 678-84.

403)   Halleck, Seymour L. "Sex Crimes and Deviation," in Psychiatry and the Dilemmas of Crime (New York: Harper and Row, 1967), pp. 176-95 at 180-88 (chap. 13).

404) Hamilton, Gilbert V. "Homosexuality, Defensive,"
      in Victor Robinson (ed.), Encyclopedia Sexualis
      (New York: Dingwall-Rock, 1936), pp. 334-42.
      (Reprinted as "Homosexuality as a Defense against
      Incest" in Masters, no. 333 above, pp. 133-48, as
      "Homosexuals and Their Mothers" in no. 172 above,
      pp. 5-15, as "Incest and Homosexuality" in Krich,
      no. 69 above, pp. 216-26, and as "Defensive Homo-
      sexuality" in Cory, no. 27 above, pp. 354-69.)

405) Hammelmann, H.A. "Homosexuality and the Law in
      Other Countries," in Rees and Usill, no. 89 above,
      pp. 143-83.

406) Hampson, John L. "Determinants of Psychosexual
      Orientation," in Beach, no. 339 above, pp. 108-32
      at 123-25 (chap. 6).

407) Hampson, John L. and Joan G. "The Ontogenesis of
      Sexual Behavior in Man," in William C. Young (ed.),
      Sex and Internal Secretions (3rd ed.; Baltimore:
      Williams and Wilkins, 1961), 2:1401-32 at 1425-28.

408) Hansard Parliamentary Debates: House of Commons.
      Debate on Homosexual Law Reform. Vol. 526: cols.
      1745-56 (Apr. 28, 1954); 589:647 (June 13, 1958);
      596:365-508 (Nov. 26, 1958); 625:1454-1514 (June 29,
      1960); 713:611-20 (May 26, 1965); 724:782-874
      (Feb. 11, 1966); 731:259-68 (July 5, 1966); 738:
      1068-1148 (Dec. 19, 1966); 748:2115-2200 (June
      23, 1967); and 749:1403-1524 (July 3, 1967).

409) Hansard Parliamentary Debates: House of Lords.
      Debate on Homosexual Law Reform.   Vol. 182: cols.
      737-67 (May 19, 1954); 206:753-832 (Dec. 4, 1957);
      266:71-172 (May 12, 1965); 266:631-712 (May 24,
      1965); 267:287-448 (June 21, 1965); 268:403-43
      (July 16, 1965); 269:677-730 (Oct. 28,1965); 270:
      28 (Nov. 10, 1965); 274:44 (Apr. 26, 1966), 605-
      52 (May 10, 1966), 1170-84 and 1190-1208 (May 23,
      1966); 275:146-78 (June 16, 1966); 284:494 (July 4,
      1967) and 1283-1323 (July 13, 1967); and 285:522-26
      (July 21, 1967) and 1324 (July 27, 1967).

410) Harper, Robert A. "The Psychological Aspects of
      Homosexuality," in Biegel, no. 358 above, pp. 187-
      97 (chap. 20).

411)   Harris, Sara. "A Homosexual is Better Off Dead"
         and "Don't Have Him Another One-Night Stand," in
         The Puritan Jungle: America's Sexual Wilderness
         (New York: Putnam, 1969), pp. 165-220 (chaps. 9-
         10).

412)   Hartwick, Alexander. "Homosexuality," in Aber-
         rations of Sexual Life After Psychopathia Sexualis
         of Dr. Richard Von Krafft-Ebing, translation by
         Arthur V. Burbury (New York: Capricorn Books,
         1962), pp. 283-311 (chap. 14). (Paperback edition--
         Capricorn CAP Giant 224.)

413)   Harvey, John F. "Homosexuality," in New Catholic
         Encyclopedia, 7:116-19 (1967).

414)   Hastings, Donald W. "Homosexuality," in Impotence
         and Frigidity (Boston: Little, Brown, 1963), pp.
         115-27 (chap. 7). (Paperback--Dell.)

415)   Hegeler, Inge and Sten. "Homosexuality," in An
         ABZ of Love, translation by David Hohnen (New
         York: Medical Press, 1963), pp. 121-31. (Paper-
         back--Alexicon.)

416)   Henry, George W. and Gross, Alfred A. "The Sex
         Offender: A Consideration of Therapeutic Principles,"
         in Dealing with Delinquency (New York: National
         Probation Association, 1941), pp. 114-37.

417)   Hiltner, Seward. "The Past and Present," in Him-
         melhoch and Fava, no. 317 above, pp. 312-25 at
         318-22.

418)   Hirning, L. Clovis. "Sex Offenders in Custody," in
         Robert M. Lindner and Robert V. Seliger (eds.),
         Handbook of Correctional Psychology (New York:
         Philosophical Library, 1947), pp. 233-56 at 244-45
         and 251-52.

419)   Hirschfeld, Magnus. "Homosexuality," in Robinson,
         no. 404 above, pp. 321-34. (Reprinted in part in
         Krich, no. 69 above, pp. 119-33.)

420)   Hirschfeld, Magnus. "Introduction to the Theory of
         Homosexuality," "Forms of Homosexuality," "Diag-
         nosis of Homosexuality," "Causes of Homosexuality,"

and "Feminine Homosexuality," in <u>Sexual Anomalies</u>
<u>and Perversions: Physical and Psychological De-</u>
<u>velopment, Diagnosis, and Treatment,</u> edited by
Norman Haire (London: Encyclopaedic Press, 1952),
pp. 225-30, 231-39, 241-51, 253-80, and 281-95
(chaps. 11-15).

421)   Hooker, Evelyn. "An Empirical Study of Some Relations between Sexual Patterns and Gender Identity in
Male Homosexuals," in John Money (ed.), <u>Sex Re-</u>
<u>search: New Developments</u> (New York: Holt, Rine-
hart, and Winston, 1965), pp. 24-52.

422)   Hooker, Evelyn. "The Homosexual Community," in
G. Nielson (ed.), <u>Personality Research</u> (vol. 2 of
<u>Proceedings of the XIVth International Congress of</u>
<u>Applied Psychology</u> [Copenhagen: Munksgaard,
1962]), pp. 40-59. (Reprinted in James C. Palmer
and Michael J. Goldstein [eds.], <u>Perspectives in</u>
<u>Psychopathology</u> [New York: Oxford, 1966], pp.
354-64; in Gagnon and Simon, no. 266 above, pp.
167-84; and Weltge, no. 116 above, pp. 25-39.)

423)   Hooker, Evelyn. "Homosexuality--Summary of
Studies," in Evelyn M. and Sylvanus M. Duvall (eds.),
<u>Sex Ways in Fact and Faith: Basis for Christian</u>
<u>Family Policy</u> (New York: Association Press, 1961),
pp. 166-83.

424)   Hooker, Evelyn. "Male Homosexual Life Styles and
Venereal Diseases," in <u>Proceedings of the World</u>
<u>Forum on Syphilis and Other Treponematoses</u> (Wash-
ington, D.C.: Public Health Service, 1964), pp.
431-37. Public Health Service Publication No. 997.

425)   Hooker, Evelyn. "Male Homosexuality," in Norman
L. Faberow (ed.), <u>Taboo Topics</u> (New York: Ather-
ton Press, 1963), pp. 44-55 (chap. 5).

426)   Hooker, Evelyn. "Male Homosexuals and their
Worlds," in Marmor, no. 75 above, pp. 83-107
(chap. 5).

427)   Hooker, Evelyn. "Sexual Behavior: Homosexuality,"
in <u>International Encyclopedia of the Social Sciences</u>
(New York: Macmillan, 1968), 14:222-33.

428)   Hooker, Evelyn and others. "Problems of Sex
        Ethics: Homosexuality," in Elizabeth S. and William
        H. Genné (eds.), Foundations for Christian Family
        Policy (New York: National Council of Churches,
        1961), pp. 167-89.

429)   James, T. E. "Law and the Sexual Offender," in
        Rosen, no. 316 above, pp. 461-92 (chap. 16).

430)   Jones, Harold J. "Sex Deviation," in Encyclopedia
        Americana, 24:629a-629b (1967).

431)   Jung, Carl G. "Analysis of Two Homosexual Dreams"
        from "The Significance of the Unconscious," in Con-
        tributions to Analytical Psychology, translation by
        H. G. and C. F. Baynes (New York: Harcourt, Brace,
        1928), pp. 391-400. (Reprinted in Krich, no. 69
        above, pp. 286-93.)

432)   Kallman, Franz J. "Genetic Aspects of Sex Deter-
        mination and Sexual Maturation Potentials in Man,"
        in Winokur, no. 287 above, pp. 5-18 (chap. 1).

433)   Kameny, Franklin E. "Gay is Good," in Weltge, no.
        116 above, pp. 129-45 (chap. 10).

434)   Kardiner, Abram. "Flight from Masculinity," in
        Sex and Morality (Indianapolis: Bobbs-Merrill Co.,
        1954), pp. 160-92. (Paperback--Charter.) (Re-
        printed in Ruitenbeek, no. 96 above, pp. 17-39.)

435)   Karpman, Benjamin. "Homosexuality," in The
        Sexual Offender and His Offenses: Etiology, Path-
        ology, Psychodynamics, and Treatment (New York:
        Julian Press, 1954), pp. 147-65 (chap. 10).

436)   Kelly, Audrey. "General Problems: Homosexuality
        and Lesbianism," in A Catholic Parent's Guide to
        Sex Education (New York: Hawthorn, 1962), pp.
        132-42.

437)   Kelly, E. Lowell and Terman, Lewis. "A Study of
        Male Homosexuals," "A Tentative Scale for the
        Measurement of Sexual Inversion," and "Case Studies
        of Homosexual Males," in Lewis M. Terman and
        Catherine C. Miles, Sex and Personality: Studies in
        Masculinity and Femininity (New York: McGraw-Hill,

1936), pp. 239-58 (chap. 11), 259-83 (chap. 12),
and 284-320 (chap. 13). (Part of chapter 13 is
reprinted in Krich, no. 69 above, pp. 88-92.)

438) Khan, Masud. "The Role of Infantile Sexuality and
Early Object Relations in Female Homosexuality,"
in Rosen, no. 316 above, pp. 221-92 (chap. 9).

439) Kinsey, Alfred C., Pomeroy, Wardell B., Martin,
Clyde E., and Gebhard, Paul H. "Concepts of
Normality and Abnormality in Sexual Behavior," in
Hoch and Zubin, no. 290 above, pp. 11-32.

440) Kinsey, Alfred C., Pomeroy, Wardell B., and
Martin, Clyde E. "Homosexual Outlet," in Sexual
Behavior in the Human Male (Philadelphia: Saunders,
1948), pp. 610-66 (chap. 21), 168-72, 259-61, 285-
89, 315, 357-62, 383-84, 455-59, and 482-83.

441) Kinsey, Alfred C., Pomeroy, Wardell B., Martin,
Clyde E., and Gebhard, Paul H. "Homosexual
Response and Contacts," in Sexual Behavior in the
Human Female (Philadelphia: Saunders, 1953), pp.
446-501 (chap. 11), 19-21, 106, 113-14, and 140.
(Paperback--Pocket Books 99700.)

442) Kirkendall, Lester A. "Adolescent Homosexual
Fears," in Isadore Rubin and Lester A. Kirkendall
(eds.), Sex in the Adolescent Years: New Directions
in Guiding and Teaching Youth (New York: Association Press, 1968), pp. 181-85 (chap. 31).

443) Klein, Leo. "Homosexuality," in Normal and Abnormal Sex Ways (New York: Belmont, 1962), pp.
93-105 (chap. 10). (Paperback: Belmont L92-552.)

444) Kling, Samuel G. "Homosexual Behavior," in
Sexual Behavior and the Law (New York: Bernard
Geis Associates, 1965), pp. 97-128 (chap. 7).
(Paperback--Pocket Books 77118.)

445) Kluckhohn, Clyde. "As an Anthropologist Views It,"
in Deutsch, no. 337 above, pp. 88-104.

446) Kluckhohn, Clyde. "Sexual Behavior in Cross-Cultural Perspective," in Himmelhoch and Fava, no.
317 above, pp. 332-45 at 339-41.

447)   Knight, Edward H.   "Overt Male Homosexuality," in
        Slovenko, no. 307 above, pp. 434-61.

448)   Kolb, Lawrence O.   "Therapy of Homosexuality," in
        Jules H. Masserman (ed.), Current Psychiatric
        Therapies (New York: Grune and Stratton, 1963),
        3:131-37.

449)   The Koran.   Surah 11:77-83 at 78;   26:160-74 at
        164-65;   29:28-35 at 29.

450)   Krafft-Ebing, Richard von.   "General Pathology:
        Antipathic Sexuality" and "Special Pathology: Un-
        natural Abuse (Sodomy)," in Psychopathia Sexualis:
        A Medico-Forensic Study, translation by Harry E.
        Wedeck and introduction by Ernest Van den Haag
        (New York: Putnam, 1965), pp. 245-383 and 469-500.
        (First published in 1886.)   (Paperback--Putnam 7160.)

451)   Krim, Seymour.   "The Press of Freedom: Revolt of
        the Homosexual," in Daniel Wolf and Edwin Fancher
        (eds.), Village Voice Reader (New York: Grove
        Press, 1955), pp. 146-51.   (Paperback--Black Cat
        BC50.)

452)   Kronhausen, Eberhard and Phyllis.   "The Psychology
        of Pornography: Homosexuality," in Pornography and
        the Law (New York: Ballantine, 1959), pp. 232-36.
        (Paperback--Ballantine S346K.)

453)   Kronhausen, Phyllis and Eberhard.   "Homosexuality,"
        in Sex Histories of American College Men (New York:
        Ballantine, 1960), pp. 168-97, 259-60, 299.   (Paper-
        back--Ballantine S389K.)

454)   Kubie, Lawrence S.   "Psychiatric Implications of the
        Kinsey Report," in Himmelhoch and Fava, no. 317
        above, pp. 270-93 at 277-79.

455)   Landers, Ann.   "What You should know about Homo-
        sexuality," in Ann Landers Talks to Teen-agers
        About Sex (New York: Prentice-Hall, 1963), pp.
        84-94 (chap. 8).   (Paperback--Fawcett Crest d1012.)

456)   Landis, Carney.   "The Homoerotic Woman," in
        Sex in Development (New York: Hoeber, 1940), pp.
        146-54.

457) Larere, Charles. "The Passage of the Angel
      through Sodom," in Peter Flood (ed.), New Prob-
      lems in Medical Ethics (Westminster, Md.: New-
      man Press, 1955), 1:108-23.

458) Laubscher, B. J. F. "Sex in a Pagan Culture," in
      Slovenko, no. 307 above, pp. 231-49 at 239 and 244-
      45.

459) Lawton, Shailer L. and Archer, Jules. "Sexual
      Deviations," in Sexual Conduct of the Teen-ager
      (New York: Greenberg, 1951), pp. 127-35 (chap.
      10).

460) Laycock, Samuel R. "Counseling Individuals with
      Sexual Difficulties," in Pastoral Counseling for
      Mental Health (Nashville, Tenn.: Abingdon Press,
      1961), pp. 78-84.

461) Legman, Gehrson. "The Guilt of the Templars," in
      The Guilt of the Templars (New York: Basic Books,
      1966), pp. 3-134 at 4-7, 54-56 and 98-134 (chap. 1).

462) LeMoal, Paul. "The Psychiatrist and the Homo-
      sexual," in Flood, no. 457 above, 1:70-89.

463) Levy, Sidney. "Figure Drawing as a Projective
      Test," in Lawrence E. Abt and Leopold Bellek
      (eds.), Projective Psychology (New York: Knopf,
      1950), pp. 257-90.

464) Lewinsohn, Richard. "Eros Astray," in History of
      Sexual Customs (New York: Harper, 1958), pp.
      328-48 at 337-46.

465) Licht, Hans [pseudonym of Paul Brandt]. "Male
      Homosexuality," in Sexual Life in Ancient Greece,
      translation by J. H. Freese (London: Routledge
      and Sons, 1932), pp. 411-98 (chap. 5). (Reprinted
      in Cory, no. 27 above, pp. 267-349.)

466) Lindner, Robert M. "Diary of a 'Wolf' and other
      Prison Documents," in Stone Walls and Men (New
      York: Complex Press, 1946), pp. 465-68. (Re-
      printed in "Sex in Prison," Complex, 6:19-20, 1951
      and in Krich, no. 69 above, pp. 99-105.)

467)   Lindner, Robert M.   "Homosexuality and the Con-
        temporary Scene," in Must You Conform? (New
        York: Holt, Rinehart, and Winston, 1956), pp. 31-
        76. (Paperback--Black Cat BB6.) (Reprinted in
        Ruitenbeek, no. 96 above, pp. 52-79.)

468)   Lindner, Robert M.   "Sexual Behavior in Penal In-
        stitutions," in Deutsch, no. 337 above, pp. 201-15.

469)   Lloyd, Charles W.   "Treatment and Prevention of
        Certain Sexual Behavior Problems," in Charles W.
        Lloyd (ed.), Human Reproduction and Sexual Be-
        havior (Philadelphia: Lea and Febiger, 1964), pp.
        490-97.

470)   London, Louis S.   "Analysis of a Homosexual Neuro-
        sis," in Abnormal Sexual Behavior (New York:
        Julian Press, 1937), pp. 149-58.

471)   London, Louis S. and Caprio, Frank S.   "Homo-
        sexuality," in Sexual Deviations (Washington, D.C.:
        Linacre Press, 1950), pp. 45-269 and 635-36. (Re-
        printed in part in Krich, no. 69 above, pp. 30-39.)

472)   Lorand, Sandor.   "The Therapy of Perversions," in
        Lorand and Balint, no. 283 above, pp. 290-307.

473)   Lowrey, Lawson G.   "Psychopathic Personality," in
        Psychiatry for Social Workers (2d ed.; New York:
        Columbia University Press, 1950), pp. 259-71 (chap.
        14).

474)   Maddocks, Lewis I.   "The Law and the Church vs.
        the Homosexual," in Weltge, no. 116 above, pp. 95-
        110 (chap. 8).

475)   Manchester, William.   "The Oscar Wilde of the
        Second Reich," in The Arms of Krupp, 1587-1968
        (Boston: Little, Brown, 1964), pp. 206-32 (chap.
        9).

476)   Mantegazza, Paolo.   "The Perversions of Love," in
        The Sexual Relations of Mankind, translation by
        Samuel Putnam, 11th edition by Victor Robinson
        (New York: Eugenics Publishing Co., 1937), pp.
        78-96 (chap. 5). (Reprinted in Cory, no. 27 above,
        pp. 248-66.)

477) Markillie, Ronald E. D. "Sex Offenders in Prison,"
in Slovenko, no. 307 above, pp. 779-804 at 785, 790,
792, 794-98, 803.

478) Marmor, Judd. "Introduction," in Marmor, no. 75
above, pp. 1-24 (chap. 1).

479) Marrou, H. I. "Pederasty in Classical Education,"
in A History of Education in Antiquity, translation
by George Lamb (New York: Sheed and Ward,
1956), pp. 50-62 (chap. 3). (Paperback--Mentor
MQ552.)

480) Martin, John B. "Sex in Prison," in Break Down
the Walls (New York: Curtis Publishing Co., 1953),
pp. 177-82. (Paperback--Ballantine S376K.)

481) Masor, N. "Psychopathology of the Social Deviate,"
in J. S. Roucek (ed.), Sociology of Crime (New York:
Philosophical Library, 1961), pp. 93-137.

482) Masters, R. E. L. "Homosexual Acts," in Forbidden
Sexual Behavior and Morality: An Objective Reex-
amination of Perverse Sex Practices (New York:
Julian Press, 1962), pp. 161-247.

483) Masters, R. E. L. "Homosexual Bestiality," in
Sex Driven People (Los Angeles: Sherbourne Press,
1966), pp. 171-209.

484) Masters, R. E. L. "The Invert's Problem," in no.
395 above, pp. 256-82 (chap. 7).

485) Mayerson, Peter and Lief, Harold I. "Psychotherapy of Homosexuals: A Follow-Up Study of
Nineteen Cases," in Marmor, no. 75 above, pp.
302-44 (chap. 17).

486) McPartland, John. "Homosexuals," in Sex in Our
Changing World (rev. ed.; New York: Macfadden,
1964), pp. 126-40 (chap. 12). (Paperback--Mac-
fadden 60-181.)

487) McReynolds, David. "The Press of Freedom: the
Gay Underworld--A Reply to Mr. Krim," in Wolf and
Fancher, no. 451 above, pp. 151-55.

488)   Mead, Margaret. "Cultural Determinants of Sexual
        Behavior," in Young, no. 407 above, pp. 1433-81
        at 1451-55 and 1471.

489)   Menninger, Karl A. "Impotence and Frigidity," in
        Man Against Himself (New York: Harcourt, Brace,
        1938), pp. 337-50. (Paperback--HB21.) (Reprinted
        in Aaron M. Krich [ed.], Men: The Variety and
        Meaning of Their Sexual Experience [New York:
        Dell, 1956], pp. 99-114 [chap. 4]. [Paperback--
        Dell D15.])

490)   Menninger, William C. "Homosexuality," in Psy-
        chiatry in a Troubled World (New York: Macmillan,
        1948), pp. 222-31 (chap. 16).

491)   Miller, Milton L. "Proust's Homosexuality: Prob-
        able Contributing Factors and How They are Ex-
        pressed in His Work," in Nostalgia: A Psycho-
        analytic Study of Marcel Proust (Boston: Houghton
        Mifflin, 1956), pp. 159-86 (chap. 12). (Reprinted
        in Ruitenbeek, no. 95 above, pp. 263-83.)

492)   Miller, Milton L. "The Relation between Submission
        and Aggression in Male Homosexuality," in Lorand
        and Balint, no. 283 above, pp. 160-79.

493)   Millett, Kate. "Sexual Politics: Miller, Mailer,
        and Genet," in New American Review (New York:
        New American Library, 1969), no. 7, pp. 7-32 at
        24-29.

494)   Money, John. "Components of Eroticism in Man:
        Cognitional Rehearsals," in Wortis, no. 375 above,
        pp. 210-25 (chap. 16).

495)   Money, John. "Factors in the Genesis of Homo-
        sexuality," in Winokur, no. 287 above, pp. 19-43
        (chap. 2).

496)   Moore, J. E. "Homosexuality and Other Problematic
        Behavior," in C. B. Broderick and J. Bernard (eds.),
        The Individual, Sex, and Society: SIECUS Handbook
        for Teachers and Counselors (Baltimore: Johns
        Hopkins University Press, 1969).

497)   Morse, Benjamin. "The Rising Tide of Homosexuality,"

in The Sexual Revolution (Derby, Conn.: Monarch
Books, 1963), pp. 66-77 (chap. 6). (Paperback--
MB531.)

498)   Mueller, Gerhard O.W. "Sexual Offenses requiring
Other than Heterosexual Connection" and "Tables of
Penalites--Sodomy," in Legal Regulation of Sexual
Conduct (New York: Oceana Publications, 1961), pp.
54-55 (chap. 8) and 127-32 (table 7).

499)   Murdoch, G.P. "The Social Regulation of Sexual
Behavior," in Hoch and Zubin, no. 290 above, pp.
256-66 at 262-63.

500)   Neustatter, W. Lindesay. "Homosexuality: the
Medical Aspects," in Rees and Usill, no. 89 above,
pp. 67-139.

501)   Odenwald, Robert P. "The Next Step: Homosexuality," in The Disappearing Sexes (New York:
Random House, 1965), pp. 139-49.

502)   Opler, Marvin K. "Anthropological and Cross-Cultural Aspects of Homosexuality," in Marmor, no.
75 above, pp. 108-23 (chap. 6).

503)   Orenstein, Leo L. "The Sex Offender," in Marjorie
Bell (ed.), Advances in Understanding the Offender,
1950 Yearbook (New York: Probation and Parole
Association, 1951), pp. 195-202.

504)   Ovesey, Lionel. "Pseudohomosexuality and Homosexuality in Men: Psychodynamics as a Guide to
Treatment," in Marmor, no. 75 above, pp. 211-33
(chap. 12).

505)   Pare, C.M.B. "Etiology of Homosexuality: Genetic
and Chromosomal Aspects," in Marmor, no. 75
above, pp. 70-80.

506)   Patai, Raphal. "Homosexuality," in Sex and Family
in the Bible and the Middle East (Garden City,
N.Y.: Doubleday, 1959), pp. 170-78 (chap. 5).
(Paperback--Dolphin C40.)

507)   Patterson, Hawood and Conrad, Earl. "Shifting
Sex Roles," in Scottsboro Boy (Garden City, N.Y.:

Doubleday, 1950), pp. 79-85. (Reprinted in Norman
Johnston, Leonard Savitz, and Marvin Wolfgang
[eds.], The Sociology of Punishment and Correction
[New York: Wiley and Sons, 1962], pp. 140-43.)

508)   Perloff, William H. "Hormones and Homosexuality,"
in Marmor, no. 75 above, pp. 44-69 (chap. 3).

509)   Ploscowe, Morris. "Homosexuality, Sodomy, and
Crimes against Nature," in Sex and the Law (rev.
ed.; New York: Ace Books, 1962), pp. 182-201
(chap. 7). (Paperback--Ace A2) (Reprinted in
Cory, no. 27 above, pp. 394-406.)

510)   Ploscowe, Morris. "Sexual Patterns and the Law,"
in Deutsch, no. 337 above, pp. 125-43.

511)   Pollens, Bertram. "Homosexuality," in The Sex
Criminal (New York: Emerson Books, 1938), pp.
131-48 (chap. 8).

512)   Pomeroy, Wardell B. "Homosexuality," in Weltge,
no. 116 above, pp. 3-13 (chap. 1).

513)   Pomeroy, Wardell B. "Human Sexual Behavior," in
Faberow, no. 425 above, pp. 22-32 (chap. 3).

514)   Pomeroy, Wardell B. "Parents and Homosexuality,"
in Rubin and Kirkendall, no. 442 above, pp. 173-81
(chap. 30).

515)   Proust, Marcel. "A Race Accursed," in On Art and
Literature, 1896-1919, translation by Sylvia T.
Warner (New York: Meridian Books, 1958), pp.
210-29.

516)   Rado, Sandor. "An Adaptational View of Sexual Behavior," in Hoch and Zubin, no. 290 above, pp.
159-89. (Reprinted in Sandor Rado, Psychoanalysis
of Behavior: Collected Papers [New York: Grune
and Stratton, 1956], pp. 186-213 and in Ruitenbeek,
no. 96 above, pp. 94-126.)

517)   Ramsey, Glenn V. "Sex Questions Asked by Clergy,"
in Beigel, no. 358 above, pp. 67-72 (chap. 7).

518)   Rees, J. Tudor. "Homosexuality and the Law," in

Rees and Usill, no. 89 above, pp. 3-20.

518a) Reuben, David R. "Male Homosexuality," in
       Everything You Always Wanted to Know about Sex
       (New York: David McKay Co., 1969), pp. 129-51
       (chap. 8).

519)   Rhymes, Douglas. "The Predicament of the Homo-
       sexual," in No New Morality: Christian Personal
       Values and Sexual Morality (Indianapolis: Bobbs-
       Merrill Co., 1964), pp. 143-46.

520)   Richmond, Winifred V. "Homosexuality as a Per-
       sonal Problem," in An Introduction to Sex Education
       (New York: Farrar and Rinehart, 1934), pp. 210-16.

521)   Robbins, Burch. "The Consummate Artist [Oscar
       Wilde]," in Sex Sinners on Trial (North Hollywood,
       Cal.: Brandon House, 1966), pp. 14-40. (Paper-
       back: Brandon 1034.)

522)   Robbins, Lewis L. Interview, in Freeman and
       Theodores, no. 294 above, pp. 192-206 (chap. 20).

523)   Robinson, Kenneth. "Parliamentary and Public
       Attitudes," in Rosen, no. 316 above, pp. 451-60
       (chap. 15).

524)   Roeburt, John. "The Homosexual Problem" and
       "Sodomy," in Sex-Life and the Criminal Law (New
       York: Belmont Books, 1963), pp. 74-108 (chaps.
       8-9). (Paperback: Belmont L92-560.)

525)   Romm, May E. "Sexuality and Homosexuality in
       Women," in Marmor, no. 75 above, pp. 282-301
       (chap. 16).

526)   Rubin, Isadore. "The Etiology of Homosexuality--
       Conflicting Theories," in Albert Ellis and Donald W.
       Cory (eds.), Encyclopedia of Homosexual Behavior
       (New York: Citadel Press, in preparation).

527)   Rubin, Isadore. "Helping the Adolescent Cope with
       Homosexual Fears, Anxieties, and Problems," in
       K. E. Krantz and J. P. Semmens (eds.), Adolescence:
       Teenagers and Their Peers (New York: Macmillan,
       1969).

528)   Rubinstein, L. H.   "The Role of Identification in
       Homosexuality and Transvestitism in Men and Women,"
       in Rosen, no. 316 above, pp. 163-95.

529)   Ruitenbeek, Hendrik M.   "The Emasculation of the
       American Male," in Hendrik M. Ruitenbeek (ed.),
       Psychoanalysis and Contemporary Culture (New
       York: Dell, 1964), pp. 184-94.   (Paperback--TM
       75-118.)

530)   Ruitenbeek,   Hendrik M.   "Homosexuality," in The
       Male Myth (New York: Dell, 1966), pp. 181-85.
       (Paperback: Dell 5488.)

531)   Ruitenbeek, Hendrik M.   "Introduction," in Ruiten-
       beek, no. 96 above, pp. xi-xviii.

532)   Ruitenbeek, Hendrik M.   "Men Alone: the Male
       Homosexual and the Disintegrated Family," in Ruiten-
       beek, no. 96 above, pp. 80-93.

533)   Sagarin, Edward.   "Homosexuals: the Many Masks
       of Mattachine," in Odd Man In: Societies of Deviants
       in America (Chicago: Quadrangle Books, 1969), pp.
       78-110.   (Abstracted in Coronet, 7:145-49, Dec.
       1969.)

534)   St. John-Stevas, Norman.   "Homosexuality" and
       "Laws of the States of the U. S. Punishing Homo-
       sexual Offences;   Laws of the United Kingdom
       Punishing Homosexual Offences;   Laws of European
       Countries concerning Homosexual Offences;   [and]
       Proposals of the American Law Institute on Homo-
       sexual Offences," in Life, Death and the Law: Law
       and Christian Morals in England and the United States
       (Bloomington: Indiana University Press, 1961), pp.
       198-231 (chap. 5) and 310-35 (Appendices 10-12).
       (Paperback--Meridian M179.)

535)   Salzman, Leon.   "Homosexuality," in Developments
       in Psychoanalysis (New York: Grune and Stratton,
       1962), pp. 199-212 (chap. 9).

536)   Salzman, Leon.   "Latent Homosexuality," in Marmor,
       no. 75 above, pp. 234-47 (chap. 13).

537)   Salzman, Leon.   "Sexuality in Psychoanalytic Theory,"

In Judd Marmor (ed.) Modern Psychoanalysis: New
Directions and Perspectives (New York: Basic
Books, 1968), pp. 123-45 at 136-39 (chap. 6).

538)   Sanders, Jacob. "Homosexual Twins," in Robinson,
       no. 404 above, pp. 342-43.

539)   Scheinfeld, Amram. "Sex Roles and Sex Life: II.
       Abnormal," in Your Heredity and Environment
       (Philadelphia: Lippincott, 1965), pp. 535-50 (chap.
       40).

540)   Schur, Edwin M.   "Homosexuality," in Crimes
       Without Victims (Englewood Cliffs, N. J.: Prentice-
       Hall, 1965), pp. 67-119 (chap. 3). (Paperback:
       Spectrum S111.)

541)   Scott, Peter D. "Definition, Classification, Prog-
       nosis, and Treatment," in Rosen, no. 316 above,
       pp. 87-119 (chap. 4).

542)   Secor, Neale A.   "A Brief for a New Homosexual
       Ethic," in Weltge, no. 116 above, pp. 67-79 (chap.
       6).

543)   Selling, Lowell S. "The Extra-Institutional Treat-
       ment of Sex Offenders," in Lindner and Seliger,
       no. 418 above, pp. 226-32 at 229-30.

544)   Sherwin, Robert V. "Sodomy," in Slovenko, no.
       307 above, pp. 425-33.

545)   Shields, James and Slater, Eliot. "Heredity and
       Psychological Abnormality," in Hans J. Eysenck
       (ed.), Handbook of Abnormal Psychology: An
       Experimental Approach (New York: Basic Books,
       1961), pp. 298-343 at 329.

546)   Shinn, Rober L. "Homosexuality: Christian Con-
       viction and Inquiry," in Weltge, no. 116 above, pp.
       43-54 (chap. 4).

547)   Shneidman, Edwin S. "Suicide," in Faberow, no.
       425 above, pp. 33-43 (chap. 4).

548)   Simon, William and Gagnon, John H. "The Les-
       bians: A Preliminary Overview," in Gagnon and

Simon, no. 266 above, pp. 247-82.

549)   Sines, Jacob O. and Pittman, David J. "Male
       Homosexuality: the Relevance of Cross-Species
       Studies of Sexual Behavior, " in Winokur, no. 287
       above, pp. 189-92 (chap. 9).

550)   Slater, Eliot. "The Sex of Sibs and Children of
       Homosexuals, " in D. R. Smith and W. M. Davidson
       (eds.), Symposium on Nuclear Sex (London: Heine-
       mann, 1958), pp. 79-83.

551)   Slovenko, Ralph. "A Panoramic View: Sexual Be-
       havior and the Law, " in Slovenko, no. 307 above,
       pp. 5-144 at 8, 69, 81-91, 110-11, 113, and 116-17.

552)   Smith, E. Parkinson and Ikin, A. Graham. "Homo-
       sexuality and Family Life, " in Sex Problems and
       Personal Relationships (London: Heinemann, 1956),
       pp. 120-23 (chap. 11).

553)   Socarides, Charles W. "Female Homosexuality, " in
       Slovenko, no. 307 above, pp. 462-77.

554)   Sprague, W. D. "The Loneliest People in the World, "
       in Sexual Rebellion in the Sixties (New York: Lan-
       cer Books, 1965), pp. 46-58 (chap. 5). (Paperback:
       Lancer 73-440.)

555)   Stekel, Wilhelm. "The Case of Miss Ilse, " in
       Stekel, no. 107 above, pp. 96-106. (Reprinted in
       Krich, no. 69 above, pp. 13-19.)

556)   Stekel, Wilhelm. "Relation of Sadomasochism to
       Homosexuality, " in Sadism and Masochism: The
       Psychology of Hatred and Cruelty, translation by
       Louis Brink (New York: Liveright, 1953), 1:137-
       201 (chap. 5).

557)   Stoller, Robert J. "Passing and the Continuum of
       Gender, " in Marmor, no. 75 above, pp. 190-210
       (chap. 11).

558)   Storr, Anthony. "Male Homosexuality, " in Sexual
       Deviation (Baltimore: Penguin, 1964), pp. 81-90
       (chap. 8). (Paperback: Pelican A649.)

559)   Sykes, Gresham. "Argot Roles: Wolves, Punks, and Fags, " in The Society of Captives (Princeton: Princeton University Press, 1958), pp. 95-99. (Reprinted in Johnson, Savitz, and Wolfgang, no. 507 above, pp. 138-39.)

560)   Symonds, John A. "On Walt Whitman, " in Ruitenbeek, no. 95 above, pp. 111-18.

561)   Szasz, Thomas S. "Legal and Moral Aspects of Homosexuality, " in Marmor, no. 75 above, pp. 124-39 (chap. 7).

561a) Szasz, Thomas S. "The Product of Conversion--From Heresy to Illness" and "The Model Psychiatric Scapegoat--The Homosexual, " in The Manufacture of Madness: A Comparative Study of the Inquisition and the Mental Health Movement (New York: Harper and Row, 1970), pp. 160-77 (chap. 10) and 242-59 (chap. 13).

562)   Taylor, Gordon R. "Historical and Mythological Aspects of Homosexuality, " in Marmor, no. 75 above, pp. 140-64 (chap. 8).

563)   Thielicke, Helmut. "The Problem of Homosexuality, " in The Ethics of Sex, translation by John W. Doberstein (New York: Harper and Row, 1964), pp. 269-92 (chap. 4D).

564)   Thoinot, L. "Perversion of the Sexual Instinct, " "Inversion of the Sexual Instinct, " and "Inversion of Degenerates, or Uranism, " in Medico-Legal Aspects of Moral Offenses, translation by A. W. Weysoe (Philadelphia: Davis Co. , 1918), pp. 267-349 (chaps. 13-15).

565)   Tiffany, L. P. , McIntyre, D. M. Jr. , and Rotenberg, D. L. "Homosexuality, " in Detection of Crime: Stopping and Questioning, Search and Seizure, Encouragement and Entrapment (Boston: Little, Brown, 1967), pp. 231-39 (chap. 17).

566)   Ullerstam, Lars. "Homosexuality, " in The Erotic Minorities, translation by Anselm Hollo (New York: Grove Press, 1966), pp. 94-103 (chap. 9). Introduction by Yves de Saint-Agnes. (Paperback--Black Cat BC126.)

567)   Van den Haag, Ernest. "Notes on Homosexuality and
       Its Cultural Setting," in Ruitenbeek, no. 96 above,
       pp. 291-302. (Reprinted in pamphlet form by Pan-
       Graphic Press, San Francisco, 1963--see no. 227
       above.)

568)   Van den Haag, Ernest. "Psychoanalysis and the
       Social Sciences: Genuine and Spurious Integration,"
       in Hendrik M. Ruitenbeek (ed.), Psychoanalysis and
       Social Science (New York: Dutton, 1962), pp. 167-
       85 at 179-81. (Paperback: Dutton D93.)

569)   Vander Veldt, James H. and Odenwald, Robert P.
       "Homosexuality," in Psychiatry and Catholicism
       (2d ed.: New York: McGraw-Hill, 1957), pp. 422-
       38 (chap. 26).

570)   Voltaire. "The Love Called Socrates," translation
       by Donald W. Cory from "Amour Socratique," in
       Dictionnaire Philosophique (Paris: Didot, 1809), 1:
       256-62. (Reprinted in Cory, no. 27 above, pp. 350-
       53.)

571)   W-----, Mrs. "One Family's View," Geddes, no.
       296 above, pp. 154-64 at 159-60.

572)   Wahl, Charles W. "The Evaluation and Treatment
       of the Homosexual Patient," in Wahl, no. 393 above,
       pp. 192-205.

573)   Walker, Kenneth. "The Problem of Homosexuality,"
       in Physiology of Sex (2d ed.; Baltimore: Penguin,
       1954), pp. 149-62 (chap. 12).

574)   Walker, Kenneth. "Sexual Deviations," in The
       Physiology of Sex and Its Sexual Implications (Har-
       mondsworth, Eng.: Penguin, 1940), pp. 124-37
       (chap. 11). (Paperback: Pelican.)

575)   Walker, Kenneth and Strauss, Eric B. "The Psycho-
       pathology of Sexual Deviation" and "Psychotherapy of
       the Commoner Sexual Neuroses and Deviations," in
       Sexual Disorders in the Male (3d ed.; Baltimore:
       Wilkins and Wilkins, 1948), pp. 170-85 (chap. 13)
       and 186-205 (chap. 14).

576)   Wegrocki, Henry J. "Defining Normality and Ab-

normality," in Melvin Zax and George Stricker (eds.),
The Study of Abnormal Behavior: Selected Readings
(New York: Macmillan, 1964), pp. 3-12 (chap. 1).

577) Weltge, Ralph W. "The Paradox of Man and Woman,"
in Weltge, no. 116 above, pp. 55-66 (chap. 5).

578) West, Donald J. "Clinical Types among Sexual
Offenders," in Slovenko, no. 307 above, pp. 413-
24 at 416-17 and 420-21.

579) West, Louis J. and Glass, Albert J. "Sexual Behavior and the Military Law," in Slovenko, no. 307
above, pp. 250-72.

580) Westermarck, Edward A. "Homosexual Love," in
The Origin and Development of Moral Ideas (London:
Macmillan, 1908), 2:456-89 (chap. 43). (Reprinted
in Cory, no. 27 above, pp. 101-38 and in Krich,
no. 489 above, pp. 216-32.)

581) Whiteley, C. H. and Winifred, M. "Unfruitful Sex,"
in Sex and Morals (London: Botsford, 1967), pp.
79-100 at 89-94.

582) Whitman, Howard. "Homosexuality," in The Sex
Age (Garden City, N. Y.: Doubleday, 1962), pp.
132-46 (chap. 10).

583) Wilbur, Cornelia B. "Clinical Aspects of Female
Homosexuality," in Marmor, no. 75 above, pp. 268-
81 (chap. 15).

584) Wilde, Gunther. "Homosexuality," in Deviation: A
Study of Abnormal Love (New York: Macfadden-
Bartell, 1966), pp. 127-37. (Paperback: Macfadden
MB75-177.)

585) Wilkerson, David. "Homosexuality Starts at Home," in
Parents on Trial (New York: Hawthorn Books,
1967), chap. 8.

586) Willis, Stanley E. "A Philosophy of Helping the
Sexual Deviate," in Wahl, no. 393 above, pp. 205-
20.

587) Wittels, Fritz. "Homosexuality," in Vernon C.

Branham and Samuel B. Kertash (eds.), Encyclopedia of Criminology (New York: Philosophical
Library, 1949), pp. 190-94.

588)   Wolfgang, Michael S. "Lesbianism" and "Male
        Homosexuality," in Male and Female Sexual Devia-
        tions (Los Angeles: Sherbourne Press, 1964), pp.
        33-44 (chap. 5) and 46-52 (chap. 6). Introduction
        by Leonard A. Lowag. (Paperback.)

589)   Woodward, L. T. "Homosexuality in the High Schools"
        and "Homosexuality on the Campus," in Sex in Our
        Schools (Derby, Conn.: Monarch Books, 1962), pp.
        89-92 (chap. 18) and 139-40 (chap. 21). (Paperback:
        Monarch MB521.)

590)   Woodward, L. T. "Homosexuals in Uniform," in
        Sex and the Armed Forces (Derby, Conn.: Mon-
        arch Books, 1960), pp. 69-79 (chap. 6). (Paper-
        back: Monarch MB507.)

591)   Wortis, Joseph and Rosenblatt, Jay S. "Sexual
        Deviation and the Plasticity of the Sex Pattern," in
        Jules H. Masserman (ed.), Biological Psychiatry
        (New York: Grune and Stratton, 1959), 1:82-89
        (chap. 7).

592)   Zarrilli, C. L. "A Critical Analysis of the Royal
        Commission Report on Homosexuality and Prostitution,"
        in Herbert A. Bloch, Crime in America (New York:
        Philosophical Library, 1961), pp. 258-81.

Newspaper Articles

593) Ackerman, Joanell. "Homosexuals Lack Help, Understanding," Daily Nebraskan, May 5, 1969, p. 5.

594) "Ada Prosecutor Files Four More Morals Charges,"
Idaho Daily Statesman, Nov. 24, 1955, p. 1.

595) Alverson, Charles A. "A Minority's Plea - U.S.
Homosexuals Gain in Trying to Persuade Society to
Accept Them," Wall Street Journal, July 17, 1968,
pp. 1, 15.

596) Auerbach, Stuart. "Panel Urges Repeal of Homosexual Laws," Washington Post, Oct. 21, 1969, pp.
1, A15.

597) Bergman, Harry. " 'Third Sex' Convention in San
Francisco," San Francisco Sunday Examiner and
Chronicle, Aug. 21, 1966, p. 15.

598) Berlandt, Konstantin. "Minorities--'2,700 Homosexuals at Cal.'," Daily Californian, Nov. 29 -
Dec. 3, 1965. (5 articles.)

599) Bess, Donovan. "Angry Ministers Rip Police," San
Francisco Chronicle, Jan. 3, 1965, p. 2.

600) Bieber, Irving. "Speaking Frankly on a Once Taboo
Subject," New York Times, Aug. 23, 1964, magazine
section, p. 75.

601) "A Big Court Victory for U.S. Homosexuals," San
Francisco Chronicle, July 2, 1969, p. 8.

602) "Biggest San Francisco Raid on Homosexuals," San
Francisco Chronicle, Feb. 14, 1965, p. 3.

603) Bird, David. "Trees in a Queens Park Cut Down
as Vigilantes Harass Homosexuals," New York Times,
July 1, 1969, pp. 1, 29.

603a) Black, Jonathan. "Gay Power Hits Back," Village
       Voice, July 31, 1969, pp. 1, 3, 38.

604)   Blumenthal, Ralph. "Bundestag Votes Penal Re-
       form," New York Times, May 10, 1969, pp. 1, 5.

605)   Bryan, John. "Police Outrages Help Create L.A.
       Homosexual Rights Drive," Los Angeles Free Press,
       Mar. 10, 1967, p. 5.

606)   Buckley, William F. Jr. "Homosexual Laws," San
       Francisco Examiner, Mar. 3, 1966, p. 34.

607)   Carroll, Jerry. "Homosexual Pickets: Gay Melee
       at Examiner," San Francisco Chronicle, Nov. 1,
       1969, p. 5.

608)   Childs, Marquis. "Much More Than Personal
       Disaster," Washington Post, Oct. 23, 1964, p. A12.

609)   "The Church and the Homosexual," San Francisco
       Chronicle, Apr. 29, 1966, p. 3.

610)   "Church for Sex Law Reform," San Francisco Ex-
       aminer, Apr. 9, 1967, p. 1.

611)   "City Lifts Job Curb for Homosexuals," New York
       Times, May 9, 1969, pp. 1, 23.

612)   "City Police Step Up Mass Arrest Here," New York
       Times, June 17, 1956, p. 66.

613)   Clines, Francis X. "Long Island Homosexuals to
       Get Legal Aid," New York Times, July 24, 1967,
       p. 19.

614)   "College Boys Help Trap Homosexuals," San Fran-
       cisco Chronicle, Dec. 29, 1965, p. 2.

615)   Collins, Carol. "Sex Deviates Menace Los Angeles,"
       Hollywood Citizen-News, Feb. 4-8, 1964. (5 arti-
       cles.)

616)   Cooney, William. "A Homosexual Bill of Rights,"
       San Francisco Chronicle, July 4, 1968, p. 4.

617)   Crane, Lionel. "How to Spot a Possible Homo,"

London Sunday Mirror, Apr. 28, 1963, p. 7.

618)   "Crush the Monster," Idaho Daily Statesman, Nov. 3,
       1955. (Editorial.)

619)   Culbert, Mike. "90,000 S.F. Perverts--Startling
       Police Report," San Francisco News Call Bulletin,
       Mar. 18, 1965, p. 3.

620)   Dart, John. "Church for Homosexuals," Los Angeles
       Times, Dec. 8, 1969, part 2, pp. 1-3.

621)   Dart, John. "Cleric Urges Churches to Give Homo-
       sexuals Aid," Los Angeles Times, Oct. 3, 1967,
       part 2, p. 6.

622)   Defrain, John. " 'Rights' Sought for Nation's Homo-
       sexuals," Lincoln Evening Journal and Nebraska
       State Journal, Oct. 5, 1968, p. 11.

623)   Denton, Charles. "A Case of Too Much Under-
       standing?" San Francisco Examiner, Jan. 28, 1965,
       p. 29.

624)   "Distribution of Report on Homosexuality," San Fran-
       cisco Chronicle, July 18, 1967, p. 40.

625)   Donaldson, Stephen. "The Anguish of the Student
       Homosexual," Columbia Daily Spectator, Apr. 11,
       1968, pp. 4, 9.

626)   Doty, Robert C. "Growth of Overt Homosexuality in
       City Provokes Wide Concern," New York Times,
       Dec. 17, 1963, pp. 1, 33.

627)   Drews, Jed. "Broward Grand Jury to Probe Homo-
       sexuals," Broward County Sun-Sentinel, Apr. 11,
       1966, p. 1.

628)   Duran, Jeanne. "Guides for the Understanding
       Parent," Detroit Free Press, Sep. 19-21, 1965.
       (3 articles.)

629)   Dusheck, George. "A Sex Treatment That is
       Shocking," San Francisco Call-Bulletin, Sep. 28,
       1963, p. 4.

630) Fiske, Edward B. "Episcopal Clergymen Here Call Homosexuality Morally Neutral," New York Times, Nov. 29, 1967, pp. 1, 39.

631) "4 Policemen Hurt in 'Village' Raid," New York Times, June 29, 1969, p. 33.

632) Freeman, Ira H. "Cafe Drive Turns to Homosexuals," New York Times, Dec. 1, 1960, p. 30.

633) Furlong, Monica. "The Law and the Homosexual," London Daily Mail, Oct. 21, 1964, p. 8.

634) Gervis, Stephanie. "The Homosexual's Labyrinth of Law and Social Custom," Village Voice, Oct. 11, 1962.

635) Gilbert, George. "Dispelling Some Myths about the Homosexual," San Francisco Chronicle, Aug. 31, 1967, p. 52.

636) Golden, Harry. "Politics and Homosexuality," Carolina Israelite, Jan.-Feb. 1961, p. 20.

637) Graham, Fred P. "The Homosexuals' Case," New York Times, July 9, 1967, sec. 4, p. E7.

638) Grigg, John. "Is Homosexuality a Crime?" New York Times, magazine section, June 27, 1965, pp. 6-7.

639) Gruenberg, Charles. "Cops Pinch 69 'Undesirables' in New West Side Roundup," New York Post, Mar. 13, 1955, pp. 3, 20.

640) Grutzner, Charles. "S.L.A. Won't Act on Deviate Bars," New York Times, Apr. 26, 1966, p. 54.

641) Hager, Philip. "Court Bars Lifting of Teacher's Credential for Homosexual Act," Los Angeles Times, Nov. 21, 1969, pp. 28, 29.

642) Hamill, Pete. "The Worst Job," New York Post, Apr. 19, 1966, p. 41.

643) Hansen, Terry. "Stanford's New Homophile League Holds Discussion about Problems," Palo Alto Times, Feb. 5, 1968, p. 3.

644)   Harris, Louis. "Public Registers Strong Disapproval
       of Nonconformity," Washington Post, Sep. 27, 1965,
       p. 2.

645)   Harris, Sidney J. "Make Homosexuality Legal,"
       Miami Herald, Dec. 23, 1964, p. 6A.

646)   Harris, Sydney J. "Who's At Fault?" San Fran-
       cisco Examiner, Dec. 23, 1964, p. 23.

647)   Hebert, Dick. "Atlanta's Lonely 'Gay' World,"
       Atlanta Journal and Constitution, Jan. 3-8, 1966.
       (6 articles.)

648)   Heyler, David. "Let's Face Our Sex Deviate Peril,"
       Hollywood Citizen-News, Feb. 1, 2, 7, 8, 11, 1964. (5
       editorials.)

649)   "High Court Denies Homosexual Plea," New York
       Times, May 23, 1967, p. 41.

650)   "High Court in Jersey Overturns a Ban on Homo-
       sexuals in Bars," New York Times, Nov. 7, 1967,
       p. 28.

651)   Hoge, Warren. "Federal Job Barriers on Homo-
       sexuals Falling," New York Post, Sep. 10, 1969, p.
       7.

652)   "Homosexuals and Crime," San Francisco News
       Call Bulletin, Mar. 19, 1965, p. 16.

653)   "The Homosexuals Reply to Doctor," San Francisco
       Chronicle, June 21, 1968, pp. 1, 21.

654)   Hunter, Charlayne. "Homosexual Presses a Security
       Clearance Probe," New York Times, Aug. 20, 1969,
       p. 38.

655)   Jenkins, Bess. "Homosexual 'Expressing Prefer-
       ence,' " Lincoln Evening Journal and Nebraska State
       Journal, Feb. 28, 1969, p. 36.

656)   Kauffmann, Stanley. "Homosexual Drama and Its
       Disguises," New York Times, Jan. 23, 1966, sec.
       2, p. 1.

657)   Kauffmann, Stanley. "On the Acceptability of the
       Homosexual," New York Times, Feb. 6, 1966, sec.
       2, p. 1.

658)   Kilpatrick, James J. "The Law and Homosexuals:
       Perhaps a Sin; Not a Crime," Miami Herald, Dec.
       16, 1964, p. 7A.

659)   Komisar, Lucy. "Three Homosexuals in Search of
       a Drink," Village Voice, May 5, 1966, p. 15.

660)   Labelle, Maurice. "Laws Needed to Force 'Homos'
       to Seek Help," Coral Gable Times, Feb. 4, 1965,
       pp. 6, 8.

661)   Lenn, Ernest. "Special Cops for 'Gay' Bars," San
       Francisco Examiner, Oct. 12, 1961, p. 3.

662)   Lewis, Anthony. "Commons Adopts Bill to Modify
       Penalty for Homosexuality," New York Times, July
       5, 1967, pp. 1, 5.

663)   Lissner, Will. "Homosexual Fights Rule in Security
       Clearance," New York Times, Nov. 26, 1967, p.
       70.

664)   McCabe, Charles. "Fear, and Be Saved," San
       Francisco Chronicle, Aug. 11, 1966, p. 28.

665)   McCabe, Charles. "Free the Queers," San Fran-
       cisco Chronicle, Mar. 11, 1969, p. 29.

666)   Merry, Howard. "Tenderloin Ministry," Wall
       Street Journal, Mar. 13, 1967, pp. 1, 14.

667)   Moorehouse, Geoffrey. "Outside of 'Normal' Society,"
       San Francisco Chronicle, Oct. 8, 1967, p. 5.

668)   Nathan, Ruth. "How Not to Marry a Homosexual,"
       San Francisco Sunday Examiner and Chronicle, Apr.
       7, 1968, Women's Section, p. 3.

669)   Nouwen, H. "Homosexuality: Prejudice or Mental
       Illness?" National Catholic Reporter, Nov. 29, 1967,
       pp. 4-8.

670)   Oppedahl, John. "Glide Church--A Bold Path to the

Fringes of Society," San Francisco Sunday Examiner and Chronicle, Sep. 10, 1967, p. 3.

671) Pace, Eric. "Police Forbidden to Lure Deviates," New York Times, May 11, 1966, p. 39.

672) Patterson, Robert. "Dreary Revels of S. F. 'Gay' Clubs," San Francisco Examiner, Oct. 25, 1969, p. 5.

673) Perlman, David. "A Medical View of the Homosexual," San Francisco Chronicle, June 19, 1968, pp. 1, 28.

674) Perlmutter, Emanuel. "Catholics and Episcopalians Differ on Law for Sex Deviates," New York Times, Nov. 26, 1964, pp. 1, 34.

675) Perlmutter, Emanuel. "Penal Law Plan Meets Objection," New York Times, Nov. 25, 1964, p. 43.

676) "Police Again Rout 'Village' Youths," New York Times, June 30, 1969, p. 22.

677) "Police Nab 109 in Raid on Club near Chicago," Arizona Daily Star, Apr. 26, 1964, p. 9A.

677a) "Police Order Renews Drive on Sex Deviates," San Francisco Chronicle, May 26, 1955, p. 1.

678) "Police with Dogs Raid a 'Gay' Bar," San Francisco Examiner, Feb. 14, 1965, p. 3.

679) Raudebaugh, Charles. "Liberalized State Sex Law Drafted," San Francisco Chronicle, July 13, 1967, pp. 1, 9.

680) Regelson, Rosalyn. "Up the Camp Staircase," New York Times, Mar. 3, 1968, sec. 2, pp. 1, 14.

680a) Ross, Nancy. "Homosexual Revolution," Washington Post, Oct. 25, 1969, pp. C1-2.

681) Roth, Jack. "Blackmail Paid by Congressman," New York Times, May 17, 1967, pp. 1, 35.

682) Roth, Jack. "National Ring Preying on Prominent

Deviates," New York Times, Mar. 3, 1966, pp. 1, 25.

683)   "Santa Ana Police Nab 40 in Drive on Homosexuals," Long Beach Press Telegram, Mar. 17, 1965, p. 2.

684)   Schott, Webster.   "Civil Rights and the Homosexual," New York Times, Nov. 12, 1967, magazine section, pp. 44-72.

685)   Schumach, Murray.   "Columbia Charters Homo-sexual Group," New York Times, May 3, 1967, pp. 1, 44.

686)   Schumach, Murray.   "Morals: On the Third Sex," New York Times, May 7, 1967, sec. 4, p. 5.

687)   "Secrecy Ruling on Homosexuals," San Francisco Chronicle, Dec. 18, 1969, p. 14.

688)   Sharpley, Anne.   "London's Hidden Problem," London Evening Standard, July 20-23, 1964. (4 articles.)

689)   Sharpley, Anne.   "The Roots of Prejudice," San Francisco Sunday Examiner and Chronicle, Dec. 25, 1966, p. 4.

690)   "Sin and the Homosexual," San Francisco Chronicle, May 2, 1968, p. 1E.

691)   Smith, Julie.   "The Lesbians' Story," San Francisco Chronicle, June 30 - July 2, 1969. (3 articles.)

692)   Speckman, James.   "500 Sex Deviates Quizzed by Police," Columbus Dispatch, Dec. 2, 1962, p. 22A.

693)   "A Stout Defense of San Francisco Homosexuals," San Francisco News Call Bulletin, Aug. 17, 1965, p. 10.

694)   "A Study of Homosexuals in America," San Francisco Chronicle, Oct. 4, 1967, p. 2.

695)   Sullivan, Dan.   "Three Plays Examine Dark Side of Gay Life," Los Angeles Times, Mar. 30, 1969, calendar section, p. 32.

696) Taubman, Howard. "Not What It Seems; Homo-
      sexual Motif Gets Heterosexual Guise, " New York
      Times, Nov. 5, 1961, sec. 2, p. 1.

697) "This Mess Must be Removed, " Idaho Daily States-
      man, Nov. 18, 1955. (Editorial.)

698) "Three Boise Men Admit Sex Charges, " Idaho Daily
      Statesman, Nov. 2, 1955, p. 1.

699) Thurber, Scott. "The City's Homosexuals and
      Police, " San Francisco Chronicle, Sep. 25, 1965,
      pp. 1, 4.

700) Trentacoste, Palma. "Charities Delegates Told
      Church Can Aid Homosexuals, " Monitor (Archdio-
      cese of San Francisco), Oct. 19, 1967, p. 7.

701) Ubell, Earl. "Sexual Deviation--Many Theories, No
      Cure, " New York Herald Tribune, Oct. 18, 1964,
      p. 45.

702) Wacker, Denise and Sutin, Philip. "Comments Dif-
      fer on Problem of Homosexuality, " Michigan Daily,
      June 29, 1962, p. 1.

703) Wacker, Denise and Sutin, Philip. "Police, 'U'
      Crack Down on Homosexual Activities, " Michigan
      Daily, June 28, 1962, p. 1.

704) Walman, Hal. " 'Police Abuse Us, ' Homophiles
      Across Nation Cry, " Los Angeles Free Press, Sep.
      8, 1967.

705) "War Role Sought for Homosexuals, " New York Times,
      Apr. 17, 1966, p. 10.

706) "Wayne U. Destroys Files Protested by Students, "
      New York Times, May 5, 1967, p. 19.

707) Wegars, Don. "Ginsberg Reports: Cuba Homosexuals,"
      San Francisco Chronicle, July 23, 1965, p. 4.

708) Wehrwein, Austin. "Minnesota U. Recognizes Club
      for Homosexuals, " Washington Post, Nov. 25, 1969,
      p. A2.

709)   Whearley, Bob. "Homosexuals in Denver," <u>Denver Post</u>, Feb. 14-19, 1965. (5 articles.)

710)   White, Jean. "Those Others: A Report on Homosexuality," <u>Washington Post</u>, Jan. 31 - Feb. 4, 1965. (5 articles.)

711)   Wickstrom, Karl. "The Life of a Homosexual: It's Sad, Not Gay," <u>Miami Herald</u>, Aug. 9, 1964, p. 9D.

712)   Wille, Lois. "Chicago's Twilight World--the Homosexuals," <u>Chicago Daily News</u>, June 20-23, 1966. (4 articles.)

713)   Wyden, Peter and Barbara. "Growing Up Straight: the Father's Role," <u>New York Times</u>, July 26, 1968, magazine section, pp. 69-72.

714)   Zane, Maitland. "Life in a World of Sexual Hostility," <u>San Francisco Chronicle</u>, Aug. 20, 1966, p. 2.

715)   Zion, Sidney E. "Albany Abandons Homosexual Bill," <u>New York Times</u>, May 28, 1965, p. 36.

Articles in Popular Magazines

716) "Adult Responsibility," Time, 67:14, Jan. 2, 1956.

717) "Against Nature," Economist, 185:844, Dec. 7, 1957.

718) "All in the Family," Time, 94:64, Aug. 29, 1969.

719) "All the Sad Young Men," Time, 81:105-08, June 14, 1963.

720) Anonymous. "Boarding School Homosexuality," Times Educational Supplement, 2220:1552, Dec. 6, 1957.

721) Anonymous. "The Homosexual in Advertising: Does It Take Men to Sell Women?" Printer's Ink, 288: 52, June 26, 1964.

722) Anonymous. "Story of a Tragic Marriage," Good Housekeeping, 167:36-46, July 1968.

723) "As Security Becomes a Growing Issue," U.S. News and World Report, 57:6, Nov. 2, 1964.

724) "Assassination: History or Headlines?" Newsweek, 69:44, 47, Mar. 13, 1967.

725) "The Ax Falls," Newsweek, 41:31, May 4, 1953.

726) Ayer, A.J. "Homosexuals and the Law," New Statesman and Nation, 56:716-17, Nov. 22, 1958. (See no. 141 above.)

727) Baldwin, James. "Gide as Husband and Homosexual," New Leader, Dec. 13, 1954. (Reprinted as "The Male Prison," in Nobody Knows My Name [New York: Dial Press, 1961], pp. 155-62 [chap. 10].) (Paperback--Dell 6435.)

728) "Battle Unjoined," Newsweek, 41:28, Mar. 23, 1953.

729)   Becker, Howard S.   "Deviance and Deviates," Na-
        tion, 201:115-19, Sep. 20, 1965.

730)   Becker, Howard S.   "Idaho's Hot Potato," Book
        Week, 4:20-21, Nov. 6, 1966.

731)   Beecher, John.   "A Little Night Music," Nation,
        199:272-75, Oct. 26, 1964.

732)   Bergler, Edmund.   "Twilight Love," Coronet, 2:32-
        38, Oct. 1964.

733)   Berkman, Ted.   "The Third Sex--Guilt or Sickness?"
        Coronet, 39:129-33, Nov. 1955.

734)   Bickel, Alexander M.   "Homosexuality as Crime in
        North Carolina," New Republic, 151:5-6, Dec. 12,
        1964.

735)   Bone, Robert A.   "The Novels of James Baldwin,"
        Tri-Quarterly, Win. 1965, pp. 3-20.

736)   "The Boys in the Band," Time, 91:97, Apr. 26,
        1968.

737)   Braine, J.   "Confession," National Review, 21:1176,
        Nov. 18, 1969.

738)   Breward, Ian.   "Hagley Park Treatment," Landfall,
        74:155-61, June 1965.

739)   "A Bridge to the Non-Church," Time, 90:86, 88,
        Oct. 20, 1967.

740)   Brien, Alan.   "Afterthought: Homosexuality,"
        Spectator, 211:542, Oct. 25, 1967.

741)   Brien, Alan.   "Campers' Guide," New Statesman,
        73:873-74, June 23, 1967.

742)   Buckley, Tom.   "The Transsexual Operation," Es-
        quire, 67:111-15, 205-08, Apr. 1967.

743)   Buckley, William F. Jr.   "Jenkins and the Public
        Concern," National Review, 16:947, Nov. 3, 1964.

744)   Buckley, William F. Jr.   "On Experiencing Gore

Vidal," Esquire, 72:108-13, 122-32, Aug. 1969.

745)   Bunzel, Peter. "Outbreak of New Films for Adults Only," Life, 52:88-102, Feb. 23, 1962.

746)   Burke, Tom. "The New Homosexuality," Esquire, 73:178, 304-18, Dec. 1969.

747)   "Calling Col. Barmitage," Time, 80:35, Nov. 16, 1962.

748)   "Camp and After," New Statesman, 68:894-95, Dec. 4, 1964.

749)   Cantor, Donald J. "The Homosexual Revolution: A Status Report," Humanist, 27:160-63, Fall 1967. (Reprinted in Social Progress, no. 208 above, pp. 5-12.)

750)   Caprio, Frank S. "How to Warn Your Kids about Homosexuals," Pageant, 24:100-07, July 1968.

751)   Carroll, Paul. "What's A Warhol?" Playboy, 16: 133-34, 140, 278-82, Sep. 1969.

752)   "The Case of the Elusive Euphemism," Time, 88: 45-46, July 22, 1966.

753)   "The Charge of Immorality," New Republic, 153: 6-7, July 3, 1965.

754)   Chataway, Christopher. "A New Deal for the Homosexual," Spectator, 216:133-34, Feb. 4, 1966.

755)   "Cheers for Democracy," Economist, 218:712, Feb. 19, 1966.

756)   Chester, Alfred. "Fruit Salad," New York Review of Books, 1:6-7, Special Issue, 1963.

757)   "A Choice, Not an Echo," Esquire, 62:97, Jan. 1965.

758)   "Cities of the Plain," Economist, 189:769-70, Nov. 29, 1958.

759)   "City Side," Newsweek, 62:42, Dec. 30, 1963.

760)   Coady, Matthew. "Civilization Marches On," New
        Statesman, 71:214, Feb. 18, 1966.

761)   Coates, Stephen. "Homosexuality," New Society,
        no. 17, pp. 19-20, Jan. 24, 1963.

762)   "Cook County Horror," Time, 90:75, Dec. 15, 1967.

763)   Crawford, Kenneth. "The Loud Silence," Newsweek,
        64:42, Nov. 2, 1964.

764)   "Crime and Sin," Time, 70:74, Oct. 7, 1957.

765)   "Crime Breeding Prisons," Newsweek, 55:108, 110-12,
        Apr. 25, 1960.

766)   "The 'Crime' of Deviation," Newsweek, 64:90, Dec.
        7, 1964.

767)   "Crimes for the Times," Time, 83:36, Mar. 27,
        1964.

768)   Cullen, Tom. "Homosexuality and British Opinion,"
        New Republic, 132:13-15, Apr. 25, 1955.

769)   "Curable Disease," Time, 68:74-76, Dec. 10, 1956.

770)   Curran, Charles. "Sex and Politics in Britain,"
        Spectator, 201:10-11, July 4, 1958.

771)   Curtler, Martin S. "The Homosexual Minority,"
        Saturday Review of Literature, 32:25, June 4, 1949.

772)   David, Lester. "Our Son Was Different," Good
        Housekeeping, 162:51, 113, 115, 120, 122-25, Jan. 1966.

773)   Davidson, Bill. "Your Eye Can't Lie," Saturday
        Evening Post, 239:76-79, Jan. 15, 1966.

774)   Davis, Alan J. "Sexual Assaults in the Philadelphia
        Prison System and Sheriff's Vans," Trans-Action,
        Dec. 1968, pp. 8-13.

775)   "Dealing with Deviates," Time, 88:17, Dec. 30,
        1966.

776)   "Death of a Playwright," Time, 90:40, Sep. 15, 1967.

777) "Death of Ahmed el Osamy," Time, 88:27, Aug. 12, 1966.

778) "The Defectors," Newsweek, 56:33-37, Sep. 19, 1960.

779) "Defectors: the Risk, the Danger," Newsweek, 56: 58, Sep. 26, 1960.

780) "A Delicate Problem," Newsweek, 43:99-102, June 14, 1954.

781) Deutsch, Albert. "Vice Squad," Colliers, 133:66-70, May 28, 1954.

782) Diotima. "Roots of Homosexualism," Contemporary Review, 207:5-7, July 1965.

783) Disney, D.C. "Alma Hid from the Truth," Ladies Home Journal, 85:30ff., Oct. 1968.

784) "Dr. Kinsey's Misrememberers," Time, 51:76, June 14, 1948.

785) Donnelly, Desmond. "Blackmailer's Charter," Spectator, 208:232, Feb. 23, 1962.

786) "A Double Crown," Time, 94:71-72, Sep. 19, 1969.

787) Dove, Tom. "Homosexuals in U.S. Army!" Confidential, 17:46-49, Jan. 1969.

788) "Dramatically Different," Time, 84:52-53, Aug. 14, 1964.

789) Elemen, Ormen. "Truth about that Homosexual Blackmail Ring," Confidential, 15:14-15, 48, Oct. 1967.

790) "Equality for Your Fellow Man," Time, 89:52, May 12, 1967.

791) Evans, Bergen. "That Homosexuals are Always Effeminate," American Mercury, 64:598, May 1947.

792) "Facing the Facts," Newsweek, 50:50, Sep. 16, 1957.

793)   Farnham, Marynia F.   "The Unmentionable Minority,"
       Cosmopolitan, May 1948.

794)   "Fascination with the Deviate," Time, 93:68, Jan.
       10, 1969.

795)   "The Fear," International Nudist Sun, 4:11-12, 1964.

796)   Fermor, Patrick L.   "Homosexuals and the Law,"
       Spectator, 192:460, Apr. 16, 1954.

797)   "Files on Parade," Time, 61:26, Feb. 16, 1953.

798)   "Filling in the Blanks," Time, 84:52, Aug. 14, 1964.

799)   Fitzgibbon, Constantine.   "Politics and Sex," Spec-
       tator, 210:563-64, May 3, 1963.

800)   Fonzi, Gaeton J.   "The Furtive Fraternity," Greater
       Philadelphia Magazine, Dec. 1962. (See no. 159
       above.)

801)   Forster, E. M.   "A Magistrate's Figures," New
       Statesman and Nation, 46:508-09, Oct. 31, 1953.

802)   "425 Homosexuals," Time, 61:26, Apr. 20, 1953.

803)   Frankenheimer, Anna.   "A Much-Needed Upbraiding
       of Long-Hair Music," Fact, 1:11-17, Nov.-Dec. 1964.

804)   "Fundamental Right," Newsweek, 50:58-59, Dec. 16,
       1957.

805)   "Funny Business," Time, 57:22, Apr. 9, 1951.

806)   Furlong, Monica.   "Crime and Canterbury," Spec-
       tator, 203:818-20, Dec. 4, 1959.

807)   "Games Lesbians Play," Time, 88:93, Oct. 14, 1966.

808)   Gebhard, Paul.   "The 1965 Kinsey Report: Our
       Dangerous Sex Laws," Ladies Home Journal, 82:66-
       67,121 and 82:42-44, May and June 1965.

809)   "George and the Leprechauns," Time, 85:23B, Mar.
       26, 1965.

810)   Gibbens, T. C. N.   "Is Aversion Therapy Wrong?"
       New Society, no. 250:42-43, July 13, 1967.

811)   Gilbert, Carol.   "The Homosexual in Society,"
       Insert, May 1965, pp. 16-19.

812)   Gilliatt, Penelope.   "Consenting Adults," Spectator,
       205:69, July 8, 1960.

813)   Gilmour, Ian.   "Echoes of a Report: Wolfenden
       and the 'Scandal,' " Spectator, 213:106, July 26,
       1964.

814)   "God and the Homosexual," Newsweek, 69:63, Feb.
       13, 1967.

815)   Golden, Harry.   "Politics and Homosexuality,"
       Carolina Israelite, Jan. -Feb. 1961, p. 20.

816)   Gorer, Geoffrey.   "Man to Man," Encounter, 16:73-
       79, May 1961.

817)   Gosling, Ray.   "Homosexuals Now," New Society,
       no. 309:293-94, Aug. 29, 1968.

818)   Gould, R. E.   "Understanding Homosexuality," Seven-
       teen, 28:90-91f. , July 1969.

819)   "The Great Hippie Hunt," Time, 94:22-23, Oct. 10,
       1969.

820)   Grey, Antony.   "Homosexuality: Time for Action
       Now, " Views Quarterly, 1:57-61, 1963.

821)   Grey, Antony and West, Donald J.   "Homosexuals:
       New Law but No New Deal," New Society, no. 39,
       Mar. 27, 1969, pp. 476-79.

822)   Hadden, Samuel B.   "A Way Out for Homosexuals,"
       Harper's, 234:107-08, 114-20, Mar. 1967.

823)   Hall, Wendall.   "The Fag-Jag on the Boob Tube, "
       Fact, 4:16-23, Jan. -Feb. 1967.

824)   Hanauer, Joan.   "The 'Gay' Society," Morals '68,
       pp. 52-53.

825)   Hardwick, Elizabeth. "Sex and the Single Man,"
        New York Review of Books, 3:4, Aug. 20, 1964.

826)   Hart, H. L. A. "Immorality and Treason," Listener,
        62:162-63, 1959.

827)   Haskell, Francis. "A Hidden Life," New York
        Review of Books, 4:20-21, Apr. 8, 1965.

828)   Hatterer, Lawrence and Mayer, Nancy. "What
        Every Parent Should Know about Homosexuality,"
        Parents Magazine, 43:56-57, 72, Mar. 1968.

829)   Hauser, Richard and others. "The Male Homo-
        sexual," Listener, 73:141-43, Jan. 28, 1965.

830)   Havemann, Ernest. "Homosexuality in America:
        Scientists Search for Answers to a Touchy and
        Puzzling Question--Why?" Life, 56:76-80, June 26,
        1964.

831)   Hefner, Hugh. "The Playboy Philosophy," Playboy,
        11:63-68, 176-84, Apr. 1964; 12:69-72, 159-60, Nov.
        1965; and 12:83-87, 220-25, Dec. 1965.

832)   Helmer, William J. "New York's 'Middle-Class'
        Homosexuals," Harper's, 226:85-92, Mar. 1963.

833)   Herberg, W. "The Case for Heterosexuality,"
        National Review, 21:1007-08, Oct. 7, 1969.

834)   Hicks, Granville. "The Covert Community," Satur-
        day Review, 46:23-24, June 8, 1963.

835)   "The Hidden Problem," Time, 62:28-29, Dec. 28,
        1953.

836)   Hofstadter, Samuel H. Letter to the Editor, Nation,
        201:428, Nov. 29, 1965.

837)   "Home Office," New Society, no. 45, Aug. 6, 1963,
        p. 19.

838)   "Homosexual Acts," Newsweek, 69:28, 30, Jan. 2, 1967.

839)   "The Homosexual in America," Time, 87:40-41, Jan.
        21, 1966.

840)   "The Homosexual: Newly Visible, Newly Understood, "
       Time, 94:56-67, Oct. 31, 1969.

841)   "Homosexual Wedding, " Newsweek, 70:59, July 17,
       1967.

842)   "Homosexuality: A Medical Viewpoint, " Spectator,
       193:778, Dec. 17, 1954.

843)   "Homosexuality between Wars: Preoccupations at
       Oxford and Cambridge, " Time, 91:73, Mar. 8,
       1968.

844)   "Homosexuality: Coming to Terms, " Time, 94:82,
       Oct. 24, 1969.

845)   "Homosexuality, Cont'd. , " New Republic, 152:5,
       Jan. 9, 1965.

846)   "The Homosexuality Issue, " Newsweek, 42:44-47,
       Nov. 16, 1953.

847)   "Homosexuals and the Stage, " Time, 78:78-79,
       Nov. 17, 1961.

848)   "Homosexuals can be Cured, " Time, 85:44-46, Feb.
       12, 1965.

849)   "Homosexuals in State, " Time, 61:21, Mar. 23,
       1953.

850)   "Homosexuals in Uniform, " Newsweek, 29:54, June
       9, 1947.

851)   "Homosexuals: One Soldier in 25?" Newsweek,
       57:92, 94, May 15, 1961.

852)   "Homosexuals: 28 Fired by State Department, "
       U. S. News and World Report, 61:16, Sep. 26, 1966.

853)   "Housecleaning Time, " Time, 59:22, Apr. 7, 1952.

854)   "How Secret the Confessional, " Time, 90:51, Dec.
       22, 1967.

855)   Hughes, Graham. "Law, Sin, and Private Behavior,"
       Nation, 186:57-58, Jan. 18, 1958.

856)   Hyams, Edward. "The Spurious Problem," New
        Statesman and Nation, 59:945-46, June 25, 1960.

857)   "Idaho Underworld," Time, 66:25, Dec. 12, 1955.

858)   "The Impenitent Thief," Time, 89:78, E5, Feb. 3,
        1967.

859)   "Infection from the Enemy," Time, 57:29-30, June
        25, 1951.

860)   "The Iniquitous Depths," Time 88:14, Aug. 26, 1966.

861)   Irwin, Theodore. "The 'Queer One': The Facts
        about Homosexuality," Pageant, 21:116-25, Mar. 1966.

862)   "The Jenkins Case," Nation, 199:290-91, Nov. 2, 1964.

863)   Jenkins, Roy. "A Resounding Finale," Spectator,
        205:52, July 25, 1960.

864)   "Johnson and the Jenkins Case," Time, 84:20, Nov.
        6, 1964.

865)   Joyce, Marion. "Flight from Slander; Zeal for
        Imputing Homosexuality," Forum, 100:90-94, Aug.
        1938.

866)   "Justice for Homosexuals," Nation, 201:318-19, Nov.
        8, 1965.

867)   Kameny, Franklin E. "The Federal Government
        versus the Homosexual," Humanist, 29:20-23, May-
        June, 1969.

868)   Katz, Sidney. "The Harsh Facts of Life in the 'Gay'
        World," Maclean's Magazine, 77:18, 34-38, Mar. 7,
        1964. (See no. 181 above.)

869)   Katz, Sidney. "The Homosexual Next Door," Maclean's
        Magazine, 77:10-11, 28-30, Feb. 22, 1964. (See no.
        181 above.)

870)   Kauffmann, Stanley. "Prisoners and the Law," New
        Republic, 146:35-36, Mar. 12, 1962.

871)   Kauffmann, Stanley. "Queer Lives," New York

Review of Books, 5:31-33, Nov. 11, 1965.

872)   Knight, Arthur and Alpert, Hollis. "The History of
        Sex in Cinema: Part XV: Experimental Films,"
        Playboy, 14:136-42, 196-212 at 202-12, Apr. 1967.

873)   Knight, Arthur and Alpert, Hollis. "Sex in Cinema:
        1969," Playboy, 16:168-81, 258-66, Nov. 1969.

874)   Kroll, Jack. "Chez Harry," Newsweek, 71:96, Jan.
        22, 1968.

875)   Kroll, Jack. "Decline and Fall," Newsweek, 74:
        129, Oct. 20, 1969.

876)   Kroll, Jack. "Jacks and Queens," Newsweek, 71:
        93-94, Apr. 29, 1968.

877)   Kroll, Jack. "Underground in Hell," Newsweek, 68:
        109, Nov. 14, 1966.

878)   Kurtz, Irma. "Homosexuality: the Unlocking of a
        Law," Nova, Feb. 1967, pp. 20-25.

879)   Laine, Dixie. "Cuba Plans Concentration Camp for
        Homos," Confidential, 13:34-35, 56-59, Aug. 1965.

880)   Lathbury, Vincent T. "Mothers and Sons: An In-
        timate Discussion," Ladies Home Journal, 82:43-45,
        Feb. 1965.

881)   "Lavender and Old Blues," Newsweek, 54:82, July
        20, 1959.

882)   "The Law and the Homosexual," Economist, 177:113,
        Oct. 8, 1955.

883)   "The Law and the Homosexual Problem," Life, 58:4,
        June 11, 1965.

884)   Leavitt, Jack. "The Ordinariness of Sodomy," Na-
        tion, 204:54-57, Jan. 9, 1967.

885)   Lee, Donald. "Seduction of the Guilty: Homosexuality
        in American Prisons," Fact, 2:57-61, Nov.-Dec. 1965.

886)   Lindner, Robert M. "Sex in Prison," Complex, 6:

5-20, 1951. (See no. 466 above.)

887) "Live and Let Live, " Realist, no. 36, pp. 1, 11-14,
      Aug. 1962; no. 37, pp. 9-13, Sep. 1962; and no.
      38, pp. 8-14, Oct. 1962.

888) "The Lonergan Case, " Time, 43:68-69, Apr. 3, 1944.

889) "Lord in the Dock, " Newsweek, 42:33, Dec. 28, 1953.

890) MacInnes, Colin. "English Queerdom, " Partisan
      Review, 28:146-53, Jan. 1961.

891) Magee, Bryan. "Facts about Lesbianism: A Special
      Inquiry into a Neglected Problem, " New Statesman,
      69:491-93, Mar. 6, 1965.

892) "Mail Snooping, " New Republic, 153:6-7, Aug. 21,
      1965.

893) Major, Ralph H. Jr. "New Moral Menace to our
      Youth, " Coronet, 28:101-08, Sep. 1950.

894) "Making of a Homosexual, " Newsweek, 72:63, Aug.
      5, 1968.

895) "The Male Homosexual, " Listener, 73:141-43, 1965.

896) "Man Hunt, " Time, 57:28, June 18, 1951.

897) Marine, Gene. "Who's Afraid of Little Annie Fanny?"
      Ramparts, 5:27-30, Feb. 1967.

898) Martin, Kingsley. "The Abominable Crime, " New
      Statesman and Nation, 46:508, Oct. 31, 1953.

899) Mathis, Charles V. " 'Gay Set' Influx Worries Cape
      May, " Variety, 238:54, 56, Apr. 28, 1965.

900) McIntosh, K. C. "Greek Way of Life, " Saturday Re-
      view of Literature, 33:24, Mar. 11, 1950.

901) "Men Only, " Time, 66:19, Dec. 26, 1955.

902) "Merely Unlawful?" Economist, 193:712, Nov. 21,
      1959.

903)   "The Milieu is the Meaning," Time, 79:66, June 8, 1962.

904)   Miller, Emanuel. "Sex and Society: A Psychiatrist's View," Twentieth Century, 163:16-21, 1958.

905)   "Minority Listening," Newsweek, 60:48, July 30, 1962.

906)   "Miss Mary doesn't Answer Any More," Time, 80: 41, Nov. 2, 1962.

907)   "The Missing Diplomats," Newsweek, 37:36, 41, June 18, 1951.

908)   "Modernizing Sex Laws," Time, 94:57, Aug. 8, 1969.

909)   "More Harm than Good," Time, 76:17, Aug. 22, 1960.

910)   "More Private Vices," Economist, 184:735-36, Sep. 7, 1957.

911)   Morgenstern, Joseph. "Sandy's Week," Newsweek, 71:92, Feb. 19, 1968.

912)   Murtagh, John M. "The Principle of Privacy," Saturday Review, 43:31-32, May 4, 1963.

913)   "Musica e Martini Dry," Time, 86:62, July 16, 1965.

914)   "Neo-Gothic Trend," Time, 89:96-97, May 26, 1967.

915)   "Netherlands: A Gay Place," Newsweek, 72:38, Dec. 23, 1968.

916)   "The New Morality," International Nudist Sun, 4:32, 1964.

917)   "The New Pornography," Time, 85:28-29, Apr. 16, 1965.

918)   "New Pressure to Ease Morals Laws," U.S. News and World Report, 57:12, Dec. 7, 1964.

919)   "New Shape of the Y," Newsweek, 68:86, July 7, 1966.

920)   "New Shocker," Newsweek, 35:18, May 29, 1950.

921)   "New World Cacophony," Time, 79:76, Jan. 29,
        1962.

922)   Nichols, Beverley. "The Twisted Marriage of
        Somerset Maugham," Look, 30:33-37, Oct. 18, 1966.

923)   Niemoller, A. F. "A Glossary of Homosexual Slang,"
        Fact, 2:25-27, Jan.-Feb. 1965.

924)   "Nuts from Underground," Time, 88:37, Dec. 30,
        1966.

925)   "Object Lesson," Time, 56:10, Dec. 25, 1950.

926)   "Odd Company," Time, 89:24-25, Mar. 10, 1967.

927)   "Out of the Briar Patch," Time, 84:54-55, Dec. 25,
        1964.

928)   Panter-Downs, Mollie. "Letter from London," New
        Yorker, 33:136-40, Sep. 28, 1957.

929)   Panter-Downs, Mollie. "Letter from London," New
        Yorker, 34:114-16, Dec. 13, 1958.

930)   "Parliament: Home Office," New Society, no. 72,
        Feb. 13, 1964, p. 23.

931)   Peale, Norman V. "Answers to Questions," Look,
        20:132, Dec. 11, 1956.

932)   "The Peephole Problem," Time, 86:59, 61, Nov. 12,
        1965.

933)   Perrot, Roger. "Police Getting Too Tough on Homo-
        sexuals," Observer, Mar. 31, 1968, p. 8.

934)   "The Petty Demon," Time, 84:114, Nov. 27, 1964.

935)   Pharos. "A Spectator's Notebook," Spectator, 201:
        743, Nov. 28, 1958.

936)   Phelan, James. "Rush to Judgment in New Orleans,"
        Saturday Evening Post, 240:21-25, May 6, 1967.

937)   Phillips, William. "The New Immoralists," Com-
        mentary, 39:66-69, Apr. 1965.

938)   Pickrel, Paul. "Sex: the Amateurs and the Virtuosi,"
        Harper's, 233:116-18, Dec. 1966.

939)   Pilpel, Harriet F. "Sex v. the Law: A Study in
        Hypocrisy," Harper's, 230:35-40, Jan. 1965.

940)   Plate, Thomas G. "Not So Gay," Newsweek, 72:
        108, Oct. 14, 1968.

941)   "Playboy Forum," Playboy, 12:37-39,140, Feb. 1965
        ("Air Force Psychiatrist's Dissent," "Homosexuality
        in the Military," and "The Jenkins Case").

942)   "Playboy Forum," Playboy, 12:63, May 1965 ("En-
        trapment in New Orleans").

943)   "Playboy Forum," Playboy, 12:12, Nov. 1965 ("Gay
        Say").

944)   "Playboy Forum," Playboy, 13:64, June 1966 ("Homo-
        sexual Rights").

945)   "Playboy Forum," Playboy, 13:144, Aug. 1966
        ("Menace to Homosexuals").

946)   "Playboy Forum," Playboy, 14:55-56,218, Jan. 1967
        ("Homosexual Harassment," "Vice Squad Franken-
        stein," "Homosexual Dilemma," and "Lesbian La-
        ment").

947)   "Playboy Forum," Playboy, 14:52, Apr. 1967
        ("Homosexual Harassment" and "Vice Squad Cor-
        ruption").

948)   "Playboy Forum," Playboy, 14:147, May 1967
        ("Homosexuality in Prison").

949)   "Playboy Forum," Playboy, 14:174, June 1967
        ("Fair Play for Homosexuals," "Suicide and Homo-
        sexuality," and "Survival and Homosexuality").

950)   "Playboy Forum," Playboy, 14:135, July 1967
        ("Are Homosexuals Psychopathic?").

951)   "Playboy Forum," Playboy, 14:146, Aug. 1967
        ("Sodomy Factories").

952)   "Playboy Forum," Playboy, 14:81,184, Sep. 1967
        ("A Queer Sort of Arrest," "Detecting Deviates,"
        and "Homosexuality and Hypocrisy").

953)   "Playboy Forum," Playboy, 14:56, Oct. 1967
        ("Liberals and Lesbians" and "Homosexuality and
        Manhood").

954)   "Playboy Forum," Playboy, 14:83-84, 86, Dec. 1967
        ("Homosexual Cure," "Bisexual Insecurity," "Homo-
        sexual Arrests," "Save a Queer for Me," "Hell in
        Paradise," "Lavender Bluecoat," "Psychopathic
        Homosexuals," and "Homosexual Erotica").

955)   "Playboy Forum," Playboy, 15:59-60, Jan. 1968
        ("Sodomy Factories").

956)   "Playboy Forum," Playboy, 15:41,46, Feb. 1968
        ("Life Term for Homosexual," "Homosexual Mar-
        riage," and "Dayton Doldrums").

957)   "Playboy Forum," Playboy, 15:45-47, Mar. 1968
        ("Sodomy Factories," "An Ex-Prisoner's Tale,"
        "Homosexuals and the Police," and "Pointless Law
        Reform").

958)   "Playboy Forum," Playboy, 15:63, Apr. 1968
        ("Police and Entrapment Denial").

959)   "Playboy Forum," Playboy, 15:60-61, May 1968
        ("Absalom, My Son," "Dayton Doldrums," and
        "Defenseless Male").

960)   "Playboy Forum," Playboy, 15:54-56, June 1968
        ("Homosexuals and the Draft," "Lesbians and Puri-
        tanism," and "Death for Homosexuals").

961)   "Playboy Forum," Playboy, 15:51, July 1968 ("More
        Deviation, Less Population").

962)   "Playboy Forum," Playboy, 15:82, 220-21, Sep. 1968
        ("Sodomy Factories," "Death for Homosexuals,"
        "God and the Homosexual," and "Christ A Homo-
        sexual").

963)   "Playboy Forum," Playboy, 15:179-80, Nov. 1968
        ("Behavior Therapy," "Consensual Sodomy," and
        "Crimes without Victims").

964)   "Playboy Forum," Playboy, 16:50, 54, 56, Jan. 1969
        ("Sodomy Factories" and "God and Peanut Butter").

965)   "Playboy Forum," Playboy, 16:43, 45-46, Mar. 1969
        ("WACs Fight Lesbian Charge," "Behavior Therapy,"
        "Gay is Good," and "Bus Terminal Blues").

966)   "Playboy Forum," Playboy, 16:68, 180, 182, Apr.
        1969 ("Report on Homosexuals," "Straight is Great,"
        "The Man Between," and "A Queer Sort of Fuzz").

967)   "Playboy Forum," Playboy, 16:64-65, 69, June 1969
        ("Therapy and Morality," "Citizenship for Bisexuals,"
        "Biological Predestination," "Homosexuality as a
        Compulsion," "Penalizing Heterosexuals," and "Com-
        pulsive Heterosexuals").

968)   "Playboy Forum," Playboy, 16:47-48, July 1969
        ("LSD and Homosexuality").

969)   "Playboy Forum," Playboy, 16:42, 48-50, Aug. 1969
        ("Homosexuals and the Draft," "The Nature of Homo-
        sexuality," "Army of Quacks," "A Double Life," and
        "Report on Homosexuals").

970)   "Playboy Forum," Playboy, 16:71-74, 80, Sep. 1969
        ("Nonexclusive Homosexuality," "The Morality of
        Passing," "I Dislike What I Am," "Sodomy Fac-
        tories," and "Sergeant Strangelove").

971)   "Playboy Forum," Playboy, 16:64-65, 78-80, Oct.
        1969 ("Homosexuals' Right to Work," "Queens vs.
        'Queens,' " "Infectious Homosexuality," "American
        Apartheid," "Hounding Homosexuals," and "Homo-
        sexuals and Psychiatry").

972)   "Playboy Forum," Playboy, 16:64, Nov. 1969
        ("Sex-Law Revision").

973)   "Playboy Forum," Playboy, 16:82, 84, Dec. 1969
        ("Sodomy Factories," "Sexual Preferences," "Mor-
        ality and the Homosexual," and "The Nature of
        Homosexuality").

974)   "Playboy Interview: Jean Genet," Playboy, 11:45-
       53, Apr. 1964.

975)   "Playboy Interview: Allen Ginsberg," Playboy, 16:
       81-92, 236-44 at 86-90, Apr. 1969.

976)   "Playboy Interview: Gore Vidal," Playboy, 16:77-96,
       238, at 77, 92-94, June 1969.

977)   "Playboy Panel: Religion and the New Morality,"
       Playboy, 14:55-78, 148-61 at 68, 148, 150, 155, and
       158, June 1967.

978)   Playfair, Giles.   "Sex and the Law: Beyond Wolfen-
       den," Spectator, 214:713-14, June 4, 1965.

979)   "A Plea for Perversion?" Time, 79:102, Feb. 23,
       1962.

980)   Ploscowe, Morris.   "We Must Change Our Sex Laws,"
       Coronet, 32:31-35, Oct. 1952.

981)   "The Poetry of Wasted Lives," Time, 79:93, May 18,
       1962.

982)   "Policing the Third Sex," Newsweek, 74:76, 81, Oct.
       27, 1969.

983)   Prideaux, Tom.   "What's So Funny about Sad Sister
       George?" Life, 61:6, Dec. 2, 1966.

984)   "Problem Still Plaguing the State Department," U.S.
       News and World Report, 54:8, June 17, 1963.

985)   "Prodigious Prodigy," Time, 79:86, Mar. 30, 1962.

986)   "Prosecuting Homosexuals; Greater Uniformity,"
       Economist, 212:340, July 25, 1964.

987)   "Public and Private Vice," New Statesman and Na-
       tion, 54:261, Sep. 7, 1957.

988)   "Quaking Morals," Newsweek, 61:77, Mar. 4, 1963.

989)   "Queer People," Newsweek, 34:52-54, Oct. 10, 1949.

990)   "Question of Consent," Time, 70:22, Dec. 16, 1957.

991)   "Quirks of the Mind," Newsweek, 31:46, May 31,
        1948.

992)   Raven, Simon. "Boys Will Be Boys: The Male
        Prostitute in London," Encounter, 15:19-24, Nov.
        1960. (Reprinted in Ruitenbeek, no. 96 above,
        pp. 279-90.)

993)   Raven, Simon. "Homosexuality without Cant,"
        Spectator, 220:808, June 14, 1968.

994)   Raven, Simon. "Special Occasion," Spectator,
        205:818, Nov. 25, 1960.

995)   "Reagan's Denials: to be Continued?" Newsweek,
        70:27, Nov. 20, 1967.

996)   "Resurgent Syphilis," Time, 80:74-75, Sep. 21,
        1962.

997)   Richardson, Maurice. "A Minority," New States-
        man and Nation, 59:946, June 25, 1960.

998)   Ridgeway, James. "Snooping in the Park," New
        Republic, 152:9-10, Jan. 16, 1965.

999)   "Risks of Research," Time, 90:40, Dec. 22, 1967.

1000)   Robinson, Kenneth, "The Time for Decision," New
        Statesman and Nation, 59:942-43, June 25, 1960.

1001)   "Rococo Rotter," Time, 82:71, Nov. 22, 1963.

1002)   Rodell, Fred. "Our Unlovable Sex Laws," Trans-
        action, 2:36-39, May-June 1965.

1003)   Rolph, C. H. "Homosexuality: Reform at Last?"
        New Statesman, 71:152, Feb. 4, 1966.

1004)   Rolph, C. H. "Lords Do It Again," New Statesman,
        70:148-49, July 30, 1965.

1005)   Rolph, C. H. "Parliament Must Choose," New
        Statesman, 63:293-94, Mar. 2, 1962.

1006)   Rolph, C. H. "The Problem for the Police," New
        Statesman, 59:944-45, June 25, 1960.

1007)   Rolph, C. H.   "Roy Jenkins Sets to Work," New
         Statesman, 71:35, Jan. 14, 1966.

1008)   Rolph, C. H.   "Wolfenden Revisited," New States-
         man, 54:373-74, Sep. 28, 1957.

1009)   Rolph, C. H.   "Wolfenden Revived," New Statesman,
         69:792, May 21, 1965.

1010)   "Room Service in Lausanne," Time, 83:42, Apr.
         3, 1964.

1011)   "Rooting Them Out," Time, 57:26, May 7, 1951.

1012)   Roth, Philip.   "The Play that Dare not Speak Its
         Name," New York Review of Books, 4:4, Feb. 25,
         1965.

1013)   Rowe, Dilys.   "A Quick Look at Lesbians," Twen-
         tieth Century, 171:67-72, Win. 1962-63.

1014)   Russell, Daniel.   "The Homosexual Dilemma,"
         Master Detective, 75:48-49, 53-55, Feb. 1968.

1015)   "Sacred Realm," Newsweek, 50:60, Oct. 7, 1957.

1016)   Salkeld, Pablo.   "Ugly Head," Horizon, 20:3-13,
         1949.

1017)   "Sandy's Week," Newsweek, 71:92, Feb. 19, 1968.

1018)   Sanford, David.   "Boxed In: Homosexuals' Ex-
         clusion from Military Service," New Republic, 154:
         8-9, May 21, 1966.

1019)   Sapirstein, Milton R.   "The 'Happy' Homosexual,"
         Nation, 173:551-52, Dec. 22, 1951.

1020)   Sapirstein, Milton R.   "Hindering the Search for
         Morality," Nation, 174:252-53, Mar. 15, 1952.

1021)   "Satisfaction for Kuchel," Newsweek, 65:23-24,
         Mar. 8, 1965.

1022)   "A Scandal at the Top," Newsweek, 70:15, Oct.
         30, 1967.

1023)   "Scandal on the Campus," Newsweek, 56:44, Sep.
        19, 1960.

1024)   Schickel, Richard. "Shock of Seeing a Hidden
        World," Life, 65:34-38, Nov. 1, 1968.

1025)   Schickel, Richard. "The Yawnsome Task of Waiting
        for Warhol," Life, 66:15, June 13, 1969.

1026)   Schreiber, Flora R. "I Was Raising a Homosexual
        Child," Cosmopolitan, 154:60-65, Jan. 1963.

1027)   "A Self-Corrective for the Population Explosion,"
        Time, 83:56, Feb. 28, 1964.

1028)   "The Senior Staff Man," Time, 84:19-23, Oct. 23,
        1964.

1029)   "Sex and the Church," Time, 67:33, June 4, 1956.

1030)   "Sex Spies: UCLA Study of Law Enforcement Poli-
        cies and Practices," Nation, 202:572-73, May 16,
        1966.

1031)   "Shame is Enough," Time, 90:30, July 14, 1967.

1032)   Shaw, George B. "The Cleveland Street Scandal,"
        Encounter, 3:20-21, Sep. 1954.

1033)   Sheed, Wilfrid. "Gay Life Gets a Sharp Going
        Over," Life, 64:18, May 24, 1968.

1034)   Sherrill, Robert G. "U.S. Civil Service: Wash-
        ington's Bland Bondage," Nation, 204:239-42, Feb.
        20, 1967.

1035)   "Shocker in the White House: the Jenkins Case,"
        Life, 57:43-44, Oct. 23, 1964.

1036)   "Shouldn't Prosecute Homosexuality but Church
        Should Bar Homos: Cleric," Justice Weekly, Feb.
        26, 1966, p. 11.

1037)   Sidel, Victor W. "Medical Ethics and the Cold
        War," Nation, 191:325-27, Oct. 29, 1960.

1038)   Silver, George A. "The Homosexual: Challenge to

Science," Nation, 184:451-54, May 25, 1957.

1039)   Silverstein, Shel. "Silverstein on Fire Island,"
         Playboy, 12:121-25, Aug. 1965.

1040)   "Sin and Criminality," Time, 65:13, May 30, 1955.

1041)   "Sin or Crime?" Newsweek, 67:54, Feb. 21, 1966.

1042)   "The Sins of Sodom," Time, 82:54, Sep. 6, 1963.

1043)   Smail, R. C. "Is It True about the Templars?"
         New York Review of Books, 8:14-15, Feb. 23, 1967.

1044)   Smart, Mollie S. and Bieber, Irving. "What You
         Should Know about Homosexuality," Parents Maga-
         zine, 41:31-32, 62, 104, 106, May 1966.

1045)   "The Smear," Time, 85:23, Mar. 5, 1965.

1046)   "Smeared Peer Revenged," Newsweek, 64:40, Aug.
         17, 1964.

1047)   "The Smell of Treason," Time, 80:23, Nov. 23,
         1962.

1048)   Smith, Colin. "Homosexual Clinic Opens in Hol-
         land," Observer, Dec. 1, 1968, p. 6.

1049)   "Social Lepers or Sick Men?" Spectator, 191:470,
         Oct. 30, 1953.

1050)   Sontag, Susan. "Notes on 'Camp,'" Partisan Re-
         view, 31:515-30, Fall 1964.

1051)   "Spasms of Fury," Time, 84:62-63, Dec. 25, 1964.

1052)   "Spots on Mr. Clean," Newsweek, 70:34-35, Nov.
         13, 1967.

1053)   "Staircase," Time, 91:66-67, Jan. 19, 1968.

1054)   "Stand Up and be Counted," Spectator, 204:903-04,
         June 24, 1960.

1055)   Star, Jack. "The Faces of the Boys in the Band"
         and "A Changing View of Homosexuality?" Look,
         33:62-68, Dec. 2, 1969.

1056)   Star, Jack. "The Sad 'Gay' Life," Look, 31:31-33, Jan. 10, 1967.

1057)   "Status and Sodomy," Time, 90:100, Sep. 8, 1967.

1058)   Stern, Daniel. "A Special Corner on Truth," Saturday Review, 48:32, Nov. 6, 1965.

1059)   "Still Another List," Nation, 198:615, June 22, 1964.

1060)   "The Story of Pop," Newsweek, 67:56-61, Apr. 25, 1966.

1061)   "The Strange World," Time, 74:66, Nov. 9, 1959.

1062)   "Suicidal Tendencies," Time, 88:114, Oct. 14, 1966.

1063)   "Sweeping the Streets," Spectator, 199:291, Sep. 6, 1957.

1064)   " 'Taboo' on Television," Newsweek, 50:68, Dec. 9, 1957.

1065)   Taper. "Westminster Commentary," Spectator, 201:742, Nov. 28, 1958.

1066)   Taubman, Howard. "The Subtle Persuasion in the American Theater," Cosmopolitan, 155:88-91, Nov. 1963.

1067)   Terkel, Studs. "What It's Like to be: ... A Homosexual ...," Coronet, 5:153-94 at 163-64, June 1967.

1068)   "That Kind of Love," Time, 79:83, Feb. 9, 1962.

1069)   "Their Liberal Lordships," Newsweek, 65:38, June 7, 1965.

1070)   "Therese and Isabelle," Time, 91:56, May 31, 1968.

1071)   "These Tragic Women," Newsweek, 53:62, 64, June 15, 1959.

1072)   "The Third Sex," Newsweek, 63:76, June 1, 1964.

1073)   "The Third Sex on Stage," Show Business Illustrated, 1:34-36, 40, 76-78, Apr. 1962.

1074)   "To Punish or Pity," Newsweek, 56:78, July 11,
         1960.

1075)   "Toronto Homosexual Centre in Canada, Claims
         Minister," Justice Weekly, Feb. 26, 1966, p. 11.

1076)   Towne, Alfred. "Homosexuality in American Cul-
         ture: the New Taste in Literature," American
         Mercury, 73:3-9, Aug. 1951.

1077)   "Traitor's Day in Moscow," Time, 76:20, Sep. 19,
         1960.

1078)   "Trial of Truth," Newsweek, 60:34, Nov. 26, 1962.

1079)   Trilling, Diana. "Uncomplaining Homosexuals,"
         Harper's, 239:90-95, Aug. 1969.

1080)   Trilling, Lionel. "Sex and Science: the Kinsey
         Report," Partisan Review, 15:460-76, Apr. 1948.
         (Reprinted in Bulletin of the Menninger Clinic,
         13:109-18, 1949; in Lionel Trilling, The Liberal
         Imagination [New York: Viking Press, 1950;
         Anchor Paperback A13], pp. 216-35; and in
         Geddes, no. 286 above, pp. 213-29 at 227-28.)

1081)   "Tyranny or Blaspheny," Time, 55:16, May 29,
         1950.

1082)   "Uganda's Black Saints," Time, 84:57, July 17,
         1964.

1083)   "Uncle Willie," Newsweek, 67:102,104, May 9,
         1966.

1084)   "The Unspeakable Crime," Time, 62:35-36, Nov.
         16, 1953.

1085)   "A Vest-Pocket Guide to Camp," Life, 59:84,
         Aug. 20, 1965.

1086)   "Vice Laws in Prospect," Economist, 189:881,
         Dec. 6, 1958.

1087)   "Victim," Campus Illustrated, May-June 1962, pp.
         5,34.

1088) Vidal, Gore. "But Is It Legal?" Partisan Review, 32:79-87, Win. 1965. (Reprinted as "Sex and the Law," in Gore Vidal, The City and the Pillar Revised, no. 3077 below, pp. 229-41.)

1089) Vidal, Gore. "A Distasteful Encounter with William F. Buckley, Jr." Esquire, 72:140-45, 150-51, Sep. 1969.

1090) "Viennese Drag," Time, 94:71, Oct. 17, 1969.

1091) Wainwright, Loudon. "What Road Back from Ruin?" Life, 57:31, Oct. 30, 1964.

1092) Wand, J. W. C. "Homosexuality: the Christian View," Spectator, 195:59, July 8, 1955.

1093) Warner, Rex. "Renault at Her Greek Best," Life, 61:16, Oct. 28, 1966.

1094) "Was Jesus an Outsider?" Newsweek, 70;83, Aug. 7, 1967.

1095) "The Watch on the Mails," Newsweek, 67:24, June 13, 1966.

1096) Watson, Angus. "Prison and Homosexuals," Spectator, 193:576, Nov. 12, 1954.

1097) Watts, Alan. "The Circle of Sex," Playboy, 12: 135, 166, 284, 286, at 166 and 284, Dec. 1965.

1098) Weightman, John. "Just Friends," New York Review of Books, 5:16, Jan. 6, 1966.

1099) Weightman, John. "Play as Fable [Themes of Homosexuality and Alienation]," Encounter, 28:55- 57, Feb. 1967.

1100) Welch, Paul. "Homosexuality in America: The 'Gay' World Takes to the City Streets," Life, 56: 68-74, June 26, 1964.

1101) "What Ever Happened to Childie McNaught?" Time, 92:83, Dec. 20, 1968.

1102) "What Investigators found in a Top-Secret Agency,"

U. S. News and World Report, 53:8, Aug. 27, 1962.

1103)   "What is a Homosexual?" Time, 71:44, June 16,
        1958.

1104)   "What Now?" Economist, 196:19, July 2, 1960.

1105)   "What the FBI Found in the Jenkins Case," U. S.
        News and World Report, 57:6, Nov. 2, 1964.

1106)   "Where the Boys Are," Time, 91:80-81, June 26,
        1968.

1107)   Wicker, Tom. "The Undeclared Witch-hunt,"
        Harper's, 239:108-10, Nov. 1969.

1108)   "Wife Killers," Newsweek, 43:81, May 24, 1954.

1109)   "Wild Cards," Time, 80:18, Aug. 31, 1962.

1110)   Wildeblood, Peter. "The Boys Who Cried Wolfen-
        den," Encounter, 12:61-63, 1959.

1111)   "Willie's Last Chapters," Time, 87:126, May 20,
        1966.

1112)   Woetzel, Robert K. "Do Our Homosexuality Laws
        Make Sense?" Saturday Review, 48:23-25, Oct.
        9, 1965.

1113)   Wolf, Ruth. "The Homosexual in Seattle," Seattle
        Magazine, Nov. 1967, pp. 38ff.

1114)   Wolfe, Burton H. "Gay in San Francisco," Knight,
        7:12-17, 64-65, 77-81, June 1969.

1115)   Wolfenden, John F. "Ahead of Public Opinion,"
        New Statesman and Nation, 59:941, June 25, 1960.

1116)   "The Wolfenden Report," Time, 70:39-40, Sep. 16,
        1957.

1117)   Wollheim, Richard. "Road to Toleration," Specta-
        tor, 200:435-36, Apr. 4, 1958.

1118)   "A Woman's Work," Newsweek, 68:82, July 11,
        1966.

1119)   Wootton, Barbara. "Sex and Society: a Sociolo-
         gist's View," Twentieth Century, 163:5-15, Jan.
         1958.

1120)   Wrong, Dennis H. "Homosexuality in America,"
         New Society, no. 39, June 27, 1963, p. 19.

1121)   "Wuthering Depths," Time, 83:106-08, Apr. 3,
         1964.

Articles in Religious Journals

1122)   Anderson, Camilla A. "The Church and the Homo-
        sexual," Pastoral Psychology, 2:54-56, Nov. 1951.

1123)   Anonymous. "A Very Sick Society," Christianity
        and Crisis, 26:135, June 13, 1966.

1124)   Anonymous. Letter to the Editor, Christianity
        Today, 12:23, Mar. 1, 1968.

1125)   Anonymous. Letter to the Editor, Pastoral Psy-
        chology, 8:51-52, Dec. 1957.

1126)   "Are We Post-Christian?" America, 108:394,
        Mar. 23, 1963.

1127)   Aschaffenberg, Helga. "Relationship Therapy with
        a Homosexual: A Case History," Pastoral Coun-
        selor, 4:4-12, 1966.

1128)   Ashbrook, James B. Review of Daniel Cappon's
        Toward an Understanding of Homosexuality, Pastoral
        Psychology, 16:57-58, Mar. 1965.

1129)   Bailey, Sherwin. "The Problem of Sexual Inver-
        sion," Theology, 55:47-52, 1952.

1130)   Baxbaum, R. E. "Homosexuality and Love," Jour-
        nal of Religion and Health, 6:17-32, Jan. 1967.

1131)   Bennett, J. C. "Questions on the Jenkins Case,"
        Christianity and Crisis, 24:223, Nov. 16, 1964.

1132)   Bergler, Edmund. "Homosexuality: Disease or
        Way of Life?" Pastoral Psychology, 8:49-52, June
        1957.

1133)   Bergler, Edmund. Letter to the Editor, Pastoral
        Psychology, 8:52-54, Dec. 1957.

1134)   "The Bible and the Homosexual," Christianity To-
         day, 12:24-25, Jan. 19, 1968. (Reply--12:33,
         Mar. 1, 1968.)

1135)   Bozarth, Rene and Gross, Alfred A.   "Homosexuality:
         Sin or Sickness? A Dialogue," Pastoral Psychology,
         13:35-42, Dec. 1962.

1136)   Bryce, Dean T. "The Unspeakables," St. Joseph
         Magazine, Jan.-May 1965. (5 articles.)

1137)   "California Episcopalians Would Liberalize Laws,"
         Churchman, 181:18, June-July 1967.

1138)   Canavan, Francis. "Reflections on the Revolution
         in Sex," America, 112:312-15, Mar. 6, 1965.
         (Replies--112:456-58, Apr. 3, 1965 and 112:510,
         Apr. 17, 1965.)

1139)   Casey, R. P. "The Christian Approach to Homo-
         sexuality," Theology, 58:459-63, 1955.

1140)   "Catholics Support Homosexual Law, London,"
         Ave Maria, 103:7, Mar. 26, 1966.

1141)   "Cavanagh, John R. "Problems of a Woman Homo-
         sexual," U. S. Catholic, 33:12-16, Oct. 1967.

1142)   Chikes, Thibor. "Christian Attitudes toward Homo-
         sexuality," Concern, 15:8-11, June 15, 1963.

1143)   "The Church and the Homosexual," Living Church,
         Jan. 8, 1967. (Editorial.)

1144)   "Clergy Shatter Another Taboo: Council on Religion
         and the Homosexual," Christian Century, 81:1581,
         Dec. 23, 1964.

1145)   Connery, J. R. "A Theologian Looks at the Wolfen-
         den Report," America, 98:485-86, Jan. 25, 1958.

1146)   Cotter, J. "The Homosexual Influence," Sign, 42:
         46, Aug. 1962.

1147)   "Council Talks with Homosexuals: Council on Re-
         ligion and the Homosexual, San Francisco," Ave
         Maria, 101:4, Jan. 1965.

1148)   Cromey, Robert W. "Ministry to the Homosexual,"
        Living Church, Jan. 8, 1967.

1149)   Dempsey, William. "Homosexuality," Dublin Re-
        view, 239:123-35, Sum. 1965.

1150)   Dempsey, William. "Homosexuality Today," Dub-
        lin Review, 240:289-94, Fall 1966.

1151)   "Depravity and Unbelief; the Christian Tradition
        and Unnatural Vice," Tablet, 202:570-71, Dec. 12,
        1953. (Replies--20:606, Dec. 19, 1953.)

1152)   Dolby, J. R. "Helping the Homosexual," Chris-
        tianity Today, 12:29-30, Feb. 16, 1968.

1153)   Dowell, Graham. Letter to the Editor, Theology,
        55:28-29, 1952.

1154)   Driver, Thomas F. "On Taking Sex Seriously,"
        Christianity and Crisis, 23:175-79, Oct. 14, 1963.
        (Replies--23:204-06, Nov. 11, 1963.)

1155)   Elwes, R. "Homosexuality and the Law," Tablet,
        208:538-39, Dec. 15, 1956.

1156)   "Equality for Homosexuals?" Christian Century,
        84:1587-88, Dec. 13, 1967. (Replies--85:111-12,
        Jan. 24, 1968.)

1157)   Ernst, C. "The Wolfenden Report; Mortal Sin,"
        Tablet, 212:90, July 26, 1958.

1158)   Fairfield, Letitia. "The Wolfenden Report," Tablet,
        210:204-05, Sep. 14, 1957.

1159)   Fleck, J. C. "Canada Debates Abortion and Homo-
        sexuality," Christian Century, 86:354-58, Mar. 12,
        1969.

1160)   Gagnon, John H. and Simon, William. "Perspec-
        tive on Homosexuality," Dublin Review, 241:96-114,
        Sum. 1967.

1161)   Gaylin, Willard. "Society and the Homosexual,"
        Commonweal, 91:338-39, Dec. 12, 1969.

1162) Gilby, Thomas. "Not All That Anomalous," Black-
       friars, 41:402-08, Nov. 1960.

1163) Gleason, R.W. "Homosexuality: Moral Aspects of
       the Problem," Homiletic and Pastoral Review, 58:
       272-78, Dec. 1957.

1164) Gradwell, L. "New 'Dublin,' the Catholic Report
       on Homosexuality and the Law," Tablet, 208:473,
       Dec. 1, 1956.

1165) Grey, Antony. "Homosexual Law Reform," Dublin
       Review, 239:136-42, Sum. 1965.

1166) Gross, Alfred A. "Accepting the Deviate," Chris-
       tian Century, 80:1107, Sep. 11, 1963.

1167) Gross, Alfred A. "The Homosexual in Society,"
       Pastoral Psychology, 1:38-45, Apr. 1950.

1168) Gustafson, G.J. "Homosexuality and the Law,"
       Priest, 14:21-25, Jan. 1958.

1169) Hartung, Philip T. "Lov'd Not Wisely," Common-
       weal, 87:384, Dec. 22, 1967.

1170) Hartung, Philip T. "Homosexual Movie," Common-
       weal, 89:502-03, Jan. 17, 1969.

1171) Harvey, J.F. "Counselling the Homosexual,"
       Homiletic and Pastoral Review, 62:328-35, 1962.

1172) Harvey, J.F. "Current Moral Theology," American
       Ecclesiastical Review, 158:122-29, Feb. 1968.

1173) Harvey, J.F. "Homosexuality and Marriage,"
       Homiletic and Pastoral Review, 62:227-34, 1961.

1174) Harvey, J.F. "Homosexuality as a Pastoral Prob-
       lem," Theological Studies, 16:86-108, 1955.

1175) Harvey, J.F. "Morality and Pastoral Treatment of
       Homosexuality," Continuum, 5:279-97, Sum. 1967.

1176) Harvey, J.F. Review of Michael Buckley's Mor-
       ality and the Homosexual, Theological Studies, 21:
       491-95, 1960.

1177)   Harvey, J. F.   Review of D. S. Bailey's Homo-
        sexuality and the Western Christian Tradition,
        Theological Studies, 17:128-32, 1956.

1178)   "Helping the Homosexual," Christianity Today, 12:
        29-30, Feb. 16, 1968.

1179)   Henry, George W.   "On Homosexuality," Pastoral
        Psychology, 6:50-51, Sep. 1955.

1180)   Henry, George W.   "Pastoral Counseling for Homo-
        sexuals," Pastoral Psychology, 2:33-39, Nov. 1951.
        (Reprinted in Cory, no. 27 above, pp. 384-93.)

1181)   Henry, George W.   "Punishment," Pastoral Psy-
        chology, 6:31-42, June 1955. (Reprint of pp. 427-
        41 of George W. Henry, All the Sexes, no. 53
        above.)

1182)   Henry, George W. and Gross, Alfred A.   "On
        Homosexuality," Pastoral Psychology, 6:52-53, Sep.
        1955.

1183)   Hiltner, Seward.   "The Church and the Homosexual,"
        Pastoral Psychology, 2:56-57, Nov. 1951.

1184)   Hiltner, Seward.   "On Homosexuality," Pastoral
        Psychology, 6:44-49, Sep. 1955.

1185)   "Homosexual Law Reform," America, 114:278,
        Feb. 26, 1966.

1186)   "Homosexual Offences and the Law in England,"
        New Blackfriars, 46:606-08, Aug. 1965.

1187)   "Homosexuality, Prostitution, and the Law" and
        "Report of the Roman Catholic Advisory Committee
        on Prostitution and Homosexual Offences and the
        Existing Law," Dublin Review, 230:57-65, Sum.
        1956. (See above, no. 197.)

1188)   "Homosexuality: Society's Attitude," America, 114:
        316, Mar. 5, 1966.

1188a) "How Should Homosexuality by Viewed?" Awake,
        Jan. 8, 1964, pp. 14-16.

1188b)   Kameny, Franklin E.   "Federal Government and
         Homosexuals," Concern, 8:10-11, 16, Apr. 15,
         1966.

1189)   Kane, John J.   "Understanding Homosexuality,"
         U. S. Catholic, 31:14-18, Jan. 1966. (See no. 180
         above.)

1190)   Kelsey, M. T.   "The Church and the Homosexual,"
         Journal of Religion and Health, 7:61-78, Jan. 1968.
         (Reply--7:368-70, Oct. 1968.)

1191)   Knight, James A.   Review of Alfred A. Gross'
         Strangers in Our Midst, Pastoral Psychology, 13:
         57-59, Nov. 1962.

1192)   Laforet, E.   "Casement: A Proposal to the Guild
         of St. Luke of Central City," Linacre, 34:83-84,
         Feb. 1967.

1193)   Lake, Frank.   "First Aid in Counselling; the
         Homosexual Man," Expository Times, 78:356-60,
         Sep. 1967.

1194)   "Law and Homosexuality," America, 113:71, July
         17, 1965.

1195)   "The Law as Bastion," Tablet, 219:568, May 22,
         1965.

1196)   "Laws against Homosexuals," Christianity Today,
         14:32, Nov. 7, 1969.

1197)   Leitsch, Richard.   "A New Frontier for Freedom,"
         Social Action, 34:21-29, Dec. 1967.

1198)   Lowery, Daniel.   "The Problem of Homosexuality,"
         Liguorian 54:18-24, Sep. 1966.

1199)   Maddocks, Lewis I.   "The Homosexual and the
         Law," Social Action, 34:5-20, Dec. 1967.

1200)   Malin, Irving.   Review of John Rechy's Numbers,
         Commonweal, 87:568, Feb. 9, 1968.

1201)   Marney, Carlyle.   "The Christian Community and
         the Homosexual," Religion in Life, 35:760-63, Win.

1966. (Reprinted in Social Progress, 58:31-40, Nov.-Dec. 1967.)

1202) Maves, Paul B. Review of Edmund Bergler's Homosexuality: Disease or Way of Life?, Pastoral Psychology, 8:60-63, June 1957.

1203) Maves, Paul B. Letter to the Editor, Pastoral Psychology, 8:54-55, Dec. 1957.

1204) Menninger, William C. "More on Homosexuality," Pastoral Psychology, 9:46-47, Feb. 1958.

1205) Merrill, George W. "More on Homosexuality," Pastoral Psychology, 9:47-48, Feb. 1958.

1206) Milhaven, J. "Homosexuality and the Christian," Homiletic and Pastoral Review, 68:663-69, May 1968.

1207) Millet, John A. P. "The Church and the Homosexual," Pastoral Psychology, 2:49-51, Nov. 1951.

1208) Millet, John A. P. "On Homosexuality," Pastoral Psychology, 6:49-50, Sep. 1955.

1209) Moody, Howard. "Homosexuality and Muckraking," Christianity and Crisis, 27:270-71, Nov. 27, 1967. (Reply--27:314, Jan. 8, 1968.)

1210) "The 'Mother' Image," America, 107:227, May 12, 1962.

1211) "My Question Is ...," Lutheran, 6:44, Jan. 17, 1968.

1212) Myers, C. Kilmer and Gross, Alfred A. Review of the Wolfenden Report, Pastoral Psychology, 14: 62-63, Sep. 1963.

1213) Mobile, Philip. "Patriots and Indians," Commonweal, 91:185-86, Nov. 7, 1969.

1214) "Notes and News: the Homosexual," Pastoral Psychology, 2:59, Nov. 1951.

1215) "Notes on Homosexuality: Excerpts from a Consul-

tation," Social Progress, 58:26-30, Nov. -Dec.
1967.

1216)   Odenwald, Robert. "Counseling the Homosexual,"
Priest, 9:940-44, Dec. 1953.

1217)   O'Grady, R. M. "New Zealand, Homosexuality: A
Crime?" Christian Century, 86:29-30, Jan. 1,
1969.

1218)   Overholser, Winfred. "Homosexuality: Sin or
Disease?" Christian Century, 80:1099-1101, Sep.
11, 1963.

1219)   Paine, Marcus. "Views of a Hidden Homosexual,"
Social Progress, 58:22-25, Nov. -Dec. 1967.

1220)   Palmer, Robert S. "More on Homosexuality,"
Pastoral Psychology, 9:48-49, Feb. 1958.

1221)   Parlour, R. R. and others. "Homophile Movement:
Its Impact and Implications," Journal of Religion
and Health, 6:217-34, July 1967.

1222)   Phillips, G. "Hope for the Homosexual," Homiletic
and Pastoral Review, 66:995-1001, Sep. 1966.

1223)   Ploscowe, Morris. "Homosexuality, Sodomy, and
Crimes against Nature," Pastoral Psychology, 2:40-
48, Nov. 1951. (Reprint of part of chapter 7 of
Sex and the Law, no. 509 above.)

1224)   Politzer, Jerome F. "Church Channel to Homosexuals," Christianity Today, 9:53-54, Mar. 4,
1966.

1225)   "Problems of a Woman Homosexual," U.S. Catholic, 33:12-16, Oct. 1967. (Reply--33:16, Oct.
1967.)

1226)   Rado, Sandor. "The Church and the Homosexual,"
Pastoral Psychology, 2:54, Nov. 1951.

1227)   "Reappraising the Law on Homosexuality: the
Wolfenden Committee's Recommendations," Christian Century, 82:659, May 26, 1965.

1228)   "Religious Group Urges Recognition of Homosexuals'
        Rights," Christian Century, 85:744-45, June 5, 1968.

1229)   Rhymes, Douglas. "The Church's Responsibility
        towards the Homosexual," Dublin Review, 241:83-
        114, Sum. 1967.

1230)   Roberts, David E. "On Homosexuality: the Related
        Function of the Church, the Psychiatrist, and
        Society," Pastoral Psychology, 6:43-45, Jan. 1955.

1231)   Roberts, David E. "On Homosexuality," Pastoral
        Psychology, 6:43-45, June 1955. (Reprint of fore-
        word to All the Sexes, no. 53 above, pp. vii-x.)

1232)   Roche, Philip Q. "The Church and the Homosexual,"
        Pastoral Psychology, 2:51-52, Nov. 1951.

1233)   Rosenbaum, J. "Religious and the Fear of Homo-
        sexuality," Review for Religious, 27:880-82, Sep.
        1968.

1233a) "Sexual Dialogue," Christianity Today, 9:50, Apr.
        23, 1965.

1234)   "The Sexual Revolution," America, 108:526, Apr.
        20, 1963.

1235)   Shannon, William V. "The Jenkins Case," Com-
        monweal, 81:151-52, Oct. 30, 1964.

1236)   Sheed, Wilfrid. "Heterosexual Backlash," Common-
        weal, 82:289-90, May 21, 1965.

1237)   Shinn, Roger L. "Persecution of the Homosexual,"
        Christianity and Crisis, 26:84-87, May 2, 1966.

1238)   Smith, B. L. "Homosexuality in the Bible and the
        Law," Christianity Today, 13:7-10, July 18, 1969.

1239)   "Social Effects," Tablet, 210:531-32, Dec. 14, 1957.

1240)   Stokes, Walter R. "The Church and the Homosexual,"
        Pastoral Psychology, 2:53-54, Nov. 1951.

1241)   "A Time for Moral Indignation," Christianity Today,
        9:624-26, Mar. 12, 1965.

1242)   Tinney, J. S. "Homosexuals Convene in Kansas
        City," Christian Century, 86:1436, Nov. 5, 1969.

1243)   "Treading Lightly in a Delicate Subject," Christian
        Century, 74:1092-93, Sep. 18, 1957.

1244)   Trese, Leo J. "Muted Tragedy," Commonweal,
        51:512, Feb. 17, 1950.

1245)   Trexler, Edgar R. "His Ministry Takes a Lot of
        Dimes," Lutheran 6:5-10, Jan. 17, 1968.

1246)   Tripp, C. A. "Who is a Homosexual?" Social
        Progress, 58:13-21, Nov. -Dec. 1967.

1247)   Vann, Gerald. "Anomalies and Grace," Blackfriars,
        34:424-33, Oct. 1953.

1248)   Vann, Gerald. "Moral Dilemmas: What is Na-
        tural?" Blackfriars, 35:6-7, Jan. 1954.

1249)   Vincent, Ben W. "A Knowledge of All Conditions,"
        Friends Quarterly, Jan. 1968, pp. 46-48.

1250)   "The Wicked and the Weak," America, 116:802-03,
        June 3, 1967.

1251)   Williams, Daniel D. "Three Studies of Homo-
        sexuality in Relation to the Christian Faith," Social
        Action, 34:30-37, Dec. 1967.

1252)   Williamson, H. "Sodom and Homosexuality,"
        Clergy Review, 48:507-14, Aug. 1963. (Reply--
        48:650-51, Oct. 1963.)

1253)   "The Wolfenden Report," Blackfriars, 38:402-03,
        Oct. 1957.

1254)   "The Wolfenden Report Debate; What Would Follow
        a Change," Tablet, 214:642, July 9, 1960.

1255)   "Wolfenden Report Debated," Tablet, 212:498, Dec.
        6, 1958.

1256)   "Wolfenden Report; Statement in the Westminster
        Cathedral Chronicle," Tablet, 210:523, Dec. 7,
        1957.

Articles in Legal Journals

1257) Bensing, Robert C. "A Comparative Study of
       American Sex Statutes," Journal of Criminal Law
       and Criminology, 42:57-72, 1951.

1258) Bensing, Robert C. "Sex Law Enforcement in
       Indianapolis," Western Reserve Law Review, 4:33-
       44, 1952.

1259) Bowman, Karl M. and Engle, Bernice. "A Psy-
       chiatric Evaluation of the Laws of Homosexuality,"
       Temple Law Quarterly Review, 29:273-326, 1956.

1260) Bowman, Karl M. and Engle, Bernice. "Sex
       Offenses: the Medical and Legal Implications of
       Sex Variations," Law and Contemporary Problems,
       25:293-308, 1960.

1261) Byrne, Thomas R. Jr. and Mulligan, Francis M.
       " 'Psychopathic Personality' and 'Sexual Deviation':
       Medical Terms or Catch-All--Analysis of the Status
       of the Homosexual Alien," Temple Law Quarterly
       Review, 40:328-47, 1967.

1262) Campbell, George E. "Criminal Law--Sodomy--
       The Crime and the Penalty," Arkansas Law Re-
       view, 8:497-500, 1954.

1263) Cantor, Donald J. "Deviation and the Criminal
       Law," Journal of Criminal Law, Criminology, and
       Police Science, 55:441-53, 1964.

1264) Caporale, Domenico and Hamann, Deryl F. "Sexual
       Psychopathy--A Legal Labyrinth of Medicine, Morals,
       and Mythology," Nebraska Law Review, 36:320-53,
       1957.

1265) Caron, Yves. "Legal Enforcement of Morals and
       the so-called Hart-Devlin Controversy," McGill Law
       Journal, 15:9-47, Feb. 1969.

1266)   Cavanagh, John R.   "Sexual Anomalies and the
          Law," Catholic Lawyer, 9:4-10, 1963.

1267)   Chappell, D. and Wilson, P. R.   "Public Attitudes
          to the Reform of the Law relating to Abortion and
          Homosexuality," Australian Law Journal, 42:120-21
          and 175-79, 1968.

1268)   "Clandestine Police Surveillance of Public Toilet
          Booth Held to be Unreasonable Search," Columbia
          Law Review, 63:955-61, 1963.

1269)   Clifford, W.   "Homosexuality by Consent," Justice
          of the Peace and Local Government Review, 129:
          597-98, 1965.

1270)   Coburn, Vincent.   "Homosexuality and the Invalida-
          tion of Marriage," Jurist, 20:441-59, 1960.

1271)   Cohen, Elias S.   "Administration of the Criminal
          Sexual Psychopath Statute in Indiana," Indiana Law
          Journal, 32:450-67, 1957.

1272)   "Commons Debate on the Wolfenden Report," Jus-
          tice of the Peace and Local Government Review,
          122:796, 1958.

1273)   "Crime and Sin: Reflections on Some Wolfenden
          Proposals," Law Times, 224:283-84, 1957.

1274)   "Crimes against Nature," Journal of Public Law,
          16:159-92, 1967.

1275)   "Criminal Law--Sexual Offenses--Sodomy--Cunni-
          lingus," Natural Resources Journal, 8:531-41, 1968.

1276)   Cross, Rupert.   "Regina v. Sims in England and the
          Commonwealth," Law Quarterly Review, 75:333-47,
          1959.

1276a)   Crumpler, William B.   "Is Governmental Policy
          affecting the Employment of Homosexuals Rational?"
          North Carolina Law Review, 48:912-24, 1970.

1277)   Custis, Douglass L.   "Sex Laws in Ohio: A Need
          for Revision," University of Cincinnati Law Review,
          35:211-41 at 226-28 and 239-41, 1966.

1278)   Cutler, S. Oley. "Sexual Offenses--Legal and
         Moral Considerations," Catholic Lawyer, 9:94-105,
         1963.

1279)   Davidson, Janice R. "Regulation of Sexual Conduct
         by Withholding Government Benefits and Privileges,"
         University of San Francisco Law Review, 3:372-88
         at 372-75 and 377-81, 1969.

1280)   Dean, Michael. "Similar Facts and Homosexual
         Offences: the Resurrection of Sims," Criminal
         Law Review, 1967:633-44.

1281)   DeMay, John A. "The Pennsylvania Sex Crimes
         Act," University of Pittsburgh Law Review, 13:
         739-49, 1952.

1282)   "Deportation of Homosexuals," New York University
         Law Review, 42:121-26, 1967.

1283)   "Deviate Sexual Behavior under the New Illinois
         Criminal Code," Washington University Law Quar-
         terly, 1965:220-35.

1284)   Devlin, Patrick. "Law and Morality," Manitoba
         Law Review, 1:243-54, 1962-65.

1285)   Devlin, Patrick. "Law, Democracy, and Morality,"
         University of Pennsylvania Law Review, 110:635-
         49, 1962.

1286)   Devlin, Patrick. "Mill on Liberty in Morals,"
         University of Chicago Law Review, 32:215-35, 1965.

1286a)   "Dismissal of Homosexuals from Federal Employ-
         ment: the Developing Role of Due Process in Ad-
         ministrative Adjudications," Georgetown Law Re-
         view, 58:632-45, 1970.

1287)   Dougherty, Clifford A. and Lynch, Norman B.
         "The Administrative Discharge: Military Justice?"
         George Washington Law Review, 33:498-528, 1964.

1288)   Dworkin, Ronald. "Lord Devlin and the Enforce-
         ment of Morals," Yale Law Journal, 75:986-1005,
         1966.

1289)   East, W. Norwood. "Sexual Offenders: A British
        View," Yale Law Journal, 55:527-57, 1945.

1290)   East, W. Norwood. "Sociological Aspects of Homo-
        sexuality: Introductory," Medico-Legal Journal, 15:
        11-14, 1947.

1291)   Eddy, J. P. "The Law and Homosexuality," Crimi-
        nal Law Review, 1956:22-25.

1292)   Ellis, Albert. "Interrogation of Sex Offenders,"
        Journal of Criminal Law and Criminology, 45:41-47,
        1954.

1293)   "Entrapment--Rittenour v. District of Columbia.
        163A. 2d 558 (D. C. , 1960)," Journal of Criminal
        Law, Criminology, and Police Science, 52:297, 1961.

1293a) Evans, Robert J. "Crimes against Nature," Jour-
        nal of Public Law, 16:159-92, 1967.

1294)   Everhard, John A. "Problems Involving the Dis-
        position of Homosexuals in the Service," U. S. Air
        Force Judge Advocate General's Bulletin, 2:20-23,
        1960.

1295)   "Evidence of the Absence of Fresh Complaint is
        Admissible in Sodomy Prosecutions, U. S. v. Good-
        man," Michigan Law Review, 63:732-35, 1965.

1296)   Fahr, Samuel M. "Iowa's New Sexual Psychopath
        Law--An Experiment Noble in Purpose?" Iowa
        Law Review, 41:523-57, 1956.

1297)   Fairfield, Letitia. "Sociological Aspects of Homo-
        sexuality in Women," Medico-Legal Journal, 11:
        18-20, 1947.

1297a) "Federal Employment of Homosexuals: Narrowing
        the Efficiency Standard," Catholic University Law
        Review, 19:267-75, 1969.

1298)   Fletcher, John. "Sex Offenses: An Ethical View,"
        Law and Contemporary Problems, 25:244-57, 1960.

1299)   Ford, Clellan. "Sex Offenses: An Anthropological
        Perspective," Law and Contemporary Problems, 25:
        225-43, 1960.

1300)   Ford, Stephen D. "Homosexuals and the Law:
        Why the Status Quo?" California Western Law Re-
        view, 5:232-51, 1969.

1301)   Foster, Henry H. Jr. Review of H. L. A. Hart's
        Law, Liberty, and Morality, Journal of Criminal
        Law, Criminology, and Police Science, 55:393-96,
        1964.

1302)   Fritts, Roger M. and Smith, Favor R. "Deviate
        Sexual Behavior: the Desirability of Legislative
        Proscription," Albany Law Review, 30:291-304,
        1966.

1303)   Gallo, Jon J. and Others. "The Consenting Adult
        Homosexual and the Law: An Empirical Study of
        Enforcement and Administration in Los Angeles
        County," University of California at Los Angeles
        Law Review, 13:644-832, 1966.

1304)   Glover, Edward. "The Social and Legal Aspects of
        Sexual Abnormality," Medico-Legal Journal, 13:133-
        48, 1945.

1305)   Glueck, Bernard C. Jr. "An Evaluation of the
        Homosexual Offender," Minnesota Law Review, 141:
        187-210, 1957.

1306)   Glueck, Bernard (Sr.). "Sex Offenses: A Clinical
        Approach," Law and Contemporary Problems, 25:
        279-91, 1960.

1307)   Goldman, Irv S. "Bedroom Should Not be Within
        the Province of the Law," California Western Law
        Review, 4:115-31, 1968.

1308)   Goldstein, Joseph. "Police Discretion Not to In-
        voke the Criminal Process," Yale Law Journal,
        69:543-94, 1960.

1309)   Gould, Donald B. and Hurwitz, Irving L. "Out of
        Tune with the Times: the Massachusetts SDP
        Statute," Boston University Law Review, 45:391-
        415, 1965.

1310)   "Government-created Employment Disabilities of
        the Homosexual," Harvard Law Review, 82:1738-
        51, 1969.

1311)   Gregg, James M. H.   "Other Acts of Sexual Mis-
         behavior and Perversion as Evidence in Prosecutions
         for Sexual Offenses," Arizona Law Review, 6:212-
         36, 1965.

1312)   Guttmacher, Manfred and Weihofen, Henry.   "Sex
         Offenses," Journal of Criminal Law, Criminology,
         and Police Science, 43:153-75, 1952.

1313)   Hammelmann, H. S.   "Committee on Homosexual
         Offenses and Prostitution," Modern Law Review,
         21:68-73, 1958.

1314)   Harper, Fowler W.   Review of the Kinsey Volume
         on Females, Yale Law Journal, 63:895-99, 1954.

1315)   Harris, Robert N. Jr.   "Private Consensual Adult
         Behavior: the Requirement of Harm to Others in
         the Enforcement of Morality," University of Cali-
         fornia at Los Angeles Law Review, 14:581-603,
         1967.

1316)   Hart, H. L. A.   "The Use and Abuse of the Criminal
         Law," Oxford Lawyer, 4:7-12, 1961.

1317)   Hefner, Hugh M.   "The Legal Enforcement of
         Morality," University of Colorado Law Review,
         40:199-221 at 210-20, 1968.

1318)   Hewitt, James W.   "Nebraska Statutory Revision
         of Punishment of Sex Offenders," Nebraska Law
         Review, 33:475-81, 1954.

1319)   Hodge, R. Sessions.   "Medico-Legal Aspects of the
         Treatment of the Sexual Offender," Medico-Legal
         Journal, 18:130-44, 1950.

1320)   "The Homosexual and the Military," Fordham
         Law Review, 37:465-76, 1969.

1321)   "Homosexual Delinquent," Journal of Criminal Law
         and Criminology, 32:346, 1941-42.

1322)   "Homosexual Offences," Scots Law Times, Aug.
         9, 1949, pp. 84-85.

1323)   "Homosexual Resident Alien Deportable as a Psychopathic Personality," Catholic Lawyer, 13:82-90, 1967.

1324)   "Homosexuality: A New Ground for Annulment," Catholic Lawyer, 11:158-62, 1965.

1325)   Hooker, Evelyn. Review of Hervey Cleckley's The Caricature of Love, Journal of Criminal Law, Criminology, and Police Science, 52:12-13, 1961.

1326)   Hoover, J. Edgar. "Role of the FBI in the Federal Employee Security Program," Northwestern University Law Review, 49:333-47, 1954.

1327)   Hughes, Graham. "Consent in Sexual Offenses," Modern Law Review, 25:672-86, 1962.

1328)   Hughes, Graham. "Morals and the Criminal Law," Yale Law Review, 71:662-83, 1962.

1329)   Ison, T. G. "Enforcement of Morals," University of British Columbia Law Review, 3:263-74, 1967.

1330)   Jacobs, Harold. "Decoy Enforcement of Homosexual Laws," University of Pennsylvania Law Review, 112:259-84, 1963.

1331)   Johnson, Ronald. "Sodomy Statutes--A Need for Change," South Dakota Law Review, 13:384-97, 1968.

1332)   Jones, Richard T. "Sodomy--Crime or Sin?" University of Florida Law Review, 12:83-92, 1959.

1333)   Jones, William K. "Jurisdiction of Federal Courts to Review the Character of Military Administrative Discharges," Columbia Law Review, 57:917-74 at 922, 934-37, 1957.

1334)   Karpman, Benjamin. "Considerations Bearing on Problems of Sexual Offenses," Journal of Criminal Law, Criminology, and Police Science, 43:13-28, 1952.

1335)   Karpman, Benjamin. "Psychosis as a Defense against Yielding to Perverse (Paraphiliac) Sexual Crimes," Journal of Criminal Law, Criminology, and Police Science, 44:22-29, 1953.

1336)   Karpman, Benjamin. "Psychosomatic Neurosis as an Expression of a Barrier against Indulgence in Craved but Prohibited Sexual Drives," Journal of Criminal Law, Criminology, and Police Science, 44:746-52, 1954.

1337)   Karpman, Benjamin. "Sex Life in Prison," Journal of Criminal Law and Criminology, 38:475-86, 1948.

1338)   Kozol, H. L. "Medico-Legal Problems of Sex Offenders," Acta Medicinae et Legalis Socialis, 2: 125-28, 1964.

1339)   Krahulik, John. "The Cotner Case: Indiana Witch Hunt," Indiana Legal Forum, 2:336-50, 1969.

1340)   Kyler, C. W. "Camera Surveillance of Sex Deviates," Law and Order, 11:16-18, 20, 1963.

1341)   LaFave, Wayne R. "The Police and Non-Enforcement of the Law," Wisconsin Law Review, 1962: 104-37 and 179-239 at p. 123.

1342)   Lamb, Paul L. "Criminal Law--Consensual Homosexual Behavior--the Need for Legislative Reform," Kentucky Law Journal, 57:591-98, 1968-69.

1343)   Lerner, Harry V. "Effect of Character of Discharge and Length of Service on Eligibility to Veterans' Benefits," Military Law Review, 12:121-42, 1961.

1344)   Lockhart, William B. and McClure, Robert C. "Censorship of Obscenity: the Developing Constitutional Standards," Minnesota Law Review, 45: 5-121 at 32-34, 1960.

1345)   Lockhart, William B. and McClure, Robert C. "Obscenity Censorship: the Core Constitutional Issue--What is Obscene," Utah Law Review, 7: 289-303, 1961.

1346)   Lowrey, Lawson G. Comments on Sex Psychopaths, Journal of Criminal Law, Criminology, and Police Science, 43:607-10, 1953.

1347)   Mackwood, John C.   "The Sociological Aspects of
        Homosexuality: Male Homosexuality," Medico-
        Legal Journal, 15:14-18, 1947.

1348)   Mannheim, Hermann.   "Two Reports on Sex Of-
        fences," Modern Law Review, 12:488, 1949.

1349)   "The Mayor's Committee [New York City] Reports
        on the Study of Sex Offenses," Journal of Criminal
        Law and Criminology, 34:324-27, 1944.

1349a) McConnell, J. P. and Martin, J. D.   "Judicial
        Attitudes and Public Morals," American Bar Asso-
        ciation Journal, 55:1129-33, 1969.

1350)   McKee, W. F.   "Evidentiary Problems: Camera
        Surveillance of Sex Deviates," Law and Order, 12:
        72-74, 1964.

1351)   Mewett, Alan W.   "Morality and the Criminal Law,"
        University of Toronto Law Journal, 14:213-28, 1962.

1352)   Meyers, Thomas J.   "Psychiatric Examination of
        the Sexual Psychopath," Journal of Criminal Law,
        Criminology, and Police Science, 56:27-31, 1965.

1353)   Mihm, Fred P.   "A Re-examination of the Validity
        of our Sex Psychopath Statutes in the Light of Re-
        cent Appeal Cases and Experience," Journal of
        Criminal Law, Criminology, and Police Science,
        44:716-36, 1954.

1354)   Milner, Alan.   "Sodomy as a Ground for Divorce,"
        Modern Law Review, 23:43-51, 1960.

1355)   Minow, Newton.   "The Illinois Proposal to Confine
        Sexually Dangerous Persons," Journal of Criminal
        Law and Criminology, 40:186-97, 1949-50.

1356)   Moran, J. Terry.   "Sex Offenses and Penal Code
        Revision in Michigan," Wayne Law Review, 14:
        934-69 at 948-57, 1968.

1357)   Motz, Anton.   "Criminal Law--Wisconsin's Sexual
        Deviate Act," Wisconsin Law Review, 1954:324-35.

1358)   Murphy, Arthur A.   "The Soldier's Right to a

Private Life," Military Law Review, 24:97-124, 1964.

1359)   Napley, David. "Medicine and the Law," Law Society's Gazette, 64:578-82, 1967.

1360)   Neustatter, W. Lindesey. "The Homosexual Offender," Justice of the Peace and Local Government Review, 123:480-81, 1959.

1361)   Neustatter, W. Lindesey. "Sexual Abnormalities and the Sexual Offender," Medico-Legal Journal, 29:190-99, 1961.

1362)   Neustatter, W. Lindesey. "The Wolfenden Report: I. Homosexuality," Howard Journal, 10:18-25, 1958.

1363)   "New York's New Indeterminate Sentence Law for Sex Offenders," Yale Law Review, 60:346-56, 1951.

1364)   Normanton, Helena. Discussion, Medico-Legal Journal, 15:21, 1947.

1365)   Oerton, R. T. "Medicine and Law," Law Society's Gazette, 65:52-53, 1968.

1366)   Oerton, R. T. "One Million Men: the Problem of Homosexuality," Law Society's Gazette, 57:609, 1960.

1367)   Palmer, Henry. "Evidence--Buggery--Corroboration--Direction to the Jury," Criminal Law Review, 1955:433-34.

1368)   Pederby, G. R. "Homosexuality and the Law," Medico-Legal Journal, 33:29-34, 1965.

1369)   "Pennsylvania's New Sex Crime Law," University of Pennsylvania Law Review, 100:727-50, 1952.

1370)   "Per Curiam Decisions of the Supreme Court: 1957 Term," University of Chicago Law Review, 26:279-331, at 310-12, 1959.

1371)   "Philadelphia's New Criminal Procedure for the Abnormal Sex Offender," Legal Intelligencer, Dec. 11, 1950.

1372)   Ploscowe, Morris. "Report to The Hague: Sug-
         gested Revisions of Penal Law relating to Sex
         Crimes and Crimes against the Family," Cornell
         Law Quarterly, 50:425-45, 1956.

1373)   Ploscowe, Morris. "Sex Offenses in the New Penal
         Code," Brooklyn Law Review, 32:274-86, 1966.

1374)   Ploscowe, Morris. "Sex Offenses: the American
         Legal Context," Law and Contemporary Problems,
         25:217-24, 1960.

1375)   "Post Kinsey: Voluntary Sex Relations in Criminal
         Offenses," University of Chicago Law Review, 17:
         162-82, 1950.

1376)   "Private Consensual Homosexual Behavior: the
         Crime and Its Enforcement," Yale Law Journal,
         70:623-35, 1961.

1377)   Puxon, Margaret. "Not as Other Men," Solicitor's
         Journal, 101:735-37, 1957.

1378)   Rabinovitch, Ralph D. "The Sexual Psychopath,"
         Journal of Criminal Law, Criminology, and Police
         Science, 43:610-21, 1953.

1379)   Reinhardt, James M. and Fisher, Edward C. "The
         Sexual Psychopath and the Law," Journal of Crimi-
         nal Law and Criminology, 39:734-42, 1949.

1380)   Reiss, Albert J. "Sex Offenses: the Marginal
         Status of the Adolescent," Law and Contemporary
         Problems, 25:309-33, 1960.

1381)   Renshaw, Vernon and Goldrein, Eric. "Soliciting
         by Men," Criminal Law Review, 1959:276-79.

1382)   Rich, C. S. A. "Sexual Offences Act of 1967," New
         Law Journal, 118:451, 1968.

1383)   Rigg, Budd M. "New Jersey's Treatment of Sex
         Offenders: Some Recommended Improvements,"
         Rutgers Law Review, 9:567-75, 1955.

1384)   Ritty, Charles G. "Invalidity of Marriage by
         Reason of Sexual Anomalies," Jurist, 23:394-422,

1963. (Reprinted in Catholic Lawyer, 10:90-108,
1964.)

1385)   Roberts, G. D. "The Sociological Aspects of Homosexuality: the Legal Position with Regard to Offenders, " Medico-Legal Journal, 15:20-23, 1947.

1386)   Sadoff, Robert L. " 'Psychopathic Personality' and
'Sexual Deviation': Medical Terms or Legal Catch-
alls--Analysis of the Status of the Homosexual
Alien, " Temple Law Quarterly, 40:305-15, 1967.

1387)   Schmitthoff, C. M. "Law Reform in England, "
Manitoba Law School Journal, 1:225, 1964-65.

1388)   Schwartz, Louis B. "The Model Penal Code: An
Invitation to Reform, " American Bar Association
Journal, 49:452-55, 1963.

1389)   Schwartz, Louis B. "Morals, Offenses and the
Model Penal Code, " Columbia Law Review, 63:
669-86, 1963.

1390)   "Sex and the Law, " Solicitor's Journal, 74:717-18,
1930.

1391)   "Sexual Offences Act, 1966, " Magistrate, 23:129-31,
1967.

1392)   Sheedy, Charles. "Law and Morals, " Chicago Bar
Record, 43:373-78, 1962.

1393)   Slough, M. C. and Schwinn, Tom L. "The Sexual
Psychopath, " University of Kansas City Law Review, 19:131-53, 1950-51.

1394)   Slovenko, Ralph. "Sex Mores and the Enforcement of the Law on Sex Crimes: A Study of the
Status Quo, " University of Kansas Law Review,
15:265-86 at 276-81, 1966.

1395)   Slovenko, Ralph. "Sexual Deviation: Response to
an Adaptational Crisis, " University of Colorado
Law Review, 40:222-41, 1968.

1396)   Slovenko, Ralph and Phillips, Cyril. "Psychosexuality and the Criminal Law, " Vanderbilt Law

Review, 15:797-828, 1962.

1397)   Smith, Charles E. "The Homosexual Federal Of-
         fender, A Study of 100 Cases," Journal of Criminal
         Law, Criminology, and Police Science, 44:582-91,
         1954.

1398)   "Sodomy--People v. Randall. 174 N. E. 2d 507,
         N. Y., 1961," Journal of Criminal Law, Criminology,
         and Police Science, 52:432, 1961.

1399)   Sontag, L. W. "The Sexual Psychopath," Journal of
         Criminal Law, Criminology, and Police Science, 43:
         606-07, 1952.

1400)   Spence, James R. "The Law of Crime against
         Nature," North Carolina Law Review, 32:312-24,
         1954.

1401)   Stafford-Clark, David. "Homosexuality," Medico-
         Legal Journal, 25:65-81, 1957.

1402)   "State v. Green. 388 P. 2d 362, Mont., 1964,"
         Journal of Criminal Law, Criminology, and Police
         Science, 55:390, 1964.

1403)   Stebbins, Phillip E. "Sexual Deviation and the Laws
         of Ohio," Ohio State Law Journal, 20:346-60, 1959.

1404)   Stürup, Georg K. "Sex Offenses: the Scandinavian
         Experience," Law and Contemporary Problems, 25:
         361-75, 1960.

1405)   Sutherland, Edwin H. "The Sexual Psychopath
         Laws," Journal of Criminal Law and Criminology,
         40:543-54, 1950.

1406)   Swanson, Alan H. "Sexual Psychopath Statutes:
         Summary and Analysis," Journal of Criminal Law,
         Criminology, and Police Science, 51:215-35, 1960.

1407)   Tenney, Charles W. Jr. "Sex, Sanity, and Stu-
         pidity in Massachusetts," Boston University Law
         Review, 42:1-31, 1962.

1408)   Thornton, Nathaniel. "The Relation between Crime
         and Psychopathic Personality," Journal of Criminal

Law and Criminology, 42:199-204, 1951.

1408a) Vacek, Albert E. "Constitutionality of the Texas
Sodomy Statute--in the Recent Case of Buchanan
v. Batchelor," Baylor Law Review, 22:300-03, 1970.

1409) Wells, W. T. "Homosexuality," Oxford Lawyer,
3:21-24, 1961.

1410) Wertham, Frederic. "A Psychiatrist Looks at
Psychiatry and the Law," Buffalo Law Review, 3:
41-51, 1953.

1411) Wheeler, Stanton. "Sex Offenses: A Sociological
Critique," Law and Contemporary Problems, 25:
258-78, 1960. (Reprinted in Wolfgang, Savitz, and
Johnston, no. 507 above, pp. 397-411.)

1412) White, Doyle E. and Wilson, Paul E. "New Criminal Code for Kansas," Journal of the Bar Association of Kansas, 34:308-10 and 357-62, 1965.

1413) Williams, D. G. T. "Sex and Morals in the Criminal Law," Criminal Law Review, 1964:253-68.

1414) Williams, G. "Victims as Parties to Crimes--A
Further Comment," Criminal Law Review, 1964:
686-91.

1415) Williams, Glanville. "Corroboration--Sexual Cases,"
Criminal Law Review, 1962:662-71.

1416) Williams, J. E. Hall. "The Proper Scope and
Function of the Criminal Law," Law Quarterly
Review, 74:76-81, 1958.

1417) Williams, J. E. Hall. "Sex Offenses: the British
Experience," Law and Contemporary Problems, 25:
334-60, 1960.

1418) "Wolfenden Report," Criminal Law Review, 1957:
665-68.

1419) "The Wolfenden Report," Law Times, 224:182,
1957.

1420) "The Wolfenden Report in Parliament," Criminal

Law Review, 1959:38.

1421)   "The Wolfenden Report: A Review of the Main
         Recommendations," Justice of the Peace and Local
         Government Review, 121:607-08, 1957.

1422)   The Wolfenden Report: the Wider Aspects," Jus-
         tice of the Peace and Local Government Review,
         121:623-25, 1957.

1423)   Zoghby, Guy A. "Is There a Military Common
         Law of Crimes?" Military Law Review, 27:75-
         109, 1965.

Court Cases Involving Consenting Adults

1424)   Adams v. Laird. 420 F. 2d 230. (D.C. Cir.,
        1969) - revocation of security clearance.

1424a) Alexander v. U.S. 187 A. 2d 901. (D.C., 1963)
        - solicitation of police decoy.

1425)   Anonymous v. Macy. 398 F. 2d 317. (5th Cir.,
        1968) - federal employment.

1426)   Avanzi, People v. 77 P. 2d 237. (Cal., 1938) -
        homosexual act.

1427)   Babb, People v. 229 P. 2d 843. (Cal., 1951) -
        lewd vagrancy.

1428)   Beard v. Stahr. 200 F. Supp. 766. (D.C., 1961);
        370 U.S. 41. (1962) - solicitation of police decoy
        and military discharge.

1429)   Benites, In re. 140 P. 436. (Nev., 1914) -
        homosexual act.

1430)   Bennett v. Abram. 253 P. 2d 359. (N. Mex.,
        1953) - homosexual acts.

1431)   Bentley, People v. 226 P. 2d 669. (Cal., 1951) -
        public acts.

1432)   Berneau v. U.S. 188 A. 2d 301. (D.C., 1963) -
        solicitation of police decoy.

1433)   Bicksler v. U.S. 90 A. 2d 233. (D.C., 1952) -
        solicitation of police decoy.

1434)   Bielicki and Welch v. Superior Court. 371 P. 2d
        288. (Cal., 1962) - clandestine police observation.

1435)   Blake v. State. 124 A. 2d 273. (Md., 1956) -
        homosexual act.

127

1436)   Boutlier v. Immigration and Naturalization Service.
             363 F. 2d 488. (2d Cir., 1966); 387 U.S. 118.
             (1967) - deportation of homosexual alien.

1437)   Brass, Teper v. Hoberman. U.S. Dist. Ct., SD
             NY, Civ. 68-2993; 1969 - employment.

1438)   Brenke v. U.S. 78 A. 2d 677. (D.C., 1951) -
             solicitation of police decoy.

1439)   Britt v. Superior Court. 374 P. 2d 817. (Cal.,
             1962) - clandestine police observation.

1439a)   Buchanan v. Batchelor. 308 F. Supp. 729. (Tex.,
             1970) - unconstitutionality of sodomy statute.

1440)   Canter v. Maryland. 168 A. 2d 385. (Md., 1961)
             - public acts.

1441)   Caplan v. Karth. 373 U.S. 917. (1963) - federal
             employment.

1442)   Chamberlain, People v. 249 P. 2d 562. (Cal.,
             1952) - public act.

1443)   Chapman, People v. 4 N.W. 2d 18. (Mich., 1942)
             - gross indecency and sex psychopathy.

1444)   Clackum v. U.S. 148 Ct. of Claims 404. (1960)
             - military discharge.

1445)   Cook, U.S. v. 15 U.S.C.M.A. 436; 35 C.M.R.
             408. (1965) - military discharge.

1446)   Courtney v. Secretary of the Air Force. 267 F.
             Supp. 305. (Cal., 1967) - military discharge.

1447)   Dew v. Halaby. 317 F. 2d 582. (D.C., 1963) -
             federal employment.

1448)   Dresselhaus v. Pugh. 250 F. Supp. 721. (Cal.,
             1965) - military discharge.

1449)   Dyson v. U.S. 97 A. 2d 135. (D.C., 1953) -
             solicitation of policy decoy.

1450)   Earl, People v. 216 Cal. App. 2d 607. (1963) -
             private acts.

1451)   Ephraim v. State. 89 So. 344. (Fla., 1921) -
          homosexual act.

1452)   Feliciano, People v. 173 N. Y. S. 2d 123. (N. Y.,
          1958) - solicitation of police decoy.

1453)   Ficklin, State v. 67 P. 2d 897. (Wash., 1937) -
          homosexual act.

1454)   Fletcher, State v. 256 P. 2d 847. (Kans., 1953)
          - homosexual act.

1455)   Fleuti v. Rosenberg. 302 P. 2d 652. (9th Cir.,
          1962); 374 U. S. 449 (1963) - deportation of homo-
          sexual alien.

1456)   Flores-Rodriguez, U. S. v. 237 F. 2d 405. (2d
          Cir., 1956) - deportation of homosexual alien.

1456a)   Frazier, People v. 64 Cal. Rptr. 447. (1967) -
          homosexual act in prison.

1457)   Funches, People v. 162 N. E. 2d 393. (Ill., 1959)
          - public act.

1458)   Ganduxe y Marino v. Murff. 183 F. Supp. 565.
          (N. Y., 1959); 278 F. 2d 330. (2d Cir., 1960) -
          deportation of homosexual alien.

1459)   Giani, People v. 302 P. 2d 813. (Cal., 1956) -
          homosexuality and sex psychopathology.

1460)   Goldstein, People v. 303 P. 2d 892. (Cal., 1956)
          - homosexual acts.

1461)   Guarro v. U. S. 116 A. 2d 408. (D. C., 1955) -
          assault and solicitation of police decoy.

1462)   Guerin, State v. 152 P. 747. (Mont., 1915) -
          homosexual act.

1463)   H. v. H. 157 A. 2d 721. (N. J., 1959) - divorce.

1463a)   Heath, People v. 72 Cal. Rptr. 457. (Cal., 1968)
          - clandestine police observation.

1464)   Henderson v. U. S. 117 A. 2d 456. (D. C., 1955)

- assault and solicitation of police decoy.

1464a)   Hensel, People v.   43 Cal. Rptr. 865.   (Cal.,
         1965) - clandestine police observation.

1465)   Hickey, People v.   41 P. 1027.   (Cal., 1895) -
         attempted homosexual assault.

1466)   Holloday, U. S. v.   36 C. M. R. 598.   (1966) -
         military discharge.

1467)   Hooper, U. S. v.   9 U. S. C. M. A. 637;   26 C. M. R.
         417.   (1958) - service retirement pay and associa-
         tion with homosexuals.

1468)   Humphrey, People v.   111 N. Y. S. 2d 450.   (N. Y.,
         1952) - breach of the peace and solicitation of
         police decoy.

1469)   Ingalls v. Brown.   377 F. 2d 151.   (D. C., 1967)
         - military discharge.

1470)   Jackson v. State.   94 So. 505.   (Fla., 1922) -
         homosexual act.

1471)   Jacquith v. Commonwealth.   120 N. E. 2d 189.
         (Mass., 1954) - unnatural act.

1472)   Jones v. State.   88 S. E. 712.   (Ga., 1916) -
         homosexual act.

1473)   Jordan, People v.   74 P. 2d 519.   (Cal., 1937) -
         clandestine police observation.

1474)   Justus v. Zimny.   250 F. Supp. 719.   (Cal., 1965)
         - military discharge.

1475)   Katt, People v.   234 N. Y. S. 2d 988.   (N. Y., 1962)
         - homosexual act.

1476)   Kehm, State v.   103 A. 2d 781.   (Del., 1954) -
         homosexual act.

1477)   Kelly v. Municipal Court.   160 Cal. App. 2d 38.
         (1958) - registration of sex offenders.

1478)   Kelly v. U. S.   194 F. 2d 150.   (D. C., 1952) -

solicitation of police decoy.

1479)   Kelly and Washington, U. S. v.   119 F. Supp. 217.
          (D. C. , 1954) - homosexual act.

1480)   Kershaw v. Department of Alcoholic Beverage Con-
          trol. 318 P. 2d 494. (Cal. , 1957) - gay bar
          license.

1481)   King v. U. S. 90 A. 2d 229. (D. C. , 1952) -
          solicitation of police decoy.

1482)   Langelier, State v. 8 A. 2d 897. (Me. , 1939) -
          homosexual act.

1483)   Lavoie v. U. S. Immigration and Naturalization
          Service. 360 F. 2d 27. (9th Cir. , 1966) - de-
          portation of homosexual alien.

1484)   Louisiana v. Bonanno. 163 So. 2d 72. (1964) -
          homosexual acts.

1484a)   Maldonado, People v. 50 Cal. Rptr. 45. (Cal. ,
          1966) - clandestine police observation.

1485)   Manual Enterprises, Inc. v. Day. 370 U. S. 478.
          (1962) - homosexual erotica.

1486)   Marion v. Gardner. 359 F. 2d 175. (8th Cir. ,
          1966) - social security benefits.

1487)   Massie, People v. 264 P. 2d 671. (Cal. , 1953)
          - homosexual act.

1488)   Maurer, Commonwealth v. 74 A. 2d 732 and 734.
          (Pa. , 1950) - homosexual act.

1489)   McDermott v. U. S. 98 A. 2d 287. (D. C. , 1953)
          - solicitation of police decoy.

1490)   Michalis, State v. 122 A. 538. (N. J. , 1923) -
          private act.

1491)   Mishkin v. State of New York. 383 U. S. 502.
          (1966) - homosexual erotica.

1492)   Morrison v. State Board of Education. 74 Cal.

Rptr. 116 and 82 Cal. Rptr. 175 (1969) - employment and teacher certification.

1493)   Mundy, In re. 85 A. 2d 371. (N. H., 1952) - homosexuality and sex psychopathology.

1494)   Murray v. U. S. 154 Ct. of Claims 185. (1961) - military discharge.

1495)   Nickola v. Munro. 328 P. 2d 271. (Cal., 1958) - gay bar license.

1496)   Norton v. Macy. 417 F. 2d 1161 (D. C., 1969) - federal employment.

1497)   Norton, People v. 25 Cal. Rptr. 676. (Cal., 1962) - clandestine police observation.

1498)   Odorizzi v. State Board of Education. 54 Cal. Rptr. 533. (Cal., 1966) - teacher certification and employment.

1499)   One Eleven Wines and Liquors, Inc. v. Division of Alcoholic Beverage Control; Val's Bar v. Division of Alcoholic Beverage Control; and Murphy's Tavern v. Division of Alcoholic Beverage Control. 235 A. 2d 12. (N. J., 1967) - gay bar license.

1500)   One, Inc. v. Olesen. 241 F. 2d 772. (9th Cir., 1957); 355 U. S. 371. (1958) - homophile publications.

1501)   Paddock Bar, Inc. v. Division of Alcoholic Beverage Control. 134 A. 2d 779. (N. J., 1957) - gay bar license.

1502)   Perkins v. North Carolina. 234 F. Supp. 333. (N. Car., 1964) - private act.

1503)   Poindexter, Commonwealth v. 118 S. W. 943. (Ky., 1909) - homosexual act.

1504)   Polls, State v. 254 P. 2d 1023. (Ariz., 1953) - homosexual act.

1505)   Provoo, U. S. v. 215 F. 2d 531. (2d Cir., 1954) - homosexual condition.

1506)   Quiroz v. Neelly.   291 F. 2d 906.   (5th Cir.,
        1961) - deportation of homosexual alien.

1506a) Ragsdale, People v.   2 Cal. Rptr. 640.   (Cal.,
        1960) - homosexual act in prison.

1507)   Ramos, People v.   270 P. 2d 540.   (Cal., 1954) -
        crime against nature.

1508)   Reed v. U. S.   93 A. 2d 568.   (D. C., 1953) -
        solicitation of police decoy.

1509)   Rittenour v. District of Columbia.   163 A. 2d 558.
        (D. C., 1960) - private act and solicition by police
        decoy.

1509a) Roberts, People v.   64 Cal. Rptr. 70.   (Cal.,
        1967) - clandestine police observation.

1510)   Sarac v. State Board of Education.   57 Cal. Rptr.
        69.   (1967) - employment and teacher certification.

1511)   Schlegel v. U. S.   U. S. Ct. of Claims.   No. 369-63
        (Oct. 1969) - federal employment.

1512)   Schwartz v. Covington.   341 F. 2d 537.   (9th Cir.,
        1965) - military discharge.

1513)   Scott v. Macy.   349 F. 2d 182.   (D. C., 1965);
        402 F. 2d 644.   (D. C., 1968) - federal employ-
        ment.

1514)   Seitner v. U. S.   143 A. 2d 101.   (D. C., 1958);
        262 F. 2d 710.   (D. C., 1958) - assault and solici-
        tation of police decoy.

1515)   Sellers, People v.   230 P. 2d 398.   (Cal., 1951)
        - public act.

1516)   Sheehan, U. S. v.   29 C. M. R. 887 (1960) - mili-
        tary discharge.

1517)   Shields v. Sharp.   366 U. S. 917.   (1961) - federal
        employment.

1518)   Short, State v.   181 A. 2d 225.   (Conn., 1962) -
        homosexual acts.

1519)   Smayda v. U.S.   352 F. 2d 251.   (9th Cir. , 1965)
         - clandestine police observation.

1520)   Spaulding, People v.   254 P. 614.   (Cal. , 1927) -
         public act with police decoy.

1521)   Spinar and Germain, U.S. v.   U.S.D.C. , Min. ,
         4th Div. (1967) - homosexual erotica.   (Reprinted
         in One Confidential, July 1967, pp. 4-11.)

1522)   Stoumen v. Reilly.   234 P. 2d 969.   (Cal. , 1951)
         - gay bar license.

1523)   Strauss, People v.   114 N. Y. S. 2d 322.   (N. Y. ,
         1952) - disorderly conduct.

1524)   Strum v. State.   272 S. W. 359.   (Ark. , 1925) -
         homosexual act.

1525)   Sultan Turkish Bath, Inc. v. Board of Police Com-
         missioners.   337 P. 2d 203.   (Cal. , 1959) -
         Turkish bath license.

1526)   Tarbox v. Board of Supervisors.   329 P. 2d 553.
         (Cal. , 1958) - theater license and lewd vagrancy.

1526a)   Taylor v. Civil Service Commission.   374 F. 2d
         466.   (9th Cir. , 1967) - federal employment.

1527)   Townsend, State v.   71 A. 2d 517.   (Me. , 1950)
         - crime against nature.

1528)   Unglesby v. Zimny.   250 F. Supp. 714.   (Cal. ,
         1965) - military discharge.

1529)   Vallerga and Azar v. Department of Alcoholic
         Beverage Control.   347 P. 2d 909.   (Cal. , 1959)
         - gay bar license.

1529a)   Vigil v. Post Office Department.   406 F. 2d 921.
         (10th Cir. , 1969) - federal employment.

1530)   White, State v.   217 A. 2d 212.   (Me. , 1966) -
         private act.

1531)   Wildeblood v. U.S.   284 F. 2d 592.   (D.C. , 1960)
         - solicitation of police decoy.

1532)   Yeast, U. S. v.   36 C. M. R. 890.   (1966) - con-
        duct unbecoming an officer.

1533)   Young, People v.   29 Cal. Rptr. 492.   (Cal. , 1963)
        - clandestine police observation.

Articles in Medical and Scientific Journals

1534)   Aaronson, B. S. and Grumpelt, H. R.   "Homo-
         sexuality and Some MMPI Measures of Masculinity-
         Femininity," Journal of Clinical Psychology, 17:245-
         47, 1961.

1535)   Abe, K. and Moran, P. A. P.   "Parental Age of
         Homosexuals," British Journal of Psychiatry, 115:
         313-17, 1969.

1536)   Abe, K. and Moran, P. A. P.   "Parental Loss in
         Homosexuals," British Journal of Psychiatry, 115:
         319-20, 1969.

1537)   Abraham, Karl.   "The Psychological Relations be-
         tween Sexuality and Alcoholism," International
         Journal of Psychoanalysis, 7:2-10, 1926.

1538)   Abrams, Albert.   "Homosexuality--A Military
         Menace," Medical Review of Reviews, 24:528-29,
         1918.

1539)   Abramson, Harold A.   "Lysergic Acid Diethylamide
         (LSD-25): III. As an Adjunct to Psychotherapy with
         Elimination of Fear of Homosexuality," Journal of
         Psychology, 39:127-55, 1955.

1540)   Adler, Alfred.   "The Homosexual Problem," Alienist
         and Neurologist, 38:268-87, 1917.

1541)   Adler, Kurt A.   "Life Style, Gender Role, and the
         Symptoms of Homosexuality," Journal of Individual
         Psychology, 23:67-78, 1967.

1542)   Alexander, Leo.   "Psychotherapy of Sexual Devia-
         tion with the Aid of Hypnosis," American Journal of
         Clinical Hypnosis, 9:181-83, 1967.

1543)   Alexander, Michail.   "Homosexuality and the Arts,"
         International Journal of Sexology, 8:26-27, 1954.

136

1544)   Allen, Clifford. "The Homosexual," Medical World,
        78:144-48, 1953.

1545)   Allen, Clifford. "Homosexuality and Oscar Wilde:
        A Psychological Study," International Journal of
        Sexology, 2:205-15, 1949.

1546)   Allen, Clifford. "Homosexuality: the Psychological
        Factor," Medical Press, 218:222-23, 1947.

1547)   Allen, Clifford. "The Meaning of Homosexuality,"
        International Journal of Sexology, 7:207-12, 1954.

1548)   Allen, Clifford. "The Meaning of Homosexuality,"
        Medical World, 80:9-16, 1954.

1549)   Allen, Clifford. "On the Cure of Homosexuality,"
        International Journal of Sexology, 5:148-50, 1952.

1550)   Allen, Clifford. "The Problem of Homosexuality,"
        International Journal of Sexology, 6:40-42, 1952.

1551)   Allen, Clifford. "The Treatment of Homosexuality,"
        Medical Press, 235:441-50, 1956.

1552)   Allen, Frederick H. "Homosexuality in Relation to
        the Problem of Human Difference," American Jour-
        nal of Orthopsychiatry, 10:129-35, 1940.

1553)   Alman, C., Barker, J., Mathis, J. K., and Powers,
        C. A. "Drawing Characteristics of Male Homo-
        sexuals," Journal of Clinical Psychology, 9:185-
        88, 1953.

1554)   Anant, S. S. "Former Alcoholics and Social
        Drinking," Canadian Psychologist, 9:1-35, 1968.

1555)   Anant, S. S. "The Use of Verbal Aversion (Nega-
        tive Conditioning) with an Alcoholic: A Case Re-
        port," Behaviour Research and Therapy, 6:395-96,
        1968.

1556)   Anderson, C. "On Certain Conscious and Uncon-
        scious Homosexual Responses to Warfare," British
        Journal of Medical Psychology, 20:161-74, 1944.

1557)   Anonymous. "The Feelings of a Fetishist,"

Psychiatric Quarterly, 31:742-58, 1957.

1558)   Anonymous. "Living with Homosexuality," Canadian Medical Association Journal, 86:875-78, 1962.

1559)   Anonymous. "Male Homosexuality," Lancet, no. 7111:1077-80, 1959. (See no. 141 above.)

1560)   Apfelberg, B., Sugar, C., and Pfeffer, A.A. "A Psychiatric Study of 250 Sex Offenders," American Journal of Psychiatry, 100:762-70, 1944.

1561)   Appel, K.E. and Flaherty, J.A. "Endocrine Studies in Cases of Homosexuality," Archives of Neurology and Psychiatry, 37:1206-07, 1937.

1562)   Apperson, L.B. and McAdoo, W.G. Jr. "Parental Factors in the Childhood of Homosexuals," Journal of Abnormal Psychology, 73:201-06, 1968.

1563)   Arlow, J.A. "Report on Panel, Perversion: Theoretical and Therapeutic Aspects," Journal of the American Psychoanalytic Association, 2:336-45, 1954.

1564)   Arlow, J.A. "Report on Panel, Psychodynamics and Treatment of Perversions," Bulletin of the American Psychoanalytic Association, 8:315-27, 1952.

1565)   Armon, Virginia. "Some Personality Variables in Overt Female Homosexuality," Journal of Projective Techniques, 24:292-309, 1960.

1566)   Armstrong, C.N. "Diversities of Sex," British Medical Journal, 2:1173-77, 1955.

1567)   Aronson, Gerald J. "Delusion of Pregnancy in a Male Homosexual with an Abdominal Cancer," Bulletin of the Menninger Clinic, 16:159-66, 1952.

1568)   Aronson, Marvin L. "A Study of the Freudian Theory of Paranoia by Means of the Blacky Pictures," Journal of Projective Techniques, 17:3-19, 1953.

1569)   Aronson, Marvin L. "A Study of the Freudian

Theory of Paranoia by Means of the Rorschach Test," Journal of Projective Techniques, 16:397-411, 1952.

1569a)   Athaniasiou, Robert; Shaver, Philip; and Tavris, Carol. "Sex [Attitudes]," Psychology Today, 4:39-52 at 50-51, July 1970.

1570)   Atia, I. M. and Muftic, M. K. "Hypnosis in the Psychosomatic Investigation of Female Homosexuality," British Journal of Medical Hypnosis, 9:41-46, 1957.

1571)   Bak, R. C. "Fetishism," Journal of the American Psychoanalytic Association, 1:285-98, 1953.

1572)   Bak, R. C. "Masochism in Paranoia," Psychoanalytic Quarterly, 15:285-301, 1946.

1573)   Bakwin, Harry. "Deviant Gender-Role Behavior in Children: Relation to Homosexuality," Pediatrics, 41:620-29, 1968.

1574)   Bakwin, Harry and Ruth M. "Homosexual Behavior in Children," Journal of Pediatrics, 43:108-11, 1953.

1575)   Banay, R. S. and Davidoff, L. "Apparent Recovery of a Sex Psychopath after Lobotomy," Journal of Criminal Psychopathology, 4:59-66, 1942.

1576)   Barahal, Hyman S. "Constitutional Factors in Male Homosexuals," Psychiatric Quarterly, 13:391-400, 1939.

1577)   Barahal, Hyman S. "Female Transvestism and Homosexuality," Psychiatric Quarterly, 27:390-438, 1953.

1578)   Barahal, Hyman S. "Testosterone in Psychotic Male Homosexuals," Psychiatric Quarterly, 14:319-29, 1940.

1579)   Barker, A. J., Mathis, J. K., and Powers, C. A. "Drawing Characteristics of Male Homosexuals," Journal of Clinical Psychology, 9:185-88, 1953.

1580)   Barker, J. G. "Behaviour Therapy for Transves-

tism: A Comparison of Pharmacological and Elec-
trical Aversion Techniques," British Journal of
Psychiatry, 111:268-76, 1965.

1581)   Barnes, J.   "Rape and Other Sexual Offences,"
British Medical Journal, 2:293-95, 1967.

1582)   Barnes, J.   "The Unmarried Woman," Practitioner,
172:405-10, 1954.

1583)   Barnette, W. L.   "Study of an Adult Male Homosexual and Terman-Miles M-F Scores," American
Journal of Orthopsychiatry, 12:346-52, 1942.

1584)   Barr, M. L. and Hobbs, G. E.   "Chromosomal Sex
in Transvestites," Lancet, 266:1109-10, 1954.

1585)   Barr, R. H. and Hill, G.   "Acquired Spasmodic
Torticollis in a Male Homosexual," Journal of
Nervous and Mental Disease, 130:325-30, 1960.

1586)   Bartholomew, A. A.   "A Long-Acting Phenothiazine
as   a Possible Agent to Control Deviant Sexual Behavior," American Journal of Psychiatry, 124:917-
23, 1968.

1587)   Bauer, Julius.   "Homosexuality as an Endocrino-
logical, Psychological, and Genetic Problem,"
Journal of Criminal Psychopathology, 2:188-97,
1940.

1588)   Baumeyer, F.   "The Schreber Case," International
Journal of Psychoanalysis, 37:61-74, 1956.

1589)   Beach, Frank A.   "Experimental Studies of Sexual
Behavior in Male Animals," Journal of Clinical
Endocrinology, 4:126-34, 1944.

1590)   Beach, Frank A.   "A Review of Physiological and
Psychological Studies of Sexual Behavior in Mam-
mals," Physiological Reviews, 27:240-307, 1947.

1591)   Becher, A. L.   "A Third Sex? Some Speculations
on a Sexuality Spectrum," M. D. , 16:366-78, 1967.

1592)   Bell, D. S. and Trethowan, W. H.   "Amphetamine
Addiction and Disturbed Sexuality," Archives of

General Psychiatry, 4:74-78, 1961.

1593)   Benda, C. E. "Existential Psychotherapy of Homo-
        sexuality, " Review of Existential Psychology and
        Psychiatry, 3:133-52, 1963.

1594)   Bendel, R. "The Modified Szondi Test in Male
        Homosexuality, " International Journal of Sexology,
        8:226-27, 1955.

1595)   Bender, Lauretta and Blau, Abram. "The Re-
        action of Children to Sexual Relations with Adults, "
        American Journal of Orthopsychiatry, 7:500-18,
        1937.

1596)   Bender, Lauretta and Grugett, Alvin E. Jr. "A
        Follow-Up Report on Children Who had Atypical
        Sexual Experience, " American Journal of Ortho-
        psychiatry, 22:825-37, 1952.

1597)   Bender, Lauretta and Paster, Samuel. "Homo-
        sexual Trends in Children, " American Journal of
        Orthopsychiatry, 11:730-43, 1941.

1598)   Bene, Eva. "On the Genesis of Female Homo-
        sexuality, " British Journal of Psychiatry, 111:815-
        21, 1965. (Abstracted in Psychiatry Digest, 27:
        23-24, May 1966.)

1599)   Bene, Eva. "On the Genesis of Male Homosexuality:
        An attempt at Clarifying the Role of Parents, " Brit-
        ish Journal of Psychiatry, 111:803-13, 1965.

1600)   Benedict, Ruth. "Continuities and Discontinuities
        in Cultural Conditioning, " Psychiatry, 1:161-67,
        1938. (Reprinted in Edgar A. Schuler and others
        [eds.], Readings in Sociology [2d ed. ; New York:
        Crowell, 1960], pp. 166-75.)

1601)   Benedict, Ruth. "Sex in Primitive Society, "
        American Journal of Orthopsychiatry, 9:570-74,
        1939.

1602)   Benjamin, Harry. "Clinical Aspects of Trans-
        sexualism in the Male and Female, " American
        Journal of Psychotherapy, 18:458-69, 1964.

142   Homosexuality

1603)   Benjamin, Harry. "An Echo of and an Addendum
         to 'For the Sake of Morality,' " Medical Journal
         and Record, 134:118-20, 1931.

1604)   Benjamin, Harry. "For the Sake of Morality,"
         Medical Journal and Record, 133: 380-82, 1931.

1605)   Benjamin, Harry. "Transsexualism and Transves-
         tism as Psychosomatic and Somatopsychic Syn-
         dromes," American Journal of Psychotherapy, 8:
         219-30, 1954.

1606)   Bennet, E. A. "The Social Aspects of Homosex-
         uality," Medical Press, 218:207-10, 1947. (Ab-
         stracted in Proceedings of the Royal Society of
         Medicine, 40:585-92, 1947.)

1607)   Bennet, E. A. , Mannheim, H. , Stanley-Jones, D. ,
         East, W. N. , and Mackwood, J. C. "Homosexuality,"
         British Medical Journal, 1:691-92, 1947.

1608)   Bentler, P. M. "A Note on the Treatment of Ado-
         lescent Sex Problems," Journal of Child Psy-
         chology and Psychiatry, 9:125-29, 1968.

1609)   Benton, Arthur L. "The Minnesota Multiphasic
         Personality Inventory in Clinical Practice," Journal
         of Nervous and Mental Disease, 102:416-20, 1945.

1610)   Berg, Charles. "The Problem of Homosexuality,"
         American Journal of Psychotherapy, 10:696-708,
         1956 and 11:65-79, 1957.

1611)   Berger, L. and Liverant, S. "Homosexual Pre-
         judice and Perceptual Defense," Journal of Con-
         sulting Psychology, 25:459, 1961.

1612)   Bergler, Edmund. "Contributions to the Psycho-
         genesis of Alcohol Addiction," Quarterly Journal of
         Studies on Alcoholism, 5:434-49, 1944.

1613)   Bergler, Edmund. "Contributions to the Psychology
         of Homosexuals," Samiska, 8:205-09, 1954.

1614)   Bergler, Edmund. "D. H. Lawrence's 'The Fox' and
         the Psychoanalytic Theory of Lesbianism," Journal
         of Nervous and Mental Disease, 126:488-91, 1958.

1615)   Bergler, Edmund. "Differential Diagnosis between
        Spurious Homosexuality and Perversion Homosex-
        uality," Psychiatric Quarterly, 21:399-409, 1947.

1616)   Bergler, Edmund. "Eight Prerequisites for the
        Psychoanalytic Treatment of Homosexuality,"
        Psychoanalysis and the Psychoanalytic Review, 31:
        253-86, 1944.

1617)   Bergler, Edmund. "The Myth of a New National
        Disease: Homosexuality and the Kinsey Report,"
        Psychiatric Quarterly, 22:66-88, 1948. (Reprinted
        in Krich, no. 69 above, pp. 226-50.)

1618)   Bergler, Edmund. "Psychological Factors in the
        Decline of an Industry," Diseases of the Nervous
        System, 21:461-63, 1960.

1619)   Bergler, Edmund. "Psychology of Friendship and
        Acquaintanceship," Medical Record, 159:101-04,
        1946.

1620)   Bergler, Edmund. "The Respective Importance of
        Reality and Phantasy in the Genesis of Female
        Homosexuality," Journal of Criminal Psychopathology,
        5:27-30, 1943.

1621)   Bergler, Edmund. "Spurious Homosexuality,"
        Psychiatric Quarterly Supplement, 28:68-77, 1954.

1622)   Bergler, Edmund. "Suppositions about the Mech-
        anism of Criminosis," Journal of Criminal Psycho-
        pathology, 5:215-46, 1943.

1623)   Bergler, Edmund. "What Every Physician Should
        Know about Homosexuality," International Record of
        Medicine, 171:685-90, 1958.

1624)   Bergmann, M.S. "Homosexuality in the Rorschach
        Test," Bulletin of the Menninger Clinic, 9:78-83,
        1945.

1625)   Bernstein, I.C. "Homosexuality in Gynecologic
        Practice," South Dakota Journal of Medicine, 21:
        33-37, 1968.

1626)   Beukenkamp, Cornelius. "Phantom Patricide,"

Archives of General Psychiatry, 3:282-88, 1960.

1627)   Bieber, Irving. "Changing Concepts of the Genesis
         and Therapy of Male Homosexuality," American
         Journal of Orthopsychiatry, 35:203, 1965.

1628)   Bieber, Irving; Gershman, Harry; Ovesey, Lionel;
         and Weiss, Frederick A. "The Meaning of Homo-
         sexual Trends in Therapy: A Round Table Dis-
         cussion," American Journal of Psychoanalysis, 24:
         60-76, 1964.

1629)   Bieber, Toby. "On Treating Male Homosexuals,"
         Archives of General Psychiatry, 16:60-63, 1967.

1630)   Bien, Ernest. "Why do Homosexuals Undergo
         Treatment?" Medical Review of Reviews, 40:10-
         18, 1934.

1631)   Bird, M. S. "Some Emotional Problems Dealt with
         in the Special Clinic," British Journal of Venereal
         Diseases, 41:217-20, 1965.

1632)   The Bishop of Rochester. "The Church and Sex,"
         Practitioner, 172:350-54, 1954.

1633)   Blackman, Nathan J. "The Culpability of the Homo-
         sexual," Missouri Medicine, 50:27-29, 1953.

1634)   Blackman, Nathan J. "The Genesis of Homosex-
         uality," Journal of the Missouri Medical Associa-
         tion, 47:814-17, 1950.

1635)   Blakemore, C. B., Thorpe, J. G., Barker, J. C.,
         Conway, C. G., and Lavin, N. I. "The Application
         of Faradic Aversion Conditioning in a Case of
         Transvestism," Behaviour Research and Therapy,
         1:29-34, 1963.

1636)   Blakemore, C. B. and others. "Follow-Up Note to:
         The Application of Faradic Aversion Conditioning in
         a Case of Transvestism," Behaviour Research and
         Therapy, 1:191, 1963.

1637)   Bloch, Herbert A. "Social Pressures of Confine-
         ment toward Sexual Deviation," Journal of Social
         Therapy, 1:112-25, 1955.

1638)   Bluestone, Harvey; O'Malley, Edward; and Connell,
          Sydney. "Homosexuals in Prison," Corrective Psy-
          chiatry and Journal of Social Therapy, 12:13-24,
          1966. (Abstracted in Psychiatry Digest, 27:13,
          Sep. 1967.)

1639)   Bollmeier, L. N. "A Paranoid Mechanism in Male
          Overt Homosexuality," Psychoanalytic Quarterly, 7:
          357-67, 1938.

1640)   Bonime, Walter. "A Case of Depression in a
          Homosexual Young Man," Contemporary Psycho-
          analysis, 3:1-14, 1966.

1641)   "The Borstal Puzzle," Lancet, 260:1399-1400, 1951.

1642)   Borstelman, L. J. and Klopfer, W. G. "Does the
          Szondi Test Reflect Individuality? The Affective
          Valences of the Szondi Pictures," Journal of
          Personality, 19:421-39, 1951.

1643)   Bose, G. "The Genesis of Homosexuality,"
          Samiksa, 4:66-75, 1950.

1644)   Botwinick, J. and Machover, S. "A Psychometric
          Examination of Latent Homosexuality in Alcoholism,"
          Quarterly Journal of Studies on Alcohol, 12:268-72,
          1951.

1645)   Bowman, Karl M. "The Problem of the Sex Of-
          fender," American Journal of Psychiatry, 108:250-
          57, 1951.

1646)   Bowman, Karl M. and Engle, Bernice. "A Psy-
          chiatric Evaluation of Laws of Homosexuality,"
          American Journal of Psychiatry, 112:577-83, 1956.

1647)   Bowman, Karl M. and Jellinek, E. Morton. "Al-
          cohol Addiction and its Treatment," Quarterly
          Journal of Studies on Alcohol, 2:98-176, 1941.

1648)   Braaten, Leif J. and Darling, C. Douglas. "Overt
          and Covert Homosexual Problems among Male
          College Students," Genetic Psychology Monographs,
          71:269-310, 1965.

1649)   Bradshaw, W. V. "Homosexual Syphilis Epidemic,"

Texas State Journal of Medicine, 57:907-09, 1961.

1650)   Brady, J. P. and Levitt, E. E.   "The Relation of
          Sexual Preferences to Sexual Experiences," Psycho-
          logical Record, 15:377-84, 1965.

1651)   Braff, Erwin H.   "Venereal Disease, Sex Positions,
          and Homosexuality," British Journal of Venereal
          Diseases, 38:165-66, 1962.

1652)   Bragman, Louis J.   "The Case of John Addington
          Symonds: A Study in Aesthetic Homosexuality,"
          American Journal of Psychiatry, 43:375-98, 1936.
          (Reprinted in Ruitenbeek, no. 95 above, pp. 87-
          111.)

1653)   Bramanti, R. M.   "Letter to a Probation Officer
          on a Case of Homosexuality," Southwest Medical
          Journal, 46:253-57, 1965.

1654)   Brancale, R., Ellis, A., and Doorbar, R.   "Psy-
          chiatric and Psychological Investigations of Con-
          victed Sex Offenders: A Summary Report," Ameri-
          can Journal of Psychiatry, 109:17-21, 1952.

1655)   Breger, L. and Liverant, S.   "Homosexual Pre-
          judice and Perceptual Defense," Journal of Con-
          sulting Psychology, 25:459, 1961.

1656)   Brill, A. A.   "The Conception of Homosexuality,"
          Journal of the American Medical Association, 61:
          335-40, 1913.

1657)   Brill, A. A.   "Homoerotism and Paranoia," Ameri-
          can Journal of Psychiatry, 90:957-74, 1934.

1658)   Brill, A. A.   "The Psychiatric Approach to the
          Problem of Homosexuality," Psychiatric Association
          and Student Health Association, 15:31-34, 1934.
          (Reprinted in Journal-Lancet, 55:249-52, 1935.)

1659)   Brill, A. A.   "The Psychological Mechanisms of
          Paranoia," New York Medical Journal, 94:1209-13,
          1911.

1660)   Brill, A. A.   "Sexual Manifestations in Neurotic and
          Psychotic Symptoms," Psychiatric Quarterly, 14:9-
          16, 1940.

1661)   British Medical Association and Magistrates' Asso-
          ciation. "The Criminal Law and Sexual Offenders,"
          British Medical Journal Supplement, 1:135-40, 1949.

1662)   British Psychological Society Council. "Memoran-
          dum of Evidence to the Home Office Departmental
          Committee on the Law relating to Homosexual Of-
          fences and Prostitution," Bulletin of the British
          Psychological Society, 29:1-8, 1956.

1663)   Brody, E. B. "From Schizophrenic to Homosexual:
          A Crisis in Role and Relating," American Journal
          of Psychotherapy, 17:579-95, 1963.

1664)   Brody, M. W. "An Analysis of the Psychosexual
          Development of a Female--with special Reference to
          Homosexuality," Psychoanalysis and the Psycho-
          analytic Review, 30:47-58, 1943. (Reprinted in
          Krich, no. 69 above, pp. 312-24.)

1665)   Bromberg, Walter. "Sex Deviation and Therapy,"
          Journal of Social Therapy, 1:203-10, 1955.

1666)   Bromberg, Walter. "Sex Offense as a Disguise,"
          Corrective Psychiatry and the Journal of Social
          Therapy, 11:293-98, 1965.

1667)   Bromberg, Walter and Franklin, Girard H. "The
          Treatment of Sexual Deviates with Group Psycho-
          drama," Group Psychotherapy, 4:274-89, 1952.

1668)   Bromberg, Walter and Schilder, Paul. "Psychologic
          Considerations in Alcoholic Hallucinations," Interna-
          tional Journal of Psychoanalysis, 14:206-24, 1933.

1669)   Broster, L. R. and Vines, H. W. C. "A Note on the
          Adrenal Cortex," British Medical Journal, 1:662,
          1937.

1670)   Brown, Daniel G. "The Development of Sex-Role
          Inversion and Homosexuality," Journal of Pediatrics,
          50:613-14, 1957.

1671)   Brown, Daniel G. "Homosexuality and Family
          Dynamics," Bulletin of the Menninger Clinic, 27:
          227-32, 1963.

1672)   Brown, Daniel G.   "Inversion and Homosexuality,"
         American Journal of Orthopsychiatry, 28:424-29,
         1958.

1673)   Brown, Daniel G.   "Masculinity-Femininity De-
         velopment in Children," Journal of Consulting
         Psychology, 21:197-202, 1957.

1674)   Brown, Daniel G.   "Sex Role Preference in Young
         Children," Psychological Monographs, vol. 70, no.
         14, pp. 1-19, 1956.

1675)   Brown, Daniel G. and Tolor, Alexander.   "Human
         Figure Drawings as Indicators of Sexual Identifica-
         tion and Inversion," Perceptual and Motor Skills
         (Monograph Supplement No. 3), 7:199-211, 1957.

1676)   Brown, J. H.   "Homosexuality as an Adaptation in
         Handling Aggression," Journal of the Louisiana
         Medical Society, 115:304-11, 1963.

1677)   Brown, P. T.   "On the Differentiation of Homo- or
         Hetero-erotic Interest in the Male: An Operant
         Technique Illustrated in the Case of a Motor-cycle
         Fetishist," Behaviour Research and Therapy, 2:31-
         35, 1964.

1678)   Brown, P. T.   A Reply to Koenig (see no. 2105
         below), Behaviour Research and Therapy, 2:309-11,
         1965.

1679)   Brussel, J. A.   "The Tschaikowsky Troika," Psy-
         chiatric Quarterly Supplement, 36:304-22, 1962.

1680)   Bryan, Douglas.   "Bisexuality," International Jour-
         nal of Psychoanalysis, 11:150-66, 1930.

1681)   Buki, Rudolph A.   "A Treatment Program for
         Homosexuals," Diseases of the Nervous System, 25:
         304-07, 1964.

1682)   Buki, Rudolph A.   "The Use of Psychotropic Drugs
         in the Rehabilitation of Sex-Deviated Criminals,"
         American Journal of Psychiatry, 120:1170-75, 1964.

1683)   Burrow, Trigant.   "The Genesis and Meaning of
         'Homosexuality' and Its Relation to the Problem of

Introverted Mental States," Psychoanalysis and the
Psychoanalytic Review, 4:272-84, 1917.

1684)   Burtchaell, James.   Review of Michael Buckley's
         Morality and the Homosexual, Bulletin of the Guild
         of Catholic Psychiatrists, 7:193-96, 1960.

1685)   Burton, Arthur.   "The Use of the Masculinity-
         Femininity Scale of the Minnesota Multiphasic Per-
         sonality Inventory as an Aid in the Diagnosis of
         Sexual Inversion," Journal of Psychology, 24:161-
         64, 1947.

1686)   Butts, William M.   "Boy Prostitutes of the Me-
         tropolis," Journal of Clinical Psychopathology, 8:
         673-81, 1947.

1687)   Bychowski, Gustav.   "The Ego and the Introjects,"
         Psychoanalytic Quarterly, 25:11-36, 1956.

1688)   Bychowski, Gustav.   "The Ego and the Object of
         the Homosexual," International Journal of Psycho-
         analysis, 42:255-59, 1961.

1689)   Bychowski, Gustav, "The Ego of Homosexuals,"
         International Journal of Psychoanalysis, 26:114-27,
         1945.

1690)   Bychowski, Gustav.   "The Structure of Homosexual
         Acting-Out," Psychoanalytic Quarterly, 23:48-61,
         1954.

1691)   Bychowski, Gustav.   "Walt Whitman: A Study in
         Sublimation," Psychoanalysis and the Social Sciences,
         3:223-61, 1951.   (Reprinted in Ruitenbeek, no. 95
         above, pp. 140-80.)

1692)   Cabeen, C.W. and Coleman, J.C.   "Group Therapy
         with Sex Offenders: Description and Evaluation of
         Group Therapy in an Institutional Setting," Journal
         of Clinical Psychology, 17:122-29, 1961.

1693)   Cabeen, C.W. and Coleman, J.C.   "The Selection
         of Sex-Offender Patients for Group Psychotherapy,"
         International Journal of Group Psychotherapy, 12:
         326-34, 1962.

1694)   Caldwell, Alexander B.   "Sexual Behavior and Its
          Deviations," Trauma: A Journal of Medicine,
          Anatomy, and Surgery for Lawyers, 6:7-55, 1964.

1695)   Carpenter, C. R.   "Sexual Behavior of the Free
          Ranging Rhesus Monkeys (Macaca Mulatta) II.
          Periodicity of Estrus, Homosexual, Autoerotic, and
          Non-Conformist Behavior," Journal of Comparative
          Psychology, 33:143-62, 1942.

1696)   Carr, Arthur C.   "Symposium on 'Reinterpretation
          of the Screber Case: Freud's Theory of Paranoia.'
          II. Observations on Paranoia and their Relationship
          to the Schreber Case," International Journal of
          Psychoanalysis, 44:195-200, 1963.

1697)   Carstairs, G. M.   "Hinjra and Jiryan: Two Derivi-
          tives of Hindu Attitudes to Sexuality," British Jour-
          nal of Medical Psychology, 29:128-38, 1956.

1698)   Carstairs, G. M. and Grygier, T.   "Anthropological,
          Psychometric, and Psychotherapeutic Aspects of
          Homosexuality," Bulletin of the British Psychological
          Society, 32:46-47, 1957.

1699)   "Case of Oscar Wilde," Lancet, 2:440, 1948.

1700)   Cason, Hulsey.   "A Case of Sexual Psychopathy,"
          Journal of Clinical Psychopathology, 8:785-800,
          1947.

1701)   Cassity, John H.   "Personality Study of 200 Mur-
          derers," Journal of Criminal Psychopathology, 2:
          296-304, 1941.

1702)   Castelnuovo-Tedesco, P.   "Ulcerative Colitis in an
          Adolescent Boy Subjected to Homosexual Assault,"
          Psychosomatic Medicine, 24:148-56, 1962.

1703)   "Castration of a Male Homosexual," British Medical
          Journal, 2:1001 and 2:1562, 1954.

1704)   Cattell, R. S. and Morony, J. H.   "The Use of 16
          PF in Distinguishing Homosexuals, Normals, and
          General Criminals," Journal of Consulting Psy-
          chology, 26:531-40, 1962.

1705)   Catterall, R. D.   "Anorectal Gonorrhea, " Pro-
        ceedings of the Royal Society of Medicine, 55:871-
        73, 1962.

1706)   Cautela, J. R.   "Covert Sensitization, " Psychological
        Reports, 20:459-68, 1967.

1707)   Cavanagh, John R.   "Homosexuality as an Impediment
        to Marriage, " Bulletin of the Guild of Catholic Psy-
        chiatrists, 7:96-109, 1960.

1708)   Cavanagh, John R.   "Latent Homosexuality as a
        Cause of Marital Discord, " Bulletin of the Guild of
        Catholic Psychiatrists, 12:33-42, 1965.

1709)   Chang, Judy and Block, Jack.   "Study of Identifica-
        tion in Male Homosexuals, " Journal of Consulting
        Psychology, 24:307-10, 1960.

1710)   Chapman, A. H. and Reese, D. C.   "Homosexual
        Signs in the Rorschach of Early Schizophrenics, "
        Journal of Clinical Psychology, 9:30-32, 1953.

1711)   Chapman, Diana.   "What is a Lesbian?" Family
        Doctor, Aug. 1965, pp. 474-75.

1712)   Chatterji, N. N.   "Auto-eroticism in Paranoia, "
        Samiska, 1:149-56, 1947.

1713)   Chatterji, N. N.   "Drug Addiction, " Indian Journal
        of Psychology, 32:101-04, 1957.

1714)   Chesser, Eustace.   "Society and the Homosexual, "
        International Journal of Sexology, 7:213-16, 1954.

1715)   Clark, D. F.   "A Note on Avoidance Conditioning
        Techniques in Sexual Disorder, " Behaviour Re-
        search and Therapy, 3:203-06, 1965.

1716)   Clarke, R. V. G.   "The Slater Selective Vocabulary
        Test and Male Homosexuality, " British Journal of
        Medical Psychology, 38:339-40, 1965.

1717)   Coates, Stephen.   "Homosexuality and the Rorschach
        Test, " British Journal of Medical Psychology, 35:
        177-90, 1962.

1718)   Cohen, M. M.   "New Innoculation Sites resulting
         from New Adventures," Maryland State Medical
         Journal, 11:128-29, 1962.

1719)   Comfort, Alex.   "A Matter of Science and Ethics:
         Reflections on the British Medical Association Com-
         mittee's Report on Homosexuality and Prostitution,"
         Lancet, 270:147-49, 1956.

1720)   "Committee on Homosexuality," Lancet, 266:986,
         1954.

1721)   "Committee on Homosexuality and Prostitution,"
         British Medical Journal, 2:603, 1954, and 1:799,
         1955.

1722)   Conn, J. H.   "Hypnosynthesis: the Dynamic Psycho-
         therapy of the Sex Offender Utilizing Hypnotic Pro-
         cedures," Journal of the American Society of Psy-
         chosomatic Dentistry and Medicine, 15:18-27, 1968.

1723)   Cooke, R. A. and Rodrigue, R. B.   "Amoebic
         Balantis," Medical Journal of Australia, 51:114-16,
         1964.

1724)   Coon, Earl O.   "Homosexuality in the News,"
         Archives of Criminal Psychodynamics, 2:843-65,
         1957.

1725)   Cooper, W. L.   "Sex Hormone Assays as Expert
         Evidence (in Cases associated with Homosexuality),"
         Medico-Legal and Criminological Review, 7:374-77,
         1939.

1726)   Coppen, A. J.   "Body Build of Homosexuals,"
         Psychosomatic Medicine, 1:154-60, 1960.

1727)   Coppen, A. J.   "Body Build of Male Homosexuals,"
         British Medical Journal, 2:1443-45, 1959.

1728)   Coriat, Isador H.   "Homosexuality: Its Psycho-
         genesis and Treatment," New York Medical Jour-
         nal, 97:589-94, 1913.

1729)   Cornsweet, A. C. and Hayes, M. F.   "Conditioned
         Response to Fellatio," American Journal of Psy-
         chiatry, 103:76-78, 1946.

1730)   Cory, Donald W.   "Homosexual Attitudes and
        Heterosexual Prejudices," International Journal of
        Sexology, 5:151-53, 1952. (Reprinted in Cory, no.
        27 above, pp. 420-26.)

1731)   Cory, Donald W.   "Homosexuality in Prison," Jour-
        nal of Social Therapy, 1:137-40, 1955.

1732)   "The Court and the Sexual Offender," British Medi-
        cal Journal, 2:1459-60, 1951.

1733)   Craft, Michael.   "Boy Prostitutes and their Fate,"
        British Journal of Psychiatry, 112:1111-14, 1966.

1734)   Crane, Harry W.   "The Environmental Factor in
        Sexual Inversion," Journal of the Elisha Mitchell
        Scientific Society, 61:243-48, 1945. (Reprinted in
        William C. Coker [ed.], Studies in Science [Chapel
        Hill: University of North Carolina Press, 1946],
        pp. 243-48.)

1735)   Creadick, R. N.   "Management of Homosexuals,"
        Southern Medical Journal, 46:455-60, 1953.

1736)   "Crime and Sin: Sir John Wolfenden at Winchester,"
        British Medical Journal, 2:140-42, 1960.

1737)   Crooke, A. C.   "The Androgens," Practitioner,
        180:13-21, 1958.

1738)   Crowley, R. M.   "The Courts and Psychiatry,"
        Psychiatry, 1:265-68, 1938.

1739)   Cupp, M. E. and Sachs, L. B.   "A Possible Ex-
        planation of the Excessive Brother-to-Sister Ratios
        reported in Siblings of Male Homosexuals," Jour-
        nal of Nervous and Mental Disease, 140:305-06,
        1965.

1740)   Curran, Desmond.   "Homosexuality," Practitioner,
        141:280-87, 1938.

1741)   Curran, Desmond.   "Sexual Perversions and their
        Treatment," Practitioner, 158:343-48, 1947.

1742)   Curran, Desmond and Parr, Denis.   "Homosexuality:
        An Analysis of 100 Male Cases seen in Private

Practice," British Medical Journal, 1:797-801, 1957.

1743)   Cutter, Fred. "Sexual Differentiation in Figure Drawings and Overt Deviation," Journal of Clinical Psychology, 12:369-72, 1956.

1744)   Daly, Claude D. "The Mother Complex in Literature," Samiska, 1:157-90, 1947. (Reprinted in Ruitenbeek, no. 95 above, pp. 20-58.)

1745)   Daniel, S. "The Homosexual Woman in Present Day Society," International Journal of Sexology, 7: 223-24, 1954.

1746)   Darke, Roy A. "Heredity as an Etiological Factor in Homosexuality," Journal of Nervous and Mental Disease, 107:251-68, 1948.

1747)   Darke, Roy A. and Geil, George A. "Homosexual Activity: Relation of Degree and Role to the Goodenough Test and to the Cornell Selectee Index," Journal of Nervous and Mental Disease, 108:217-40, 1948.

1748)   David, Henry P. and Rabinowitz, William. "Szondi Patterns in Epileptic and Homosexual Males," Journal of Consulting Psychology, 16:247-50, 1952.

1749)   Davids, A., Joelson, M., and McArthur, C. "Rorschach and TAT Indices of Homosexuality in Overt Homosexuals, Neurotics, and Normal Males," Journal of Abnormal and Social Psychology, 53:161-72, 1956.

1750)   Davies-Jones, C. W. S. "A Case of War Shock Resulting from Sex Inversion," International Journal of Psychoanalysis, 1:240-44, 1920.

1751)   Dean, Robert B. and Richardson, Harold. "Analysis of MMPI Profiles of 40 College-Educated Overt Male Homosexuals," Journal of Consulting Psychology, 28:483-86, 1964.

1752)   Dean, Robert B. and Richardson, Harold. "On MMPI High-Point Codes of Homosexual versus Heterosexual Males," Journal of Consulting Psychology, 30:558-60, 1966.

1753)   DeLuca, Joseph N.   "Performance of Overt Male
         Homosexuals and Controls on the Blacky Test,"
         Journal of Clinical Psychology, 23:497, 1967.

1754)   DeLuca, Joseph N.   "The Structure of Homosexuality,"
         Proceedings of the 73rd Annual Convention of the
         American Psychological Association, 1965, pp. 205-
         06.   (Reprinted in Journal of Projective Techniques
         and Personality Assessments, 30:187-91, 1966.)

1755)   Demaria, L. A. de.   "Homosexual Acting Out,"
         International Journal of Psychoanalysis, 49:219-20,
         1968.

1756)   DeMartino, M. F.   "Human Figure Drawings by
         Mentally Retarded Males," Journal of Clinical
         Psychology, 10:241-44, 1954.

1757)   DeMonchy, R.   "A Clinical Type of Homosexuality,"
         International Journal of Psychoanalysis, 46:218-25,
         1965.

1758)   Denford, J. D.   "The Psychodynamics of Homo-
         sexuality," New Zealand Medical Journal, 66:743-
         44, 1967.

1759)   Deri, Susan K.   "The Szondi Test," American Jour-
         nal of Orthopsychiatry, 19:447-54, 1949.

1760)   Deschin, C. S.   "VD and the Adolescent Personality,"
         American Journal of Nursing, 63:58-63, Nov. 1963.

1761)   Deutsch, Helene.   "On Female Homosexuality,"
         Psychoanalytic Quarterly, 1:484-510, 1932 (transla-
         tion by Edith B. Jackson).   (Reprinted in Inter-
         national Journal of Psychoanalysis, 14:34-56, 1933
         and in Robert Fliess [ed.], The Psychoanalytic
         Reader [New York: International Universities
         Press, 1948], pp. 237-60.)

1762)   Devereux, George.   "Institutionalized Homosexuality
         of the Mohave Indians," Human Biology, 9:498-527,
         1937.   (Reprinted in Ruitenbeek, no. 96 above,
         pp. 183-226.)

1763)   Devereux, George.   "Mohave Indian Autoerotic Be-
         havior," Psychoanalytic Review, 37:201-20, 1950.

1764)   Devereux, George. "Retaliatory Homosexual
        Triumph over the Father," International Journal
        of Psychoanalysis, 41:157-61, 1960.

1765)   Devereux, George. "The Significance of the Ex-
        ternal Female Genitalia and of Female Orgasm for
        the Male," Journal of the American Psychoanalytic
        Association, 8:278-86, 1958.

1766)   Devereux, George and Moos, Malcolm C. "The
        Social Structure of Prisons and the Organic Ten-
        sions," Journal of Criminal Psychopathology, 4:
        306-24, 1942.

1767)   Devine, Henry. "A Study of Hallucinations in a
        Case of Schizophrenia," Journal of Mental Science,
        67:172-86, 1921.

1768)   Dickey, Brenda A. "Attitudes toward Sex Roles and
        Feelings of Adequacy in Homosexual Males," Jour-
        nal of Consulting Psychology, 25:116-22, 1961.

1769)   Diefenbach, W. C. L. "Gonorrheal Parotitis (ac-
        quired in Homosexual Practices)," Oral Surgery,
        Oral Medicine, and Oral Pathology, 6:974-75, 1953.

1770)   Dinerstein, Russell H. and Glueck, Bernard C. Jr.
        "Sub-coma Insulin Therapy in the Treatment of
        Homosexual Panic States," Journal of Social Thera-
        py, 1:182-86, 1955.

1771)   DiScipio, William J. "Modified Progressive De-
        sensitization and Homosexuality," British Journal
        of Medical Psychology, 41:267-72, 1968.

1772)   Doe, J. C. "Autobiography of a Transsexual,"
        Diseases of the Nervous System, 28:251-55, 1967.

1773)   Doidge, William T. and Holtzman, Wayne H. "Im-
        plications of Homosexuality among Air Force
        Trainees," Journal of Consulting Psychology, 24:9-
        13, 1960.

1774)   Don, A. M. "Transvestism and Transsexualism: A
        Report of Four Cases and Problems Associated with
        their Management," South Africa Medical Journal,
        37:479-85, 1963.

1775)   Dörner, G. "Hormonal Induction and Prevention
         of Female Homosexuality," Journal of Endocrinology,
         42:163-64, 1968.

1776)   Dörner, G. and Hinz, G. "Induction and Prevention
         of Male Homosexuality by Androgen," Journal of
         Endocrinology, 40:387-88, 1968.

1777)   Dörner, G. and others. "Homo- and Hypersexuality
         in Rats with Hypothalamic Lesions," Neuroendo-
         crinology, 4:20-24, 1969.

1778)   Dörner, G. and others. "Homosexuality and Neo-
         natally Castrated Male Rats following Androgen
         Substitution in Adulthood," German Medical Monthly,
         12:281-83, 1967.

1779)   Dörner, G. and others. "Homosexuality in Female
         Rats following Testosterone Implantation in the
         Anterior Hypothalamus," Journal of Reproduction
         and Fertility, 17:173-75, 1968.

1780)   Dougherty, William J. "Epidemiologic Treatment
         of Syphilis Contacts," Journal of the Medical
         Society of New Jersey, 59:564-67, 1962.

1781)   Doyle, T. L. "Homosexuality and Its Treatment,"
         Nursing Outlook, 15:38-40, Aug. 1967.

1782)   Druss, Richard G. "Cases of Suspected Homo-
         sexuality seen at an Army Mental Hygiene Con-
         sultation Service," Psychiatric Quarterly, 4:62-
         70, 1967.

1783)   Due, F. O. and Wright, M. E. "The Use of Content
         Analysis in Rorschach Interpretations: 1. Differ-
         ential Characteristics of Male Homosexuals,"
         Rorschach Research Exchange, 9:169-77, 1945.

1784)   East, W. Norwood. "Homosexuality," Medical
         Press, 218:215-17, 1947.

1785)   East, W. Norwood. "Sexual Offenders," Journal
         of Nervous and Mental Disease, 103:626-66 at 647-
         51, 1946.

1786)   Editorial, Psychiatric Quarterly, 25:156-57, 1951.

1787)   Ehrenwald, Jan. "The Symbiotic Matrix of Para-
         noid Delusions and the Homosexual Alternative,"
         American Journal of Psychoanalysis, 20:49-65,
         1960.

1788)   Eliasberg, W. G. "Group Treatment of Homosexuals
         on Probation," Group Psychotherapy, 7:218-26, 1954.

1789)   Ellis, Albert. "The Effectiveness of Psychotherapy
         with Individuals Who have Severe Homosexual Prob-
         lems," Journal of Consulting Psychology, 20:191-95,
         1956. (Reprinted in Ruitenbeek, no. 96 above, pp.
         175-82.)

1790)   Ellis, Albert. "A Homosexual Treated with Ra-
         tional Psychotherapy," Journal of Clinical Psy-
         chology, 15:338-43, 1959.

1791)   Ellis, Albert. "Homosexuality and Creativity,"
         Journal of Clinical Psychology, 15:376-79, 1959.

1792)   Ellis, Albert. "Homosexuality: the Right to be
         Wrong," Journal of Sex Research, 2:96-107, 1968.

1793)   Ellis, Albert. "The Influence of Heterosexual
         Culture on the Attitude of Homosexuals," Interna-
         tional Journal of Sexology, 5:77-79, 1951. (Re-
         printed in Cory, no. 27 above, pp. 415-19.)

1794)   Ellis, Albert. "Masturbation," Journal of Social
         Therapy, 1:141-43, 1955.

1795)   Ellis, Albert. "On the Cure of Homosexuality,"
         International Journal of Sexology, 5:135-38, 1952.

1796)   Ellis, Albert. "The Sexual Psychology of Human
         Hermaphrodites," Psychosomatic Medicine, 7:108-
         25, 1945.

1797)   Emde Boas, C. V. "The Connection between
         Shakespeare's Sonnets and his 'Travestidouble'
         Plays," International Journal of Sexology, 4:67-72,
         1950.

1798)   "Endocrines and Disordered Sexual Behavior,"
         British Medical Journal, 1:574, 1957.

1799)   English, O. Spurgeon. "A Primer on Homosex-
        uality," GP [General Practice], 7:55-60, Spring
        1953.

1800)   Ernst, John R. "Dementia Praecox Complexes,"
        Medical Journal and Record, 128:381-86, 1928.

1801)   Ernst, John R. "Dementia Praecox Complexes
        (Oedipus and Homosexual)," Medical Annals of the
        District of Columbia, 12:343, 1943.

1802)   Ernst, John R. "Homosexuality and Crime,"
        Journal of Clinical Psychopathology, 8:763-69, 1947.

1803)   Evans, Ray B. "Childhood Parental Relationships
        of Homosexual Men," Journal of Consulting and
        Clinical Psychology, 33:129-35, 1969.

1804)   Fain, M. and Marty, P. "The Synthetic Function
        of Homosexual Cathexis in the Treatment of Adults,"
        International Journal of Psychoanalysis, 41:101-06,
        1960.

1805)   Fairbairn, W. R. D. "A Note on the Origins of
        Male Homosexuality," British Journal of Medical
        Psychology, 37:31-32, 1964.

1806)   Farina, A. and others. "Role of the Stigmatized
        Person in Affecting Sex Relationships," Journal of
        Personality, 36:169-82, 1968.

1807)   Farnell, F. J. "Eroticism as Portrayed in Litera-
        ture," International Journal of Psychoanalysis, 1:
        396-413, 1920. (Reprinted in Ruitenbeek, no. 95
        above, pp. 3-20.)

1808)   "Fatal Emetive Poisoning from Aversion Treat-
        ment," Medicolegal Journal, 32:95, 1964.

1809)   Feigen, Gerald M. "Proctologic Disorders in Sex
        Deviates: A Study of 68 Cases of Sodomy," Cali-
        fornia Medicine, 81:79-83, 1954.

1810)   Fein, Leah G. "Rorschach Signs of Homosexuality
        in Male College Students," Journal of Clinical Psy-
        chology, 6:248-53, 1950.

1811)   Feldman, M. P. "Aversion Therapy for Sexual
        Deviation: a Critical Review," Psychological
        Bulletin, 65:65-79, 1966.

1812)   Feldman, M. P. and MacCulloch, M. J. "The
        Application of Anticipatory Avoidance Learning to
        the Treatment of Homosexuality: 1. Theory, Tech-
        nique, and Preliminary Results," Behaviour Re-
        search and Therapy, 2:165-83, 1965.

1813)   Feldman, M. P. and MacCulloch, M. J. "A Syste-
        matic Approach to the Treatment of Homosexuality
        by Conditioned Aversion: Preliminary Report,"
        American Journal of Psychiatry, 121:167-71, 1964.

1814)   Feldman, M. P. , MacCulloch, M. J. , Mellor, V.,
        and Pinschof, J. M. "The Application of Anticipa-
        tory Avoidance Learning to the Treatment of Homo-
        sexuality: III. The Sexual Orientation Method,"
        Behaviour Research and Therapy, 4:289-99, 1966.

1815)   "Female Homosexuality," British Medical Journal,
        1:330-31, 1969.

1816)   Fenichel, Otto. "Outline of Clinical Psychoanalysis:
        The Sexual Perversions," Psychoanalytic Quarterly,
        2:260-308 at 270-90, 1933.

1817)   Fenichel, Otto. "The Psychology of Transvestism,"
        International Journal of Psychoanalysis, 11:211-27,
        1930.

1818)   Ferenczi, Sandor. "On the Part Played by Homo-
        sexuality in the Pathogenesis of Paranoia," Jahr-
        buch der Psychoanalyse, 3:103-06 (translation by
        Ernest Jones). (Reprinted in Krich, no. 69 above,
        pp. 48-51 and 105-09.)

1819)   Fine, Reuben. "Apparent Homosexuality in the
        Adolescent Girl," Diseases of the Nervous System,
        21:634-37, 1960.

1820)   Fine, Reuben. "The Case of El: The MAPS
        Test," Journal of Projective Techniques, 25:383-
        89, 1961.

1821)   Fine, Reuben. "A Transference Manifestation of

Male Homosexuals," Psychoanalysis and The Psychoanalytic Review, 48:116-20, 1961.

1822) Finger, Frank W. "Sex Beliefs and Practices among Male College Students," Journal of Abnormal and Social Psychology, 42:57-67, 1947.

1823) Fink, Maximilian and others. "Clinical Conference: Homosexuality with Panic and Paranoid States," Journal of the Hillside Hospital, 2:164-90, 1953.

1824) Finney, J. C. "Homosexuality Treated by Combined Psychotherapy," Journal of Social Therapy, 6:27-34, 1960.

1825) Fischoff, Joseph. "Pre-Oedipal Influences in a Boy's Determination to be 'Feminine' during the Oedipal Period," Journal of the American Academy of Child Psychiatry, 3:273-86, 1964.

1826) Fitzgerald, Thomas K. "A Theoretical Typology of Homosexuality in the United States," Corrective Psychiatry and Journal of Social Therapy, 9:28-35, 1963.

1827) Fiumara, N. J., Wise, H. M. Jr., and Many, M. "Gonorrheal Pharyngitis," New England Journal of Medicine, 276:1248-50, 1967.

1828) Fluker, J. L. "Recent Trends in Homosexuality in West London," British Journal of Venereal Diseases, 42:48-49, 1966.

1829) Fodor, Nandor. "Homosexuality in an Identical Twin," Psychoanalysis and the Psychoanalytic Review, 45:105-24, 1958.

1830) Fookes, B. H. "Some Experiences in the Use of Aversion Therapy in Male Homosexuality, Exhibitionism, and Fetish Transvestism," British Journal of Psychiatry, 115:339-41, 1969.

1831) Ford, C. A. "Homosexual Practices of Institutionalized Females," Journal of Abnormal and Social Psychiatry, 23:442-48, 1929.

1832) Forer, B. R. "The Case of El: Vocational Choice,"

Journal of Projective Techniques, 25:371-74, 1961.

1833)   Fox, Beatrice and DiScipio, William J. "An Ex-
        ploratory Study in the Treatment of Homosexuality
        by Combining Principles from Psychoanalytic Theory
        and Conditioning: Theoretical and Methodological
        Considerations," British Journal of Medical Psy-
        chology, 41:273-82, 1968.

1834)   Foxe, Arthur N. "Psychoanalysis of a Sodomist,"
        American Journal of Orthopsychiatry, 11:132-42,
        1941.

1835)   Frank, George H. "A Test of the Use of a Figure
        Drawing Test as an Indicator of Sexual Inversion,"
        Psychological Reports, 1:137-38, 1955.

1836)   Freed, L. F. "Homosexuality and the Bill," South
        African Medical Journal, 42:457-58 and 567, 1968.

1837)   Freed, L. F. "Medico-sociological Data in the
        Therapy of Homosexuality," South African Medical
        Journal, 28:1022-23, 1954.

1838)   Freed, S. C. "Estrogens and Androgens," American
        Journal of Medical Sciences, 205:735-47, 1943.

1839)   Freedman, Lawrence Z. "Sexual, Aggressive, and
        Acquisitive Deviates; A Preliminary Note," Journal
        of Nervous and Mental Disease, 132:47, 1961.

1840)   Freeman, Hal E. "Cleveland City Hospital Obser-
        vation on Sources of Infection in Syphilis," Ohio
        State Medical Journal, 36:616-19, 1940.

1841)   Freeman, Thomas. "Clinical and Theoretical Ob-
        servations on Male Homosexuality," International
        Journal of Psychoanalysis, 36:335-47, 1955.

1842)   Frei, W. "Combatting Lymphogranuloma Venereum
        --Role of Latent Forms and Pederasty in Spread,"
        Archives of Dermatology and Syphilology, 47:830-
        42, 1943.

1843)   Freud, Anna. "Clinical Observations on the Treat-
        ment of Manifest Male Homosexuality," Psycho-
        analytic Quarterly, 20:337-38, 1951.

1844) Freud, Anna. "Problems of Technique in Adult Analysis," Bulletin of the Philadelphia Association of Psychoanalysis, 4:44-70, 1954.

1845) Freud, Anna. "Some Clinical Remarks concerning the Treatment of Cases of Male Homosexuality," International Journal of Psychoanalysis, 30:195, 1949. (Reprinted in Bulletin of the American Psychoanalytic Association, 7:117-18, 1951.)

1846) Freud, Sigmund. "Letter to an American Mother," American Journal of Psychiatry, 107:786-87, 1951. (Reprinted in International Journal of Psychoanalysis, 32:331, 1951 and in Ruitenbeek, no. 96 above, pp. 1-2.)

1847) Freund, Kurt. "Diagnosing Homo- or Heterosexuality and Erotic Age Preference by Means of a Psychophysiological Test," Behaviour Research and Therapy, 5:209-28, 1967.

1848) Freund, Kurt. "Erotic Preference in Pedophilia," Behaviour Research and Therapy, 5:339-48, 1967.

1849) Freund, Kurt. "Laboratory Differential Diagnosis of Homo- and Heterosexuality--An Experiment with Faking," Review of Czechoslovak Medicine, 7:20-31, 1961.

1850) Freund, Kurt. "A Laboratory Method for Diagnosing Predominance of Homo- or Hetero-erotic Interest in the Male," Behaviour Research and Therapy, 1:85-93, 1963.

1851) Freund, Kurt. "On the Problem of Male Homosexuality," Review of Czechoslovak Medicine, 11: 11-17, 1965.

1852) Freund, Kurt; Diamant, J.; and Pinkava, V. "On the Validity and Reliability of the Phalloplethysmographic (Php) Diagnosis of Some Sexual Deviations," Review of Czechoslovak Medicine, 4:145-51, 1958.

1853) Freund, Kurt and Pinkava, V. "Homosexuality in Man and Its Association with Parental Relationships," Review of Czechoslovak Medicine, 7:32-40, 1961.

1854)   Frey, Egon C. "Dreams of Male Homosexuals and
         the Attitude of Society," Journal of Individual Psy-
         chology, 18:26-34, 1962.

1855)   Freyhan, F. A. "Homosexual Prostitution: A Case
         Report," Delaware State Medical Journal, 19:92-
         94, 1947.

1856)   Friberg, R. R. "Measures of Homosexuality: Cross-
         Validation of Two MMPI Scales and Implications for
         Usage," Journal of Consulting Psychology, 31:88-91,
         1967.

1857)   Friedman, Joel and Gassel, Sylvia. "Orestes: A
         Psychoanalytic Approach to Dramatic Criticism,"
         Psychoanalytic Quarterly, 20:423-33, 1951.

1858)   Fromm, Erika O. and Elonen, Anna S. "The Use
         of Projective Techniques in the Study of a Case of
         Female Homosexuality," Journal of Projective
         Techniques, 15:185-230, 1951.

1859)   Frosch, Jack and Bromberg, Walter. "The Sex
         Offender: A Psychiatric Study," American Journal
         of Orthopsychiatry, 9:761-77, 1939.

1860)   Gadpaille, Warren J. "Homosexual Experience in
         Adolescence," Medical Aspects of Human Sexuality,
         Oct. 1968.

1861)   Gardner, G. E. "Evidences of Homosexuality in 120
         Unanalyzed Cases with Paranoid Content," Psycho-
         analysis and the Psychoanalytic Review, 18:57-62,
         1931.

1861a)   Gardner, James M. "Indicators of Homosexuality
         in the Human Figure Drawings of Heroin and Pill-
         using Addicts," Perceptual and Motor Skills, 28:
         705-06, 1969.

1862)   Garma, A. "The Psychosomatic Shift through
         Obesity, Migraine, Peptic Ulcer, and Myocardial
         Infarction in a Homosexual," International Journal
         of Psychoanalysis, 49:241-45, 1968.

1863)   Gaylin, Willard M. "The Homosexual Act as a
         Symptom," Psychiatry Digest, 25:25-30, Dec. 1964.

1864) Geil, G. A. "The Goodenough Test as Applied to
       Adult Delinquents," Journal of Clinical Psycho-
       pathology, 9:62-82, 1948.

1865) Geil, G. A. "The Use of the Goodenough Test for
       Revealing Male Homosexuality," Journal of Clinical
       Psychopathology and Psychotherapy, 6:307-21, 1944.

1866) "Genesis of Homosexuality," Canadian Medical
       Association Journal, 93:1041, 1965.

1867) "Genetic Sex of Homosexuals," British Medical
       Journal, 1:969-70, 1963.

1868) Gentele, H., Lagerholm, B., and Lodin, A. "The
       Chromosomal Sex of Male Homosexuals," Acta
       Dermato-Venerologica, 40:470-73, 1960.

1869) Gershman, Harry. "Considerations of Some As-
       pects of Homosexuality," American Journal of Psy-
       choanalysis, 13:82-83, 1953.

1870) Gershman, Harry. "Homosexuality and Some As-
       pects of Creativity," American Journal of Psycho-
       analysis, 24:29-38, 1964, with commentary by
       Irving Bieber.

1871) Gershman, Harry. "Psychopathology of Compulsive
       Homosexuality," American Journal of Psychoanaly-
       sis, 17:58-77, 1957, with commentary by Silvano
       Arieti and Frederick A. Weiss.

1872) Gershman, Harry. "Reflections on the Nature of
       Homosexuality," American Journal of Psychoanaly-
       sis, 26:46-62, 1966.

1873) Giannell, A. S. "Giannell's Criminosynthesis
       Theory Applied to Female Homosexuality," Journal
       of Psychology, 64:213-22, 1966.

1874) Gibbens, T. C. N. "The Sexual Behaviour of Young
       Criminals," Journal of Mental Science, 103:527-40
       at 528, 535-37, 1957.

1875) Gibbins, R. J. and Walters, R. H. "Three Pre-
       liminary Studies of a Psychoanalytic Theory of
       Alcohol Addiction," Quarterly Journal of Studies on

Alcohol, 21:618-41, 1960.

1876)   Giese, Hans. "Differences in the Homosexual Re-
         lations of Man and Woman," International Journal
         of Sexology, 7:225-27, 1954.

1877)   Gilbert, S. F. "Homosexuality and Hypnotherapy,"
         British Journal of Medical Hypnosis, 5:2-7, 1954.

1878)   Gillespie, W. H. "Notes on the Analysis of Sexual
         Perversion," International Journal of Psychoanalysis,
         33:397-402, 1952.

1879)   Gillespie, W. H., Pasche, F., Wiedman, G. H.,
         and Greenson, R. R. "Symposium on Homosexuality:
         I-IV," International Journal of Psychoanalysis, 45:
         203-19, 1964.

1880)   Ginsburg, Kenneth N. "The 'Meat Rack': A Study
         of Male Homosexual Prostitution," American Jour-
         nal of Psychotherapy, 21:170-85, 1967.

1881)   Gioscia, Nicolai. "The Gag Reflex and Fellatio,"
         American Journal of Psychiatry, 107:380, 1950.

1882)   Glass, S. J., Deuel, H. J., and Wright, C. A. "Sex
         Hormone Studies in Male Homosexuality," Endoc-
         rinology, 26:590-94, 1940.

1883)   Glass, S. J. and Johnson, R. W. "Limitations and
         Complications of Organotherapy in Male Homo-
         sexuality," Journal of Clinical Endocrinology, 4:540-
         44, 1944.

1884)   Glass, S. J. and McKennon, B. J. "The Hormonal
         Aspects of Sex Reversal States," Western Journal
         of Surgery, Obstetrics, and Gynecology, 45:467-
         73, 1937.

1885)   Glauber, I. P. "The Rebirth Motif in Homosexuality
         and Its Teleological Significance," International
         Journal of Psychoanalysis, 37:416-21, 1956.

1886)   Glick, Burton S. "Homosexual Panic: Clinical
         and Theoretical Considerations," Journal of Nervous
         and Mental Disease, 129:20-28, 1959. (Abstracted
         in Journal of Clinical and Experimental Psycho-

pathology and Quarterly Review of Psychiatry and Neurology, 21:60, 1960.)

1887)   Glover, Benjamin H. "Observations on Homo-sexuality among University Students," Journal of Nervous and Mental Disease, 113:377-87, 1951. (Reprinted in Krich, no. 69 above, pp. 141-53.)

1888)   Glover, Edward G. "The Aetiology of Alcoholism," Proceedings of the Royal Society of Medicine, 21: 1351-56, 1928.

1889)   Glover, Edward G. "The Social and Legal Aspects of Sexual Abnormality," Medico-Legal and Crimino-logical Review, 13:133-48, 1945.

1890)   Gluckman, L. K. "Lesbianism--A Clinical Ap-proach," New Zealand Medical Journal, 65:443-49, 1966.

1891)   Gluckman, L. K. "Lesbianism in the Maori: A Series of Three Interconnected Clinical Studies," Australian and New Zealand Journal of Psychiatry, 1:98-103, 1967.

1892)   Glueck, Bernard C. Jr. "Psychodynamic Patterns in the Homosexual Sex Offender," American Jour-nal of Psychiatry, 112:584-90, 1956.

1893)   Goitein, P. L. "A Diary of Fellatio; Terroriza-tion and Its Unconscious Counterpart," Journal of Criminal Psychopathology, 5:95-113, 1943.

1894)   Gold, S. and Neufeld, I. L. "A Learning Approach to the Treatment of Homosexuality," Behaviour Re-search and Therapy, 2:201-04, 1965.

1895)   Goldberg, J. and Bernstein, R. "Studies on Granu-loma Inguinale: Two Cases of Perianal Granuloma Inguinale in Male Homosexuals," British Journal of Venereal Diseases, 40:137-39, 1964.

1896)   Goldberg, P. A. and Milstein, J. T. "Perceptual Investigation of Psychoanalytic Theory Concerning Latent Homosexuality in Women," Perceptual and Motor Skills, 21:645-46, 1965.

1897)   Goldfried, Marvin R.   "On the Diagnosis of Homo-
         sexuality from the Rorschach," Journal of Con-
         sulting Psychology, 30:338-49, 1966.

1898)   Goldschmidt, R.   "Analysis of Intersexuality in
         the Gypsy-moth," Quarterly Review of Biology, 6:
         125-42, 1931.

1899)   Goodman, Herman.   "An Epidemic of Genital
         Chancres from Perversion," American Journal of
         Syphilis, Gonorrhea, and Venereal Disease, 28:
         310-14, 1944.

1900)   Goodman, Herman.   "The Esoteric Male as a Focus
         for Spread of Venereal Disease," Acta Dermatologica-
         Venereologica, 37:483-86, 1957.

1901)   Goodman, Herman.   "The Male Homosexual and
         Venereal Diseases," Acta Dermatologica-Venereo-
         logica, 38:274-82, 1958.

1902)   Goodman, Herman.   "The Male Homosexual and
         Venereal Disease," Acta Dermatologica-Venereo-
         logica, 42:256-64, 1962.

1903)   Goodman, Herman.   "Public Health Aspects of an
         Epidemic of Genital Chancres from Perversion,"
         Urologic and Cutaneous Review, 48:267-70, 1944.

1904)   Gordon, Alfred.   "The History of a Homosexual:
         His Difficulties and Triumphs," Medical Journal
         and Record, 131:152-56, 1930.

1905)   Gough, Harrison G.   "Diagnostic Patterns on the
         Minnesota Multiphasic Personality Inventory,"
         Journal of Clinical Psychology, 2:23-37, 1946.

1906)   Grace, A. W. and Henry, G. W.   "The Mode of
         Acquisition of Lymphogranuloma Venereum of the
         Anorectal Type," New York State Journal of Medi-
         cine, 40:285-89, 1940.

1907)   Grams, Armin and Rinder, Lawrence.   "Signs of
         Homosexuality in Human-Figure Drawings," Journal
         of Consulting Psychology, 22:394, 1958.

1908)   Granick, Samuel and Smith, Leon J.   "Sex Sequence

in the Draw-a-Person Test and Its Relation to the MMPI Masculinity-Femininity Scale," Journal of Consulting Psychology, 17:71-73, 1953.

1909) Grauer, David. "Homosexuality and the Paranoid Psychoses as Related to the Concept of Narcissism," Psychoanalytic Quarterly, 24:516-26, 1955.

1910) Grauer, David. "Homosexuality in Paranoid Schizophrenics as Revealed by the Rorschach Test," Journal of Consulting Psychology, 18:459-62, 1954.

1911) Greco, Marshall C. "Social-Psychological Differentials in the Intiation and Retention of Chronic Homosexuality," American Psychologist, 1:240, 1946.

1912) Greco, Marshall C. and Wright, James C. "The Correctional Institution in the Etiology of Chronic Homosexuality," American Journal of Orthopsychiatry, 14:295-308, 1944.

1913) Green, Eugene W. and Johnson, L. G. "Homosexuality," Journal of Criminal Psychopathology, 5: 467-80, 1944.

1914) Green, M. and Moore, S. "The Homosexual in the VD Clinic," British Journal of Venereal Diseases, 40:135-36, 1964.

1915) Green, Richard and Money, John. "Stage-acting, Role-taking, and Effeminate Impersonation during Boyhood," Archives of General Psychiatry, 15: 535-38, 1966.

1916) Greene, R. A. and Breazeale, E. L. "Gonorrhea acquired via Rectal Intercourse: A Case Report," Arizona Medicine, 7:48-49, Nov. 1950.

1917) Greenson, Ralph R. "On Homosexuality and Gender Identity," International Journal of Psychoanalysis, 45:217-19, 1964.

1918) Greenspan, Herbert and Campbell, John D. "The Homosexual as a Personality Type," American Journal of Psychiatry, 101:682-89, 1945.

1919) Greenstein, Jules M. "Father Characteristics and

Sex Typing," Journal of Personality and Social
Psychology, 3:271-74, 1966.

1920)   Gross, Alfred A.   "An Ethical Approach to the
Problem of Sexual Deviation," Psychological Service
Center Journal, 9:59-70, 1959.

1921)   Gross, Alfred A.   "An Introduction to the Study of
Homosexuality," Psychological Service Center
Journal, 12:1-87, 1961.

1922)   Gross, Alfred A.   "The Persistent Problem of
the Homosexual--A Social Approach," Psychological
Service Center Journal, 9:25-36, 1959.

1923)   Grygier, T. G.   "Psychometric Aspects of Homosexuality," Journal of Mental Science, 103:514-26,
1957.   (Abstracted in American Journal of Psychotherapy, 12:182-83, 1958.)

1924)   Gundlach, Ralph H.   "Childhood Parental Relation-
ships and the Establishment of Gender Role of
Homosexuals," Journal of Consulting and Clinical
Psychology, 33:136-39, 1969.

1925)   Gundlach, Ralph S. and Riess, Bernard F.   "Birth
Order and Sex of Siblings in a Sample of Lesbians
and Non-Lesbians," Psychological Reports, 20:61-
62, 1967.

1926)   Gutheil, Emil A.   "The Exhibitionism of Jean
Jacques Rousseau: An Abstract of Stekel's Analysis,"
American Journal of Psychotherapy, 16:266-77, 1962.

1927)   Gutheil, Emil A.   "The Psychologic Background of
Transsexualism and Transvestism," American
Journal of Psychotherapy, 8:231-39, 1954.

1928)   Guttmacher, Manfred S.   "The Homosexual in
Court," American Journal of Psychiatry, 112:591-
98, 1956.

1928a) Guze, Samuel B., Goodwin, Donald W., and Crane,
J. Bruce.   "Criminality and Psychiatric Disorders,"
Archives of General Psychiatry, 20:583-91, 1969.

1929)   Hacker, Helen M.   "The Ishmael Complex," American Journal of Psychotherapy, 6:494-513, 1952.

1930)   Hadden, Samuel B.   "Attitudes toward and Ap-
        proaches to the Problem of Homosexuality,"
        Pennsylvania Medical Journal, 60:1195-98, 1957.

1931)   Hadden, Samuel B.   "Group Psychotherapy for
        Sexual Maladjustments," American Journal of
        Psychiatry, 125:83-88, 1968.

1932)   Hadden, Samuel B.   "Group Psychotherapy of
        Male Homosexuals," Current Psychiatric Therapy,
        6:177-86, 1966.

1933)   Hadden, Samuel B.   "Male Homosexuality,"
        Pennsylvania Medical Journal, 70:78-80, Feb. 1967.

1934)   Hadden, Samuel B.   "Newer Treatment Techniques
        for Homosexuality," Archives of Environmental
        Health, 13:284-88, 1966.

1935)   Hadden, Samuel B.   "Treatment of Homosexuality
        by Individual and Group Therapy," American Jour-
        nal of Psychiatry, 114:810-14, 1958.

1936)   Hadden, Samuel B.   "Treatment of Male Homo-
        sexuals in Groups," International Journal of Group
        Psychotherapy, 16:13-22, 1966. (Abstracted in
        Psychiatry Digest, 27:15, June 1967.)

1937)   Hader, M.   "Homosexuality as Part of Our Aging
        Process," Psychiatric Quarterly, 40:515-24, 1966.

1938)   Hadfield, J. A.   "The Cure of Homosexuality,"
        British Medical Journal, 1:1323-26, 1958. (Ab-
        stracted in Medico-Legal Journal, 26:113, 1958.)

1939)   Hadfield, J. A.   "Origins of Homosexuality,"
        British Medical Journal, 1:678, 1966.

1940)   Hagopian, John V.   "A Psychological Approach to
        Shelley's Poetry," American Imago, 12:25-45, 1955.
        (Reprinted in Ruitenbeek, no. 95 above, pp. 293-
        310.)

1941)   Haines, William H.   "Homosexuality," Journal of
        Social Therapy, 1:132-36, 1955.

1942)   Haines, W. H., Hoffman, H. R., and Esser, R. A.

"Commitments under the Criminal Sexual Psychopath Law in the Criminal Court of Cook County,
Illinois," American Journal of Psychiatry, 105:420-
25, 1948.

1943)   Haines, W. H. and McLaughlin, J. J.   "Treatment
of the Homosexual in Prison," Diseases of the
Nervous System, 13:85-87, 1952.

1944)   Halleck, Seymour and Hersko, Marvin.   "Homosexual Behavior in a Correctional Institution for
Adolescent Girls," American Journal of Orthopsychiatry, 32:911-17, 1962.

1945)   Hamburger, C., Stürup, G. K., and Dahl-Iversen,
E.   "Transvestism: Hormonal, Psychiatric, and
Surgical Treatment," Journal of the American
Medical Association, 152:391-96, 1953.   (Reprinted
in Krich, no. 69 above, pp. 293-308.)

1946)   Hamilton, Donald M.   "Some Aspects of Homosexuality in Relation to Total Personality Development,"
Psychiatric Quarterly, 13:229-44, 1939.   (Abstracted
in Journal of Criminal Psychopathology, 2:554-55,
1941.)

1947)   Hamilton, Gilbert V.   "A Study of Sexual Tendencies
in Monkeys and Baboons," Journal of Animal Behavior, 4:295-318, 1914.

1948)   Hammer, Emanuel F.   "Relationship between
Diagnosis of Psychosexual Pathology and the Sex
of the First Drawn Person," Journal of Clinical
Psychology, 10:168-70, 1954.

1949)   Hammer, Emmanuel F.   "Symptoms of Sexual
Deviation: Dynamics and Etiology," Psychoanalytic
Review, 55:5-27, 1968.

1950)   Hammer, Max.   "Homosexuality in a Women's Reformatory," Corrective Psychiatry and Journal of
Social Therapy, 11:168-69, 1965.

1951)   Hammer, Max.   "Homosexuality and the Reversed
Oedipus Complex," Corrective Psychiatry and Journal of Social Therapy, 14:45-47, 1968.

1952)   Harms, Ernest. "Homo-Anonymous," Diseases of
         the Nervous System, 14:318-19, 1953.

1953)   Harrison, S. I. and Klopman, H. J. "Relationships
         between Social Forces and Homosexual Behavior
         Observed in a Children's Psychiatric Hospital,"
         Journal of the American Academy of Child Psychia-
         try, 5:105-10, 1966.

1954)   Hartman, A. A. and Nicolay, R. C. "Sexually De-
         viant Behavior in Expectant Fathers," Journal of
         Abnormal Psychology, 71:232-34, 1966.

1955)   Hartman, Bernard J. "Comparison of Selected
         Experimental MMPI Profiles of Sexual Deviates
         and Sociopaths without Sexual Deviation," Psycho-
         logical Reports, 20:234, 1967.

1956)   Hartogs, Renatus. "Discipline in Early Life of
         Sex Delinquents and Sex Criminals," The Nervous
         Child, 9:167-72, 1951.

1957)   Harvey, John F. "Counselling the Apparent Ado-
         lescent Homosexual," Bulletin of the Guild of Catho-
         lic Psychiatrists, 10:204-14, 1963.

1958)   Harvey, John F. "Counselling the Invert in Re-
         ligious Life," Bulletin of the Guild of Catholic Psy-
         chiatrists, 9:210-21, 1962.

1959)   Haselkorn, Harry. "The Vocational Interests of a
         Group of Male Homosexuals," Journal of Counselling
         Psychology, 3:8-11, 1956. (See no. 246 above.)

1960)   Hastings, Donald W. "A Paranoid Reaction with
         Manifest Homosexuality," Archives of Neurology and
         Psychiatry, 45:379-81, 1941.

1961)   Haupt, T. D. and Allen, R. M. "A Multi-variate
         Analysis of Variance of Scale Scores on the Sex
         Inventory, Male Form," Journal of Clinical Psy-
         chology, Supplement, 21:23-31, 1966.

1962)   Hayward, Sumner C. "Modification of Sexual Be-
         havior of the Male Albino Rat," Journal of Com-
         parative and Physiological Psychology, 50:70-73,
         1957.

1963)   Hecht, H. "Venereal Diseases in Homosexuals,"
         Acta Dermatologica-Venereologica, 37:182-90, 1957.

1964)   Heersema, Philip H. "Homosexuality and the
         Physician," Journal of the American Medical Asso-
         ciation, 193:815-17, 1965.

1965)   Heibrunn, G. "Psychoanalysis of Yesterday, Today,
         and Tomorrow," Archives of General Psychiatry,
         4:321-30, 1961.

1966)   Heller, Arthur D. "The Problem of Homosexuality,"
         Medical Press, 239:36-38, 1958.

1967)   Hemphill, R. E. , Leitch, A. , and Stuart, J. R.   "A
         Factual Study of Male Homosexuality," British
         Medical Journal, 1:1317-23, 1958.

1968)   Hennessey, M. A. R. "Homosexual Charges against
         Children," Journal of Criminal Psychopathology, 2:
         524-32, 1941.

1969)   Henry, George W. "Constitutional Factors in
         Psychosexual Development: Comparative Study of
         Heterosexual, Homosexual and Narcissistic Types
         of Adjustment," Proceedings of the Association for
         Research in Nervous and Mental Disease, 14:287-
         300, 1933.

1970)   Henry, George W. "A Decade of Helpfulness: the
         Tenth Annual Report of the George W. Henry Foun-
         dation, Inc. , for the Year ending April 1, 1958,"
         Psychological Service Center Journal, 9:73-87, 1959.

1971)   Henry, George W. "The Eighth Annual Report of
         the George W. Henry Foundation," Psychological
         Service Center Journal, 9:37-49, 1959.

1972)   Henry, George W. "The Eleventh Annual Report
         of the George W. Henry Foundation," Psychological
         Service Center Journal, 9:89-100, 1959.

1973)   Henry, George W. "The Ninth Annual Report of
         the George W. Henry Foundation," Psychological
         Service Center Journal, 9:50-57, 1959.

1974)   Henry, George W. "Psychogenic and Constitutional

Factors in Homosexuality," Psychiatric Quarterly, 8:243-63, 1934. (Reprinted in Krich, no. 69 above, pp. 153-74.)

1975)   Henry, George W.   "Psychogenic Factors in Overt Homosexuality," American Journal of Psychiatry, 93:889-908, 1937.

1976)   Henry, George W.   "The Seventh Annual Report of the George W. Henry Foundation," Psychological Service Center Journal, 9:1-24, 1959.

1977)   Henry, George W. and Galbraith, Hugh M.   "Constitutional Factors in Homosexuality," American Journal of Psychiatry, 90:1249-70, 1934, with comment by Ben Karpman and Philip Trentzsch.

1978)   Hermans, E. H. and DeCock, P.   "Homosexuality and Venereal Disease," Dermatologica, 127:278-88, 1963.

1979)   Hermans, E. H. and others.   "Homosexuality and Venereal Diseases," Acta Leidensia, 33:107-16, 1964-65.

1980)   Hess, E. H., Seltzer, A. L., and Shlien, J. M. "Pupil Response of Hetero- and Homosexual Males to Pictures of Men and Women: A Pilot Study," Journal of Abnormal Psychology, 70:165-68, 1965.

1981)   Heston, L. L. and Shields, J.   "Homosexuality in Twins: A Family Study and a Registry Study," Archives of General Psychiatry, 18:149-60, 1968.

1982)   Hewitt, Charles C.   "On the Meaning of Effeminacy in Homosexual Men," American Journal of Psychotherapy, 15:592-602, 1961.

1983)   Higley, H. E.   "100 Males Arrested for Homosexuality," Journal of the American Osteopathic Association, 54:194-97, 1954.

1984)   Hinrichsen, Josephine.   "The Importance of a Knowledge of Sexual Habits in the Diagnosis and Control of Venereal Disease, with Special Reference to Homosexuals," Urologic and Cutaneous Review, 48:469-86, 1944.

1985)   Hirsh, H. "The Homosexual and the Family
         Doctor, " GP [General Practice], 26:103-07, Nov.
         1962.

1986)   Hobbs, A. M. and Lambert, R. D. "An Evaluation
         of Sexual Behavior in the Human Male, " American
         Journal of Psychiatry, 104:758-64, 1958.

1987)   Hoffman, Martin. "Homosexual, " Psychology
         Today, 3:43-45, 70-71, July 1969.

1988)   Holden, H. M. "Psychotherapy of a Shared Syn-
         drome in Identical Twins, " British Journal of
         Psychiatry, 111:859-64, 1965.

1989)   Holemon, R. Eugene and Winokur, George. "Ef-
         feminate Homosexuality: A Disease of Childhood, "
         American Journal of Orthopsychiatry, 35:48-56, 1965.

1990)   Holtzman, W. H. "The Examiner as a Variable in
         the Draw-A-Person Test, " Journal of Consulting
         Psychology, 16:145-48, 1952.

1991)   Holz, W. C. , Harding, G. F. , and Glassman, S. M.
         "A Note on the Clinical Validity of the Marsh-
         Hilliard-Liechti MMPI Sexual Deviation Scale, "
         Journal of Consulting Psychology, 21:326, 1957.

1992)   "Homosexual Body-Build, " GP [General Practice],
         21:131, June 1960.

1993)   "Homosexual Fantasies in Heterosexuals, " Journal
         of the American Medical Association, 183:7:42-43,
         1963.

1994)   "Homosexual Offences, " British Medical Journal,
         2:393, 1963.

1995)   "Homosexual Offences and Prostitution, " Lancet,
         273:527-29, 1957.

1996)   "Homosexual Practice and Venereal Disease, "
         British Medical Journal, 1:5-6, 1967.

1997)   "Homosexual Practice and Venereal Disease, "
         Lancet, 1:481-82, 1964.

1998)   "Homosexual Scandals: Some Misconceptions,"
         Corrective Psychiatry and Journal of Social Therapy,
         11:1-2, 1965.

1999)   "Homosexuality," Bulletin of the New York Academy
         of Medicine, 40:576-80, 1964.

2000)   "Homosexuality," GP [General Practice], 16:132,
         Oct. 1957.

2001)   "Homosexuality," Lancet, 269:1288, 1955.

2002)   "Homosexuality," Practitioner, 172:346-47, 1954.

2003)   "Homosexuality," Practitioner, 179:349, 1957.

2004)   "Homosexuality and Left-Handedness," British
         Medical Journal, 1:91, 1966.

2005)   "Homosexuality and Moral Welfare," Lancet, 266:
         505-06, 1954.

2006)   "Homosexuality and Prostitution," British Medical
         Journal, 2:1492-93, 1955.

2007)   "Homosexuality and Prostitution," British Medical
         Journal, 1:988, 1956.

2008)   "Homosexuality and Prostitution: B. M. A. Memo-
         randum of Evidence for the Departmental Com-
         mittee," British Medical Journal Supplement, 2:
         165-70, 1955.   (See no. 143 above.)

2009)   "Homosexuality and the Law," Lancet, no. 7111:
         1071, 1959.   (Reprinted in no. 141 above.)

2010)   "Homosexuality as a Crime," Lancet, no. 7396:
         1151-52, 1965.

2011)   "Homosexuality as a Detrimental Factor," Lancet,
         228:1536, 1935.

2012)   "Homosexuality as a Ground for Divorce," Medico-
         Legal and Criminological Review, 5:405-06, 1937.

2013)   "Homosexuality in Society," British Medical Jour-
         nal, 1:631-32, 1957.

2014)   "Homosexuals," Science News, 96:373, Oct. 25,
         1969.

2015)   "Homosexuals Need Help," Science News Letter,
         87:102, Feb. 13, 1965.

2016)   "Homosexuals Played with Dolls, not Baseballs,"
         Science News Letter, 69:313, May 19, 1956. (See
         also Science Digest, 40:37, Sep. 1956.)

2017)   Hooker, Evelyn. "The Adjustment of the Male
         Overt Homosexual," Journal of Projective Tech-
         niques, 21:18-31, 1957. (Reprinted in Mattachine
         Review, Dec. 1957, pp. 33-39 and Jan. 1958, pp.
         4-11 and in Ruitenbeek, no. 96 above, pp. 141-
         61.)

2018)   Hooker, Evelyn. "The Case of El: A Biography,"
         Journal of Projective Techniques, 25:252-67, 1961.

2019)   Hooker, Evelyn. "Male Homosexuality in the
         Rorschach," Journal of Projective Techniques, 22:
         33-54, 1958. (Reprinted in Murray H. Sherman
         [ed.], A Rorschach Reader [New York: Interna-
         tional Universities Press, 1960], pp. 14-44.)

2020)   Hooker, Evelyn. "Parental Relations and Male
         Homosexuality in Patient and Non-Patient Samples,"
         Journal of Consulting and Clinical Psychology, 33:
         140-42, 1969.

2021)   Hooker, Evelyn. "A Preliminary Analysis of
         Group Behavior of Homosexuals," Journal of
         Psychology, 42:217-25, 1956.

2022)   Hooker, Evelyn. "What is a Criterion?" Journal
         of Projective Techniques, 23:278-81, 1958.

2023)   "Hormone Treatment for Lesbianism," British
         Medical Journal, 1:175, 1963.

2024)   Hornstra, L. "Homosexuality," International Jour-
         nal of Psychoanalysis, 48:394-402, 1967.

2025)   Horowitz, M. J. "The Homosexual's Image of Him-
         self," Mental Hygiene, 48:197-201, 1964.

2026)   Hoskins, R. G. and Pincus, Gregory. "Sex-Hor-
         mone Relationships in Schizophrenic Men," Psycho-
         somatic Medicine, 11:102-12, 1949.

2027)   Housden, J. "An Examination of the Biological
         Etiology of Transvestism," International Journal of
         Social Psychiatry, 11:301-05, 1965.

2028)   Houston, L. N. "Vocational Interest Patterns of
         Institutionalized Youthful Offenders as Measured by
         a Nonverbal Inventory," Journal of Clinical Psy-
         chology, 21:213-14, 1965. (See no. 247 above.)

2029)   Hubble, D. "Medicine and Society," Lancet, 1:
         995-1000, 1964.

2030)   Huffman, Arthur V. "Problems Precipitated by
         Homosexual Approaches on Youthful First Offenders,"
         Journal of Social Therapy, 7:216-22, 1961.

2031)   Huffman, Arthur V. "Sex Deviation in a Prison
         Community," Journal of Social Therapy, 6:170-81,
         1960.

2032)   Hughes, C. H. "An Emasculated Homosexual,"
         Alienist and Neurologist, 35:278, 1914.

2033)   Hulbeck, Charles R. "Emotional Conflicts in
         Homosexuality," American Journal of Psychoanalysis,
         8:72-73, 1948.

2034)   Hunter, T. A. A. "Sex and Its Problems. III.
         Sexual Problems of Adolescence," Practitioner,
         198:453-58, 1967.

2035)   Hutchinson, G. E. "A Speculative Consideration of
         Certain Possible Forms of Selection in Man,"
         American Naturalist, 93:81-91, 1959.

2036)   "Incidence of Homosexuality," Lancet, 257:919,
         1949.

2037)   Ive, F. A. "Bikini Drawers: A Vestimentary Aid
         to the Diagnosis of Secondary Syphilis," Trans-
         actions of St. John's Hospital Dermatological Society,
         50:162-63, 1964.

2038)   Jackson, C. Colin. "Gonorrheal Proctitis,"
          Rocky Mountain Medical Journal, 60:36-37, 1963.

2039)   Jackson, C. Colin. "Homosexual Transmission
          of Infectious Syphilis," California Medicine, 99:95-
          97, 1963.

2040)   Jackson, C. Colin. "Syphilis: the Role of the
          Homosexual," Medical Service Journal, Canada,
          19:631-38, 1963.

2041)   Jackson, C. Colin. "The Venereal Esoteric,"
          Canadian Medical Association Journal, 87:716-17,
          1962.

2042)   Jacobi, Jolande. "A Case of Homosexuality,"
          Journal of Analytic Psychology, 14:48-64, 1969.

2043)   James, Anatole. "Homosexuality and the 'Artistic'
          Professions," International Journal of Sexology,
          8:24-25, 1954.

2044)   James, Basil. "Behaviour Therapy Applied to
          Homosexuality," New Zealand Medical Journal,
          66:752-54, 1967.

2045)   James, Basil. "Case of Homosexuality Treated
          by Aversion Therapy," British Medical Journal,
          1:768-70, 1962.

2046)   James, Basil. "Learning Theory and Homosex-
          uality," New Zealand Medical Journal, 66:748-51,
          1967.

2047)   James, Basil and Early, Donal F. "Aversion
          Therapy for Homosexuality," British Medical Jour-
          nal, 1:538, 1963.

2048)   James, Robert E. "Precipitating Factors in Acute
          Homosexual Panic (Kempf's Disease), with a Case
          Presentation," Quarterly Review of Psychiatry and
          Neurology, 2:530-33, 1947.

2049)   Jefferiss, F. J. G. "Homosexually-acquired Venereal
          Disease," British Journal of Venereal Diseases, 42:
          46-47, 1966.

2050) Jefferiss, F. J. G. "The Return of the Venereal Diseases," British Medical Journal, 1:1751-53, 1962.

2051) Jefferiss, F. J. G. "Venereal Disease and the Homosexual," British Journal of Venereal Diseases, 32:17-20, 1956.

2052) Jenkins, Marion. "The Effect of Segregation on the Sex Behavior of the White Rat as Measured by the Obstruction Method," Genetic Psychology Monographs, 3:455-568, 1928.

2053) Jens, R. "Male Hypersexual Behavior: Suggested Treatment: Report of 15 Cases," Journal of the American Medical Women's Association, 19:208-13, 1964.

2054) Joelson, M. and McArthur, C. "Rorschach and TAT Indices of Homosexuality in Overt Homosexuals, Neurotics, and Normal Males," Journal of Abnormal Psychology, 53:161-72, 1956.

2055) Johnson, Adelaide M. and Robinson, David B. "The Sexual Deviant--Causes, Treatment, and Prevention," Journal of the American Medical Association, 164:1559-65, 1957.

2056) Jolles, I. "A Study of the Validity of Some Hypotheses for the Qualititative Interpretation of the H-T-P for Children of Elementary School Age: I. Sexual Identification," Journal of Clinical Psychology, 8:113-18, 1952.

2057) Jonas, C. H. "An Objective Approach to the Personality and Environment in Homosexuality," Psychiatric Quarterly, 18:626-41, 1944.

2058) Jones, A. J. and Janis, Lee. "Primary Syphilis of the Rectum and Gonorrhea of the Anus in a Male Homosexual Playing the Role of a Female Prostitute," American Journal of Syphilis, Gonorrhea, and Venereal Disease, 28:453-57, 1944.

2059) Jones, E. "The Death of Hamlet's Father," International Journal of Psychoanalysis, 29:174-76, 1948.

2060)   Jones, Ernest. "Recent Advances in Psycho-
        Analysis," International Journal of Psychoanalysis,
        1:161-85, 1920.

2061)   Jowitt, Earl. "The 28th Maudsley Lecture: Medi-
        cine and the Law," Journal of Mental Science, 100:
        351-59, 1954.

2062)   Juzwiak, Marijo. "Understanding the Homosexual
        Patient," RN [Registered Nurse], 27:53-59,118,
        Apr. 1964.

2063)   Kahn, Eugene and Lion, Ernest G. "Clinical Note
        on a Self-Fellator," American Journal of Psychiatry,
        95:131-33, 1938.

2064)   Kallmann, Franz J. "Comparative Twin Study on
        the Genetic Aspects of Male Homosexuality," Jour-
        nal of Nervous and Mental Disease, 115:283-98,
        1952.

2065)   Kallman, Franz J. "Twin and Sibship Study of
        Overt Male Homosexuality," American Journal of
        Human Genetics, 4:136-46, 1952.

2066)   Kanee, B. and Hunt, C. L. "Homosexuality as a
        Source of Venereal Disease," Canadian Medical
        Association Journal, 65:138-40, 1951.

2067)   Kaplan, Eugene A. "Homosexuality: A Search
        for the Ego-Ideal," Archives of General Psychiatry,
        16:355-58, 1967.

2068)   Karon, Bertram P. and Rosberg, Jack. "The
        Homosexual Urges in Schizophrenia," Psychoanalysis
        and the Psychoanalytic Review, 45:50-56, 1958.

2069)   Karpman, Benjamin. "Dream Life in a Case of
        Transvestism; with Particular Attention to the
        Problem of Latent Homosexuality," Journal of
        Nervous and Mental Disease, 106:292-337, 1947.

2070)   Karpman, Benjamin. "The Kreutzer Sonata: A
        Problem in Latent Homosexuality and Castration,"
        Psychoanalysis and the Psychoanalytic Review, 25:
        20-48, 1938.

2071)   Karpman, Benjamin. "Mediate Psychotherapy and
         the Acute Homosexual Panic (Kempf's Disease),"
         Journal of Nervous and Mental Disease, 98:493-
         506, 1943.

2072)   Karpman, Benjamin. "A Paranoic Murder,"
         Archives of Criminal Psychodynamics, 1:908-39,
         1955.

2073)   Karpman, Benjamin. "The Structure of Neurosis:
         with special Differentials between Neurosis, Psy-
         chosis, Homosexuality, Alcoholism, Psychopathy,
         and Criminality," Archives of Criminal Psycho-
         dynamics, 4:599-646, 1961.

2074)   Kasanin, Jacob and Biskind, Gerson R. "Per-
         sonality Changes following Substitution Therapy in
         Preadolescent Eunochoidism," Journal of the Ameri-
         can Medical Association, 121:1319-21, 1943.

2075)   Kates, Elizabeth M. "Sexual Problems in Women's
         Institutions," Journal of Social Therapy, 1:187-91,
         1955.

2076)   Kaufmann, M. Ralph. "Projection, Heterosexual
         and Homosexual," Psychoanalytic Quarterly, 3:134-
         36, 1934.

2077)   Kaye, Harvey E. and others. "Homosexuality in
         Women," Archives of General Psychiatry, 17:626-
         34, 1967.

2078)   Keiser, Sylvan and Schaffer, Dora. "Environmental
         Factors in Homosexuality in Adolescent Girls,"
         Psychoanalytic Review, 36:283-95, 1949.

2079)   Kemp, G. T. "The Homophiles in Society," Inter-
         national Journal of Sexology, 7:217-19, 1954.

2080)   Kempf, Edward J. "The Social and Sexual Be-
         havior of Infrahuman Primates with Some Compara-
         ble Facts in Human Behavior," Psychoanalytic Re-
         view, 4:127-54, 1917.

2081)   Kemph, J. P. and Schwerin, E. "Increased Latent
         Homosexuality in a Woman during Group Therapy,"
         Journal of Group Psychotherapy, 16:217-24, 1966.

2082)   Kendler, Howard H. "S. F., a Case of Homosex-
        ual Panic," Journal of Abnormal and Social Psy-
        chology, 42:112-19, 1947.

2083)   Kendrick, D. C. and Clarke, R. V. "Attitudinal
        Differences between Heterosexually and Homosex-
        ually Oriented Males," British Journal of Psychi-
        atry, 113:95-99, 1967.

2084)   Kenyon, F. E. "Physique and Physical Health of
        Female Homosexuals," Journal of Neurology,
        Neurosurgery, and Psychiatry, 31:487-89, 1968.

2085)   Kenyon, F. E. "Studies in Female Homosexuality:
        VI. The Exclusively Homosexual Group," Acta
        Psychiatrica Scandinavica, 44:224-37, 1968.

2086)   Kenyon, F. E. "Studies in Female Homosexuality:
        Psychological Test Results," Journal of Consulting
        and Clinical Psychology, 32:510-13, 1968.

2087)   Kenyon, F. E. "Studies in Female Homosexuality:
        IV. Social and Psychiatric Aspects. V. Sexual
        Development, Attitudes, and Experience," British
        Journal of Psychiatry, 114:1337-50, 1968.

2088)   Ketterer, Warren A. "Venereal Disease and
        Homosexuality," Journal of the American Medical
        Association, 188:11-12, 1964.

2089)   Khan, M. Masud R. "Foreskin Fetishism and Its
        Relation to Ego Pathology in a Male Homosexual,"
        International Journal of Psychoanalysis, 46:64-80,
        1965.

2090)   Kiefer, J. H., Bronstein, P., Rosenthal, I. M., and
        Hyde, J. S. "Male or Female? The Problem of
        Indeterminate Sex," Medical Clinics of North Ameri-
        ca, 43:1685, 1959.

2091)   King, A. J. "The Complications of Homosexuality:
        Introduction," Proceedings of The Royal Society of
        Medicine, 55:869-70, 1962.

2092)   Kinsey, Alfred C. "Homosexuality: Criteria for
        a Hormonal Explanation of the Homosexual," Jour-
        nal of Clinical Endocrinology, 1:424-28, 1941. (Re-

printed in Cory, no. 27 above, pp. 370-83.)

2093)   Kitay, P. M.   "Symposium on Reinterpretations of
the Schreber Case," International Journal of Psychoanalysis, 44:191-94, 1963.

2094)   Klaf, Franklin S.   "Evidence of Paranoid Ideation
in Overt Homosexuals," Journal of Social Therapy,
7:48-51, 1961.

2095)   Klaf, Franklin S.   "Female Homosexuality and
Paranoid Schizophrenia: A Survey of 75 Cases and
Controls," Archives of General Psychiatry, 4:84-
90, 1961.

2096)   Klaf, Franklin S. and Davis, Charles A. "Homosexuality and Paranoid Schizophrenia: A Survey of
150 Cases and Controls," American Journal of Psychiatry, 116:1070-75, 1960.

2097)   Klein, H. R. and Horwitz, W. A.   "Psychosexual
Factors in the Paranoid Phenomena," American
Journal of Psychiatry, 105:697-701, 1949.

2098)   Klein, Melanie.   "Notes on Some Schizoid Mechanisms," International Journal of Psychoanalysis,
27:99-110, 1946.

2099)   Klintworth, Gordon K.   "A Pair of Male Mono-
zygotic Twins discordant for Homosexuality," Journal of Nervous and Mental Disease, 135:113-25,
1962.

2100)   Klopfer, W. G. and Borstelman, L. J.   "Associative
Valences of the Szondi Pictures," Journal of Personality, 19:172-88, 1951.

2101)   Knight, J. A.   "False Pregnancy in a Male," Psychosomatic Medicine, 22:260-66, 1960.

2102)   Knight, Robert P.   "The Relationship of Latent
Homosexuality to the Mechanism of Paranoid Delusions," Bulletin of the Menninger Clinic, 4:149-
59, 1940.

2103)   Knox, Stuart C.   "Another Look at Homosexuality,"
Journal of the American Medical Association, 193:
831, 1965.

2104)   Koegler, Ronald R. and Kline, Lawrence Y.   "Psy-
         chotherapy Research: An Approach Utilizing Auto-
         nomic Response Measurements," American Journal
         of Psychotherapy, 19:268-79, 1965.

2105)   Koenig, K. P.   "The Differentiation of Hetero- or
         Homo-erotic Interests in the Male: Some Comments
         on Articles by Brown and Koenig," Behaviour Re-
         search and Therapy, 2:305-07, 1965.

2106)   Kolb, L. C.   "Therapy of Homosexuality," Current
         Psychiatric Therapy, 3:131-37, 1963.

2107)   Kolb, L. C. and Johnson, A. M.   "Etiology and
         Therapy of Overt Homosexuality," Psychoanalytic
         Quarterly, 24:506-15, 1955.

2108)   Kraff-Ebing, Richard von.   "Perversion of the
         Sexual Instinct--Report of Cases," Alienist and
         Neurologist, 9:565-81, 1888.

2109)   Kraft, I. A.   "Pseudo-Homosexuality as Studied in
         Group Psychotherapy," American Journal of Psycho-
         analysis, 20:207-11, 1960.

2110)   Kraft, Tom.   "Behaviour Therapy and the Treat-
         ment of Sexual Perversions," Psycho-Therapy and
         Psychosomatics, 15:351-57, 1967.

2111)   Kraft, Tom.   "A Case of Homosexuality Treated
         by Systematic Desensitization," American Journal of
         Psychotherapy, 21:815-21, 1967.

2112)   Krausz, Erwin O.   "Homosexuality as Neurosis,"
         International Journal of Individual Psychology, 1:
         30-39, 1935.

2113)   Kremer, M. W. and Rifkin, A. H.   "The Early
         Development of Homosexuality: A Study of Adoles-
         cent Lesbians," American Journal of Psychiatry,
         126:91-96, 1969.

2114)   Krieger, M. H. and Worchel, P.   "A Test of the
         Psychoanalytic Theory of Identification," Journal of
         Individual Psychology, 16:56-63, 1960.

2115)   Krinsky, C. M. and Michaels, J. J.   "A Survey of

100 Sex Offenders Admitted to the Boston Psychiatric
Hospital," Journal of Criminal Psychopathology, 2:
199-201, 1940.

2116)   Krippner, Stanley. "The Identification of Male
         Homosexuality with the MMPI," Journal of Clinical
         Psychology, 20:159-61, 1964.

2117)   Kubie, L. S. "The Psychiatric Implication of the
         Kinsey Report," Psychosomatic Medicine, 10:95-
         106, 1948.

2118)   Kuethe, J. L. and Weingartner, H. "Male-Female
         Schemata of Homosexual and Non-homosexual Peni-
         tentiary Inmates," Journal of Personality, 32:23-31,
         1964.

2119)   Kurzrok, R. "Physiological Approach to the Prob-
         lem of Homosexuality," Journal-Lancet, 55:417-19,
         1935.

2120)   Kvorning, S. A. "Clinical Comments on the Start
         of an Epidemic of Syphilis," British Journal of
         Venereal Diseases, 39:261-63, 1963.

2121)   LaBarre, Weston. "The Psychopathology of Drinking
         Songs," Psychiatry, 2:203-12, 1939.

2122)   Lagache, Daniel. "From Homosexuality to Jeal-
         ousy," International Journal of Psychoanalysis, 30:
         195-96, 1949.

2123)   Lagache, Daniel. "Homosexuality and Jealousy,"
         International Journal of Psychoanalysis, 31:24-31,
         1950.

2124)   Laird, S. M. "Present Patterns of Early Syphilis
         in the Manchester Region: III. Homosexual In-
         fections," British Journal of Venereal Diseases,
         38:82-85, 1962.

2125)   Lambert, Carl. "Homosexuals," Medical Press,
         232:523-26, 1954.

2126)   Landes, Ruth. "A Cult Matriarchate and Male
         Homosexuality," Journal of Abnormal and Social
         Psychology, 35:386-97, 1940.

2127)   Landis, J. T.   "Experiences of 500 Children with
        Adult Sexual Deviation," Psychiatric Quarterly
        Supplement, 30:91-109, 1956.

2128)   Landsman, Arthur A.   "Chancre of the Anus,"
        Medical Journal and Record, 133:328, 1931.

2129)   Lang, Theo.   "Studies on the Genetic Determination
        of Homosexuality," Journal of Nervous and Mental
        Disease, 92:55-64, 1940.

2130)   Langsley, D. G. , Schwartz, M. N. , and Fairburn,
        R. H.   "Father-Son Incest," Comprehensive Psychia-
        try, 9:218-26, 1968.

2131)   Larsen, Anthony A.   "The Transmission of Venere-
        al Diseases through Homosexual Practices," Cana-
        dian Medical Association Journal, 80:22-25, 1959.

2132)   Lazlo, Carl.   "Notes on Various Phenomena in
        Male Homosexuality," International Journal of
        Sexology, 8:220-25, 1955.

2133)   Lavin, N. I. , Thorpe, J. G. , Barker, J. C. , Blake-
        more, C. B. , and Conway, C. G.   "Behaviour
        Therapy in a Case of Transvestism," Journal of
        Nervous and Mental Disease, 133:346-53, 1961.

2134)   "The Law and the Homosexual," Lancet, 267:500-
        01, 1954.

2135)   "Law on Homosexuality," Lancet, 269:781 and
        934, 1955.

2136)   Layard, John.   "Homo-eroticism in a Primitive
        Society as a Function of the Self," Journal of
        Analytic Psychology, 4:101-15, 1959.

2137)   Laycock, S. R.   "Homosexuality--A Mental Hygiene
        Problem," Canadian Medical Association Journal,
        63:245-50, 1950.

2138)   Learoyd, C. G.   "The Problem of Homosexuality,"
        Practitioner, 172:355-63, 1954.

2139)   Leitch, A.   "Male Homosexuality as a Medico-
        Legal and Sociological Problem in the United

Kingdom," International Journal of Social Psychiatry, 5:98-106, 1959.

2140)   "Lesbianism as Cruelty," British Medical Journal, 2:472, 1947.

2141)   Levin, S. M. , Hirsch, I. S. , Shugar, G. , and Kapche, R. "Treatment of Homosexuality and Heterosexual Anxiety with Avoidance Conditioning and Systematic Desensitization: Data and Case Report," Psychotherapy: Therapy Research and Practice, 5:160-68, 1968.

2142)   Levine, Jacob. "The Sexual Adjustment of Alco-holics--A Clinical Study of a Selected Sample," Quarterly Journal of Studies on Alcohol, 16:675-80, 1955.

2143)   Levitt, E. E. and Brady, J. P. "Sexual Preferences in Young Adult Males and Some Correlates," Jour-nal of Clinical Psychology, 21:347-54, 1965.

2144)   Lewinsky, Hilde. "Features from a Case of Homo-sexuality," Psychoanalytic Quarterly, 21:344-54, 1952.

2145)   Lewinsky, Hilde. "Notes on Two Special Features in a Homosexual Patient," International Journal of Psychoanalysis, 30:56, 1949.

2146)   Lewis, G. M. Jr. and Rowe, C. J. "The Sexual Offender as Seen in a Municipal Court," Minnesota Medicine, 45:1113-16, 1962.

2147)   Lichtenstein, Perry M. "The 'Fairy' and the 'Lady Lover,' " Medical Review of Reviews, 27: 369-74, 1921.

2148)   Liddicoat, Renee. "Homosexuality: Results of a Survey as Related to Various Theories," British Medical Journal, 2:1110-11, 1957. (See no. 251 above.)

2149)   Lieberman, Daniel and Siegel, Benjamin A. "A Program for 'Sexual Psychopaths' in a State Mental Hospital," American Journal of Psychiatry, 113: 801-07, 1957.

2150)   Liebman, Samuel. "Homosexuality, Transvestism, and Psychosis: Study of a Case Treated with Electro-Shock," Journal of Nervous and Mental Disease, 99:945-58, 1944.

2151)   Lief, H. I., Dingham, J. F., and Bishop, M. P. "Psychoendocrinologic Studies in a Male with Cyclic Changes in Sexuality," Psychosomatic Medicine, 24:357-69, 1962.

2152)   Lindner, Robert M. "Content Analysis in Rorschach Work," Rorschach Research Exchange, 10:121-30, 1946.

2153)   Lindzey, Gardner. "Seer versus Sign," Journal of Experimental Research in Personality, 1:17-26, 1965.

2154)   Lindzey, Gardner; Bradford, Jean; Tejessy, Charlotte; and Davids, Anthony. "Thematic Apperception Test: An Interpretive Lexicon for Clinician and Investigator," Journal of Clinical Psychology, Monograph Supplement, No. 12, pp. 1-98 at 27-28 and 65-67, 1959.

2155)   Lindzey, Gardner; Tejessy, Charlotte; and Zemansky, Harold S. "Thematic Apperception Test: An Empirical Examination of Some Indices of Homosexuality," Journal of Abnormal and Social Psychology, 57:67-75, 1958.

2156)   Lipkowitz, M. H. "Homosexuality as a Defense against Feminine Strivings: A Case Report," Journal of Nervous and Mental Diseases, 138:394-98, 1964.

2157)   Lipton, H. R. "Stress in Correctional Institutions," Journal of Social Therapy, 6:216-23, 1960.

2158)   Lister, John. "Morals and the Law: the Doctor's Office," New England Journal of Medicine, 251:1104-05, 1954.

2159)   "Literature and Sexual Inversion," Urologic and Cutaneous Review, 37:820-21, 1933.

2160)   Litin, E. M., Griffin, M. D., and Johnson, A. M.

"Parental Influence in Unusual Sexual Behavior in Children," Psychoanalytic Quarterly, 25:37-55, 1956.

2161)   Litkey, L. J. and Feniczy, P. "An Approach to the Control of Homosexual Practices," International Journal of Neuro-Psychiatry, 3:20-23, 1967.

2162)   Litman, Robert E. "Psychotherapy of a Homosexual Man in a Heterosexual Group," International Journal of Group Psychotherapy, 11:440-48, 1961.

2163)   "Living with Homosexuality," Canadian Medical Association Journal, 86:875-78, 1962.

2164)   Loeser, Lewis H. "The Sexual Psychopath in the Military Service; A Study of 270 Cases," American Journal of Psychiatry, 102:92-101, 1945.

2165)   Loewenstein, R. "Phallic Passivity in Men," International Journal of Psychoanalysis, 16:334-40, 1935.

2166)   Lolli, Giorgio. "Alcoholism and Homosexuality in Tennessee Williams' 'Cat on a Hot Tin Roof,'" Quarterly Journal of Studies on Alcohol, 17:543-53, 1956.

2167)   London, Louis S. "Analysis of a Homosexual Neurosis," Urologic and Cutaneous Review, 37:93-97, 1933.

2168)   London, Louis S. "Homosexual Panic with Hallucinations--A Case Study," Medical Times, 92:175-89, 1964.

2169)   Lorand, Alexander S. "Fetishism in Statu Nascendi," International Journal of Psychoanalysis, 11:419-27, 1930.

2170)   Lorand, Sandor. "Perverse Tendencies and Fantasies: Their Influence on Personality," Psychoanalysis and the Psychoanalytic Review, 26:178-90, 1939.

2171)   "Lords Vote on Homosexual Law Reform," British Medical Journal, 2:1131, 1965.

2172)   Lubin, A. and Malloy, M. "An Empirical Test of
         Some Assumptions Underlying the Szondi Test,"
         Journal of Abnormal and Social Psychology, 46:
         480-84, 1951.

2173)   Lundberg, E. "Folliculin Test for Determination
         of Homosexuality in Men," Hygeia, 96:561-67, 1934.

2174)   Lurie, Louis A. "The Endocrine Factor in Homo-
         sexuality," American Journal of Medical Science,
         208:176-86, 1944.

2175)   Lurie, Louis A. "Somatopsychic Aspects of Be-
         havior Disorders of Children," Medical Clinics of
         North America, 31:668-79, 1947.

2176)   MacCulloch, M. J. and Feldman, M. P. "Aversion
         Therapy in Management of 43 Homosexuals," Brit-
         ish Medical Journal, 2:594-97, 1967. (Abstracted
         in Psychiatry Digest, 29:39, 43, Mar. 1968.)

2177)   MacCulloch, M. J. and Feldman, M. P. "Personality
         and Treatment of Homosexuality," Acta Psychiatrica
         Scandinavica, 43:300-17, 1967.

2178)   MacCulloch, M. J., Feldman, M. P., and Pinshoff,
         J. M. "The Application of Anticipatory Learning to
         the Treatment of Homosexuality--II. Avoidance
         Response Latencies and Pulse Rate Changes," Be-
         haviour Research and Therapy, 3:21-44, 1965.

2179)   MacDonald, F. G. "The Problem of the Homosex-
         ual with Venereal Disease," British Journal of
         Venereal Diseases, 25:13-15, 1949.

2180)   MacDonald, John M. "Homosexuality in Ex-Pris-
         oners," Journal of the American Medical Associa-
         tion, 175:834, 1961.

2181)   MacDonald, John W. "Homosexuality," Journal of
         the American Medical Association, 180:707, 1962.

2182)   MacDonald, M. W. "Criminally Aggressive Be-
         havior in Passive, Effeminate Boys," American
         Journal of Orthopsychiatry, 8:70-78, 1938.

2183)   Machover, S., Puzzo, F. S., Machover, K., and

Plumeau, F. "Clinical and Objective Studies of Personality Variables in Alcoholism," Quarterly Journal of Studies on Alcohol, 20:528-42, 1959.

2184) MacKenzie, D. F. "Homosexuality and the Justice Department," New Zealand Medical Journal, 66:745-48, 1967.

2184a) MacKinnon, J. "The Homosexual Woman," American Journal of Psychiatry, 103:661-64, 1947.

2185) Maclay, D. T. "Boys Who Commit Sexual Misdemeanors," British Medical Journal, 1:186-90, 1960.

2186) Mackwood, J. C. "A Note on the Psychotherapeutic Treatment of Homosexuality in Prison," Medical Press, 218:217-19, 1947.

2187) MacNamara, Donald E. J. "Male Prostitution in American Cities: A Socioeconomic or Pathological Phenomenon?" American Journal of Orthopsychiatry, 35:204, 1965.

2188) Mainord, Florence R. "A Note on the Use of Figure Drawings in the Diagnosis of Sexual Inversion," Journal of Clinical Psychology, 9:188-89, 1953.

2189) "Male and Female Homosexuality," British Medical Journal, 1:748, 1946.

2190) "The Male Homosexual," British Medical Journal, 2:1304, 1960.

2191) "Male Homosexuality," Lancet, 269:291-93, 1955.

2192) "Male Homosexuality," Lancet, 2:1077-80, 1959. (Reprinted in no. 141 above.)

2193) "Male Homosexuality," Medical Journal of Australia, 54:651-52, 1967.

2194) Mannheim, Hermann. "Some Criminological Aspects of Homosexuality," Medical Press, 218:210-12, 1947.

2195) Marino, A. W. M. Jr. "Proctologic Lesions Observed

in Male Homosexuals," Diseases of the Colon and
Rectum, 7:121-28, 1964.

2196) Marison, R. C. and Trice, E. R. "The Changing
Pattern of Syphilis," Southern Medical Journal, 56:
705-10, 1963.

2197) Marks, B. "Homosexuality," Harper Hospital
Bulletin, 26:242-47, 1968.

2198) Marks, I. M. "Aversion Therapy," British Journal
of Medical Psychology, 41:47-52, 1968.

2199) Marmell, M. "Donovanosis of the Anus in the
Male: An Epidemiological Consideration," British
Journal of Venereal Diseases, 34:213, 1958.

2200) Marone, Silvio. "Homosexuality and Art," International Journal of Sexology, 7:175-90, 1954.

2201) Marsh, J. T., Hilliard, J., and Liechti, R. A. "A
Sexual Deviation Scale for the MMPI," Journal of
Consulting Psychology, 19:55-59, 1955.

2202) Martensen-Larsen, O. "The Family Constellation
and Homosexualism," Acta Genetica et Statistica
Medica, 7:445-46, 1957.

2203) Martin, Agnes J. "A Case of Homosexuality and
Personality Disorder in a Man of 36 Treated by
LSD and Resolved within Two Months," Psycho-
therapy and Psychodynamics, 15:44, 1967.

2204) Martin, Agnes J. "The Treatment of 12 Male
Homosexuals with L.S.D.," Acta Psychotherapeutica,
10:394-402, 1962.

2205) Martin, E. G. and Kallett, H. I. "Primary Syphilis
of the Anorectal Region," Journal of the American
Medical Association, 84:1556-58, 1925.

2206) Mason, S. C., Jacob, J. S., Himler, L. E., Gould,
S. M. Jr., and Bird, H. W. "Homosexuality: A
Medico-Legal Problem," Journal of the Michigan
State Medical Society, 60:635-38, 1961.

2207) Masserman, Jules H. "Some Current Concepts of

Sexual Behavior," Psychiatry, 14:67-72, 1951.

2208)   Massett, Lawrence. "Homosexuality: Changes on
        the Way," Science News, 96:557-59, Dec. 13, 1969.

2209)   Mather, N. J. deV. "The Treatment of Homosexuality
        by Aversion Therapy," Medicine, Science, and Law,
        6:200-05, 1966.

2210)   Maude, John. "Homosexuality and the Criminal
        Law," Practitioner, 172:378-80, 1954.

2211)   Max, Louis W. "Breaking-Up a Homosexual Fix-
        ation by the Conditioned Reaction Technique: A
        Case Study," Psychological Bulletin, 32:734, 1935.

2212)   Mayer, Edward E. "The Sex Deviate," Pennsylvania
        Medical Journal, 53:32-38, 1950, with discussion by
        Rodney H. Kiefer.

2213)   Mayne, D. G. "Homosexuality," British Journal of
        Psychiatry, 114:125, 1968.

2214)   McConaghy, N. "Penile Volume Change to Moving
        Pictures of Male and Female Nudes in Heterosexual
        and Homosexual Males," Behaviour Research and
        Therapy, 5:43-48, 1967.

2215)   McCord, W., McCord, J., and Verden, P. "Family
        Relationships and Sexual Deviance in Lower Class
        Adolescents," International Journal of Social Psy-
        chiatry, 8:165-79, 1962.

2216)   McCreary, John K. "Psychopathia Homosexualis,"
        Canadian Journal of Psychology, 4:63-74, 1950.

2217)   McDonald, F. G. "Homosexuality and Venereal
        Disease," Indian Journal of Venereal Disease, 18:
        57-61, 1952.

2218)   McGuire, R. J. "Sexual Deviation as Conditioned
        Behaviour: A Hypothesis," Behaviour Research
        and Therapy, 2:185-90, 1965.

2219)   McGuire, R. J. and Vallance, M. "Aversion
        Therapy by Electric Shock: A Simple Technique,"
        British Medical Journal, 1:151-53, 1964.

2220)   McHenry, F. A.   "A Note on Homosexuality, Crime,
         and the Newspapers," Journal of Criminal Psycho-
         pathology, 2:533-48, 1941.

2221)   McKinnon, Jane.   "The Homosexual Woman,"
         American Journal of Psychiatry, 103:661-64, 1947.
         (Reprinted in Krich, no. 69 above, pp. 3-10.)

2222)   McLaughlin, F.   "Vice and the Law: Some Aspects
         of the Wolfenden Report," Journal of the Irish
         Medical Association, 42:78-82, 1958.

2223)   McLeish, John.   "The Homosexual," Medical World,
         93:237-39, 1960.

2224)   McMurtie, Douglas C.   "Notes on Homosexuality:
         An Attempt at Seduction;   An Example of Acquired
         Homosexuality in Prison;   A Commentary on the
         Prevalence of Inversion in Germany," Vermont
         Medical Monthly, 19:66-68, 1913.

2225)   McMurtie, Douglas C.   "Notes on Pederastic
         Practices in Prison," Chicago Medical Recorder, 36:
         15-17, 1914.

2226)   Meagher, John F. W.   "Homosexuality: Its Psycho-
         logical and Psychopathological Significance," Uro-
         logic and Cutaneous Review, 33:505-18, 1929.

2227)   Meketon, B. W., Griffith, R. M., Taylor, V. H.,
         and Wiedeman, J. S.   "Rorschach Homosexual Signs
         in Paranoid Schizophrenics," Journal of Abnormal
         and Social Psychology, 65:280-84, 1962.

2228)   Melikian, Levon.   "Social Change and Sexual Be-
         havior of Arab University Students," Journal of
         Social Psychology, 73:169-75, 1967.

2229)   Melikian, Levon and Prothro, E. Terry.   "Sexual
         Behavior of University Students in the Arab Near
         East," Journal of Abnormal and Social Psychology,
         49:59-64, 1954.

2230)   Mendelsohn, F. and Ross, M.   "An Analysis of 133
         Homosexuals Seen at a University Student Health
         Service," Diseases of the Nervous System, 20:246-
         50, 1959.

2231)   Merricks, J. W. and Papierniak, F. B.   "Gonorrhea,"
         Journal of the American Medical Association, 177:
         225, 1961.

2232)   Merrill, Lilburn.   "A Summary of Findings in a
         Study of Sexualism among a Group of 100 Delinquent
         Boys," American Journal of Urology and Sexology,
         15:259-69, 1919.

2233)   Mesnikoff, A. M., Rainer, J. D., Kolb, L. C., and
         Carr, A. C.   "Intrafamilial Determinants of Diver-
         gent Sexual Behavior in Twins," American Journal
         of Psychiatry, 119:732-38, 1963.

2234)   Messer, Alfred A.   "The British Family and the
         'Vice Scandals,' " Psychiatry Today, 28:41, 44-46,
         Mar. 1967.

2235)   Meyer, Adolf E.   "Psychoanalytic versus Be-
         havior Therapy of Male Homosexuals: A Statistical
         Evaluation of Clinical Outcome," Comprehensive
         Psychiatry, 7:110-17, 1966.

2236)   Meyer, Mortimer M.   "The Case of El: Blind
         Analysis of the Tests of an Unknown Patient,"
         Journal of Projective Techniques, 25:375-82, 1961.

2237)   Miller, A. and Caplan, J.   "Sex-Role Reversal
         Following Castration of a Homosexual Transvestite
         with Klinefelder's Syndrome," Canadian Psychiatric
         Association, 10:223-27, 1965.

2238)   Miller, Charles W.   "The Paranoid Syndrome,"
         Archives of Neurology and Psychiatry, 45:953-63,
         1941.

2239)   Miller, M. M.   "Hypnotic-Aversion Treatment of
         Homosexuality," Journal of the National Medical
         Association, 55:411-15, 436, 1963.

2240)   Miller, Paul R.   "The Effeminate Passive Obliga-
         tory Homosexual," Archives of Neurology and Psy-
         chiatry, 80:612-18, 1958.

2241)   Miller, P. M., Bradley, J. B., Gross, R. S., and
         Wood, G.   "Review of Homosexuality Research
         (1960-66) and Some Implications for Treatment,"

Psychotherapy: Theory, Research, and Practice,
5:3-6, 1968.

2242)   Miller, W. G. and Hannum, T. E.   "Characteristics
of Homosexually Involved Incarcerated Females,"
Journal of Consulting Psychology, 27:277, 1963.

2243)   Mintz, Elizabeth E.   "Overt Male Homosexuals in
Combined Group and Individual Treatment," Journal
of Consulting Psychology, 30:193-98, 1966.

2244)   Mohr, J. W. and Turner, R. E.   "Sexual Deviations:
I. Introduction," Applied Therapeutics, 9:78-81, 1967.

2245)   Mohr, J. W. and Turner, R. E.   "Sexual Deviations:
II. Homosexuality," Applied Therapeutics, 9:165-68,
1967.

2246)   Mohr, J. W. , Turner, R. E. , and Ball, R. B.   "Exhibitionism and Pedophilia," Journal of Social
Therapy, 8:172-83, 1962.

2247)   Moir, J. L.   "Homosexual Offences," Medico-Legal
and Criminological Review, 8:121-22, 1940.

2248)   Monchy, Rene de.   "A Clinical Type of Homosexuality," International Journal of Psychoanalysis,
46:218-25, 1965.

2249)   Money, John.   "The Genetics of Homosexuality,"
New Zealand Medical Journal, 66:745-48, 1967.

2250)   Money, John and Alexander, Duane.   "Psychosexual Development and Absence of Homosexuality in
Males with Precocious Puberty," Journal of Nervous
and Mental Disease, 148:111-23, 1969.

2251)   Money, John and Wang, Christine.   "Human Figure
Drawings: II. Quality Comparison in Gender-
Identity Anomalies, Klinefelder's Syndrome, and
Precocious Puberty," Journal of Nervous and
Mental Disease, 144:55-58, 1967.

2252)   Monroe, Russell R. and Enelow, Morton L.   "The
Therapeutic Motivation in Male Homosexuals,"
American Journal of Psychotherapy, 14:474-90,
1960.

2253)   Monsour, Karen J. "Migraine: Dynamics and
         Choice of Symptoms," Psychoanalytic Quarterly,
         26:476-93, 1957.

2254)   Moore, K. R. and Query, W. T. "Group Psycho-
         therapy as a Means of Approaching Homosexual Be-
         havior among Hospitalized Psychiatric Patients,"
         Journal of the Kentucky Medical Association, 61:
         403-07, 1963.

2255)   Moore, R. A. and Selzer, M. L. "Male Homosex-
         uality, Paranoia, and the Schizophrenias," American
         Journal of Psychiatry, 119:743-47, 1963. (Ab-
         stracted in Psychiatry Digest, 24:12-13, Mar. 1963.)

2256)   Moore, Thomas V. "The Pathogenesis and Treat-
         ment of Homosexual Disorders: A Digest of Some
         Pertinent Evidence," Journal of Personality, 14:47-
         83, 1945.

2257)   Morris, Desmond. "Homosexuality in the Ten-
         Spined Stickleback (Pygosteus Pungitius L)," Be-
         havior, 4:233-61, 1952.

2258)   Morrow, J. E. , Cupp, M. E. , and Sachs, L. B.
         "A Possible Explanation of the Excessive Brother-
         to-Sister Ratios Reported in Siblings of Male Homo-
         sexuals," Journal of Nervous and Mental Disease,
         140:305-06, 1965.

2259)   Morson, B. C. "Anorectal Venereal Disease,"
         Proceedings of the Royal Society of Medicine, 57:
         179-80, 1964.

2260)   Mulcock, Donald. "A Study of 100 Non-Selected
         Cases of Sexual Assaults on Children," International
         Journal of Sexology, 7:126, 1954.

2261)   Murray, G. B. "Learning in Homosexuality," Psycho-
         logical Reports, 23:659-62, 1968.

2262)   Murray, Henry A. "Commentary on the Case of
         El," Journal of Projective Techniques, 25:404-11,
         1961.

2263)   Musaph, H. "On Homosexuality," Psychiatria,
         Neurologia, Neurochirugia, 63:203-11, 1960.

2264)   Myerson, Abraham and Neustadt, Rudolph. "An-
         drogen Excretion in Urine in Various Neuropsy-
         chiatric Conditions: A Preliminary Report," Ar-
         chives of Neurology and Psychiatry, 44:689-91,
         1940.

2265)   Myerson, Abraham and Neustadt, Rudolph. "Bi-
         sexuality and Male Homosexuality: Their Biologic
         and Medical Aspects," Clinics, 1:932-57, 1942.

2266)   Myerson, Abraham and Neustadt, Rudolph. "The
         Bisexuality of Man," Journal of the Mt. Sinai Hos-
         pital, 9:668-78, 1942.

2267)   Myerson, Abraham and Neustadt, Rudolph. "Es-
         sential Male Homosexuality and Results of Treat-
         ment," Archives of Neurology and Psychiatry, 55:
         291-93, 1946.

2268)   Myerson, Abraham, Neustadt, Rudolph, and Rak,
         I. P. "The Male Homosexual: Hormonal and
         Clinical Studies," Journal of Nervous and Mental
         Disease, 93:209-12, 1941.

2269)   Nacht, S., Diatkine, R., and Favreau, J. "The
         Ego in Perverse Relationships," International Jour-
         nal of Psychoanalysis, 37:404-13, 1956.

2270)   Nagler, S. H. "Fetishism: A Review and A Case
         Study," Psychiatric Quarterly, 31:713-41, 1957.

2270a)   Naiman, James. "Short Term Effects as Indicators
         of the Role of Interpretations in Psychoanalysis,"
         International Journal of Psychoanalysis, 49:353-57,
         1968.

2271)   Nash, John and Hayes, Frank. "The Parental
         Relationship of Male Homosexuals: Some Theoretical
         Issues and a Pilot Study," Australian Journal of Psy-
         chology, 17:35-43, 1965.

2272)   Nedoma, Karel. "Homosexuality in Sexological
         Practice," International Journal of Sexology, 4:219-
         24, 1951.

2273)   Neser, W. B. and others. "Importance of Homo-
         sexuals and Bisexuals in the Epidemiology of Syphilis,"

Southern Medical Journal, 62:177-80, 1969.

2274)   Neustadt, Rudolph and Myerson, Abraham. "Quanti-
        tative Sex Hormone Studies in Homosexuality, Child-
        hood, and Various Neuropsychiatric Disorders,"
        American Journal of Psychiatry, 97:524-51, 1940.

2275)   Neustatter, W. Lindesay. "Homosexuality: the
        Medical Aspect," Practitioner, 172:364-73, 1954.

2276)   Neustatter, W. Lindesay. "The Medical Aspects of
        Homosexuality," Practitioner, 199:704-10, 1967.

2276a) Neustatter, W. Lindesay. "Psychiatry and Crime:
        Some Aspects of Sexual Perversion," Practitioner,
        170:395-97, 1953.

2277)   New York Academy of Medicine, Committee on
        Public Health. "Homosexuality: A Report," Bulle-
        tin of the New York Academy of Medicine, 40:576-
        80, 1964. (See no. 208 above.)

2278)   Nichols, Robert C. "Subtle, Obvious, and Stereo-
        type Measures of Masculinity-Femininity," Educa-
        tional and Psychological Measurement, 22:449-61,
        1962.

2279)   Nicol, C. S. "Anal Syphilis," Proceedings of the
        Royal Society of Medicine, 55:870-71, 1962.

2280)   Nicol, C. S. "Homosexuality and Venereal Dis-
        ease," Practitioner, 184:345-49, 1960. (Abstracted
        in Medico-Legal Journal, 28:225, 1960.)

2281)   Nielson, Nils. "What Is Homosexuality?" Interna-
        tional Journal of Sexology, 6:188, 1953.

2282)   Nitsche, C. J., Robinson, J. F., and Parsons, E. T.
        "Homosexuality and the Rorschach," Journal of
        Consulting Psychology, 20:196, 1956.

2283)   Norman, Herbert J. "Sexual Anomalies and Per-
        versions," Practitioner, 126:251-58, 1931.

2284)   Norman, Jacob P. "Evidence and Clinical Signifi-
        cance of Homosexuality in 100 Unanalyzed Cases of
        Dementia Praecox," Journal of Nervous and Mental

Disease, 107:484-89, 1948.

2285) Novey, R. "The Artistic Communication and the
Recipient: 'Death in Venice' as an Integral Part
of a Psychoanalysis," Psychoanalytic Quarterly, 33:
25-52, 1964.

2286) Nunberg, Herman. "Circumcision and Problems of
Bisexuality," International Journal of Psychoanalysis,
28:145-79, 1947.

2287) Nunberg, Herman. "Homosexuality, Magic, and
Aggression," International Journal of Psychoanalysis,
19:1-16. 1938.

2288) Nydes, Jule. "Symposium on 'Reinterpretation of
the Schreber Case: Freud's Theory of Paranoia,'
IV. Schreber, Parricide, and Paranoid-Masochism,"
International Journal of Psychoanalysis, 44:208-12,
1963.

2289) Oberndorf, C. P. "Diverse Forms of Homosexuality,"
Urologic and Cutaneous Review, 33:518-23, 1929.

2290) O'Connor, P. J. "Aetiological Factors in Homosexuality as Seen in Royal Air Force Psychiatric Practice," British Journal of Psychiatry, 110:381-91,
1964.

2291) Oldershaw, H. L. "Outbreak of Gonorrhea in a
Residential Boys' School," British Journal of Venereal Diseases, 5:302, 1929.

2292) Oliver, W. A. and Mosher, D. L. "Psychopathology
and Guilt in Heterosexuals and Sub-groups of Homosexual Reformatory Inmates," Journal of Abnormal
Psychology, 73:323-29, 1968.

2293) Orgel, S. Z. "A Case of Male Homosexuality,"
Samiska, 17:43-61, 1963.

2294) "Origins of Homosexuality," British Medical Journal, 2:1077-78, 1965.

2295) Ortega, M. J. "Delusions of Jealousy," Psychoanalysis and the Psychoanalytic Review, 46:102-03,
1959.

2296)   Oswald, Ian. "Induction of Illusory and Hallucina-
        tory Voices with Considerations of Behavior Thera-
        py," Journal of Mental Science, 108:196-212, 1962.

2297)   Ovesey, Lionel. "The Homosexual Conflict: An
        Adaptational Analysis," Psychiatry, 17:243-50, 1954.
        (Reprinted in Ruitenbeek, no. 96 above, pp. 127-
        40.)

2298)   Ovesey, Lionel. "Homosexuality in Men," Mani-
        toba Medical Review, 48:94-99, Mar. 1968.

2299)   Ovesey, Lionel. "Masculine Aspirations in Women:
        An Adaptional Analysis," Psychiatry, 19:340-51,
        1956.

2300)   Ovesey, Lionel. "The Pseudohomosexual Anxiety,"
        Psychiatry, 18:17-26, 1955.

2301)   Ovesey, Lionel. "Pseudohomosexuality in Men,"
        Manitoba Medical Review, 48:89-93, Mar. 1968.

2302)   Ovesey, Lionel. "Pseudohomosexuality, the Para-
        noid Mechanism, and Paranoia," Psychiatry, 18:
        163-73, 1955.

2303)   Ovesey, Lionel and Gaylin, Willard. "Psycho-
        therapy of Male Homosexuality: Prognosis, Selec-
        tion of Patients, Technique," American Journal of
        Psychotherapy, 19:382-96, 1965.

2304)   Ovesey, Lionel; Gaylin, Willard, and Hendin,
        Herbert. "Psychotherapy of Male Homosexuality,"
        Archives of General Psychiatry, 9:19-31, 1963.

2305)   Owensby, N. M. "The Correction of Homosexuality,"
        Urologic and Cutaneous Review, 45:494-96, 1941.

2306)   Owensby, N. M. "Homosexuality and Lesbianism
        Treated with Metrazol," Journal of Nervous and
        Mental Disease, 92:65-66, 1940.

2307)   Page, James and Warkentin, John. "Masculinity
        and Paranoia," Journal of Abnormal and Social
        Psychology, 33:527-31, 1938.

2308)   Panton, James H. "New MMPI Scale for the Identi-

fication of Homosexuality," Journal of Clinical
Psychology, 16:17-21, 1960.

2309)   Pardes, H. , Steinberg, J. , and Simons, R. C.   "A
         Rare Case of Overt and Mutual Homosexuality in
         Female Identical Twins," Psychiatric Quarterly, 41:
         108-33, 1967.

2310)   Paré, C. M. B.   "Homosexuality and Chromosomal
         Sex," Journal of Psychosomatic Research, 1:247-
         51, 1956.

2311)   Parker, Neville.   "Homosexuality in Twins; A Re-
         port on Three Discordant Pairs," British Journal of
         Psychiatry, 110:489-95, 1964.

2312)   Parr, Denis.   "Homosexuality in Clinical Practice,"
         Proceedings of the Royal Society of Medicine, 50:
         651-54, 1957.

2313)   Parr, Denis and Swyer, G. I. M.   "Seminal Analysis
         in 22 Homosexuals," British Medical Journal, 2:
         1359-61, 1960.

2314)   Pascal, G. R. and Herzberg, F. C.   "The Detection
         of Deviant Sexual Practice from Performance on
         the Rorschach Test," Journal of Projective Tech-
         niques, 13:366-73, 1952.

2315)   Pasche, Francis.   "Symposium on Homosexuality,"
         International Journal of Psychoanalysis, 45:210-13,
         1964.

2316)   Pascoe, H.   "Deviant Sexual Behavior and the Sex
         Criminal," Canadian Medical Association Journal,
         84:206-11, 1961.

2317)   Paul, R.   "Problems of Psycho-Sexual Orientation,"
         Guy's Hospital Reports, 114:333-36, 1965.

2318)   Pauly, Ira B.   "Male Psychosexual Inversion:
         Transsexualism, A Review of 100 Cases," Archives
         of General Psychiatry, 13:172-81, 1965.

2319)   Payne, C. R.   "Some Freudian Contributions to the
         Paranoia Problem," Psychoanalysis and the Psycho-
         analytic Review, 1:76-93, 187-202, 308-21, 445-51,
         1913-14 and 2:93-101, 200-02, 1915.

2320)   Pearce, John D. W.   "Clinical Aspects of Psychia-
         tric Problems in the Army," Practitioner, 154:33-
         38, 1945.

2321)   Pearce, John D. W.   "Problems of Sex in the
         Services," Practitioner, 172:436-39, 1954.

2322)   Peck, J. S.   "Anti-Intellectualism: Psychoanalytic
         Notes on a Cultural Trait," American Imago, 20:
         385-91, 1963.

2323)   Peek, Roland M. and Storms, Lowell H.   "Validity
         of the Marsh-Hilliard-Liechti MMPI Sexual Devia-
         tion Scale in a State Hospital Population," Journal
         of Consulting Psychology, 20:133-36, 1956.

2324)   Perloff, William H.   "The Role of Hormones in
         Homosexuality," Journal of the Einstein Medical
         Center, 11:165-78, 1963.

2325)   Perloff, William H.   "The Role of Hormones in
         Human Sexuality," Psychosomatic Medicine, 11:133-
         39, 1949.

2326)   Pertinax.   "Without Prejudice," British Medical
         Journal, 1:1225, 1963.

2327)   Philip, H. L.   "Homosexuality," British Medical
         Journal, 1:550, 1946.

2328)   Philipp, E.   "Homosexuality as Seen in a New
         Zealand City Practice," New Zealand Medical Jour-
         nal, 67:397-401, 1968.

2329)   Piotrowski, Z. A.   "Inadequate Heterosexuality,"
         Psychiatric Quarterly, 41:360-65, 1967.

2330)   Planansky, Kabel and Johnston, Roy.   "The Inci-
         dence and Relationship of Homosexual and Paranoid
         Features in Schizophrenia," Journal of Mental Sci-
         ence, 108:604-10, 1962.

2331)   Podolsky, E.   "Several Aberrations of Sexual
         Emotion," Medical Press, 2:57-62, 1931.

2332)   Poe, John S.   "The Successful Treatment of a 40-
         Year Old Passive Homosexual Based on an Adapta-

tional View of Sexual Behavior," Psychoanalysis and
the Psychoanalytic Review, 39:23-33, 1952.

2333)   "Points from Parliament," British Medical Journal,
        1:621, 1966.

2334)   Pollock, C. B. R.   "Types of Male Homosexuals,"
        Medical Press, 235:197-201, 1956.

2335)   Polozker, I. L.   "Report of a Case of a Patient who
        Considers Himself a Hermaphrodite," Journal of
        Nervous and Mental Disease, 75:1-21, 1932.

2336)   Popkess, Athelstan.   "Some Criminal Aspects of
        Abnormalities of Sex," Practitioner, 172:446-50,
        1954.

2337)   Pottenger, F. M. Jr. and Simonsen, D. G.   "A
        Male Sex-Stimulating and Female Sex-Repressing
        Fraction from the Adrenal Gland," Endocrinology,
        22:197-202, 1938.

2338)   Praetorius, Numa.   "The Dispute about Walt Whit-
        man's Homosexuality," Zeitschrift für Sexual-Wis-
        senschaft, 3:326-39, 1916.   Translation by Helene
        Zahler.   (Reprinted in Ruitenbeek, no. 95 above,
        pp. 121-39.)

2339)   Praetorius, Numa.   "A Seventeenth Century Homo-
        sexual Poet: Saint-Pavin, the 'King of Sodom,' A
        Psychological Study," Zeitschrift für Sexual-Wis-
        senschaft, 5:261-71, 1918.   Translation by Helene
        Zahler.   (Reprinted in Ruitenbeek, no. 95 above,
        pp. 191-202.)

2340)   Primost, Norman.   "Homosexual Tendencies not
        Cruelty," Lancet, no. 7133:1068, 1960.

2341)   Prince, C. V.   "Homosexuality, Transvestism, and
        Transsexualism: Reflections on their Etiology and
        Differentiation," American Journal of Psychotherapy,
        11:80-85, 1957.   (Abstracted in Marriage and
        Family Living, 20:88-89, 1958.)

2342)   Prince, G. Stewart.   "The Therapeutic Function of
        Homosexual Transference," Journal of Analytic Psy-
        chology, 4:117-24, 1959.

2343) Prince, Morton. "Sexual Perversion or Vice? A Pathological and Therapeutic Inquiry," Journal of Nervous and Mental Disease, 25:237-56, 1898.

2344) Pritchard, Michael. "Homosexuality and Genetic Sex," Journal of Mental Science, 108:616-23, 1962.

2345) Pritchard, Michael and Graham, P. "An Investigation of a Group of Patients Who have Attended both the Child and Adult Department of the Same Psychiatric Hospital," British Journal of Psychiatry, 112:603-12, 1966.

2346) "Privilege Complaints Fail," British Medical Journal, 2:1626, 1955.

2347) "Psychiatric Treatment for Prisoners," Lancet, 256:632, 1949.

2348) "Psychopathology and Treatment of Sexual Deviation," British Medical Journal, 2:1303, 1960.

2349) Purpon, I., Jimenez, D., and Engelking, R. L. "Amebiasis of the Penis," Journal of Urology, 98:372-74, 1967.

2350) "Qualified Privilege of Medical Records," British Medical Journal, 2:596, 1961.

2351) "Queries and Minor Notes: Homosexuality," Journal of the American Medical Association, 128:1132, 1945.

2352) "Query: Endocrine Imbalance and Homosexuality," Practitioner, 178:254-55, 1957.

2353) "Query: Ethinyloestradiol in Homosexuality," Practitioner, 170:311-12, 1953.

2354) "Query: Latent Homosexuality," Practitioner, 167:559-60, 1951.

2355) "Questions and Answers: Homosexuality in Ex-Prisoners," Journal of the American Medical Association, 175:834, 1961.

2356) Rabinowitz, S. "Developmental Problems in Catholic

Seminarians," Psychiatry, 32:107-17, 1969.

2357)   Raboch, Jan and Nedoma, Karel. "Sex Chromatin
        and Sexual Behavior: A Study of 36 Men with
        Female Nuclear Pattern and of 194 Homosexuals,"
        Psychosomatic Medicine, 20:55-59, 1958.

2358)   Rachman, S. "Sexual Disorders and Behavior
        Therapy," American Journal of Psychiatry, 118:
        235-40, 1961.

2359)   Rado, Sandor. "A Critical Examination of the
        Concept of Bisexuality," Psychosomatic Medicine,
        2:459-67, 1940. (Reprinted in Marmor, no. 75
        above, pp. 175-89 [chap. 10].)

2360)   Rainer, J.D., Mesnikoff, A., Kolb, L.C., and
        Carr, A. "Homosexuality and Heterosexuality in
        Identical Twins," Psychosomatic Medicine, 22:251-
        60, 1960, with discussion by Franz J. Kallmann.

2361)   Ramsey, Glenn V. "The Sexual Development of
        Boys," American Journal of Psychology, 56:217-33,
        1943.

2362)   Ramsey, R.W. and VanVelzen, V. "Behaviour
        Therapy for Sexual Perversions," Behaviour Re-
        search and Therapy, 6:233, 1968.

2363)   Rancourt, Rejane and Limoges, Therese. "Homo-
        sexuality among Women," Canadian Nurse, 63:42-
        44, Dec. 1967.

2364)   Randell, J.B. "Transvestism and Transsexualism:
        A Study of 50 Cases," British Medical Journal, 2:
        1448-52, 1959.

2365)   Rapaport, Walter and Lieberman, Daniel. "The
        Sexual Psychopath in California," California Medi-
        cine, 85:232-34, 1956.

2366)   Rappaport, E.A. "A Case of Facultative Sexual
        Identity," University of Chicago Medical School
        Quarterly, 26:145-51, 1966.

2367)   Rashman, S. "Sexual Deviation and Behavior Thera-
        py," American Journal of Psychiatry, 118:235-40,
        1961.

2368)   Rasmussen, E. Wulff. "Experimental Homosexual
         Behavior in Male Albino Rats," Acta Psychologica,
         11:303-34, 1955.

2369)   "Rational Psychotherapy Cures One Homosexual,"
         Science News Letter, 74:230, 1958.

2370)   Raybin, James B. "Homosexual Incest," Journal of
         Nervous and Mental Disease, 148:105-09, 1969.

2371)   Read, C. S. "The Psycho-pathology of Alcoholism
         and Some so-called Alcoholic Psychoses," Journal
         of Mental Science, 66:233-44, 1920.

2372)   Rees, J. R. "Prognosis in the Sexual Neurosis,"
         Lancet, 228:948-49, 1935.

2373)   Rees, J. R. "The Unwilling Patient (Especially
         the Homosexual)," British Journal of Medical
         Psychology, 17:69-70, 1937.

2374)   Regardie, Francis I. "Analysis of a Homosexual,"
         Psychiatric Quarterly, 23:548-66, 1949.

2375)   Reider, Norman. "Problems of Homosexuality,"
         California Medicine, 86:381-84, 1957.

2376)   Reitzell, Jeanne M. "A Comparative Study of
         Hysterics, Homosexuals, and Alcoholics Using
         Content Analysis of Rorschach Responses," Ror-
         schach Research Exchange, 13:127-41, 1949. (See
         no. 258 above.)

2377)   "Report of the Departmental Committee on Homo-
         sexual Offences and Prostitution," British Medical
         Journal, 2:639-40, 1957.

2378)   "Research with Adolescents Sheds New Light on
         Early Lesbianism," Science News, 96:45, July 19,
         1969.

2379)   "Resurgence of Venereal Disease," Bulletin of the
         New York Academy of Medicine, 40:802-23, 1964.

2380)   Riggall, Robert M. "Homosexuality and Alcoholism,"
         Psychoanalysis and the Psychoanalytic Review, 10:
         157-69, 1923.

2381)   Robbins, Bernard S.   "Psychological Implication of
        the Male Homosexual 'Marriage,' " Psychoanalysis
        and the Psychoanalytic Review, 30:428-37, 1943.

2382)   Robertiello, R. C.   "Clinical Notes: Female Homo-
        sexual Panic," Psychoanalytic Review, 51:67-72,
        1964-65.

2383)   Robie, Theodore R.   "The Investigation of the
        Oedipus and Homosexual Complexes in Schizo-
        phrenia," Psychiatric Quarterly, 1:231-41, 1927.

2384)   Robie, Theodore R."The Oedipus and Homosexual
        Complexes in Schizophrenia," Psychiatric Quarterly,
        1:468-84, 1927.

2385)   Robinson, William J.   "An Essay on Sexual Inver-
        sion, Homosexuality, and Hermaphroditism," Medi-
        cal Critic and Guide, 25:247, 1923.

2386)   Robinson, William J.   "My Views on Homosexuality,"
        American Journal of Urology, 10:550-52, 1914.

2387)   Roheim, Geza.   "Ceremonial Prostitution in Duau,"
        Journal of Clinical Psychopathology, 7:753-64, 1946.

2388)   Roman, M.   "The Treatment of the Homosexual in
        Group Psychotherapy," Topical Problems in Psycho-
        therapy, 5:170-75, 1965.

2389)   Rood, Reginald S.   "Forensic Psychiatry and the
        State Hospital System," Journal of Social Therapy,
        4:257-62, 1956.

2390)   Rood, Reginald S.   "The Nonpsychotic Offender and
        the State Hospital," American Journal of Psychiatry,
        115:512-13, 1958.

2391)   Roper, Peter.   "The Effects of Hypnotherapy on
        Homosexuality," Canadian Medical Association
        Journal, 96:319-27, 1967.

2392)   Rosanoff, Aaron J.   "Human Sexuality, Normal and
        Abnormal, from a Psychiatric Standpoint," Urologic
        and Cutaneous Review, 33:523-30, 1929.

2393)   Rosanoff, Aaron J.   "A Theory of Chaotic Sexuality,"

American Journal of Psychiatry, 92:35-41, 1935.

2394)   Rosanoff, W. R. and Murphy, F. E. "The Basal
        Metabolic Rate, Fasting Blood Sugar, Glucose
        Tolerance, and Size of the Sella Tirica in Homo-
        sexuals," American Journal of Psychiatry, 101:
        97-99, 1944.

2395)   Rosenfeld, Herbert. "Remarks on the Relation of
        Male Homosexuality to Paranoia, Parnoid Anxiety,
        and Narcissism," International Journal of Psycho-
        analysis, 30:36-47, 1949.

2396)   Rosenzweig, Saul. "An Hypothesis regarding Cycles
        of Behavior in a Schizophrenic," Psychiatric Quar-
        terly, 16:463-68, 1942.

2397)   Rosenzweig, Saul and Hoskins, R. G. "A Note on
        the Ineffectualness of Sex-hormone Medication in a
        Case of Pronounced Homosexuality," Psychosomatic
        Medicine, 3:87-89, 1941.

2398)   Ross, Mathew and Mendelsohn, Fred. "Homosexuality
        in College: A Preliminary Report of the Data Ob-
        tained from 133 Students Seen in a University Student
        Health Center and Review of Pertinent Literature,"
        Archives of Neurology and Psychiatry, 80:253-63,
        1958.

2399)   Ross, Robert T. "Measures of the Sex Behavior of
        College Males Compared with Kinsey's Results,"
        Journal of Abnormal and Social Psychology, 45:753-
        55, 1950.

2400)   Ross, T. A. "A Note on 'The Merchant of Venice,' "
        British Journal of Medical Psychology, 14:303-11,
        1934.

2401)   Rottersman, W. "Homosexuality," Journal of the
        Medical Association of Georgia, 50:245-46, 1961.

2402)   Rowe, W. S. "The Treatment of Homosexuality and
        Associated Perversions by Psychotherapy and Aver-
        sion Therapy," Medical Journal of Australia, 54:
        637-39, 1967.

2403)   Rubins, Jack L. "The Neurotic Personality and

Certain Sexual Perversions," Contemporary Psychoanalysis, 4:53-72 at 67-68, 1967.

2404)   Rubinstein, L. H.   "Psychotherapeutic Aspects of
        Male Homosexuality," British Journal of Medical
        Psychology, 31:14-18, 1958.

2405)   Rudolf, G. deM.   "The Experimental Effect of
        Sex-Hormone Therapy upon Anxiety in Homosexual
        Types," British Journal of Medical Psychology, 18:
        317-22, 1941.

2406)   Rudolf, G. deM.   "Sex Perversion in Fighting
        Services and Isolated Stations," British Journal of
        Medical Psychology, 21:127-34, 1948.

2407)   Ruskin, Samuel H.   "Analysis of Sex Offenses
        among Male Psychiatric Patients," American Jour-
        nal of Psychiatry, 97:955-68, 1941.

2408)   Saghir, M. T. and Robins, E.   "Homosexuality: I.
        Sexual Behavior of the Female Homosexual," Ar-
        chives of General Psychiatry, 20:192-201, 1969.

2409)   Saghir, M. T., Robins, E., and Walbran, B.
        "Homosexuality: II. Sexual Behavior of the Male
        Homosexual," Archives of General Psychiatry, 21:
        219-29, 1969.

2410)   Salzman, Leon.   "The Concept of Latent Homo-
        sexuality," American Journal of Psychoanalysis,
        17:161-69, 1957.

2411)   Salzman, Leon.   "Paranoid State, Theory, and
        Therapy," Archives of General Psychiatry, 2:679-
        93, 1960.

2412)   Samuels, A. S.   "Use of Group Balance as a
        Therapeutic Technique," Archives of General Psy-
        chiatry, 11:411-20, 1964.

2413)   Sappenfield, B. R.   "A Proposed Heterosexual
        Theory of Delusions," Psychological Reports, 16:
        84-86, 1965.

2414)   Saul, Leon J. and Beck, Aaron T.   "Psychody-
        namics of Male Homosexuality," International Journal

of Psychoanalysis, 42:43-48, 1961.

2415)   Savalle, H. J. "Some Psychodynamic Aspects of a
         Case of Spontaneous Pairing (Couple Formation),"
         Topical Problems of Psychotherapy, 4:212-18, 1963.

2416)   Sawyer, G. I. M. "Homosexuality: the Endocrino-
         logical Aspects," Practitioner, 172:374-77, 1957.

2417)   Schamberg, I. L. "Syphilis and Sisyphus," British
         Journal of Venereal Diseases, 39:87-97, 1963.

2418)   Schilder, Paul. "On Homosexuality," Psychoanaly-
         sis and the Psychoanalytic Review, 16:377-89, 1929.
         (Reprinted in Krich, no. 69 above, pp. 201-14.)

2419)   Schilder, Paul. "The Psychogenesis of Alcoholism,"
         Quarterly Journal of Studies on Alcoholism, 2:277-
         92, 1941.

2420)   Schmideberg, Melitta. "A Note on Homosexuality
         and Circumcision," Psychoanalysis and the Psycho-
         analytic Review, 35:183-84, 1948.

2421)   Schmidt, E. and Brown, P. "Experimental Testing
         of Two Psychoanalytic Hypotheses," British Journal
         of Medical Psychology, 38:177-80, 1965.

2422)   Schmidt, E., Castell, D., and Brown, P. "A
         Retrospective Study of 42 Cases of Behaviour
         Therapy," Behaviour Research and Therapy, 3:91-9,
         1965.

2423)   Schmidt, H., Hauge, L., and Schonning, L. "In-
         cidence of Homosexuals among Syphilitics," British
         Journal of Venereal Diseases, 39:264-65, 1963.

2424)   Schneck, Jerome M. "Notes on the Homosexual
         Component of the Hypnotic Transference," British
         Journal of Medical Hypnosis, 1:24-26, 1950.

2425)   Schneck, Jerome M. "Sleep Paralysis: Psycho-
         dynamics," Psychiatric Quarterly, 22:462-69, 1948.

2426)   Schneck, Jerome M. "Some Aspects of Homosex-
         uality in Relation to Hypnosis," Psychoanalysis and
         the Psychoanalytic Review, 37:351-57, 1950.

2427)   Schockley, Francis M.   "The Role of Homosexuality
         in the Genesis of Paranoid Conditions," Psycho-
         analysis and the Psychoanalytic Review, 1:431-38,
         1913-14.

2428)   Schofield, Michael.   "Social Aspects of Homosex-
         uals," British Journal of Venereal Diseases, 40:
         129-34, 1964.

2429)   Schreiber, Flora R.   "Homosexual Men and
         Women: How They Get that Way and How They
         can be Treated," Science Digest, 55:55-65, Apr.
         1964.

2430)   Schufeldt, R. W.   "Biography of a Passive Peder-
         ast," American Journal of Urology and Sexology,
         13:451-60, 1917.

2431)   Schwarz, Hedwig.   "A Case of Character Dis-
         order," Bulletin of the Menninger Clinic, 16:20-30,
         1952.

2432)   Scott, Edward M.   "Psychosexuality of the Alco-
         holic," Psychological Reports, 4:599-602, 1958.

2433)   Scott, Peter D.   "Homosexuality with Special
         Reference to Classification," Proceedings of the
         Royal Society of Medicine, 50:655-60, 1957, with
         comment by T. C. N. Gibbens.

2434)   Scott, T. R. , Wells, W. H. , Wood, D. Z. , and
         Morgan, D. I.   "Pupillary Response and Sexual In-
         terest Reexamined," Journal of Clinical Psychology,
         23:433-38, 1967.

2435)   Sechrist, Lee and Flores, Luis.   "Homosexuality
         in the Philippines and the United States: the Hand-
         writing on the Wall," Journal of Social Psychology,
         79:3-12, 1969.

2436)   Segal, M. M.   "Transvestitism as an Impulse and
         as a Defense," International Journal of Psycho-
         analysis, 46:209-17, 1965.

2437)   Segard, C. P.   "Male Sexual Relationships; Devia-
         tions from Normal," Postgraduate Medicine, 7:36-
         39, 1950.

2438)   Seidenberg, R.   "A Note on the Theory of Homo-
        sexuality: The Body as Object," Journal of Nervous
        and Mental Disease, 128:179-81, 1959.

2439)   Selling, Lowell S.   "The Results of Therapy in
        Cases of Sex Deviation," Journal of Criminal
        Psychopathology, 3:477-93, 1942.

2440)   Serban, George.   "The Existential Therapeutic Ap-
        proach to Homosexuality," American Journal of
        Psychotherapy, 22:491-501, 1968.

2441)   Severinghaus, E. L. and Chornyak, John.   "A
        Study of Homosexual Adult Males," Psychosomatic
        Medicine, 7:302-05, 1945.

2442)   Seward, G. H. , Bloch, S. K. , and Heinrich, J. F.
        "The Question of Psychophysiologic Infertility:
        Some Negative Answers," Psychosomatic Medicine,
        29:151-52, 1967.

2443)   "Sex Life in Prison," Journal of the American
        Medical Association, 138:298, 1948.

2444)   "Sexual Aberration," British Medical Journal, 1:
        974, 1961.

2445)   "Sexual Abnormality and the Law," Lancet, 253:
        661, 1947.

2446)   "Sexual Deviation," Lancet, no. 7156:922-24, 1960.

2447)   "Sexual Deviations," Medical Press, 216:257-58,
        1946.

2448)   "Sexual Offences," British Medical Journal, 2:1328,
        1953.

2449)   "Sexual Offences," Lancet, 261:221, 1951.

2450)   "Sexual Offences," Lancet, 265:1269-70, 1953.

2451)   "Sexual Offences," Lancet, 273:843, 1957.

2452)   "Sexual Offenders," Lancet, 256:449, 1949.

2453)   "Sexual Pervert Probe," Science News Letter, 58:
        5, July 1, 1950.

2454)   "Sexual Promiscuity," British Medical Journal,
        1:1308, 1963.

2455)   Shaskan, Donald. "100 Sex Offenders," American
        Journal of Orthpsychiatry, 9:565-69, 1939.

2456)   Shearer, M. "Homosexuality and the Pediatrician;
        Early Recognition and Preventive Counselling,"
        Clinical Pediatrician, 5:514-18, 1966. (Abstracted
        in Psychiatry Digest, 28:14, Mar. 1967.)

2457)   Sheppe, William M. "The Problem of Homosexuality
        in the Armed Forces," Medical Aspects of Human
        Sexuality, 3:65, 69-88, Oct. 1969.

2458)   Sherman, Irene C. and Sherman, Mandel. "The
        Factor of Parental Attachment in Homosexuality,"
        Psychoanalysis and the Psychoanalytic Review, 13:
        32-37, 1926.

2459)   Sherwin, Robert V. "Sex Expression and Law. II:
        Sodomy;   A Medico-Legal Enigma," International
        Journal of Sexology, 5:10-13, 1951.

2460)   Sherwin, Robert V. "Some Legal Aspects of Homo-
        sexuality," International Journal of Sexology, 4:22-
        26, 1950.

2461)   Shneidman, Edwin S. "The Case of El: Psycho-
        logical Test Data," Journal of Projective Tech-
        niques, 25:131-54, 1961.

2462)   Shneidman, Edwin S. "The Logic of El: A Psycho-
        Logical Approach to the Analysis of Test Data,"
        Journal of Projective Techniques, 25:390-403, 1961.

2463)   Siegal, Lewis J. "Homosexuality--Psychothera-
        peutic Approach to Its Criminologic Challenge,"
        Group Psychotherapy, 8:321-26, 1955.

2464)   Silber, A. "Object Choice in a Case of Male
        Homosexuality," Psychoanalytic Quarterly, 30:497-
        503, 1961.

2465)   Silverberg, William V. "The Personal Basis and
        Social Significance of Passive Male Homosexuality,"
        Psychiatry, 1:41-53, 1938.

2466)   Silverman, Daniel and Rosanoff, William B.
        "Electroencephalographic and Neurologic Studies
        of Homosexuals," Journal of Nervous and Mental
        Disease, 101:311-21, 1945.

2467)   Simon, Robert I. "A Case of Female Transsex-
        ualism," American Journal of Psychiatry, 123:
        1598-1601, 1967.

2468)   Singer, M. and Fischer, R. "Group Psychotherapy
        of Male Homosexuals by a Male and Female Co-
        Therapy Team," International Journal of Group
        Psychotherapy, 17:44-52, 1967.

2469)   Sipprelle, Carl N. and Swenson, Clifford H. "Re-
        lationship of Sexual Adjustment to Certain Sexual
        Characteristics of Human Figure Drawings, Jour-
        nal of Consulting Psychology, 20:197-98, 1956.

2470)   Sjostedt, Elsie M. and Hurwitz, Irving. "A De-
        velopmental Study of Sexual Functioning by Means
        of a Cognitive Analysis," Journal of Projective
        Techniques, 23:237-46, 1959.

2471)   Slater, Eliot. "Birth Order and Maternal Age of
        Homosexuals," Lancet, no. 7220:69-71, 1962.

2472)   Slater, Eliot. "A Demographic Study of a Psycho-
        pathic Population," Annals of Eugenics, 12:121-37,
        1944.

2473)   Slater, Eliot and Slater, Patrick. "A Study in the
        Assessment of Homosexual Traits," British Journal
        of Medical Psychology, 21:61-74, 1947.

2474)   Slavson, S. R. "Criteria for Selection and Rejection
        of Patients for Various Types of Group Therapy,"
        International Journal of Group Psychotherapy, 5:3-
        30, 1955.

2475)   Slochower, Harry. "Thomas Mann's 'Death in
        Venice,' " American Imago, 26:99-122, 1969.

2476)   Smalldon, John L. "The Etiology of Chronic Al-
        coholism," Psychiatric Quarterly, 4:640-61 at 647,
        1933.

2477)   Smith, Alexander B. and Bassin, Alexander.
         "Group Therapy with Homosexuals," Journal of
         Social Therapy, 5:225-32, 1959.

2478)   Smith, A. P. Jr.   "Pseudohomosexual Anxiety,"
         Journal of the National Medical Association, 50:
         201-06, 1958.

2479)   Smith, Charles E.   "Prison Pornography," Journal
         of Social Therapy, 1:126-28, 1955.

2480)   Smith, Charles E.   "Some Problems in Dealing
         with Homosexuals in the Prison Situation," Journal
         of Social Therapy, 2:37-45, 1956.

2481)   Smith, Durand.   "Infectious Syphilis of the Anal
         Canal," Diseases of the Colon and Rectum, 6:7-
         14, 1963.

2482)   Smith, Durand.   "Infectious Syphilis of the Anal
         Canal," Modern Medicine, 31:141, 1963.

2483)   Smith, Groves B.   "The Law and Morals," Cor-
         rective Psychiatry and Journal of Social Therapy,
         12:315-22, 1966.

2484)   Smitt, Jarl W.   "Homosexuality in a New Light,"
         International Journal of Sexology, 6:36-39, 1952.

2485)   Socarides, Charles W.   "The Historical Develop-
         ment of Theoretical and Clinical Concepts of Overt
         Female Homosexuality," Journal of the American
         Psychoanalytic Association, 11:386-414, 1963.

2486)   Socarides, Charles W.   "A Provisional Theory of
         Aetiology in Male Homosexuality: A Case of Pre-
         Oedipal Origin," International Journal of Psycho-
         analysis, 49:27-37, 1968.   (Abstracted in Psy-
         chiatry Digest, 30:33, Jan. 1969.)

2487)   Socarides, Charles W.   "Psychoanalytic Therapy
         of a Male Homosexual," Psychoanalytic Quarterly,
         38:173-90, 1969.

2488)   Socarides, Charles W.   "Theoretical and Clinical
         Aspects of Overt Female Homosexuality," Journal
         of the American Psychoanalytic Association, 10:
         579-92, 1962.

2489)   Socarides, Charles W. "Theoretical and Clinical
        Aspects of Overt Male Homosexuality," Journal of
        the American Psychoanalytic Association, 8:552-66,
        1960.

2490)   "The Social Problem of Homosexuality," Medical
        Press, 218:203-04, 1947.

2491)   Soddy, Kenneth. "Homosexuality," Lancet, 266:541-
        46, 1954.

2492)   Soddy, Kenneth. "Not Yet ... ?" Lancet, no. 7143:
        197-99, 1960.

2493)   Solyom, L. and Miller, S. "A Differential Condi-
        tioning Procedure as the Initial Phase of Behaviour
        Therapy of Homosexuality," Behaviour Research
        and Therapy, 3:147-60, 1965.

2494)   Sonenschein, David. "The Ethnography of Male
        Homosexual Relationships," Journal of Sex Re-
        search, 4:69-83, 1968.

2495)   Spencer, S. J. G. "Homosexuality among Oxford
        Undergraduates," Journal of Mental Science, 105:
        393-405, 1959. (Abstracted in Medico-Legal Jour-
        nal, 28:52-53, 1960.)

2496)   Speyer, N. and Stokis, B. "The Psycho-Analytical
        Factor in Hypnosis," British Journal of Medical
        Psychology, 17:217-22, 1938.

2497)   Spiegel, Leo A. "Comments on the Psychoanalytic
        Psychology of Adolescence," Psychoanalytic Study
        of the Child, 13:296-308, 1958.

2498)   Sprague, George S. "Varieties of Homosexual
        Manifestation," American Journal of Psychiatry,
        92:143-54, 1935, with discussion by Karl Men-
        ninger, Isador Coriat, Charles Lambert, Ernest
        Poate, and S. W. Hartwell. (Reprinted in Krich,
        no. 69 above, pp. 174-87.)

2499)   Sprince, Marjorie P. "A Contribution to the Study
        of Homosexuality in Adolescence," Journal of Child
        Psychology and Psychiatry and Allied Disciplines,
        5:103-17, 1964.

2500)   Srnec, J. and Freund, Kurt. "Treatment of Male
         Homosexuality through Conditioning," International
         Journal of Sexology, 7:92-93, 1953.

2501)   Stafford-Clark, David. "Homosexuality," Medico-
         Legal and Criminological Review, 25:65-81, 1957.

2502)   Stafford-Clark, David. "The Medico-Legal Prob-
         lem of Homosexuality," Medical Press, 218:220-22,
         1947.

2503)   Stanley-Jones, D. "Homosexuality and Prostitution:
         Progress and Reaction," Medical Press, 235:318-
         24, 1956.

2504)   Stanley-Jones, D. "Justice and the Homosexual,"
         Medical Press, 229:7-9, 1953.

2505)   Stanley-Jones, D. "Sexual Inversion: An Ethical
         Study," Lancet, 252:366-69, 1947.

2506)   Stanley-Jones, D. "Sexual Inversion and the
         English Law: A Study in the History of Culture,"
         Medical Press, 215:391-98, 1946.

2507)   Stanley-Jones, D. "Sexual Inversion: the Prob-
         lem of Treatment," Medical Press, 218:212-15,
         1947.

2508)   Stanley-Jones, D. "The Study of Homosexuality,"
         Medical Press, 221:32-38, 1949.

2509)   Stekel, Hilda. "Short-term Psychotherapy of a
         Case of Conversion Hysteria," American Journal
         of Psychotherapy, 7:302-09, 1953.

2510)   Stekel, Wilhelm. "Is Homosexuality Curable?"
         Psychoanalysis and the Psychoanalytic Review, 17:
         443-51, 1930.

2511)   Stevenson, Ian and Wolpe, Joseph. "Recovery
         from Sexual Deviations through Overcoming non-
         sexual Neurotic Responses," American Journal of
         Psychiatry, 116:737-42, 1960.

2512)   Stokes, R. E. "Sexual Deviation and Venereal Dis-
         ease; A Report from the Forensic Clinic, Toronto,"
         Medical Digest, 31:93-98, 1963.

2513)   Stoller, Alan. "Sexual Deviation in the Male,"
        Medical Press, 216:262-68, 1946.

2514)   Stone, Calvin P. "Physiological Psychology,"
        Annual Review of Physiology, 7:623-52, 1945.

2515)   Stone, Mayer B. "Homosexuality in a Borderline
        Mental Defective: Rehabilitation through Hypnosis
        and Re-education," Pennsylvania Psychiatric Quar-
        terly, 4:42-53, 1964.

2516)   Stone, Walter N.: Schergber, John; and Seifried,
        Stanley, F. "The Treatment of a Homosexual Woman
        in a Mixed Group," International Journal of Group
        Psychotherapy, 16:425-33, 1966.

2517)   Storr, A. "The Psychopathology of Fetishism and
        Transvestitism," Journal of Analytic Psychology,
        21:153-66, 1957.

2518)   Strzyzewsky, Janusz and Zierhoffer, Marion.
        "Aversion Therapy in a Case of Fetishism with
        Transvestistic Component," Journal of Sex Re-
        search, 3:163-67, 1967.

2519)   "Study Homosexual Pattern," Science News Letter,
        73:390, 1958.

2520)   Stumper, E. "The Modified Szondi Test in Male
        Homosexuality," International Journal of Sexology,
        8:228-29, 1955.

2521)   Stürup, Georg K. "The Management and Treat-
        ment of Psychopaths in a Special Institution in
        Denmark," Proceedings of the Royal Society of
        Medicine, 41:765-68, 1948.

2522)   Stürup, Georg K. "A Psychiatric Establishment
        for Investigation, Training, and Treatment of
        Psychologically Abnormal Criminals," Acta Psy-
        chiatrica et Neurologica Scandinavica, 21:781-93,
        1946.

2523)   Sulzberger, C. F. "An Undiscovered Source of
        Heterosexual Disturbance," Psychoanalytic Review,
        42:435-37, 1955.

2524)   Swenson, Clifford H.   "Sexual Behavior and Psycho-
        pathology: A Study of College Men," Journal of
        Clinical Psychology, 19:403-04, 1963.

2525)   Swenson, Clifford H.   "Sexual Differentiation in the
        Draw-A-Person Test," Journal of Clinical Psy-
        chology, 11:37-40, 1955.

2526)   Swenson, Clifford H. and Newton, Kenneth P.
        "The Development of Sexual Differentiation on the
        Draw-A-Person Picture Test," Journal of Clinical
        Psychology, 11:417-19, 1955.

2527)   Swyer, G. I. M.   "Homosexuality: the Endocrino-
        logical Aspects," Practitioner, 172:374-77, 1954.

2528)   "Syphilis and Homosexuality," Journal of the Medi-
        cal Society of New Jersey, 59:578, 1962.

2529)   Szasz, Thomas S.   "The Psychology of Bodily
        Feelings in Schizophrenia," Psychosomatic Medi-
        cine, 19:11-16, 1957.

2530)   Tappan, Paul W.   "Treatment of the Sex Offender
        in Denmark," American Journal of Psychiatry,
        108:241-49, 1951.

2531)   Tarbox, Raymond.   " 'Death in Venice': The
        Aesthetic Object as Dream Guide," American
        Imago, 26:123-44, 1969.

2532)   Tarr, John D. F.   "The Male Homosexual and
        Venereal Disease," GP [General Practice], 25:91-
        97, June 1962.

2533)   Tarr, John D. F. and Lugar, Robert L.   "Early
        Infectious Syphilis: Male Homosexual Relations as
        Mode of Spread," California Medicine, 93:35-37,
        1960.

2534)   Taylor, A. J. W. and McLachlan, D. G.   "Clinical
        and Psychological Observations on Transvestism,"
        New Zealand Medical Journal, 61:496-506, 1962.

2535)   Taylor, A. J. W. and McLachlan, D. G.   "Further
        Observations and Comments on Transvestism," New
        Zealand Medical Journal, 62:527-29, 1963.

2536)   Taylor, A. J. W. and McLachlan, D. G.   "MMPI
        Profiles of Six Transvestites," Journal of Clinical
        Psychology, 19:330-32, 1963.

2537)   Taylor, F. H.   "Homosexual Offences and their
        Relation to Psychotherapy," British Medical Journal,
        2:525-29, 1947.   (Abstracted in Medico-Legal and
        Criminological Review, 16:80-81, 1948.)

2438)   Taylor, F. Kraüpl.   "Experimental Investigation of
        Collective Social and Libidinal Motivations in Thera-
        peutic Groups," British Journal of Medical Psychol-
        ogy, 22:169-82, 1949.

2539)   Taylor, F. Kraüpl.   "Homosexuality," British
        Journal of Psychiatry, 111:196-97 and 548-49, 1965.

2540)   "The Theater and the Homosexual," Journal of the
        American Medical Association, 198:1027-28, 1966.

2541)   Thomas, E. W.   "Syphilis: the New Epidemic,"
        Illinois Medical Journal, 124:436-39, 1963.

2542)   Thompson, Clara.   "Changing Concepts of Homo-
        sexuality in Psychoanalysis," Psychiatry, 10:183-
        89, 1947.   (Reprinted in Maurice R. Green [ed.],
        Interpersonal Psychoanalysis: The Selected Papers
        of Clara Thompson [New York: Basic Books,
        1964], pp. 3-12 [chap. 1]; in Patrick Mullahy
        [ed.], A Study of Interpersonal Relations [New
        York: Hermitage Press, 1949], pp. 211-22; in
        Ruitenbeek, no. 96 above, pp. 40-51; and in
        Krich, no. 69 above, pp. 251-61.)

2543)   Thompson, George N.   "Electroshock and Other
        Therapeutic Considerations in Sexual Psychopathy,"
        Journal of Nervous and Mental Disease, 109:531-
        39, 1949.

2544)   Thomson, P. G.   "Forensic Clinic at Toronto,"
        Journal of Social Therapy, 4:96-103, 1958.

2545)   Thomson, P. G.   "Vicissitudes of the Transference
        in a Male Homosexual," International Journal of
        Psychoanalysis, 49:629-39, 1968.

2546)   Thorne, Frederick C.   "A Factorial Study of

Sexuality in Males," Journal of Clinical Psychology, Monograph Supplement No. 21, pp. 14-22, 1966.

2547)   Thorne, Frederick C. and Haupt, Thomas D. "The Objective Measurement of Sex Attitudes and Behavior in Adult Males," Journal of Clinical Psychology, Monograph Supplement No. 21, pp. 31-39, 1966.

2548)   Thorner, H. A. "Notes on a Case of Male Homosexuality," International Journal of Psychoanalysis, 30:31-35, 1949.

2549)   Thornton, Nathaniel. "Some Mechanisms of Paranoia," Psychoanalysis and the Psychoanalytic Review, 35:290-94, 1948.

2550)   Thorpe, J. G. and Schmidt, E. "Therapeutic Failure in a Case of Aversion Therapy," Behavior Research and Therapy, 1:293-96, 1963.

2551)   Thorpe, J. G., Schmidt, E., Brown, P. T., and Castell, D. "Aversion-Relief Therapy: A New Method for General Application," Behaviour Research and Therapy, 2:71-82, 1964.

2552)   Thorpe, J. G., Schmidt, E., and Castell, D. "A Comparison of Positive and Negative (Aversive) Conditioning in the Treatment of Homosexuality," Behaviour Research and Therapy, 1:357-62, 1963.

2553)   Timm, Oreon K. "Psychodynamics of Alcoholism and Its Relation to Therapy," Medical Bulletin, 20:42-48, 1943.

2554)   Tong, J. E. "Galvanic Skin Response Studies of Sex Responsiveness in Sex Offenders and Others," Journal of Mental Science, 106:1475-85, 1960.

2555)   "Transvestism," British Medical Journal, 2:1186, 1963.

2556)   "Treatment for Homosexuality," British Medical Journal, 1:300, 1946.

2557)   "Treatment for Homosexual Tendencies," British Medical Journal, 1:1234, 1953.

2558)   "Treatment of Homosexuality," British Medical
         Journal, 2:1347, 1958.

2559)   Trice, E. R. "Homosexual Transmission of Vene-
         real Disease," Medical Times, 85:1286-88, 1960.

2560)   Trice, E. R. and Clark, F. A. Jr. "Transmission
         of Venereal Disease through Homosexual Practices,"
         Southern Medical Journal, 54:76-79, 1961.

2561)   Trice, E. R., Gayle, S. Jr., and Clark, F. A. Jr.
         "The Transmission of Early Infectious Syphilis
         through Homosexual Practice," Virginia Medical
         Monthly, 87:132-34, 1960.

2562)   Tufo, G. F. "The Genesis of Homosexuality,"
         Journal of the American Institute of Homeophathy,
         57:33-34, Apr. 1964.

2563)   Turner, R. E. "The Sexual Offender," Canadian
         Psychiatric Association Journal, 9:533-40, 1964.

2564)   "Two Valuable Pamphlets," Lancet, 272:845, 1957.

2565)   Ujhely, Valentine A. "An Unusual Case of Reni-
         fleurism," American Journal of Psychotherapy, 7:
         68-71, 1953.

2566)   VandenBergh, R. L. and Kelly, J. F. "Vampirism:
         a Review with New Observations," Archives of
         General Psychiatry, 11:543-47, 1964.

2567)   Velikovsky, I. "Tolstoy's 'Kreutzer Sonata' and
         Unconscious Homosexuality," Psychoanalysis and
         the Psychoanalytic Review, 24:18-25, 1937.

2568)   "Venereal Disease," British Medical Journal Sup-
         plement, 2:261, 1960.

2569)   Vilhotti, A. J. "An Investigation of the Use of the
         D. A. P. in the Diagnosis of Homosexuality in
         Mentally Deficient Males," American Journal of
         Mental Deficiency, 62:708-11, 1958.

2570)   Waggoner, R. W. and Boyd. D. A. Jr. "Juvenile
         Aberrant Sexual Behavior," American Journal of
         Orthopsychiatry, 11:275-92, 1941.

2571)   Wagner, Edwin W. "Hand Test Content Indicators
         of Overt Psychosexual Maladjustment in Neurotic
         Males," Journal of Projective Techniques, 27:357-
         58, 1963.

2572)   Waldhorn, H. W. "Clinical Observations on the
         Treatment of Manifest Male Homosexuality," Psycho-
         analytic Quarterly, 20:337-38, 1951. (Digest of no.
         1843 above.)

2573)   Walker, Edward L. "The Terman-Miles 'M-F'
         Test and the Prison Classification Program," Jour-
         nal of Genetic Psychology, 59:27-40, 1941.

2574)   Walker, Kenneth. "Priest and Physician on Homo-
         sexuality," British Medical Journal, 2:892, 1955.

2575)   Walker, W. H. "Homosexuality: Current Concepts
         and Attitudes," Rocky Mountain Medical Journal,
         66:42-43, 1969.

2576)   Walters, O. S. "A Methodological Critique of
         Freud's Schreber Analysis," Psychoanalytic Review,
         42:321-42, 1955.

2577)   Ward, Jack L. "Homosexual Behavior of the In-
         stitutionalized Delinquent," Psychiatric Quarterly
         Supplement, 32:301-14, 1958.

2578)   Wasserman, S. "Casework Treatment of a Homo-
         sexual Acting-out Adolescent in a Treatment Center,"
         Mental Hygiene, 44:18-29, 1960.

2579)   Watson, C. G. "A Test of the Relationship between
         Repressed Homosexuality and Paranoid Mechanisms,"
         Journal of Clinical Psychology, 21:380-84, 1965.

2580)   Wattron, John B. "Validity of the Marsh-Hilliard-
         Liechti MMPI Sexual Deviation Scale in a State
         Prison Population," Journal of Consulting Psy-
         chology, 22:16, 1958.

2581)   Watts, Virginia N. "The Effect of Therapy on the
         Creativity of a Writer," American Journal of Ortho-
         psychiatry, 32:186-92, 1962.

2582)   Wayne, D. M., Adams, M., and Rowe, L. A. "A

Medical/Scientific Articles   227

Study of Military Prisoners at a Disciplinary Bar-
racks Suspected of Homosexual Activities," Military
Surgeon, 107:499-504, 1947.

2583)   Weijl, Simon. "Theoretical and Practical Aspects of
Psychoanalytic Therapy of Problem Drinkers," Quarterly Journal of Studies on Alcohol, 5:200-11, 1944.

2584)   Weiss, Isidore I. "Homosexuality with Special
Reference to Military Prisoners," Psychiatric
Quarterly, 20:485-523, 1946. (Abstracted in Jour-
nal of Clinical Psychopathology, 9:161-62, 1948.)

2585)   Weissman, Philip. "Structural Considerations in
Overt Male Bisexuality," International Journal of
Psychoanalysis, 43:159-68, 1962. (Abstracted in
Psychiatry Digest, 25:14-15, Feb. 1964.)

2586)   Wellman, M. "Overt Homosexuality with Spontane-
ous Remission," Canadian Medical Association Journal, 75:273-79, 1956.

2587)   Wells, B. T., Kierland, R. R., and Jackman, R. J.
"Rectal Chancre: Report of a Case," Archives of
Dermatology, 79:719-21, 1959.

2588)   West, Donald J. "Parental Figures in the Genesis
of Male Homosexuality," International Journal of
Social Psychiatry, 5:85-97, 1959.

2589)   West, L. J., Doidge, W. T., and Williams, R. L.
"An Approach to the Problem of Homosexuality in
the Military Service," American Journal of Psychiatry, 115:392-401, 1958.

2590)   Westphal, Robert S. "Report of an Outbreak of
Gonorrhea at a Boys' School," New York State
Journal of Medicine, 44:493-96, 1944.

2591)   Wheeler, William M. "An Analysis of Rorschach
Indices of Male Homosexuality," Rorschach Research Exchanges, 13:97-126, 1949. (See no. 263
above.)

2592)   Whitaker, L. Jr. "The Use of Extended Draw-A-
Person Test to Identify Homosexual and Effeminate
Men," Journal of Consulting Psychology, 25:482-
85, 1961.

2593)   Whitener, R. W. and Nikelly, Arthur. "Sexual
        Deviation in College Students," American Journal
        of Orthopsychiatry, 34:386-92, 1964.

2594)   Wiedeman, George H. "Survey of Psychoanalytic
        Literature on Overt Male Homosexuality," Journal
        of the American Psychoanalytic Association, 10:
        386-409, 1962.

2595)   Wiedeman, George H. "Symposium on Homosex-
        uality: Some Remarks on the Aetiology of Homo-
        sexuality," International Journal of Psychoanalysis,
        45:214-16, 1964.

2596)   Wiens, A. N., Matarazzo, J. D., and Gaver, K. D.
        "Performance and Verbal IQ in a Group of Socio-
        paths," Journal of Clinical Psychology, 15:191-93,
        1959.

2597)   Wile, Ira S. "Sex Offenders and Sex Offenses;
        Classification and Treatment," Journal of Criminal
        Psychopathology, 3:11-32, 1941.

2598)   Wile, U. J. and Holman, H. H. "A Survey of 68
        Cases of Extragenital Chancres," American Journal
        of Syphilis, Gonorrhea, and Venereal Disease, 25:
        58-66, 1941.

2599)   Willcox, R. R. "Immigration and Venereal Disease
        in Great Britain," British Journal of Venereal Dis-
        eases, 42:225-37, 1966.

2600)   Williams, Edwin G. "Homosexuality: A Biological
        Anomaly," Journal of Nervous and Mental Disease,
        99, 65-73, 1944.

2601)   Willis, S. E. "Understanding and Counseling the
        Male Homosexual," International Psychiatry Clinics,
        4:3-225, 1967. (See no. 124 above.)

2602)   Winner, Albertine L. "Homosexuality in Women,"
        Medical Press, 218:219-20, 1947.

2603)   "Winter Talks," British Medical Journal, 1:67,
        1964.

2604)   Winterstein, Alfred. "On the Oral Basis of a Case

of Male Homosexuality," International Journal of
Psychoanalysis, 37:298-302, 1956.

2605)   Winterstein, Lambert E.   "Observations on Homosexuals," Bulletin de la Faculté de Medicine de
Istanbul, 12:216-20, 1949.

2606)   Witschi, Emil and Mengert, William F.   "Endocrine
Studies on Human Hermaphrodites and Their Bearing
on the Interpretation of Homosexuality," Journal of
Clinical Endocrinology, 2:279-86, 1942.

2607)   Wittels, Fritz.   "Collective Defense Mechanisms
against Homosexuality," Psychoanalysis and the
Psychoanalytic Review, 31:19-33, 1944.

2608)   Wittels, Frtiz.   "Heinrich Von Kleist--Prussian
Junker and Creative Genius: A Study in Bisexuality,"
American Imago, 11:11-31, 1954.

2609)   Wittels, Fritz.   "The Libidinous Structure of the
Criminal Psychopath," Journal of Criminal Psychopathology, 1:363-65, 1940.

2610)   Wittels, Fritz.   "Psychoanalysis and History--The
Nibelungs and the Bible," Psychoanalytic Quarterly,
15:88-103, 1946.

2611)   Wittels, Fritz.   "Struggles of a Homosexual in Pre-
Hitler Germany," Journal of Criminal Psychopathology, 4:408-23, 1943.

2612)   Wittenberg, Rudolph.   "Lesbianism as a Transitory
Solution of the Ego," Psychoanalytic Review, 43:
348-57, 1956.

2613)   Wohl, R. R. and Trosman, H.   "A Retrospect of
Freud's 'Leonardo,' " Psychiatry, 18:27-39, 1955.

2614)   Wolbarst, A. L.   "Sexual Perversions: Their
Medical and Social Implications," Medical Journal
and Record, 134:5-9 and 62-65, 1931.

2615)   Wolfenden, John.   "Evolution of British Attitudes
toward Homosexuality," American Journal of Psychiatry, 125:792-97, 1968.

2616)   "Wolfenden Committee and the Press," Lancet,
        273:549, 1957.

2617)   "The Wolfenden Report," Lancet, no. 7058:1228-
        30, 1958.

2618)   "Wolfenden Report Still in Advance of Opinion,"
        British Medical Journal, 2:154-55, 1960.

2619)   Wolfson, William and Gross, Alfred. "A Footnote
        to the Etiological Study of the Homosexual Syn-
        drome," International Journal of Sexology, 6:178-79,
        1953.

2620)   Wolman, Benjamin B. "Interactional Treatment of
        Homosexuality," Psychotherapy and Psychosomatics,
        15:70, 1967.

2621)   Wolowitz, Howard M. "Attraction and Aversion to
        Power: A Psychoanalytic Conflict Theory of Homo-
        sexuality in Male Paranoids," Journal of Abnormal
        Psychology, 70:360-70, 1965. (See no. 264 above.)

2622)   Wortis, Joseph. "Intersexuality and Effeminacy in
        the Male Homosexual," American Journal of Ortho-
        psychiatry, 10:567-70, 1940.

2623)   Wortis, Joseph. "A Note on the Body Build of the
        Male Homosexual," American Journal of Psychiatry,
        93:1121-25, 1937.

2624)   Wortis, Joseph. "Sex Taboos, Sex Offenders and
        the Law," American Journal of Orthopsychiatry, 9:
        554-64, 1939.

2625)   Wright, Clifford A. "Endocrine Aspects of Homo-
        sexuality: Preliminary Report," Medical Record,
        142:407-10, 1935.

2626)   Wright, Clifford A. "Endocrine Treatment in
        Homosexual Men," Therapeutic Notes, Feb., 1942,
        p. 65.

2627)   Wright, Clifford A. "Further Studies of Endocrine
        Aspects of Homosexuality," Medical Record, 147:
        449-52, 1938.

2628)   Wright, Clifford A.   "Results of Endocrine Treat-
          ment in a Controlled Group of Homosexual Men, "
          Medical Record, 154:60-61, 1941.

2629)   Wright, Clifford A.   "The Sex Offender's Hor-
          mones, " Medical Record, 149:399-402, 1939.

2630)   Wright, Clifford A. , Glass, S. J. , and Deuel, H. J.
          "Sex Hormone Studies in Male Homosexuality, " En-
          docrinology, 26:590-94, 1940.

2631)   Wulff, Moshe.   "A Case of Male Homosexuality, "
          International Journal of Psychoanalysis, 23:112-20,
          1942.   (Reprinted in Krich, no. 69 above, pp. 324-
          42 and abstracted in Journal of Criminal Psycho-
          pathology, 4:757-58, 1943.)

2632)   Yalom, Irvin D.   "Group Therapy of Incarcerated
          Sexual Deviants, " Journal of Nervous and Mental
          Disease, 132:158-70, 1961.

2633)   Yamahiro, R. S. and Griffith, R. M.   "Validity of
          Two Indices of Sexual Deviancy, " Journal of Clinical
          Psychology, 16:21-24, 1960.

2634)   Yarnell, Helen.   "Firesetting in Children, " Ameri-
          can Journal of Orthopsychiatry, 10:272-86, 1940.

2635)   Young, W. C. and Rundlett, B.   "The Hormonal In-
          duction of Homosexual Behavior in the Spayed Fe-
          male Guinea Pig, " Psychosomatic Medicine, 1:449-
          60, 1939.

2636)   Zamansky, Harold S.   "Investigation of the Psycho-
          analytic Theory of Paranoid Delusions, " Journal of
          Personality, 26:410-25, 1958.

2637)   Zamansky, Harold S.   "A Technique for Assessing
          Homosexual Tendencies, " Journal of Personality,
          24:436-48, 1956.

2638)   Zeichner, Abraham M.   "Psychosexual Identifica-
          tion in Paranoid Schizophrenia, " Journal of Pro-
          jective Techniques, 19:67-77, 1955.

2639)   Zlotlow, M. and Paganini, A. E.   "Autoerotic and
          Homoerotic Manifestations in Hospitalized Male

Post-Lobotomy Patients," Psychiatric Quarterly, 33:490-97, 1959.

2640)   Zucker, Robert A. and Manosevitz, Martin.
"MMPI Patterns of Overt Male Homosexuals: Re-interpretation and Comment on Dean and Richardson's Study," Journal of Consulting Psychology, 30:555-57, 1966.

2641)   Zuckerman, Stanley B.   "Sex in Prison," Journal of Social Therapy, 1:129-31, 1955.

2642)   Zuger, B.   "Effeminate Behavior Present in Boys from Early Childhood: the Clinical Syndrome and Follow-up Studies," Journal of Pediatrics, 69:1098-1107, 1966.

Articles in Other Specialized Journals

2643) Abrahamsen, David. "Study of 102 Sex Offenders at Sing Sing," Federal Probation, 14:26-32, Sep. 1950.

2644) Abse, Leo. "The Sexual Offences Act," British Journal of Criminology, 8:86-87, 1968.

2645) Adler, Martin D. "The Application of Discretion in Enforcement of the Law in Mental Health Situations," Police, 9:48-53, Nov.-Dec. 1964.

2646) Allen, Clifford. "The Problem of Homosexuality," British Journal of Delinquency, 5:157, 1954.

2647) "AEC Criteria for Security Clearance," Bulletin of the Atomic Scientists, 11:159-60, 1955.

2648) Andenaes, Johs. "Recent Trends in the Criminal Law and Penal System in Norway: I. Criminal Law," British Journal of Delinquency, 5:21-26, 1954.

2649) Anonymous. "Rebuttal: The Re-baring of 'The Secret Sharer'; Leg Pull?" College English, 27, 504-05, 1966.

2650) Balogh, J. K. "Conjugal Visitations in Prisons: A Sociological Perspective," Federal Probation, 28: 52-58, Sep. 1964.

2651) Beals, Ralph L. "Ethnology of the Nisenan," University of California Publications in American Archaeology and Ethnology, 31:335-410 at 376, 1933.

2652) Beardmore, Edward. "The Natives of Mowat, Daudai, New Guinea," Journal of the Royal Anthropological Institute of Great Britain and Ireland, 19: 459-66, 1890.

2653)   Bergler, Edmund. "Lesbianism, Facts and Fiction,"
        Marriage Hygiene, 4(NS):197-202, 1951.

2654)   Bergler, Edmund. "The Present Situation in the
        Genetic Investigation of Homosexuality," Marriage
        Hygiene, 4:16-29, 1937.

2655)   Bontecou, Eleanor. "President Eisenhower's
        'Security Program,' " Bulletin of the Atomic Scien-
        tists, 9:215-17, 220, 1953.

2656)   Bowling, R. W. "The Sex Offender and Law En-
        forcement," Federal Probation, 14:11-16 Sep.
        1950.

2657)   Bowman, Karl M. and Engle, Bernice. "The
        Problem of Homosexuality," Journal of Social Hy-
        giene, 39:2-16, 1953.

2658)   Bowman, Karl M. "The Challenge of the Sex Of-
        fenders: Psychiatric Aspects of the Problem,"
        Mental Hygiene, 22:10-20, 1938.

2659)   Brierley, J. R. "The 'Difficult' Prisoner," Ameri-
        can Journal of Correction, 23:14-19, 1961.

2660)   Broderick, Carlfred B. "Sexual Behavior among
        Pre-Adolescents," Journal of Social Issues, 22:6-
        21, 1966.

2661)   Brodwin, Leonora L. "Edward II: Marlowe's
        Culminating Treatment of Love," ELH [Journal of
        English Literary History], 31:139-55, June 1964.

2662)   Brown, Daniel G. "Psychosexual Disturbances:
        Transvestism and Sex-role Inversion," Marriage
        and Family Living, 22:218-27, 1960.

2663)   Brown, Daniel G. and Lynn, David B. "Human
        Sexual Development: An Outline of Components and
        Concepts," Journal of Marriage and the Family, 28:
        159-62, 1966.

2664)   Brown, Julia S. "A Comparative Study of Devia-
        tions of Sexual Mores," American Sociological Re-
        view, 17:135-46, 1952.

2665)   Calder, W.   "The Sexual Offender: A Prison
         Medical Officer's Viewpoint, " British Journal of
         Delinquency, 6:26-40, 1955.

2666)   Carson, Laura E.   "Are We Hiding behind a Word?"
         Mental Hygiene, 42:558-61, 1958.

2667)   Cavan, Sherri.   "Interaction in Home Territories, "
         Berkeley Journal of Sociology, 8:17-32, 1963.

2668)   Cory, Donald W.   "Homosexuality: Active and
         Passive, " Journal of Sex Education, 5:19-22, 1952.

2669)   David, W. A.   "Homosexuality: A Mode of Adapta-
         tion in a Prison for Women, " Social Problems, 12:
         159-77, 1964.

2670)   Editorial, British Journal of Delinquency, 5:1-3,
         1954.

2671)   Editorial, British Journal of Delinquency, 9:3-6,
         1958.

2672)   Erickson, Ralph J.   "Male Homosexuality and
         Society, " Bulletin of the National Association of
         Secondary School Principals, 45:128-34, Nov. 1961.

2673)   Fitch, J. H.   "Men Convicted of Sexual Offences
         against Children: A Descriptive Follow-up Study, "
         British Journal of Criminology, 3:18-37, 1962.

2674)   Forde, C. Daryll.   "Ethnography of the Yuma In-
         dians, " University of California Publications in
         American Archaeology and Ethnology, 28:83-278 at
         96, 1931.

2675)   Frisbie, Louise V.   "Studies on Sex Offending in
         California, " California Mental Health Research
         Digest, 4:135-41, 1966.

2676)   Gagnon, John H. and Simon, William.   "Social
         Meaning of Prison Homosexuality, " Federal Proba-
         tion, 32:23-29, Mar. 1968.

2677)   Gigeroff, A. K. , Mohr, J. W. , and Turner, R. E.
         "Sex Offenders on Probation: Homosexuality, "
         Federal Probation, 33:36-39, Mar. 1969.

2678)   Gilbert, G. M.   "Crime and Punishment: An
        Exploratory Comparison of Public, Criminal, and
        Penological Attitudes," Mental Hygiene, 42:550-
        57, 1948.

2679)   Ginsberg, M.   "The Enforcement of Morals,"
        British Journal of Sociology, 12:65-68, 1961.

2680)   Glover, Benjamin.   "Control of the Sex Deviate,"
        Federal Probation, 24:38-45, Sep. 1960.

2681)   Green, Harold.   "The Unsystematic Security Sys-
        tem," Bulletin of the Atomic Scientists, 11:118-22,
        1955.

2682)   Griffith, Clark.   "Sex and Death: the Significance of
        Whitman's Calamus Themes," Philological Quarterly,
        39:18-38, 1960.

2683)   Grinker, Roy R.   "Homosexuality," Counseling,
        20:1-4, Mar.-Apr. 1962.

2684)   Gross, Alfred A.   "Understanding the Homosexual,"
        National Probation and Parole Journal, 1:140-47,
        1955.

2685)   Grygier, Tadeuz.   "Homosexuality, Neurosis and
        'Normality': A Pilot Study in Psychological Meas-
        urement," British Journal of Delinquency, 9:59-61,
        1958.

2686)   Hacker, Helen.   "Homosexuals: Should They Have
        Equal Rights?" Sexology, Mar. 1969. (Reprinted
        in Vector, 5:16-17, Mar. 1969.)

2686a) Hacker, Helen M.   "The New Burden of Masculinity,"
        Marriage and Family Living, 19:227-33, 1957.

2687)   Hahn, Milton E. and Atkinson, Byron H.   "The
        Sexually Deviate Student," School and Society, 82:
        85-87, Sep. 1955.

2688)   Harkness, Bruce.   "The Secret of 'The Secret
        Sharer' Bared," College English, 27:55-61, 1965.

2689)   Hartsock, Mildred E.   "Henry James and the
        Cities of the Plain," Modern Language Quarterly,
        29:297-311, 1968.

2690)   Hartweg, Norman. "Homosexuality," Tulane
        Drama Review, 10:208-13, Fall 1965.

2691)   Henry, George W. and Gross, Alfred A.   "The
        Homosexual Delinquent," Mental Hygiene, 25:420-
        42, 1941.

2692)   Henry, George W. and Gross, Alfred A.   "Social
        Factors in the Case Histories of 100 Underprivi-
        leged Homosexuals," Mental Hygiene, 22:591-611,
        1938.

2693)   Hill, W. W. "Note on the Pima Berdache," Ameri-
        can Anthropologist, 40:338-40, 1938.

2694)   Hill, W. W. "The Status of the Hermaphrodite and
        Transvestite in Navaho Culture," American Anthro-
        pologist, 37:273-79, 1935.

2695)   Hohman, Leslie B. and Schaffner, Bertram.   "The
        Sex Lives of Unmarried Men," American Journal
        of Sociology, 52:501-07, 1947.

2696)   "Homosexuality and Prostitution," British Journal
        of Delinquency, 6:315-17, 1956.

2697)   Jepson, N. A. "Homosexuality, Capital Punishment
        and the Law," British Journal of Delinquency, 9:
        246-57, 1958.

2698)   Kaplan, Donald M. "Homosexuality and the Ameri-
        can Theater: A Psychoanalytic Comment," Tulane
        Drama Review, 9:25-55, Spring 1965.

2699)   Kempe, G. T. "The Homosexual in Society," Brit-
        ish Journal of Delinquency, 5:4-20, 1954.

2700)   Kitsuse, John I. "Societal Reaction to Deviant Be-
        havior: Problems of Theory and Method," Social
        Problems, 9:247-56, 1962. (Reprinted in Howard
        S. Becker [ed.], The Other Side: Perspectives on
        Deviance [New York: Free Press of Glencoe,
        1964], pp. 87-102.)

2701)   Kriegman, G. "Homosexuality and the Educator,"
        Journal of School Health, 39:305-11, 1969.

2702)   Lafitte, François. "Homosexuality and the Law:
        the Wolfenden Report in Historical Perspective,"
        British Journal of Delinquency, 9:8-19, 1958.

2703)   Laidlow, Robert W. "A Clinical Approach to
        Homosexuality," Marriage and Family Living, 14:
        39-45, 1952.

2704)   Lapp, J. C. "The Watcher Betrayed and the Fatal
        Woman: Some Recurring Patterns in Zola," Publi-
        cations of the Modern Language Association, 74:
        276-84, 1959. (Reprinted in Ruitenbeek, no. 95
        above, pp. 313-30.)

2705)   Levin, Harry. "Proust, Gide, and the Sexes,"
        Publications of the Modern Language Association,
        65:648-53, 1950.

2706)   Leznoff, Maurice. "Interviewing Homosexuals,"
        American Journal of Sociology, 62:202-04, 1956.

2707)   Leznoff, Maurice and Westley, William A. "The
        Homosexual Community," Social Problems, 3:257-
        62, 1956. (Reprinted in Ruitenbeek, no. 96 above,
        pp. 162-74; in Gagnon and Simon, no. 266 above,
        pp. 184-96; and in Alvin W. and Helen P. Goulder
        [eds.], Modern Society: An Introduction to the
        Study of Human Interaction [New York: Harcourt,
        Brace, and World, 1962], pp. 582-88. Abstracted
        in Marriage and Family Living, 18:373, 1956.)

2708)   Liddicoat, Renée. "A Study of Non-Institutionalized
        Homosexuals," Journal of the National Institute for
        Personnel Research [South Africa], 8:217-49, 1961.

2709)   Liddicoat, Renée. "Symposium on the Wolfenden
        Report: Psycho-social Aspects of the Wolfenden
        Report," National Union of South African Students,
        Winter School Conference, 1959-60, pp. 34-37.

2710)   MacCormick, Austin H. "The Challenge of Sex
        Offenders: New York's Present Problem," Mental
        Hygiene, 22:4-10, 1938.

2711)   Mangus, A. R. "Sexual Deviations and the Family,"
        Marriage and Family Living, 15:325-31, 1953.

2711a) McCaghy, C. H. and Skipper, J. K. Jr. "Lesbian
        Behavior as an Adaptation to the Occupation of
        Stripping," Social Problems, 17:262-70, 1969.

2712)   McIntosh, Mary. "Homosexual Role," Social Prob-
        lems, 16:182-92, Fall 1968.

2713)   Miller, Walter B. "Lower-Class Culture as a
        Generating Milieu of Gang Delinquency," Journal of
        Social Issues, 14:5-19, 1958.

2714)   Morgenthau, Hans. J. "The Impact of the Loyalty-
        Security Measures on the State Department," Bulle-
        tin of the Atomic Scientists, 11:134-40, 1955.

2715)   Mueller, Gerhard C. W. "Toward Ending the
        Double-Standard of Sexual Morality," Journal of
        Offender Therapy, 8:5-8, 1964.

2716)   Mullins, Claud. "Psychiatry in the Criminal
        Courts," Federal Probation, 14:37-45, Sep. 1950.

2716a) Munroe, R. L. and others. "Institutionalized Male
        Transvestism and Sex Distinctions," American An-
        thropologist, 71:87-91, Feb. 1969.

2717)   Needham, Merrill A. and Schur, Edwin M. "Stu-
        dent Punitiveness toward Sexual Deviation," Marri-
        age and Family Living, 25:227-29, 1963.

2718)   Nice, R. W. "The Problem of Homosexuality in
        Corrections," American Journal of Correction, 28:
        30-32, 1966.

2719)   O'Brien, Justin. "Albertine the Ambiguous: Notes
        on Proust's Transposition of Sexes," Publications
        of the Modern Language Association, 64:932-52,
        1949 and 65:653, 1950.

2720)   Oppegard, Charles R. "An Attitude toward the
        Homosexual," Federal Probation, 28:61-62, Mar.
        1964.

2721)   Parker, Frederick B. "Comparison of the Sex
        Temperament of Alcoholics and Moderate Drinkers,"
        American Sociological Review, 24:366-74, 1959.

240 Homosexuality

2722) Parr, Denis. "Psychiatric Aspects of the Wolfenden Report," British Journal of Delinquency, 9:33-43, 1958.

2723) Penrose, L. S. "Genetics and the Criminal," British Journal of Delinquency, 6:15-25, 1955.

2724) "A Psychosexual Deviation--the Homosexual," Police, 3:39, July-Aug. 1959.

2725) Raizen, Kenneth H. "A Case of Matricide-Patricide," British Journal of Delinquency, 10:277-94, 1960.

2726) Reeves, Ambrose. "Symposium on the Wolfenden Report: A Churchman's Views of the Report," National Union of South African Students, Winter School Conference, 1959-60, pp. 32-33.

2727) Reinhardt, James M. "A Critical Analysis of the Wolfenden Report," Federal Probation, 23:36-41, Sep. 1959.

2728) Reiss, Albert J. Jr. "Social Integration of Queers and Peers," Social Problems, 9:102-20, 1961. (Reprinted in Ruitenbeek, no. 96 above, pp. 249-78; in Gagnon and Simon, no. 266 above, pp. 197-228; and in Becker, no. 2700 above, pp. 181-210.)

2729) Riva, Raymond T. "Marcel Proust: An Immodest Proposal," Criticism, 10:217-24, Summer 1968.

2730) Roche, Philip W. "Sexual Deviation," Federal Probation, 14:3-11, Sep. 1950.

2731) Rooney, Elizabeth and Gibbons, Don C. "Social Reaction to 'Crimes without Victims,'" Social Problems, 34:401-10, 1966.

2732) Ross, H. Laurence. "The 'Hustler' in Chicago," Journal of Student Research, 1:13-19, 1959.

2733) Rylander, Gosta. "Treatment of Mentally Abnormal Offenders in Sweden," British Journal of Delinquency, 5:262-68, 1954.

2734) Saville, Eve. "I. S. T. D. Week-end Conference on

2

1

2735) Schechner, Richard. "Who's Afraid of Edward Albee?" Tulane Drama Review, 7:7-10, Spring 1963.

2736) Schneiders, A. "Understanding Homosexuality," Marriage, 50:46-52, Aug. 1968.

2737) Scott, Marvin B. and Lyman, Stanford M. "Paranoia, Homosexuality, and Game Theory," Journal of Health and Social Behavior, 9:179-87, 1968.

2738) Scott, Peter D. "Psychiatric Aspects of the Wolfenden Report," British Journal of Delinquency, 9:20-32, 1958.

2739) "Security Requirements for Government Employment: Executive Order 10450," Bulletin of the Atomic Scientists, 11:156-58, 1955.

2740) Seiden, Melvin. "Proust's Marcel and Saint Loup: Inversion Reconsidered," Contemporary Literature 10:220-40, 1969.

2741) Sherwin, Robert V. "The Law and Sexual Relationships," Journal of Social Issues, 22:109-22, 1966.

2742) Shils, Edward. "Security and Science Sacrificed to Loyalty," Bulletin of the Atomic Scientists, 11: 106-09, 1955.

2743) Simon, William and Gagnon, John H. "Femininity in the Lesbian Community," Social Problems, 15: 212-21, 1967.

2744) Simon, William and Gagnon, John H. "Homosexuality: the Formulation of a Sociological Perspective," Journal of Health and Social Behavior, 8: 177-85, 1967. (Reprinted with revisions in Weltge, no. 116 above, pp. 14-24.)

2745) Sonenschein, David. "Homosexuality as a Subject of Anthropological Inquiry," Anthropological Quarterly, 39:73-82, 1966.

2746)   Spencer, J. C.   "Contributions to the Symposium on
        Sexual Deviation," Canadian Journal of Corrections,
        3:481-84, 1961.

2747)   Spier, Leslie.   "Klamath Ethnography," University
        of California Publications in American Archaeology
        and Ethnology, 30:1-328 at 51-53, 1930.

2748)   Stiller, Richard.   "The Homosexual Crusaders [The
        Knights Templars]," Sexology, 34:305-07, Dec. 1967.

2749)   Stoltzfus, B. F.   "Saül: A Germinating Gide,"
        French Review, 39:49-56, Oct. 1965.

2750)   Stürup, G. K.   "Correctional Treatment and the
        Criminal Sexual Offender," Canadian Journal of
        Corrections, 3:250-65, 1961.

2751)   Sullivan, Harry S.   "The Socio-genesis of Homo-
        sexual Behavior in Males," Publications of the
        American Sociological Society: Studies in Quantita-
        tive and Cultural Sociology, 24:281-82, 1930.

2752)   "Summary of the Wolfenden Committee's Recom-
        mendations with regard to Homosexual Offences,"
        British Journal of Delinquency, 9:6-7, 1958.

2753)   Sutton, Walter.   "Melville's 'Pleasure Party' and
        the Art of Concealment," Philological Quarterly,
        30:316-27, 1951.

2754)   Szilard, Leo.   "Security Risk," Bulletin of the
        Atomic Scientists, 10:384-86, 398, 1954.

2755)   Tappan, Paul W.   "Sex Offender Laws and their
        Administration," Federal Probation, 14:32-37, Sep.
        1950.

2756)   Tappan, Paul W.   "Some Myths about the Sex Of-
        fender," Federal Probation, 19:7-12, June 1955.
        (Abstracted in Marriage and Family Living, 17:
        364, 1955.)

2757)   Tarail, M.   "New Treatments for the Homosexual,"
        Sexology, 27:674-77, 1961.

2758)   Trimbos, C. J. B. J.   "Imprisonment Harms the Bond
        of Marriage," Penal Reform News, 65:1-5, 1964.

2759)   Turner, R. E.   "The Group Treatment of Sexual
        Deviations," Canadian Journal of Corrections, 3:
        485-91, 1961.

2760)   Ullman, Paul S.   "Parental Participation in Child
        Rearing as Evaluated by Male Social Deviates,"
        Pacific Sociological Review, 3:89-95, 1960.

2761)   Vilhotti, Anthony J.   "An Investigation of the Use
        of the D. A. P. in the Diagnosis of Homosexuality in
        Mentally Deficient Males," American Journal of
        Mental Deficiency, 62:708-11, 1958.

2762)   Waggoner, Raymond W.   "The Emotional Prejudice
        of Sexuality," Journal of Social Hygiene, 38:30-31,
        1952.

2763)   Ward, David A. and Kassebaum, Gene G.   "Homo-
        sexuality: A Mode of Adoptation in a Prison for
        Women," Social Problems, 12:159-77, 1964.

2764)   Wasserman, Sidney.   "Case Work Treatment of a
        Homosexual Acting-Out Adolescent in a Treatment
        Center," Mental Hygiene, 44:18-29, 1960.

2765)   Werner, W. L.   "The Psychology of Marcel Proust,"
        Sewanee Review, 39:276-81, 1931.   (Reprinted in
        Ruitenbeek, no. 95 above, pp. 284-89.)

2766)   Westley, William A.   "Violence and the Police,"
        American Journal of Sociology, 59:34-41, 1953.
        (Reprinted in Johnston, Savitz, and Wolfgang, no.
        507 above, pp. 5-11.)

2767)   Wile, Ira S.   "Sex Offenses against Children:
        What Shall be Done about Them?" Journal of
        Social Hygiene, 25:33-44, 1939.

2768)   Williams, J. E. Hall.   "The Wolfenden Report--An
        Appraisal," Political Quarterly, 29:132-43, 1958.

2769)   Woodward, Mary.   "Diagnosis and Treatment of
        Homosexual Offenders: A Clinical Survey," British
        Journal of Delinquency, 9:44-59, 1958.

2770)   Yaker, Henri M.   "The Black Muslim in the Cor-
        rectional Institution," Welfare Reporter, 13:158-65,
        1962.

Articles in Homophile Publications

2771)   Allen, Luther. "Homosexuality--Is a Handicap or
          a Talent?" Mattachine Review, 1:6-10, July-Aug.
          1955.

2772)   Allen, Luther. "Just How Paranoid are Homo-
          sexuals?" Mattachine Review, 6:10-17, Oct. 1960.

2773)   Anderson, Ronald. "Neurosis and Homosexuals,"
          One, 3:4-7, Sep. 1955.

2774)   Argo, Jack. "The Homosexual in Germany Today,"
          One, 3:9-10, June 1955.

2775)   Atwell, Lee. "Homosexual Themes in the Cinema,"
          Tangents, 1:4-10, Mar. 1966 and 1:4-9, Apr. 1966.

2776)   Bannon, Ann. "Secrets of the Gay Novel," One, 9:
          6-12, July 1961.

2777)   Baudry, Andre. "The Homosexual in France," One,
          3:21-23, Feb. 1955.

2778)   Beardemphl, William. "Are Homosexuals Sick?"
          Vector, 5:16-18, Jan. 1969.

2779)   Beardemphl, William. "The Dilemma of Being a
          Gay Soldier," Vector, 4:5, 30, Apr. 1968.

2780)   Benjamin, Harry. "In Time We Must Accept,"
          Mattachine Review, 4:4-7, Apr. 1958 and 4:12-15,
          May, 1958.

2781)   "A Bibliography [on Homosexuality]," Vector, 4:21,
          Feb. 1968; 4:22, Mar. 1968; 4:26, Apr. 1968;
          4:26-27, May 1968; 4:24-25, June 1968; and 4:19-
          20, July 1968.

2782)   Bishop, Bob. "Discard the Mask," Mattachine Re-
          view, 4:14-16, 21-24, Apr. 1958.

                              244

2783)   Bishop, Donald. "Pussies in Boots," Amigo, no. 25, pp. 183-90, 1964.

2784)   "Boise's Boys Revisited: How Ignorance, Prejudice Tore a Quiet Town Apart," Los Angeles Advocate, 3:14-15, Aug. 1969.

2785)   Bradbury, Andrew. "Pederasty and Male Prostitution," One Institute Quarterly, 4:64-72, 1961.

2786)   Bradley, John. "The 'Sick,' 'Unhappy' Homosexual --Time to Get Well," Vector, 3:24-26, June 1967.

2787)   Bradley, John. "That 'Time-Life' Look," Vector, 3:1-3, Feb. 1967.

2788)   Branson, Helen P. "Homosexuals as I See Them," Mattachine Review, 4:8-12, Feb. 1958.

2789)   Call, Harold L. "A Decade of Progress in the Homophile Movement," Mattachine Review, 8:11-20, Oct. 1962.

2790)   Call, Harold L. "Open Letter to the Florida Legislature's 'Johns Committee,'" Mattachine Review, 10:5-8, Nov.-Dec. 1964.

2791)   "The Case of Scott v. Macy: Round and Round with CSC," Los Angeles Advocate, 3:6-7, Feb. 1969.

2792)   "The Case of the Black Cat Raid," One Confidential, 12:5-10, Apr. 1967.

2793)   Cody, Bart. "How Movies Got Gay ... and Gayer ... and Gayer," Los Angeles Advocate, 2:16-19, Aug. 1968.

2794)   Collins, Michael. "A History of Homosexuality in the Movies," Drum, no. 27:12-21, 30-32, Oct. 1967.

2795)   Coopersmith, Lewis J. "The Homosexual Problem: the Forward Look," Drum, 4:6-8, 25-29, Nov. 1964 and 4:8-11, 26-27, Dec. 1964.

2796)   "Cop-Out is Not an Out," Pride Newsletter, 2:7, 10-11, Aug. 1967.

2797)   Cory, Donald W.   "Toward a Rational Approach to
          Homosexuality," One, 10:5-11, Mar. 1962.

2798)   Craig, Alfred.   "Does Homosexuality Have a Bio-
          logical Basis?"   One Institute Quarterly, 5:32-35,
          1962.

2799)   Crowther, R. H.   "Homosexual Culture," One In-
          stitute Quarterly, 3:176-82, 1960.

2800)   Crowther, R. H.   "Sodom: A Homosexual View-
          point," One, 3:24-28, Jan. 1955.

2801)   Daniel, Marc.   "A Methodology for the Study of
          Historical Aspects of Homosexuality," One Institute
          Quarterly, 3:268-80, 1960.

2802)   Daniel, Marc.   "A Study of Homosexuality in France
          during the Reigns of Louis XIII and Louis XIV,"
          One Institute Quarterly, 4:77-93 and 125-36, 1961.

2803)   Dean, Robert B.   "Some Recent Empirical and
          Non-empirical Observations on Male Homosexuality,"
          One Institute Quarterly, 8:20-30, 1967.

2804)   Dewees, Curtis.   "On the Suppression of Homo-
          sexual Literature," Mattachine Review, 4:14-16,
          Aug. 1958 and 4:7-12, Sep. 1958.

2805)   Dickey, Brenda A.   "Attitudes toward Sex-Roles
          and Feelings of Adequacy in Homosexual Males,"
          Mattachine Review, 7:9-12, Aug. 1961.

2806)   "DOB Questionnaire Reveals Some Facts About
          Lesbians," Ladder, 3:4-26, Sep. 1959.

2807)   Edgerton, Daniel H.   "The Ambiguous Heroes of
          John Horne Burns," One, 6:6-12, Oct. 1958.

2808)   Egan, Jim.   "Homosexual Marriage--Fact or
          Fancy?"   One, 12:6-9, Dec. 1959.

2809)   Ellis, Albert.   "Are Homosexuals Necessarily
          Neurotic?"   One, 3:8-12, Apr. 1955.   (Reprinted
          in Cory, no. 27 above, pp. 407-14.)

2810)   Ellis, Albert.   "A Guide to Rational Homosexuality,"

Drum, 4:8-12, Oct. 1964.

2811)   Ellis, Albert.   "How Homosexuals Can Combat
        Anti-Homosexualism," One, 5:7-9, Feb. 1957.

2812)   Ellis, Albert.   "The Influence of Heterosexual
        Culture on Homosexual Attitudes," Mattachine
        Review, 1:11-14, Sep.-Oct. 1955.

2813)   Ellis, Albert.   "On the Cure of Homosexuality,"
        Mattachine Review, 1:6-9, Nov.-Dec. 1955.

2814)   Evans, Ray.   "Biological Factors in Sexual Be-
        havior with special Reference to Homosexuality,"
        One Institute Quarterly, 4:113-20, 1961.

2815)   Evans, Ray.   "A Serious Look at the Second Cory
        Report," One, 12:5-8, Jan. 1964.

2816)   "The Failure of the Church," One, 11:7-11, Dec.
        1963.

2817)   Finegal, Mackinneth.   "The Homosexual Veteran,"
        Mattachine Review, 1:29-31, July-Aug. 1955.

2818)   Fink, Kenneth.   "The Psychodynamics of the
        Homosexual," Mattachine Review, 6:4-11, July
        1960.

2819)   Fluckinger, Fritz A.   "Research Through a Glass,
        Darkly," Ladder, 10:16-26, July 1966; 10:18-26,
        Aug. 1966; and 10:22-26, Sep. 1966.

2820)   Freedman, Mark.   "Homosexuality Among Women
        and Psychological Adjustment," Ladder, 12:2-3,
        Jan. 1968.

2821)   Freeman, David I.   "How Much Do We Know About
        the Homosexual Male?" One, 3:4-6, Nov. 1955.

2822)   Freeman, David I.   "Literature and Homosexuality,"
        One, 3:13-15, Jan. 1955.

2823)   Friedman, Ruth M.   "To the Parent of a Homo-
        sexual," One, 6:5-8, May 1958.

2824)   Fugate, James B.   "Homosexuality and the Liberal

Mind," <u>Mattachine Review</u>, 1:18-22, 27, Sep.-Oct.
1955.

2825)   Gailey, Leah. "A Mother Gives an Answer--What
        Can I Do?" <u>Mattachine Review</u>, 4:5-8, May 1958.

2826)   "Gay Job Center Seeks Federal Funds," <u>Los An-
        geles Advocate</u>, 3:5, June 1969.

2827)   Goff, Martyn. "The Homosexual as Novelist,"
        <u>Amigo</u>, no. 14, pp. 116-17, 1963.

2828)   Golden, Harry. "The Homosexual in North Carolina,"
        <u>New York Mattachine Newsletter</u>, 10:4-5, Jan. 1965.
        (Reprinted from <u>The North Carolina Israelite</u>.)

2829)   Golovitz, Frank. "Gay Beach," <u>One</u>, 6:5-10, July
        1958.

2830)   Gregory, Robert. "The Gay Bar," <u>One</u>, 6:5-8,
        Feb. 1958.

2831)   Gregory, Robert. "The Homosexual Draftee," <u>One</u>,
        8:8-13, Aug. 1960.

2832)   Grey, Antony. "Attitudes to Homosexuality," <u>Man
        and Society</u>, no. 8, pp. 23-25, Spring 1965.

2833)   Guerin, Daniel. "The Suppression of Homosexuality
        in France," <u>One</u>, 9:6-13, Feb. 1961.

2834)   Hamilton, W.G. "Homosexuality: A Brake on
        Overpopulation," <u>One</u>, 4:20-23, Apr.-May, 1956.

2835)   Hannon, Michael. "Victimless Crimes: A Legal
        Dilemma," <u>Tangents</u>, 2:4-8, May.-June 1968.

2836)   Hansen, Joseph. "The Homosexual Joke," <u>Tangents</u>,
        1:26-30, Feb. 1966.

2837)   Hansen, Joseph. "Suicide and the Homosexual,"
        <u>One</u> [<u>Tangents</u>], 13:5-7, May 1965.

2838)   Harding, Carl B. "Whom Shall We Tell?" <u>Matta-
        chine Review</u>, 2:8-14, Aug. 1956.

2839)   Hauser, Richard. "The Drug of Self-Pity," <u>Man</u>

and Society, no. 6, pp. 14-16, Aut. 1963.

2840)   Hemsley, Howard.   " 'Homosexuality Will Not Be
          Tolerated ...,' " One, 14:11-14, Apr.-May 1966.

2841)   Highland, Jim.   "Raid!" Tangents, 2:4-7, Jan.
          1967.

2842)   Hoboken, Van.   "Mattachine Society of N.Y. Meets
          with Clergy," Eastern Mattachine Magazine, 10:4-6,
          Sep.-Oct. 1965.

2843)   "Homosexual Bill of Rights," Los Angeles Advocate,
          2:6, Oct. 1968.

2844)   "Homosexuality: Public Attitudes [CBS Survey],"
          Drum, no. 25, pp. 11-13, 29-31, Aug. 1967.

2845)   "How One Began," One, 3:8-15, Feb. 1955.

2846)   Howard, Roland.   "Are Homosexuals Criminal?"
          Mattachine Review, 5:5-10, Oct. 1959.

2847)   Howard, Rolland.   "The Homosexual's Right to
          Serve," Mattachine Review, 8:4-13, Dec. 1962.

2848)   Hunter, John S.   "Is Homosexuality an Illness?"
          Phoenix, 2:3-4, 12, July 1967.

2849)   "The Importance of Being Different," One, 3:4-6,
          Mar. 1954.

2850)   Jackson, Don.   "Gay Militants Demonstrate for
          Rights at UC, Berkeley," Los Angeles Advocate,
          3:1, 3, Dec. 1969.

2851)   Jackson, Ed.   "Gays Attack Laws, Police in Three
          Separate Court Actions," Los Angeles Advocate,
          3:1, 6, Sep. 1969.

2852)   James, Nicholas.   "Security Victim," Man and
          Society, no. 6, pp. 20-21, Aut. 1963.

2853)   Jason, Philip.   "Homosexuals in a Related Culture -
          A Brief Investigation," Mattachine Review, 4:8-10,
          July 1958 and 4:9-11, Aug. 1958.

2854)   Jennings, Dale. "To Be Accused is to be Guilty,"
         One, 1:10-13, Jan. 1953.

2855)   Kameny, Franklin E.   "Does Research into Homo-
         sexuaity Matter?" Ladder, 9:14-20, May 1965.

2856)   Kameny, Franklin E.   "Homosexual Picket in
         Washington and Philadelphia," Eastern Mattachine
         Magazine, 10:19-21, Sep.-Oct. 1965.

2857)   Kameny, Franklin E.   "Homosexuals and the Civil
         Service Commission," Drum, no. 18-19, pp. 21-24,
         Sep. 1966.

2858)   Kameny, Franklin E.   "U.S. Government Hides
         Behind Immoral Mores," Ladder, 10:17-20, June
         1966.

2859)   Kempe. G. Th.   "The Homophile in Society," One,
         3:8-15, Mar. 1955.

2860)   Kepner, Jim.   "Dr. Bieber's Enormous Carrot,"
         Tangents, 2:13-19, May-June 1968.

2861)   Kepner, Jim.   "An Examination of the Sex Theories
         of Albert Ellis," One Institute Quarterly, 1:40-51,
         1959.

2862)   Kepner, Jim.   "It Just Isn't Natural," One, 5:8-12,
         Aug.-Sep. 1957.

2863)   Kepner, Jim.   "The Posthumous Trial of Ramon
         Novarro," Los Angeles Advocate, 3:5, 20-21, 23,
         Oct. 1969; 3:1, 3, 8, Nov. 1969; and 3:5, 36-37,
         Dec. 1969.

2864)   Kepner, Jim.   "World Religions and the Homo-
         phile," One Institute Quarterly, 2:124-32, 1959.

2865)   King, G. P. T. Paget.   "The Church and the Homo-
         sexual," One, 14:8-10, Dec. 1966. (Reprinted
         from Dec. 1960 issue of One.)

2866)   Krell, Arthur B.   "God and a Homosexual," One,
         2:5-11, June 1954.

2867)   Krell, Arthur B.   "We Need a Great Literature,"

One, 2:19-23, May 1954.

2868) Kupper, William H. "Immortal Beethoven--a Repressed Homosexual?" One, 15:4-6, Feb. 1967.

2869) "The Law: Discussion of Entrapment," One, 14: 8-9, Sep. 1966.

2870) Legg, W. Dorr. "The Berdache and Theories of Sexual Inversion," One Institute Quarterly, 2:59-63, 1959.

2871) Legg, W. Dorr. "Homosexuality in History," One Institute Quarterly, 1:93-98, 1959.

2872) Legg, W. Dorr. "The Sociology of Homosexuality," One Institute Quarterly, 5:60-71, 1962 and 6:58-64, 1963.

2873) Leitsch, Dick. "N.Y. Cops Host Wild Gay Party--But Didn't Plan On It," Los Angeles Advocate, 3:2, Aug. 1969.

2874) Leitsch, Dick. "Police Raid on N.Y. Club Sets Off First Gay Riot," Los Angeles Advocate, 3:3, 11-12, Sep. 1969.

2875) LeRoy, John. "Crimes against Homosexuals: Never Pay Blackmail," Mattachine Review, 6:6-7, Apr. 1960.

2876) Lloyd, Randy. "Let's Push Homophile Marriage," One, 11:5-10, June 1963.

2877) Logan, John. "Puritan Terror--Massachusetts 1961," Mattachine Review, 7:4-7, Apr. 1961.

2878) Lucas, Donald S. "The Homosexuals' Experience of the Churches," Mattachine Review, 12:26-31, no. 2, 1966.

2879) Mailer, Norman. "The Homosexual Villain," One, 3:8-12, Jan. 1955.

2880) Makis, Sal. "How to End Hostility toward Homosexuals," One, 4:13-15, Aug.-Sep. 1956.

2881)   Margin, James D. "The Margin of Masculinity,"
        One, 3:7-18, May 1955.

2882)   Martello, Leo L. "Gay Liberators Confront N. Y.
        Mayoralty Candidates," Los Angeles Advocate, 3:3,
        12, Dec. 1969.

2883)   Martin, Del. "The Church and the Homosexual:
        A New Rapport," Ladder, 8:9-13, Sep. 1964.

2884)   Martin, Del. "Who Is a Homophile?" Ladder,
        10:14-15, Sep. 1966.

2885)   Martin, Marcel. "The Homosexual on the Job,"
        Tangents, 1:4-8, Jan. 1966.

2886)   Martin, Thomas and Newman, Bernard. "Guilt
        and the Homosexual," One, 14:12-13, Dec. 1966.

2887)   McIlvenna, Ted. "Christian Ethics and Homosex-
        uality," Citizen News, 4:2-4, Oct. 1966.

2888)   Merritt, Thomas M. "Homophile Ethics," One
        Institute Quarterly, 3:262-67, 1960.

2889)   "Miami Junks the Constitution," One, 2:16-21,
        Jan. 1954.

2890)   Michaels, Dick. "Anatomy of a Raid," Los An-
        geles Advocate, 2:6-7, July 1968 and 2:6-8, Aug.
        1968.

2891)   Mohler, Dane. "Homosexual Blackmail," Tangents,
        2:4-8, Dec. 1966.

2892)   "A Mother Speaks to Parents," Phoenix, 2:24, Aug.
        1967.

2893)   "A Mother's Viewpoint on Homosexuality," Phoenix,
        1:4, July 1966.

2894)   Nichols, Dennison W. "The Existential Approach to
        the Causation and Maintanance of Homosexuality,"
        Mattachine Review, 8 7-10, Sep. 1962; 8:4-10,
        Oct. 1962; and 8:26-30, Nov. 1962.

2895)   "One and the U. S. Post Office," One, 5:5-20, Mar.
        1957.

2896)   "Op-Op [Panel on Homosexuality]," Drum, no. 18-
         19, pp. 16-17, 34-46, Sep. 1966.

2897)   Pagari, David L. "Existentialism and the Homo-
         sexual Poet," One Institute Quarterly, 6:46-57,
         1963.

2898)   Paine, Marcus. "Views of a Hidden Homosexual,"
         Phoenix, 3:12, 14-15, 17, Mar.-Apr. 1968.

2899)   Papalas, Anthony J. "Prostitution in Ancient
         Greece," Drum, no. 28, pp. 19-21, Jan. 1968.

2900)   Pedersen, Lyn. "Bitch Fight of the Year: Buckley
         vs. Vidal," Los Angeles Advocate, 3:3, 5, Oct.
         1969.

2901)   Pedersen, Lyn. "Do Constitutional Guarantees
         Cover Homosexuals?" One, 4:6-11, Jan. 1956.

2902)   Pedersen, Lyn. "Do Homosexuals Hide Behind
         Great Men?" One, 5:4-6, May 1957.

2903)   Pedersen, Lyn. "Germany, Canada Pass 'Con-
         senting Adults' Laws," Los Angeles Advocate, 3:3,
         31, June 1969.

2904)   Pedersen, Lyn. "The Importance of Being Honest,"
         Mattachine Review, 1:28-33, Sep.-Oct. 1955.

2905)   Pedersen, Lyn. "Miami Hurricane," One, 2:4-8,
         Nov. 1954.

2906)   Pedersen, Lyn. "Miami's New Type Witch-hunt,"
         One, 4:8-12, Apr.-May 1956.

2907)   Pedersen, Lyn. "The Ordeal of Prince Eulenberg,"
         One, 4:4-11, Oct.-Nov. 1956 and 4:4-8, Dec. 1956.

2908)   Polak, Clark P. "The Fable of Fire Island,"
         Drum, 5:8-14, Nov. 1965.

2909)   Polak, Clark P. "The Homophile Puzzle," Drum,
         no. 10, pp. 13-17, 26-27, Dec. 1965 and no. 11,
         pp. 10-13, Jan. 1966.

2910)   Polak, Clark P. "On Gay Bars," Drum, no. 12,
         pp. 12-15, Feb. 1966.

2911)   Polak, Clark P.   "The Story Behind Physique
          Photography," Drum, no. 11, pp. 8-15, Oct. 1965.

2912)   Prentiss, Marlin.   "Are Homosexuals Security
          Risks?"   One, 3:4-6, Dec. 1955.

2913)   Prosin, Suzanne.   "The Homosexual Minority: A
          Sociologist's Viewpoint," One, 10:9-10, June 1962.

2914)   "Queer Hunting Among Teenagers," Mattachine Re-
          view, 7:6-15, June 1961.

2915)   Reid, R. D.   "The Police and the Homosexual,"
          Man and Society, no. 6, pp. 17-19, Aut. 1963.

2916)   "Registration Law Dealt Blow," One, 14:16, Sep.
          1966.

2917)   Reynolds, Winston.   "A History of Homosexuality
          in the Movie," Drum, no. 27, pp. 12-21, 30-32,
          Oct. 1967.

2918)   Reynolds, Winston.   "Oscar Wilde Revisited,"
          Drum, no. 22, pp. 8-9, Dec. 1966.

2919)   Ross, Jay.   "Army Doesn't Want Gays but Sandy
          Doesn't Look Gay," Los Angeles Advocate, 3:7,
          Mar. 1969.

2920)   Russell, David and McIntire, Dalvan.   "In Paths
          Untrodden: A Study of Walt Whitman," One, 2:5-
          15, July 1954.

2921)   Russell, Sten.   "The Homophile Community and
          Governmental Agencies--Can They Relate?" Ladder,
          11:18-22, Dec. 1966.

2922)   Schlegel, Richard L.   "Homosexuals in Government,"
          Mattachine Review, 8:13-26, Nov. 1962.

2923)   Sewell, Mark L.   "Society v. the Homosexual and
          the Articulate Reaction," Mattachine Review, 7:8-
          25, Aug. 1966.

2924)   "Sex in Prison," Drum, no. 18-19, pp. 49-51, Sep.
          1966 and no. 20, pp. 14-17, 1966.

2925)   Shaw, Herbert. "The Social Setting of Homosex-
        uality in the Philippines," One Confidential, 12:
        1-4, Apr. 1967.

2926)   Silver, Henry. "Vag Lewd: A Criticism of the
        California Statute," Mattachine Review, 1:3-8, Jan.-
        Feb. 1955.

2927)   Simms, Hector. "New York Gay Ghettos," Gay,
        Dec. 15, 1969, pp. 4-5.

2928)   "SIR Pushes for Murder Inquiry," Los Angeles
        Advocate, 3:10, Aug. 1969.

2929)   "S. I. R. Sues to Halt Police East Bay 'Decoy'
        Squads," Vector, 5:8, Aug. 1969.

2930)   Slater, Don. "The Gay Way to Draft Deferment,"
        Tangents, 3:4-7, Aug.-Sep. 1969.

2931)   Slater, Don. "Homosexuals and the Draft,"
        Magpie, 2:5-7, 36, Aug. 1969.

2932)   Slater, Don. "The Pressing Need for Law Re-
        form," Tangents, 1:11-13, Feb. 1966.

2933)   Slater, Don. "Victory--Supreme Court Upholds
        Homosexual Rights," One, 6:16-17, Feb. 1958.

2934)   Smith, A. E. "Peter Ilyich Tchaikovsky: His
        Life and Loves Re-examined," One Institute Quar-
        terly, 4:21-36, 1961.

2935)   "Sociologists Favor Homosexual Rights," Vector,
        5:29, Oct. 1969.

2936)   "Some Facts about Lesbians: The Bilitis Study,"
        One Institute Quarterly, 2:111-23, 1959.

2937)   "Some Things Journalists Ought to Know about
        Homosexuals," Mattachine Review, 9:4-10, Mar.
        1963.

2938)   Spevack, Norman R. "The Rights of Spring,"
        Tangents, 2:4-6, Nov. 1966.

2939)   Starr, J. P. "Ancients and the Greek Cult," One

Institute Quarterly, 5:55-59, 1962.

2940)   Steiner, Lee R. "The Homosexual as Seen by the
        Marriage Counselor," Mattachine Review, 5:9-16,
        Feb. 1959.

2941)   Stephens, Barbara. "Homosexuals in Uniform,"
        Ladder, 3:17-20, June 1959.

2942)   Stewart, Omer C. "Homosexuality among the
        American Indians and Other Native Peoples of the
        World," Mattachine Review, 6:9-15, Jan. 1960 and
        6:13-19, Feb. 1960.

2943)   Talbot, Serge. "Is Homosexuality a 'Vice'?" One,
        3:4-7, Oct. 1955.

2944)   Teller, Gary. "The Male Hustler: Four Case
        Studies," One [Tangents], July 1965, pp. 5-9.

2945)   Thorne, Gale. "Who Is a Homosexual?" Ladder,
        10:11-13, Sep. 1966.

2946)   Tietz, J. B. "You and the Law," One, 5:5-10,
        Apr. 1957 and 14:10-16, Sep. 1966.

2947)   Tripp, Clarence A. "Who Is a Homosexual?"
        Ladder, 10:15-23, Dec. 1965.

2948)   "Undesirable Discharge from the Air Force,"
        Mattachine Review, 5:18-20, Sep. 1959.

2949)   Van den Haag, Ernest. "Homosexuality--Its Cul-
        tural Setting," Drum, 5:14-15, 23-29, July 1965.

2950)   "Venereal Disease in the Homosexual," Mattachine
        Review, 6:6-7, May 1960.

2951)   "Victory: Supreme Court Upholds Homosexual
        Rights," One, 14:6-7, Sep. 1966.

2952)   " 'Vigilantes' Destroy N. Y. Park to Rout Homo-
        sexuals," Los Angeles Advocate, 3:26, Sep. 1969.

2953)   Waltrip, Bob. "The Case of the Mistreated Minis-
        ter," Tangents, 1:4-7, Sep. 1966.

2954)   Waltrip, Bob. "On Life and Art and the Homo-
        sexual," One, 12:6-9, Apr. 1964.

2955)   Wicker, Randolfe. "A Business Man Sounds Off:
        Money Offers a Key to Homosexual Freedom," Gay,
        Dec. 15, 1969, pp. 12-13.

2956)   Wilkins, Nancy. "How It Happened--A History of
        Homosexual Legislation in England," Man and
        Society, no. 6, pp. 8-13, Aug. 1963.

2957)   Willer, Shirley. "The Lesbian, the Homosexual,
        and the Homophile Movement," Vector, 2:8-9, Oct.
        1966.

2958)   Willer, Shirley. "What Concrete Steps Can Be
        Taken to Further the Homophile Movement," Ladder,
        11:17-20, Nov. 1966.

2959)   Wittman, Carl. "Refugees from Amerika: A Gay
        Manifesto," San Francisco Free Press, Dec. 22,
        1969, pp. 3-5.

2960)   Wood, Frank C. Jr. "The Homosexual and the
        Police," One, 11:21-25, May 1963.

2961)   Wood, Frank C. Jr. "The Right to be Free from
        Unreasonable Search and Seizure," One, 11:5-9,
        Apr. 1963.

2962)   Wood, Robert W. "Changing Religious Attitudes
        toward Homosexuality," Mattachine Review, 8:4-12,
        Nov. 1962 and 8:21-29, Dec. 1962.

2963)   Wood, Robert W. "Homosexual Behavior in the
        Bible," One Institute Quarterly, 5:10-19, 1962.

2964)   Wood, Robert W. "Homosexuality and the Church,"
        New York Mattachine Newsletter, 9:11-20, Dec. 1964.

2965)   Wray, David P. "The Psychopathology of Antihomo-
        sexuality," Vector, 4:20-21, Mar. 1968.

2966)   Zeff, Leo J. "Self-Acceptance v. Rejection,"
        Mattachine Review, 4:4-9, Mar. 1958.

Literary Works

I. NOVELS

2967)   Albert, Lou. Hours. New York: Award Books, 1969. (Paperback: Award A507S.) 186 pp.

2968)   Aldrich, Ann. We, Too, Must Love. Greenwich, Conn.: Fawcett Publications, 1958. 189 pp. (Paperback--Gold Medal 727.)

2969)   Andros, Phil. Stud. San Francisco: J. Brian Enterprises, 1969. (Paperback.) 130 pp.

2970)   Anonymous. A Room in Chelsea Square. Garden City, N.Y.: Doubleday, 1959. 216 pp. (Paperback--Consul 1144.)

2971)   Baldwin, James. Another Country. New York: Dial Press, 1962. 436 pp. (Paperback--Dell 0200.)

2972)   Baldwin, James. Giovanni's Room. New York: Dial Press, 1956. 221 pp. (Paperback--Signet 51559.)

2973)   Barr, James. The Occasional Man. New York: Paperback Library, 1966. 288 pp. (Paperback: PL 54-918.)

2974)   Barr, James. Quatrefoil. New York: Greenberg, 1950. 373 pp. (Paperback--Paperback Library 54-871.)

2975)   Bassani, Giorgio. The Gold Rimmed Spectacles. New York: Atheneum, 1960. 143 pp.

2976)   Blechman, Burt. Stations. New York: Random House, 1964. 138 pp. (Paperback--Mayflower 114709.)

2977)   Burgess, Anthony. The Wanting Seed. New York:
         Norton, 1963. 285 pp. (Paperback--Ballantine
         U5030.)

2978)   Cain, James. Serenade. New York: Knopf, 1937.
         314 pp.

2979)   Cameron, Bruce. The Case Against Colonel
         Sutton. New York: Coward-McCann, 1961. 320
         pp. (Paperback--Paperback Library 54-266.)

2980)   Coleman, Lonnie. Sam. New York: McKay,
         1959. 245 pp. (Paperback--Pyramid G479.)

2981)   Colton, James. Lost on a Twilight Road. New
         York: National Library Books, 1964. 156 pp.
         (Paperback--NL 100.)

2982)   Colton, James. Strange Marriage. Los Angeles:
         Argyle, 1965. 176 pp. (Paperback--Paperback
         Library 54-371.)

2983)   Coriolan, John. A Sand Fortress. New York:
         Universal Publishing and Distributing Corp., 1968.
         219 pp. (Paperback--Award A363N.)

2984)   Coulton, James. Gard. New York: Award Books,
         1969. 156 pp. (Paperback--Award A541S.)

2985)   Courage, James A. A Way of Life. New York:
         Putnam, 1959. 255 pp.

2986)   DeForrest, Michael. The Gay Year. New York:
         Woodford Press, 1949. 267 pp. (Paperback--
         Lancer 74-846.)

2987)   Deutsch, Deborah. The Flaming Heart. Boston:
         Humphries, 1958. 271 pp. (Paperback--Paperback
         Library PL 54-906.)

2988)   Doliner, Roy. Young Man Willing. New York:
         Scribner's Sons, 1960. 186 pp.

2989)   Drury, Allen. Advise and Consent. Garden City,
         N.Y.: Doubleday, 1959. 616 pp. (Paperback--
         Cardinal GC952.)

2990)   Dubus, André. The Lieutenant. New York: Dial
        Press, 1967. 199 pp. (Paperback--Dell 4779.)

2991)   Duggan, Alfred. Family Favorites. New York:
        Pantheon Books, 1960. 318 pp.

2992)   Dukahz, Casimir. The Asbestos Diary. New York:
        Oliver Layton Press, 1966. 281 pp. (Paperback--
        Tower 45-985.)

2993)   Dyer, Charles. Staircase. New York: Avon
        Books, 1969. (Paperback: Avon N230.) 287 pp.

2994)   Eekhoud, George. A Strange Love. New York:
        Panurge, 1930. 252 pp.

2995)   Elmer, Martin. My Spanish Youngster. Copen-
        hagen: Vennens Forlag, 1964. 66 pp. (Paperback.)

2996)   Engstrand, Stuart. The Sling and the Arrow.
        New York: Sun Dial Press, 1947. 354 pp. (Pa-
        perback--Signet 786 and 1176; Pyramid T1629.)

2997)   Friedman, Sanford. Totempole. New York: Dut-
        ton, 1965. 411 pp. (Paperback--Signet Q3023.)

2998)   Garland, Rodney. The Heart in Exile. New York:
        Coward McCann, 1953. 314 pp. (Paperback--
        Lion 76.)

2999)   Garner, Shelley. The Flame and the Vision. Lon-
        don: Frederick Muller, Ltd., 1962. 254 pp.

3000)   Genet, Jean. The Miracle of the Rose. Transla-
        tion by Bernard Frechtman. London: A. Blond,
        1965. 292 pp.

3001)   Genet, Jean. Our Lady of the Flowers. Trans-
        lation by Bernard Frechtman. New York: Grove
        Press, 1963. 318 pp. (Paperback--Bantam
        Q2945.)

3002)   Genet, Jean. Querelle of Brest. Translation by
        Gregory Streatham. London: A. Blond, 1966.
        320 pp. (Paperback--Panther 027467.)

3003)   Genet, Jean. The Thief's Journal. Translation by

Bernard Frechtman. New York: Grove Press, 1964. 268 pp. (Paperback--Bantam N3046.)

3004) George, Eliot. The Leather Boys. London: A. Blond, 1961. 175 pp.

3005) Gingerick, William. The Gay American. New York: Vantage Press, 1965. 186 pp.

3006) Goff, Martyn. The Plaster Fabric. London: Putnam, 1957. 255 pp.

3007) Goff, Martyn. The Youngest Director. London: Putnam, 1961. 237 pp.

3008) Gorham, Charles O. McCaffery. New York: Dial Press, n.d. 245 pp. (Paperback--Crest d587.)

3009) Hall, Radclyffe. The Well of Loneliness. New York: Covici-Friede, 1928. 506 pp. (Paperback--Permabook P112 and M5010.)

3009a) Hansen, Joseph. Fadeout. New York: Harper and Row, 1970. 187 pp.

3010) Harvey, Reginald. Park Beat. New York: Castle Books, 1959. 189 pp.

3011) Hastings, March. The Boys and Brigham Dee. New York: Tower Publications, 1968. 216 pp. (Paperback--Tower 45-182.)

3012) Hearn, Wallace. Queer Triangle. New York: Vantage Press, 1961. 84 pp.

3013) Holliday, Don. Blow the Man Down. San Diego: Phenix Publications, 1968. 159 pp. (Paperback--Late Hour Library LL763.)

3014) Holliday, Don. Color Him Gay. San Diego: Corinth Publications, 1966. 160 pp. (Paperback--Leisure Book LB1158.)

3015) Holliday, Don. Gay Dogs. San Diego: Ember Library, 1967. 160 pp. (Paperback--Ember Library EL386.)

3016)   Holliday, Don.   Gothic Gaye.   San Diego: Corinth
         Publications, 1966.   160 pp.   (Paperback--Leisure
         Book LB1184.)

3017)   Holliday, Don.   Holiday Gay.   San Diego: Phenix
         Publications, 1967.   159 pp.   (Paperback--Com-
         panion Book CB545.)

3018)   Holliday, Don.   The Man From C. A. M. P.   San
         Diego: Greenleaf Classics, 1966.   160 pp.   (Pa-
         perback--Leisure Book LB1154.)

3019)   Holliday, Don.   Rally Round the Fag.   San Diego:
         Ember Library, 1967.   160 pp.   (Paperback--
         Ember Library EL367.)

3020)   Holliday, Don.   The Son Goes Down.   San Diego:
         Greenleaf Classics, 1966.   160 pp.   (Paperback--
         Leisure Book LB1177.)

3021)   Holliday, Don.   Three on a Broomstick.   San
         Diego: Greenleaf Classics, 1967.   160 pp.   (Pa-
         perback--Adult Book AB404.)

3022)   Holliday, Don.   The Watercress File.   San Diego:
         Corinth Publications, 1966.   159 pp.   (Paperback--
         Leisure Book LB1168.)

3023)   Hutchins, Maud P.   Honey on the Moon.   New
         York: W. Morrow & Co. , 1964.   191 pp.

3024)   Isherwood, Christopher.   A Meeting by the River.
         New York: Simon and Schuster, 1967.   191 pp.
         (Paperback--Lancer 74-943.)

3025)   Isherwood, Christopher.   A Single Man.   New York:
         Simon and Schuster, 1964.   186 pp.   (Paperback--
         Lancer 72-969 and 74-913.)

3026)   Jackson, Charles.   The Fall of Valor.   New York:
         Rinehart, 1946.   310 pp.   (Paperback--Popular
         Library SP278 and Signet 715.)

3027)   Jackson, Neville.   No End to the Way.   London:
         Barrie and Rockliff, 1965.   240 pp.

3028)   Jourdan, Eric.   Two.   Translation by Richard

Howard. New York: Pyramid Publications, 1963.
150 pp. (Paperback--Pyramid R877.)

3028a) Keene, Howard. Noon and Night. New York:
Award Books, 1969. (Paperback: Award A554X.)
187 pp.

3029) Kent, Nial (pseud.). The Divided Path. New
York: Greenberg, 1949. 447 pp. (Paperback--
Pyramid AT32.)

3030) King, Francis. The Man on the Rock. London:
Longmans, Green, 1957. 247 pp. (Paperback--
Penguin 2109.)

3031) Levin, Meyer. Compulsion. New York: Simon
and Schuster, 1956. 495 pp. (Paperback--Signet
Q3141 and Cardinal GC74.)

3032) Levinson, Lew. Butterfly Man. New York:
Macaulay, 1934. 358 pp.

3033) Lindop, Audrey E. The Outer Ring. New York:
Appleton-Century-Croft, 1955. 308 pp. (Reprinted
in 1956 by Popular Library as The Tormented.)

3034) Little, Jay (pseud.). Maybe Tomorrow. New
York: Pageant Press, 1957. 345 pp. (Paperback
--Paperback Library 54-710.)

3035) Little, Jay (pseud.). Somewhere Between the Two.
New York: Pageant Press, 1956. 255 pp. (Pa-
perback--Paperback Library 54-831.)

3036) Lockwood, Tom. Destination Nowhere. New York:
Castle Books, 1966. 192 pp.

3037) Mackenzie, Compton. Thin Ice. London: Chatto
and Windus, 1956. 224 pp.

3038) Mandel, Paul. Mainside. New York: Random
House, 1962. 373 pp.

3039) Mann, Thomas. Death in Venice. Translation by
Kenneth Burke. New York: Knopf, 1965. 118 pp.

3040) Martin, Kenneth. Aubade. London: Chapman and

264   Homosexuality

Hall, 1958. 158 pp.

3041) Maugham, Robin. Behind the Mirror. London:
       Longmans, Green, 1955. 185 pp.

3042) McCoy, R. Entrapment. Los Angeles: Argyle,
       1965. 160 pp.

3043) McIntosh, Harlan C. This Finer Shadow. New
       York: Dial Press, 1941. 408 pp.

3044) Meeker, Richard. The Better Angel. New York:
       Greenberg, 1933. (Reprinted as Torment.)

3044a) Merrick, Gordon. The Lord Won't Mind. New
       York: B. Geis Associates, 1970. 280 pp.

3045) Mills, Carley. A Nearness of Evil. New York:
       Coward-McCann, 1961. 255 pp.

3046) Monsarrat, Nicholas. Smith and Jones. New York:
       Sloane Associates, 1963. 182 pp. (Paperback--
       Pocket Books 75221.)

3047) Murphy, Dennis. The Sergeant. New York:
       Viking, 1958. 254 pp. (Paperback--Macfadden
       75-201.)

3048) Packer, Vin. Whisper His Sin. New York: Faw-
       cett Publications, 1954. 160 pp.

3049) Peters, Fritz. Finistere. London: Gollancz,
       1951. 286 pp. (Paperback--Signet 930 and Lancer
       74-947.)

3050) Petronius. The Satyricon. Translation by William
       Arrowsmith. Ann Arbor: University of Michigan
       Press, 1959. 165 pp. (Paperback--Mentor MD
       283.)

3051) Peyrefitte, Roger. The Exile of Capri. Transla-
       tion by Edward Hyams. New York: Fleet Pub-
       lishing Co. , 1965. 284 pp.

3052) Peyrefitte, Roger. Special Friendships. Transla-
       tion by Edward Hyams. London: Secker and War-
       burg, 1958. 348 pp.

3053)   Plato. The Symposium. Translation by B. Jowett.
        In The Works of Plato, selected and edited by
        Irwin Edman. New York: Modern Library, 1928.
        Pp. 333-93.

3054)   Proust, Marcel. Cities of the Plain. Translation
        by C. K. Scott Moncrieff. New York: Modern
        Library, 1927. 384 pp.

3055)   Purdy, James. Eustace Chisholm and the Works.
        New York: Farrar, Straus, 1967. 241 pp. (Pa-
        perback--Bantam N3797.)

3056)   Raul, K. B. A Hidden Hunger. New York: Paper-
        back Library, 1968. 158 pp. (Paperback--PL55-
        724.)

3057)   Raul, K. B. Naked to the Night. New York: Pa-
        perback Library, 1964. 175 pp. (Paperback--
        PL53-285.)

3058)   Raven, Simon. The Feathers of Death. London:
        A. Blond, 1959. 254 pp.

3059)   Rebow, Milton. Oh Dear! New York: Key Pub-
        lishing Co., 1957. 181 pp.

3060)   Rechy, John. City of Night. New York: Grove
        Press, 1963. 410 pp. (Paperback--Black Cat
        BC1296.)

3061)   Rechy, John. Numbers. New York: Grove Press,
        1967. 256 pp. (Paperback--Black Cat BC171.)

3061a) Rechy, John. The Day's Death. New York: Grove
        Press, 1970. 255 pp.

3062)   Renault, Mary. The Charioteer. London: Long-
        mans, Green, 1953. 400 pp. (Paperback--Four
        Square 798 and Cardinal 75181.)

3063)   Renault, Mary. The Last of the Wine. New York:
        Pantheon, 1956. 389 pp. (Paperback--Cardinal
        75025 and Pocket Books 77115.)

3064)   Renault, Mary. The Mask of Apollo. New York:
        Pantheon, 1966. 371 pp. (Paperback--Pocket
        Books 95049.)

3065)   Rico, Don. The Daisy Dilemma. New York:
         Lancer Books, 1967. 222 pp. (Paperback--Lancer
         73-639.)

3066)   Rico, Don. The Man from Pansy. New York:
         Lancer Books, 1967. 224 pp. (Paperback--Lancer
         73-578.)

3067)   Rosenthal, Irving. Sheeper. New York: Grove
         Press, 1967. 304 pp.

3068)   Ross, Walter. The Immortal. London: F.
         Muller, 1958. 207 pp. (Paperback--Cardinal
         C338.)

3069)   Selby, James. Madame. New York: Dodd, Mead,
         1961. 313 pp.

3070)   Spicer, Bart. Act of Anger. New York: Athe-
         neum, 1962. 505 pp. (Paperback--Bantam S2607
         and N4016.)

3071)   Storey, David. Radcliffe. London: Longmans,
         1963. 376 pp.

3072)   Tellier, Andre. Twilight Men. New York:
         Greenberg, 1931. 223 pp. (Paperback--Lion 24
         and Pyramid G262.)

3073)   Tesch, Gordon. Never the Same Again. New
         York: Putnam, 1956. 318 pp. (Paperback--
         Pyramid G342.)

3074)   Thorp, Roderick. The Detective. New York:
         Dial Press, 1966. 598 pp. (Paperback--Avon
         N156 and W159.)

3075)   Turnell, John. The Stringed Lute. London:
         Rider and Co., 1955. 191 pp.

3076)   Vidal, Gore. The City and the Pillar. New York:
         Dutton, 1948. 314 pp. (Paperback--Signet 1218.)

3077)   Vidal, Gore. The City and the Pillar Revised.
         New York: Dutton, 1965. 226 pp. (Paperback--
         Signet T3603.)

3078)   Vidal, Gore. <u>Myra Breckinridge.</u> Boston: Little,
        Brown, 1968. 264 pp. (Paperback--Bantam
        Q3910.)

3079)   Wahl, Loren. <u>The Invisible Glass.</u> New York:
        Greenberg, 1950. 230 pp.

3079a) Walker, Gerald. <u>Cruising.</u> New York: Stein
        and Day, 1970. 192 pp.

3080)   Wilde, Oscar (?). <u>Teleny or the Reverse of the</u>
        <u>Medal.</u> London: Icon Books, 1966. 172 pp.
        (Paperback--Brandon House 2016.)

3081)   Williamson, Hugh Ross. <u>A Wicked Pack of Cards.</u>
        London: Michael Joseph, 1961. 205 pp.

3082)   Windham, Donald. <u>Two People.</u> New York:
        Coward-McCann, 1965. 252 pp.

3083)   Yourcenar, Marguerite. <u>Memoirs of Hadrian.</u>
        London: Secker and Warburg, 1955. 320 pp.
        (Paperback--Noonday N258.)

                            PLAYS

3084)   Anderson, Robert W. <u>Tea and Sympathy.</u> New
        York: Random House, 1953. 182 pp. (Paperback--
        Signet S1343.)

3085)   Chayefsky, Paddy. <u>The Latent Heterosexual.</u> New
        York: Random House, 1967. 115 pp.

3086)   Coward, Noel. "A Song at Twilight" in <u>Suite in</u>
        <u>Three Keys.</u> London: Heinemann, 1966. Pp. 1-
        85.

3087)   Crowley, Mart. <u>The Boys in the Band.</u> London:
        Secker and Warburg, 1969. 182 pp. (Paperback--
        Dell 0773.)

3088)   Delaney, Shelagh. <u>A Taste of Honey.</u> New York:
        Grove Press, 1959. 87 pp. (Paperback--Ever-
        green E159.)

3089)   Dyer, Charles. <u>Staircase.</u> New York: Grove

Press, 1966.   88 pp.

3090)   Fugate, James B.   Game of Fools.   Los Angeles:
        One, Inc., 1954.   100 pp.

3091)   Gaard, David.   And Puppy Dog Tales.   1969.

3092)   Herbert, John.   Fortune and Men's Eyes.   New
        York: Grove Press, 1967.   96 pp.   (Paperback.)

3093)   Hellman, Lillian.   The Children's Hour.   New
        York: Knopf, 1936.   115 pp.

3094)   Marcus, Frank.   The Killing of Sister George.
        London: Samuel French, 1965.   80 pp.   (Paper-
        back.)

3095)   Osborne, John.   A Patriot for Me.   London:
        Faber, 1965.   128 pp.

3095a) Raad, Gerry.   Circle in the Water.   1970.

3096)   Vidal, Gore.   The Best Man.   Boston: Little,
        Brown, 1960.   168 pp.

3097)   Weil, Gus.   Geese and Parents and Children.
        1969.

3098)   Williams, Tennessee.   Cat on a Hot Tin Roof.
        New York: New Directions, 1955.   197 pp.   (Pa-
        perback--Signet P2855.)

3099)   Williams, Tennessee.   Suddenly, Last Summer.
        New York: New Directions, 1958.   90 pp.   (Pa-
        perback--Signet D2494.)

3100)   Wilson, Lanford.   The Madness of Lady Bright.
        1969.

                        SHORT STORIES

3101)   Barr, James.   Derricks.   New York: Pan Books,
        1957.

3102)   Burns, John Horne.   The Gallery.   New York:
        Harper, 1947.   (Paperback--Bantam A1146.)

3103) Cory, Donald W. (ed.) Twenty-One Variations on a Theme. New York: Greenberg, 1953.

3104) Dunsmore. Six. Washington, D. C.: Guild Press, 1966. (Paperback.)

3105) Four From the Circle. San Francisco: Pan-Graphic Press, 1959. (Paperback.)

3106) Goodman, Alexander. "Blaze of Summer," "Carnal Matters," "The First Time," "Handsome Is," "Mercenary Affections," "A Sliver of Flesh," "Soft Spot," "A Sweet Gentle Boy." Washington, D. C.: Guild Press, 1966-67. (Paperback.)

3107) Harry's Fare and Other Stories. San Francisco: Pan-Graphic Press, 1960. (Paperback.)

3108) House of Dreams. San Francisco: Pan-Graphic Press, 1964. (Paperback.)

3109) Otis, Harry. Camel's Farewell. San Francisco: Pan-Graphic Press, 1961. (Paperback.)

3110) Otis, Harry. The Keval and Other Stories. Los Angeles: One, Inc., 1959. (Paperback.)

3111) Overture in G Minor. San Francisco: Pan-Graphic Press, 1964. (Paperback.)

3112) Proferes, James J. "Hellbound in Leather," "Navy Blues," "Of Greenbacks and Dress Blues," "Of Hot Nights and Damp Beds," "Weep No More My Laddie." Washington, D. C.: Guild Press, 1966-67. (Paperback.)

3113) Ramp, James H. Wild Strawberry Patch. San Francisco: Fanfare Publications, 1966. (Paperback.)

3114) Randolph, Peter. Sextet: Six Short Stories. Washington, D. C.: Guild Press, 1967. (Paperback.)

3115) Selby, Hubert Jr. Last Exit to Brooklyn. New York: Grove Press, 1957. (Paperback--Black Cat BC153.)

3116)   Vidal, Gore. A Thirsty Evil: Seven Short Stories.
        New York: Zero Press, 1956. (Reprinted in part
        in Three [New York: New American Library,
        1962]. (Paperback--Signet S1535.)

3117)   Williams, Tennessee. Hard Candy. New York:
        New Directions, 1954. (Paperback.)

3118)   Williams, Tennessee. One Arm. New York: New
        Directions, 1948. (Paperback.)

3119)   Wilson, Sandy. The Poodle from Rome. London:
        Michael Joseph, 1962.

Miscellaneous Works

MOVIES

With major homosexual theme

3120) Advise and Consent

3121) Always on Sunday
(underground)

3122) The Best Man

3123) Bike Boy (under-
ground)

3124) Blow Job (under-
ground)

3124a) The Boys in the
Band

3125) Brothel (underground)

3126) Catullus Silent (experimental)

3127) Un Chant d'Amour
(underground)

3128) The Chelsea Girls
(underground)

3129) The Children's Hour

3130) Compulsion

3131) The Detective

3132) Drag '69 (under-
ground)

3133) Fireworks (under-
ground)

3134) Flaming Creatures
(underground)

3135) Flesh (underground)

3136) The Fox

3137) The Gay Deceivers

3138) Inauguration of the
Pleasure Dome
(underground)

3139) Julietta of the Spirits

3140) The Killing of Sister
George

3141) The Leather Boys

3142) Lonesome Cowboys
(underground)

3143) Marco of Rio (underground)

3144) My Hustler (under-
ground)

3145) Passion in a Seaside
Slum (underground)

3146) Portrait of Jason
(underground)

3147) The Queen (under-
       ground)

3148) Scorpio Rising
       (underground)

3149) The Secret of Wen-
       dell Sampson
       (underground)

3150) The Sergeant

3150a) Something for Every-
       one

3151) Spy on the Fly
       (underground)

3152) Staircase

3153) Sticks and Stones
       (underground)

3154) A Taste of Honey

3155) Therese et Isabelle

3156) The Third Sex
       (German)

3157) This Sporting Life

3158) The Trials of Oscar
       Wilde (or, The
       Man with a Green
       Carnation)

3159) Vapors (underground)

3160) Victim

3161) Walk on the Wild Side

With minor homosexual theme

3162) Beckett

3163) Cat on a Hot Tin Roof

3164) The Damned

3165) Darling

3166) La Dolce Vita

3167) The Hill

3168) If

3169) King Rat

3170) The Lion in Winter

3171) Midnight Cowboy

3172) The Pawnbroker

3173) Reflections in a
       Golden Eye

3174) Rocco and His Broth-
       ers

3175) The Servant

3176) Suddenly, Last Sum-
       mer

3177) Tea and Sympathy

3178) A View from the
       Bridge

TELEVISION PROGRAMS

3179)   ABC "Weep the Weary Hunter Home," Judd for
         the Defense, Nov. 8, 1968.

3180)   BBC "One in Twenty." 1966.

3180a)   CBS "Medical Center - Undercurrent." Sep. 23,
         1970.

3181)   CBS. "CBS Report: The Homosexuals,"
         Mar. 7, 1967.

3182)   Intertel. "Every Tenth Man," Apr. 12, 1965.

3183)   KCOP (Los Angeles). "The Homosexual: Couch,
         Campus, and Courtroom," Aug. 28, 1966.

3183a)   KNBC (Los Angeles). "Out of the Shadows,"
         June 26, 1970.

3184)   KRON (San Francisco). "Homosexual." 1965.

3185)   National Educational Television - KQED (San Fran-
         cisco). "The Rejected," Sep. 11, 1961. (See no.
         191 above.)

3186)   WRCA (New York City). "Homosexuality: the
         Psychological Approach," The Open Mind, Aug. 4,
         1956.

PHONOGRAPH RECORDS

3187)   Ardery, Breck and William (privately recorded).
         "June 28, 1970 - Gay and Proud."

3188)   Probe T-2652 (Capitol Records Documentary).
         "Homosexuality in the American Male."

Appendix

AMERICAN LAWS APPLICABLE TO CONSENSUAL
ADULT HOMOSEXUAL ACTS (1970)

State & Statute	Offense	Status of Offense
ALABAMA		
14. 42 & 15. 327	attempt to commit crime against nature	misdemeanor
14. 106	crime against nature	felony
14. 326(1)	indecent exposure	misdemeanor
14. 437 & 438	vagrancy	misdemeanor
ALASKA		
11. 40. 080	indecent exposure	misdemeanor
11. 40. 120	unnatural crime - sodomy, crime against nature	felony
ARIZONA		
13. 371	disorderly conduct	misdemeanor
13. 651	sodomy - crime against nature	felony
13. 652	lewd acts committed in an unnatural manner	felony
13. 993	vagrancy - loitering near public toilet	misdemeanor
	(if previous conviction of sex offense)	felony
13. 1271-74 & 13. 1645	failure to register as sex offender	misdemeanor
ARKANSAS		
41. 813	sodomy or buggery	felony
41. 2701 & 41. 196	indecent exposure	misdemeanor
41. 3202	lewdness and lewd solicitation	misdemeanor
CALIFORNIA		
286	sodomy or crime against nature	felony

CALIFORNIA (cont.)

288a	sex perversion - oral copulation	felony or misdemeanor
290 & 19	failure to register as sex offender	misdemeanor
314	lewd conduct and indecent exposure (if already convicted of this offense)	misdemeanor felony
415	disturbing the peace	misdemeanor
647(a)	disorderly conduct - soli- citation, lewdness	misdemeanor
647(b)	disorderly conduct - pros- titution	misdemeanor
647(d)	disorderly conduct - loi- tering, lewd intent	misdemeanor
647b	loitering near adult school	misdemeanor
650 1/2 & 19	outraging public decency	misdemeanor

COLORADO

40. 2. 31(1)	crime against nature	felony
40. 2. 31(2)	solicitation for unnatural copulation	misdemeanor or felony
40. 8. 19	vagrancy	misdemeanor
40. 9. 15	lewdness and public in- decency	misdemeanor

CONNECTICUT

53. 175	disorderly conduct	misdemeanor
53. 216	sodomy	felony
53. 220	indecent exposure	misdemeanor
53. 226	lewdness, prostitution, assignation	misdemeanor
53. 235	lewd and lascivious persons	misdemeanor

(Note: new criminal code effective October 1, 1971 only applicable offense will be:

| 188 | public indecency and lewd- ness | misdemeanor) |

DELAWARE

| 11. 731-732 | lewdness | misdemeanor |
| 11. 831 | sodomy, crime against nature | felony |

DISTRICT OF COLUMBIA

| 22. 1112 | lewd, indecent, and ob- scene acts | misdemeanor |
| 22. 1121(1) | disorderly conduct | misdemeanor |

State & Statute	Offense	Status of Offense
DISTRICT OF COLUMBIA (cont.)		
22. 3302, 3304	vagrancy	misdemeanor
22. 3502	sodomy	felony
FLORIDA		
796. 07	lewdness, prostitution, assignation	misdemeanor
800. 01	crime against nature	felony
800. 02	unnatural and lascivious acts	misdemeanor
800. 03	indecent exposure	misdemeanor
856. 02-03	vagrancy - lewd persons	misdemeanor
GEORGIA		
26. 1001	attempt to commit sodomy	felony
26. 2002	sodomy (including lesbian acts)	felony
26. 2003 & 27. 2506	solicitation of sodomy	misdemeanor
26. 2011	public indecency	misdemeanor
HAWAII		
702. 1 and 5	attempt to commit sodomy	felony
727. 1	lewdness, indecent exposure	misdemeanor
768. 71	sodomy or crime against nature	felony
772. 1	vagrancy - lewd persons	misdemeanor
772. 2(7) and 3	disorderly conduct - loitering, lewdness, soliciting, wearing clothing of opposite sex with intent to deceive	misdemeanor
IDAHO		
18. 4101 & 18. 113	indecent exposure and obscenity	misdemeanor
18. 6605	crime against nature	felony
ILLINOIS		
38. 11. 2	deviate sexual conduct in private	no offense
38. 11. 9	public indecency	misdemeanor
INDIANA		
10. 2801	public indecency	misdemeanor
10. 4221	sodomy or crime against nature	felony

IOWA

705. 1 and 2	sodomy	felony
725. 1	lewdness, indecent exposure	misdemeanor

KANSAS

21. 3505 & 21. 4502-03	(Consensual) sodomy	misdemeanor
21. 3508 & 21. 4502-03	lewd behavior	misdemeanor
21. 4108(d) & 21. 4502	loitering for immoral purpose	misdemeanor

KENTUCKY

435. 105(2)	indecent or immoral practices	felony
436. 050	sodomy or buggery	felony
436. 075	lewdness	misdemeanor

LOUISIANA

14. 89	crime against nature	felony
14. 106	indecent exposure, lewdness, solicitation	misdemeanor

MAINE

17. 1001	crime against nature	felony
17. 1901	indecent exposure	misdemeanor
17. 3758	vagrants - wanton and lascivious persons	misdemeanor

MARYLAND

27. 122	disorderly conduct, indecent exposure	misdemeanor
27. 553	sodomy	felony
27. 554	unnatural or perverted sexual practices	felony

MASSACHUSETTS

272. 16	lewdness	felony
272. 34	sodomy, buggery, crime against nature	felony
272. 35	unnatural and lascivious acts	felony
272. 53	lascivious behavior, indecent exposure	misdemeanor

State & Statute	Offense	Status of Offense
MICHIGAN		
28.355	sodomy, crime against nature (special provision for sexually delinquent person)	felony
28.364-365 & 28.772	disorderly persons - indecent conduct	misdemeanor
28.567	lewdness, lascivious behavior	misdemeanor
28.567(1) & 28.200(1)	indecent exposure (special provision for sexually delinquent person)	misdemeanor
28.570 & 28.200(1)	gross indecency between males, and attempts (special provision for sexually delinquent person)	felony
28.570(1)	gross indecency between females, & attempts (special provision for sexually delinquent person)	felony
MINNESOTA		
609.293.5	Consensual sodomy	gross misdemeanor
617.23 & 609.03(2)	indecent exposure, lewdness, public indecency	gross misdemeanor
MISSISSIPPI		
2290	lewd exposure	misdemeanor
2413	unnatural intercourse, crime against nature	felony
MISSOURI		
563.150 & 556.270	lewdness	misdemeanor
563.230	crime against nature	felony
MONTANA		
94.3603 & 94.116	indecent exposure	misdemeanor
94.4118	crime against nature	felony
NEBRASKA		
28.919	crime against nature, sodomy	felony
28.920	indecent exposure	misdemeanor

NEBRASKA (cont.)

28. 920. 01	procuring, counseling, aiding exposure	misdemeanor

NEVADA

201. 190(b)	crime against nature	felony
201. 210, 193. 130 &	lewdness- first offense	gross misdemeanor
193. 140	lewdness- subsequent offense	felony
201. 220	indecent exposure - first offense	gross misdemeanor
	indecent exposure- subsequent offense	felony
207. 151 and 157 & 193. 150	failure to register as a sex offender	misdemeanor
207. 030 & 193. 150	vagrancy - solicitation or loitering for lewd conduct	misdemeanor
208. 070	attempt to commit crime against nature etc.	felony or misdemeanor

NEW HAMPSHIRE

570. 1 and 22	disorderly conduct	misdemeanor
570. 6 and 22	indecent exposure	misdemeanor
570. 25	vagrancy - lascivious behavior	misdemeanor
579. 3	lewdness	misdemeanor
579. 9	unnatural and lascivious acts	felony

NEW JERSEY

2A:85. 5	attempt to commit sodomy, etc.	misdemeanor (= felony)
2A:115. 1 & 85. 7	lewdness or indecency	misdemeanor (= felony)
2A:143. 1	sodomy or crime against nature	high misdemeanor (= felony)
2A:170. 1 & 169. 4	disorderly persons with unlawful purpose	misdemeanor
2A:170. 5 & 169. 4	lewd solicitation	misdemeanor

NEW MEXICO

40A. 9. 6 & 40A. 29. 3C	sodomy	felony
40A. 9. 8 & 40A. 29. 4B	indecent exposure	petty misdemeanor

State & Statute	Offense	Status of Offense
NEW YORK		
130. 38 and 130. 00. 2	consensual sodomy	misdemeanor
240. 35. 3	loitering for deviate sexual purposes	violation
245. 00	public lewdness	misdemeanor
(for penalities, see 60. 10. 2(d), 70. 15. 2 & 4, 80. 05. 2 & 4, and 80. 15. 2)		
NORTH CAROLINA		
14. 177 & 14. 2	crime against nature	felony
14. 190 & 14. 3	indecent exposure	misdemeanor
NORTH DAKOTA		
12. 21. 10 & 12. 06. 14	indecent exposure	misdemeanor
12. 22. 01 & 12. 06. 14	public indecency	misdemeanor
12. 22. 07	sodomy	felony or misdemeanor
12. 42. 04. 5	vagrancy - lewd behavior	misdemeanor
OHIO		
2905. 30	indecent exposure, solicitation or attempt for unnatural act	misdemeanor
2905. 44	sodomy	felony
2909. 09	nuisance, trespass	misdemeanor
2950. 01-08	failure to register as habitual sex offender	misdemeanor
OKLAHOMA		
21. 22 and 21. 10	outraging public decency	misdemeanor
21. 42	attempt to commit crime against nature	felony
21. 886	crime against nature	felony
21. 1029-31	lewdness, prostitution, assignation	misdemeanor
OREGON		
166. 060	vagrancy - loitering, disorderly conduct	misdemeanor
167. 040	sodomy, crime against nature, sexually perverse acts	felony
167. 145	indecent exposure	misdemeanor

PENNSYLVANIA

18. 4501	sodomy	felony
18. 4502	solicitation for sodomy	felony
18. 4519	public indecency, lewd-ness	misdemeanor

RHODE ISLAND

11. 10. 1	crime against nature	felony
11. 45. 1	vagrancy - lewd or in-decent behavior	misdemeanor

SOUTH CAROLINA

16. 409 & 16. 411	lewdness, indecent ex-posure	misdemeanor
16. 412	buggery	felony
16. 413 & 17. 553	indecent exposure	misdemeanor
16. 565	vagrancy - leading a disorderly life	misdemeanor

SOUTH DAKOTA

22. 22. 21	crime against nature	felony
22. 24. 1 & 22. 24. 2. 1	indecent exposure	misdemeanor
22. 24. 6 & 22. 6. 2	outraging public decency	misdemeanor

TENNESSEE

39. 707	crime against nature	felony

TEXAS

524	sodomy	felony
607(16) & (20) & 608	vagrancy - lewdness	misdemeanor

UTAH

76. 39. 5(1), 76. 1. 16 and 76. 39. 13	lewdness, indecent expo-sure, and obscene be-havior	misdemeanor
76. 53. 22	(consensual) sodomy	misdemeanor
76. 61. 1(5)	vagrancy - lewd persons	misdemeanor

VERMONT

13. 2601	lewd and lascivious conduct	felony
13. 2603	fellation	felony

VIRGINIA

18. 1. 212	crime against nature	felony
18. 1. 236 & 18. 1. 9	indecent exposure	misdemeanor

State & Statute	Offense	Status of Offense
WASHINGTON		
9. 79. 080(2)	indecent exposure	felony or misdemeanor
9. 79. 100	sodomy	felony
9. 79. 120 & 9. 92. 020	lewdness	gross misdemeanor
9. 87. 010(7)	vagrancy - lewd persons	misdemeanor
WEST VIRGINIA		
61. 8. 4	lewd and lascivious conduct	misdemeanor
61. 8. 13	crime against nature	felony
61. 8. 28	indecent exposure	misdemeanor
WISCONSIN		
944. 17	sexual perversion	felony
944. 20	lewd behavior, indecent exposure	misdemeanor
WYOMING		
6. 98	sodomy	felony
6. 102	public indecency, indecent exposure	misdemeanor
UNITED STATES UNIFORM CODE OF MILITARY JUSTICE		
80	attempt to commit acts below	felony or misdemeanor
125	sodomy	felony
134	conduct to the discredit of the service	misdemeanor
	indecent exposure	misdemeanor
	indecent and lewd acts	felony

(Note: In addition to the criminal statutes listed here, in approximately two-thirds of the states, homosexuals may also be committed under a variety of conditions to hospitals or prisons for indefinite terms, extending up to life, as sexually dangerous persons, sex psychopaths, or mentally disordered offenders.)

Index of Subjects

(Numbers are entry numbers, not page numbers)

Adolescents--see Children and Adolescents
Advertising, 721
Aging process, 1937
Aggression, dependency, and power, 84a, 1666, 1676,
    2182, 2287, 2297, 2621
Alcoholism, 235, 239, 258, 1537, 1554, 1555, 1612, 1644,
    1647, 1668, 1875, 1888, 2060, 2115, 2142, 2166, 2183,
    2371, 2376, 2380, 2419, 2432, 2476, 2553, 2583, 2721
American Civil Liberties Union, 135-37, 190
Ancient Greece, 110, 370, 372, 465, 479, 1857, 2899,
    2939
Animals, Homosexuality in, 24, 290, 345, 1589, 1590,
    1695, 1777-79, 1898, 1947, 1962, 2052, 2080, 2207,
    2257, 2337, 2368, 2635
Anthropological and sociological aspects and factors, 8, 24,
    27, 52, 98, 111, 120, 121, 227, 234a, 235a, 287, 317,
    327, 336, 339, 355, 359, 375, 376, 382, 401, 445, 446,
    499, 502, 549, 567, 1119, 1239, 1290, 1297, 1299, 1304,
    1320, 1333, 1343, 1349, 1385, 1411, 1600, 1601, 1606,
    1697, 1698, 1762, 1763, 1793, 1826, 1837, 1891, 2126,
    2136, 2139, 2387, 2494, 2614, 2650-52, 2664, 2667,
    2674, 2676, 2678, 2684, 2692-94, 2700, 2706, 2707,
    2712, 2713, 2728, 2744, 2745, 2747, 2751, 2870, 2872,
    2913, 2942
Anti-homosexuality, 561a, 677a, 2965
The Armed Services, 178, 202, 203, 204, 218, 219, 219a,
    220, 220a, 220b, 220c, 222, 223, 579, 590, 705, 787,
    797, 850, 851, 941, 965, 1287, 1294, 1358, 1423, 1428,
    1444, 1445, 1446, 1448, 1466, 1467, 1469, 1474, 1494,
    1512, 1516, 1528, 1532, 1538, 1556, 1750, 1773, 1782,
    2164, 2290, 2320, 2321, 2406, 2457, 2582, 2584, 2589,
    2695, 2779, 2817, 2831, 2847, 2919, 2941, 2948. See
    also Draft.
Arts, Homosexuality and, 916, 1060, 1146, 1543, 2043,
    2200, 2613. See also, "Camp," Fashions, Homosexuality
    in Literature, Literature on a Homosexual Theme, Movies,
    Music, Homosexuals in Television, and Theater.

Atlanta, 647

Attitudes of Homosexuals, 2083

Autobiographies, 1, 30, 32, 34a, 59, 71, 74, 92, 122, 622, 720, 1219, 1558, 1772, 2191, 2854

Aversion or behavior therapy, 365, 810, 963, 965, 1365, 1555, 1580, 1635, 1636, 1678, 1715, 1771, 1808, 1811-14, 1830, 1894, 2044-47, 2105, 2110, 2111, 2133, 2141, 2150, 2176-78, 2198, 2209, 2211, 2218, 2219, 2235, 2239, 2296, 2306, 2358, 2362, 2367, 2402, 2422, 2493, 2500, 2511, 2518, 2543, 2550-52, 2757

The Bible, 298, 299, 329, 457, 962, 1042, 1094, 1134, 1238, 1252, 2610, 2726, 2963

Bibliography, 142, 163, 188, 194, 2781

Biography, 31, 42 (da Vinci) 43, 44, 48, 51, 59a, 60 (Wilde), 67, 74, 95, 97 (Genet), 270 (Wilde), 272, 309 (Symonds), 342 (Wilde), 377 (Wilde), 383 (Rimbaud), 393a 411, 475 (Krupp), 491 (Proust), 521 (Wilde), 560 (Whitman), 727 (Gide), 843, 1545 (Wilde), 1652 (Symonds), 1691 (Whitman), 1699 (Wilde), 1904, 1926 (Rousseau), 2338 (Whitman), 2339 2608 (von Kleist), 2613 (da Vinci), 2682 (Whitman), 2729 (Proust), 2765 (Proust), 2868 (Beethoven), 2907 (Prince Eulenberg), 2918 (Wilde), 2920 (Whitman), 2934 (Tchaikovsky), 2991 (Heliogabalus)

Biological factors, 2798, 2814

Bisexuality, 1680, 2265, 2266, 2273, 2286, 2359, 2585, 2608

Blackmail, 681, 682, 785, 789, 860, 870, 1078, 1250, 2061, 2875, 2891

Body build, 1726, 1727, 1992, 2084, 2433, 2622, 2623

Boise, Idaho, 44, 716, 730, 857

Book reviews, 812, 816, 825, 827, 834, 858, 871, 884, 894, 914, 921, 934, 938, 940, 997, 1019, 1020, 1057, 1058, 1061, 1071, 1079, 1080, 1083, 1093, 1098, 1111, 1121, 1128, 1139, 1161, 1166, 1176, 1177, 1191, 1200, 1202, 1212, 1244, 1301, 1314, 1325, 1410, 1684, 2574, 2720

British Magistrates' Report, 2135

British Medical Association Report, 143, 1719, 2006, 2008, 2346

British Parliament, 59a, 408, 409, 523, 662, 930, 1004, 1005, 1069, 1391, 1420, 2171, 2333, 2644. See also Wolfenden Committee and Report.

"Camp," 680, 741, 748, 1050, 1085

Canada, 46a, 956, 1159, 2903

Case histories, 45, 69, 114, 141, 229, 233, 234, 356, 357, 363, 373, 374, 379, 411, 431, 437, 453, 470, 485, 1127, 1559, 1622, 1694, 1700, 1713, 1742, 1750, 1774, 1800, 1801, 1802, 1820, 1823, 1832, 1834, 1841, 1855, 1861, 1893,

1904, 2018, 2042, 2053, 2082, 2144, 2145, 2168, 2170,
2236, 2262, 2270, 2374, 2420, 2430, 2431, 2461, 2462,
2509, 2548, 2604, 2631, 2725
Castration, 1703, 2070
Causation or genesis, 2, 18, 25, 39, 53-56, 75, 99, 101,
133, 172, 230, 271, 348, 358, 360, 367a, 387, 406, 407,
420, 432, 434, 495, 526, 529, 782, 1576, 1598, 1599,
1600, 1627, 1634, 1643, 1683, 1728, 1734, 1747, 1805,
1863, 1866, 1911, 1939, 1949, 1956, 1969, 1974, 1975,
1977, 2024, 2055, 2067, 2090, 2107, 2112, 2156, 2256,
2290, 2294, 2341, 2414, 2429, 2486, 2562, 2588, 2595,
2619, 2894. See also Constitutional factors and General
surveys of homosexuality.
Chicago, 712
Children and adolescents, 46a, 62, 63, 78. 84, 132, 247,
376, 384, 390, 393, 442, 455, 459, 527, 589, 716, 720,
750, 857, 893, 1026, 1312, 1327, 1352, 1364, 1369,
1380, 1573, 1574, 1595-97, 1608, 1673, 1674, 1686,
1702, 1733, 1760, 1786, 1819, 1825, 1860, 1874, 1953,
1957, 1968, 1989, 2016, 2030, 2034, 2056, 2078, 2113
2127, 2159, 2175, 2182, 2185, 2215, 2232, 2250, 2251,
2260, 2291, 2345, 2361, 2433, 2497, 2499, 2570, 2577, 2578,
2590, 2634, 2642, 2660, 2673, 2713, 2728, 2764, 2767,
2914. See also Pedophilia.
The Christian Church and the homosexual, 6, 7, 17, 21,
49, 64, 85a, 116, 128, 147, 148, 149, 153, 160, 166,
167, 168, 174, 179, 180, 183, 185, 196, 197, 206, 207,
208, 231, 284, 288, 298, 299, 309, 329, 389, 400, 428,
457, 474, 506, 517, 519, 542, 546, 561a, 563, 609, 610,
620, 621, 624, 630, 658, 670, 674, 690, 693, 739, 764,
804, 814, 854, 962, 1029, 1036, 1042, 1092, 1094, 1122-
1256, 1632, 2005, 2816, 2842, 2865, 2866, 2878, 2883,
2887, 2962, 2964. See also Bible, Church of England,
English Roman Catholic Advisory Committee, Morality
and Sin, Quaker Report, and Roman Catholic Attitudes.
Church of England, Moral Welfare Council Report, 7
Civil Liberties, 135, 136, 137, 156, 190, 207, 213, 561a,
603a, 605, 616, 622, 659, 684, 712, 866, 944, 998, 2850,
2851, 2856, 2874, 2875, 2882, 2889, 2901, 2933, 2935,
2951, 2961. See also American Civil Liberties Union,
Homosexual Bill of Rights.
Civil Service Commission--see Federal policy.
College students, 260, 303, 313, 394, 589, 598, 622, 685,
703, 706, 708, 790, 843, 881, 1648, 1650, 1655, 1751,
1810, 1822, 1887, 2228-30, 2398, 2399, 2495, 2524,
2593, 2687
Consensual homosexual acts, 812, 956, 963, 990, 1269,
1303, 1315, 1327, 1342, 1356, 1372, 1375, 1389, 2731,
2824, 2835

Constitutional factors, 1576, 1969, 1974, 1977
Council on Religion and the Homosexual, 146-51, 179, 183,
185, 206, 1143, 1144, 1147, 1148, 1228, 1245
Counseling, 21, 124, 460, 586, 1152, 1180, 1193, 1216,
1957, 1958, 2601, 2940
Court cases, 32, 44, 60, 122, 351, 561a, 594, 601, 641,
642, 649, 650, 687, 860, 888, 889, 932, 954, 1261,
1276, 1293, 1295, 1323, 1370, 1375, 1386, 1398, 1402,
1424-1533, 2791, 2851, 2863, 2895, 2922, 2933, 2951
Courts, 561a, 1732, 1738, 1928, 2146, 2716
Creativity, 95, 916, 1791, 1870, 2581, 2608. See also
Homosexuality and the Arts.
Cuba, 707, 879
Cure--see Therapy

Defense of homosexuality, 9, 26, 38, 46, 79, 86, 122,
123, 152, 561a
Dementia praecox, 1800, 1801, 2284
Denmark, 2521, 2522, 2530, 2750
Denver, 709
Depression, 1640
Detecting the homosexual--tests:
    DAP, 1553, 1579, 1908, 2525, 2526, 2569, 2592, 2671
    Goodenough, 1747, 1864, 1865
    Human figure drawing, 463, 1675, 1756, 1835, 1861a,
    1907, 1948, 2188, 2251, 2469
    Lie detector, 1034
    MAPS, 1820, 2017, 2236, 2461, 2462
    Penile volume, 1847-50, 1852, 2214
    Pupil response, 773, 1980, 2434
    Szondi, 237, 1594, 1642, 1748, 1759, 2100, 2172, 2520
    TAT, 1749, 2017, 2054, 2154, 2155, 2236, 2461, 2462
    others, 617, 668, 772, 932, 1704, 1729, 1743, 1753,
    1782, 1858, 1881, 1923, 1961, 1991, 2017, 2104, 2118,
    2143, 2173, 2201, 2313, 2571, 2573, 2579, 2580, 2582,
    2636-38, 2685
See also MMPI, Rorschach, Drawing Characteristics.
Disease, Homosexuality as--see Psychopathology.
Diseases (physical), 1567, 1585, 1702, 1809, 1862, 2531.
See also Venereal diseases.
Draft (Selective Service), 155, 199a, 205, 705, 960, 969,
1018, 2919, 2930, 2931. See also the Armed Services.
Drawing characteristics, 1553, 1579, 1756, 1835, 1861a,
1864, 1907, 1908, 2188, 2251, 2469
Dreams, 1854, 2069, 2342, 2374

Effeminacy, 393, 1915, 1982, 1989, 2016, 2182, 2240,
2592, 2622, 2642. See also Gender identity and role.

Gay life--see Homosexual community and gay life.

Gender identity and role, 235a, 248, 255, 393, 1541, 1573, 1670, 1674, 1768, 1915, 1917, 1924, 2090, 2237, 2251, 2335, 2385, 2662, 2805

General surveys of homosexuality, 2, 3, 8, 10-14, 18-20, 23-26, 28, 39, 40, 53-56, 68-70, 72, 75, 76, 81-83, 85-87, 89, 93, 94, 96, 99, 101-04, 106-08, 115-19, 133, 268, 273, 276, 280, 282, 285, 297, 301, 302, 312, 315, 321, 324-26, 328, 334, 338, 341, 350, 354, 366, 367, 381, 410, 412-15, 419, 420, 423, 425, 427, 430, 435-37, 440, 441, 443, 447, 464, 471, 476, 486, 490, 496, 511-13, 518a, 530, 535, 539, 540, 544, 558, 570, 573, 574, 580, 582, 587, 701, 709, 710, 761, 830, 839, 861, 895, 1014, 1623, 1656, 1913, 1921, 2148, 2212, 2216, 2223, 2263, 2283, 2439, 2513, 2657, 2703, 2708, 2709, 2736, 2744

Genetic factors, 257, 432, 505, 545, 1584, 1587, 1742, 1829, 1867, 1868, 2035, 2060, 2064, 2065, 2099, 2129, 2249, 2309-11, 2344, 2357, 2360, 2471, 2654, 2723 See also Twins.

George W. Henry Foundation, 1970-73, 1976

Germany, 604, 2224, 2611, 2774, 2903

Graffiti, 2435

Harassment--see Police practices.

Historical novels and plays, 2991, 2999, 3032, 3045, 3063, 3064, 3083, 3095

History, homosexuality in, 1, 30-32, 43, 44, 48, 56, 59a, 67, 88, 122, 171, 214, 440, 441, 461, 465, 475, 562, 1043, 1368, 2506, 2607, 2608, 2610-12, 2702, 2748, 2801, 2802, 2871, 2902, 2956. See also Ancient Greece.

Holland, 915, 1048

Homophile movement, 33, 66, 77, 79, 126, 130, 171, 173, 259, 261, 397, 451, 467, 533, 595, 597, 603a, 607, 616, 643, 653, 659, 680a, 684, 685, 693, 705, 708, 712, 749, 790, 1221, 1242, 1500, 2015, 2686, 2789, 2842, 2845, 2850, 2851, 2856, 2874, 2875, 2882, 2928, 2929, 2957-59, 3187

Homophile organizations--see Homophile movement.

Homosexual Bill of Rights, 616, 2843. See also American Civil Liberties Union, Civil liberties, Police practices.

Homosexual community and gay life, 26, 29, 37, 47, 56, 57, 61, 73, 120, 122, 123, 129, 159, 181, 182, 191, 422, 424, 426, 433, 487, 595, 622, 634, 647, 666, 667, 688, 693, 709, 711, 712, 714, 746, 749, 759, 790, 800, 817, 824, 829, 832, 839, 840, 868, 869, 887, 915, 943, 994, 1039, 1056, 1067, 1075, 1100, 1113, 1114, 1118, 1120, 1541, 1826, 1921, 2125, 2667, 2707, 2799, 2829, 2908, 2927. See also Gay bars.

Homosexual offenses and offenders, 46a, 50a, 58, 127, 177,
249, 304, 310, 331, 333, 361, 384, 392, 398, 403, 416,
418, 429, 482, 483, 498, 503, 543, 578, 594, 652, 698,
703, 716, 764, 766, 774, 777, 801, 837, 845, 846, 889,
954, 956, 960, 986, 1030, 1257, 1260, 1262, 1263, 1274,
1275, 1277, 1278, 1280, 1281, 1289, 1292, 1293a, 1295,
1298, 1299, 1305, 1306, 1311, 1312, 1318, 1319, 1322,
1327, 1331, 1332, 1334, 1338, 1348, 1349, 1356, 1357,
1360, 1361, 1363, 1369, 1371, 1373, 1374, 1380-83,
1385, 1389, 1390, 1394, 1397, 1400, 1403, 1404, 1417,
1424-1533, 1560, 1581, 1645, 1653, 1654, 1661, 1666,
1682, 1692, 1693, 1732, 1785, 1788, 1859, 1892, 1942,
1968, 1983, 1994, 1995, 2036, 2115, 2146, 2185, 2247,
2260, 2276a, 2316, 2333, 2336, 2390, 2407, 2448-52,
2455, 2521, 2530, 2537, 2554, 2563, 2597, 2624, 2643,
2656, 2658, 2673, 2675, 2677, 2678, 2680, 2691, 2710,
2733, 2746, 2750, 2756, 2767, 2769, 2835
Homosexual panic,   1770, 1886, 2048, 2071, 2082, 2168,
2382
Homosexuality as seen by homosexuals,   69, 74, 86, 91,
205a, 653, 2771-73, 2782, 2783, 2786, 2787, 2795, 2796,
2800, 2810-12, 2824, 2838, 2846, 2849, 2860-62, 2867,
2884, 2886, 2888, 2898, 2904, 2909, 2945-47, 2954,
2955, 2959, 2966, 3186a
Hooker Report,   221, 596, 844, 2014
Hormones--see Endocrine factors.
Hospitalization,   2254, 2389, 2390, 2407, 2521, 2522, 2596,
2639
Hypnosis,   1542, 1570, 1722, 1877, 2239, 2391, 2424, 2426,
2496, 2515

Immigration and naturalization,   139, 195, 210, 561a, 649,
752, 967, 1261, 1282, 1323, 1386, 1436, 1455, 1456,
1458, 1483, 1506
Incest,   333, 2130, 2370

Jealousy,   2122, 2123, 2295
Jokes,   2836

The Kinsey Reports,   286, 317, 337, 369, 384, 385, 386,
439, 440, 441, 454, 571, 694, 784, 808, 966, 969, 1080,
1617, 2117
Klinefelder's syndrome,   2237, 2251
The Koran,   449

Latent homosexuality,   536, 1644, 1896, 1926, 2069, 2070,

Literature on a homosexual theme: novels, 2967-3083; plays, 251a, 3084-3100; short stories, 3101-19. See also Literature, homosexuality in.

Lobotomy, 1575, 2639

London, 688, 928, 929, 1828

LSD, 968, 1539, 2203, 2204

Magic, 2287

Marriage and divorce, 668, 720, 727, 841, 922, 956, 1173, 1179, 1270, 1324, 1354, 1384, 1463, 1707, 1708, 1851, 2012, 2340, 2381, 2808, 2876

Masculinity-Femininity, 256a, 1534, 1583, 1673, 1685, 1908, 2278, 2307, 2394, 2573, 2686a, 2743, 2881

Mattachine societies, 186, 187, 533, 2834. See also Homophile movement.

Minority, 26, 49, 56, 77, 120, 146, 151, 169, 209, 254, 566, 595, 598, 603a, 616, 622, 680a, 749, 771, 790, 793, 2508, 2699, 2913, 2935, 3187

MMPI (Minnesota Multiphasic Personality Inventory), 1534, 1609, 1685, 1751, 1752, 1856, 1905, 1908, 1955, 1991, 2116, 2201, 2308, 2323, 2461, 2462, 2536, 2580, 2633, 2638, 2640. See also Detecting the homosexual.

Model Penal Code, 138, 1388, 1389

Morality and sin. 6, 7, 9, 17, 21, 59a, 85a, 92, 100, 127, 154, 158, 174, 197, 200, 206, 226, 231, 284, 288, 328, 344, 351, 388, 400, 413, 428, 519, 542, 561, 561a, 563, 630, 648, 674, 677a, 686, 690, 733, 753, 764, 806, 826, 855, 909, 910, 916, 959, 970, 973, 977, 987, 988, 1020, 1037, 1040, 1041, 1086, 1135, 1151, 1154, 1157, 1163, 1164, 1172, 1175, 1176, 1188a, 1195, 1211, 1215, 1218, 1233a, 1241, 1247, 1248, 1250, 1265, 1273, 1278, 1284-86, 1288, 1298, 1300, 1301, 1315-17, 1328, 1329, 1334, 1339, 1344, 1345, 1349a, 1351, 1389, 1392, 1394, 1413, 1736, 1920, 2005, 2158, 2222, 2483, 2505, 2679, 2715, 2887, 2943. See also Christian Church, Roman Catholic attitudes, and Wolfenden Committee and Report.

Movies, 736, 745, 751, 870, 872-77, 903, 911, 924, 979, 981, 983, 1017, 1024, 1025, 1055, 1068, 1070, 1087, 1101, 1106, 1169, 1170, 2775, 2793, 2794, 2917, 3120-78

Music, 803, 913, 1679, 2070, 2567, 2868

Narcissism, 1909, 1969, 2060, 2395

National Institute of Mental Health Report--see Hooker Report.

Nature and types of homosexuality, 2, 18, 20, 22, 25, 39, 40, 53-55, 65, 69, 70, 72, 75-77, 79, 81, 82, 84a, 85, 87, 93, 94, 96, 99, 101, 104, 117-19, 133, 208, 235a,

238, 251, 262, 271, 379a, 387, 492, 494, 500, 564, 576,
584, 591, 733, 746, 791, 818, 835, 842, 904, 967, 973,
1027, 1038, 1097, 1103, 1246, 1266, 1564, 1591, 1633,
1672, 1687-90, 1754, 1757, 1758, 1799, 1869, 1872,
1873, 1876, 1878, 1879, 1885, 1893, 1930, 1937, 1967,
2011, 2033, 2073, 2091, 2132, 2137, 2138, 2147, 2148,
2167, 2248, 2269, 2275-77, 2281, 2315, 2334, 2386,
2392, 2393, 2414, 2418, 2428, 2438, 2446, 2489, 2498,
2500, 2542, 2575, 2584, 2594, 2605, 2646, 2665, 2668,
2685, 2797, 2803, 2818, 2949
New York City,   603a, 627, 759, 832
New Zealand,   2328
North Carolina,   734, 845, 927, 2828
Norway,   2648
Novels--see Literature on a homosexual theme.

Obscenity,   954, 1344, 1345, 1370, 1485, 1491, 1500, 1521,
2895, 2933, 2951. See also Pornography.
Oedipus complex,   1801, 1825, 1951, 2165, 2384, 2486,
2585

Paranoia,   235, 243, 255, 264, 278, 311, 367a, 378, 1108,
1568, 1569, 1572, 1588, 1639, 1657-60, 1696, 1712, 1787,
1818, 1861, 1909, 1910, 1960, 2060, 2072, 2083, 2093-
97, 2102, 2227, 2238, 2255, 2288, 2302, 2307, 2319,
2330, 2395, 2411, 2427, 2549, 2576, 2579, 2607, 2621,
2636, 2638, 2737, 2772
Parents--see Family.
Passivity,   2165, 2240, 2253, 2332, 2465
Pedophilia,   62, 63, 384, 390, 750, 1839, 1846, 2246.
See also Children and adolescents.
Personality of homosexuals,   12-14, 18, 20, 36, 39, 53,
54, 56, 75, 84a, 133, 235, 238, 240, 242, 251, 255,
279, 347, 362, 421, 434, 472, 1565, 1701, 1918, 1946,
2021, 2057, 2074, 2170, 2177, 2240
Philippines,   2435, 2925
The physician and the homosexual,   1037, 1964, 1985,
2009, 2103, 2158, 2375
Physique photography,   2911
Playboy Interviews,   974 (Genet), 975 (Ginsberg), 976
(Vidal)
Playboy Panel on Religion and the New Morality,   977
Playboy Forum,   941-73
Plays--see Literature on a homosexual theme.
Police practices,   44, 146, 157, 158, 184, 561a, 599, 602,
603, 605, 612-15, 618, 627, 631, 632, 639, 640, 642,
648, 650, 661, 671, 676, 677, 677a, 678, 680a, 683, 692,
697, 699, 702-04, 706, 707, 712, 724, 730, 731, 781,

800, 819, 821, 866, 899, 932, 933, 936, 942, 945-47,
949, 952, 954, 956-59, 965, 966, 971, 982, 998, 1018,
1023, 1030, 1095, 1112, 1118, 1237, 1268, 1293, 1298,
1302, 1303, 1305, 1330, 1340, 1350, 1376, 1424, 1428,
1432, 1433, 1434, 1438, 1439, 1449, 1452, 1461, 1464,
1468, 1473, 1478 1481, 1489, 1497, 1508, 1509, 1514,
1519, 1520, 1531, 1533, 2645, 2724, 2741, 2766, 2792,
2796, 2841, 2854, 2869, 2874, 2875, 2877, 2889, 2890,
2895, 2905, 2906, 2914, 2915, 2926, 2928, 2933, 2951-
53, 2960, 2961. See also Solicitation and entrapment.
Politics, Homosexuality and, 32, 59a, 60, 89, 158, 213,
217, 351, 408, 409, 493, 523, 561a, 594, 603a, 615,
627, 636, 648, 681, 697, 698, 715, 716, 724, 730, 743,
753, 763, 770, 798, 799, 815, 826, 862, 864, 890, 926,
936, 941, 995, 1021, 1022, 1028, 1035, 1045, 1046,
1052, 1059, 1081, 1091, 1138, 1209, 1235, 1334, 1396,
1998, 2326, 2453, 2790, 2882, 2889, 2905, 2989. See
also Wolfenden Committee and Report, Security.
Population control, 961, 1027, 2834, 2977
Pornography, 452, 917, 954, 2479. See also Obscenity.
The press--see Public attitudes and Scandals.
Prevention of Homosexuality--see Therapy.
Prison and reform schools, 113, 256a, 267, 353, 371,
466, 468, 477, 480, 559, 762, 765, 774, 885, 886, 948,
951, 955, 957, 962, 964, 970, 973, 1096, 1321, 1337,
1369, 1397, 1456a, 1637, 1638, 1641, 1731, 1766, 1831,
1912, 1928a, 1941, 1943, 1944, 1950, 1967, 2030, 2031,
2157, 2161, 2180, 2186, 2224, 2225, 2242, 2292, 2347,
2355, 2394, 2433, 2443, 2466, 2479, 2480, 2573, 2577,
2580, 2582, 2584, 2632, 2641, 2643, 2650, 2659, 2665,
2669, 2676, 2691, 2718, 2758, 2763, 2767, 2924
Pro-health vs. pro-sickness argument, 127, 152, 240, 245,
251, 399, 439, 440, 441, 478, 561a, 655, 1160, 1846,
2017, 2208, 2778, 2848
Prostitution (male), 8, 62, 292, 992, 1604, 1686, 1733, 1855,
1880, 2058, 2187, 2387, 2433, 2503, 2728, 2732, 2785,
2899, 2944
Pseudohomosexuality, 84a, 305, 504, 1615, 1621, 2109,
2300-02, 2478. See also aggression, dependency, and
power.
Psychological factors, 1546, 1587, 2086. See also Psychopathology.
Psychopathology (disease), 12, 13, 14, 25, 36, 39, 50, 53,
54, 55, 69, 81, 84a, 99, 101, 107, 138a, 208, 260, 300,
307, 319, 331, 450, 472, 481, 485, 516, 561a, 575, 653,
660, 669, 673, 769, 950, 954, 989, 1072, 1132, 1135,
1142, 1174, 1175, 1575, 1700, 1816, 1871, 1999, 2071,
2089, 2108, 2149, 2164, 2226, 2277, 2289, 2292, 2348,

Index of Authors

A

Aaronson, B. S. , 1534
Abe, K. , 1535, 1536
Abraham, Karl, 1537
Abrahamsen, David, 2643
Abrahamson, H. A. , 1539
Abrams, Albert, 1538
Abse, Leo, 2644
Achilles, Nancy, 232, 266
Ackerley, J. R. , 1
Ackerman, Joannell, 593
Adams, M. 2582
Adams, Mark E. , 267
Adler, Alfred, 268, 1540, 1541
Adler, Martin D. , 2645
Albany Trust, 134
Albert, Lou, 2967
Aldrich, Ann, 2968
Alexander, Duane, 2250
Alexander, Leo, 1542
Alexander, Michail, 1543
Allen, Clifford, 2, 10, 269-73, 1544-51, 2646
Allen, Frederick H. , 1552
Allen, Luther, 2771, 2772
Allen, R. M. , 1961
Alman, C. , 1553
Alpert, Hollis, 872, 873
Alverson, Charles A. , 595
American Civil Liberties Union, 135-37
American Law Institute, 274
American Psychiatric Association, 138a
Anant, S. S. , 1554, 1555
Andenaes, Johs, 2648
Anderson, C. , 1556

Anderson, Camilla A. 1122
Anderson, Patrick, 109
Anderson, Robert W. 3084
Anderson, Ronald, 2773
Andros, Phil, 2969
Anomaly, 3
Anonymous, 4, 140, 141, 275-77, 720-22, 1123-25, 1557-59, 2649, 2970
Apfelberg, B. , 1560
Appel, K. E. , 1561
Apperson, L. B. , 1562
Archer, Jules, 459
Ardery, Breck & Wm. , 3186
Argo, Jack, 1774
Arlow, J. A. , 1563, 1564
Armon, Virginia, 1565
Armstrong, C. N. , 1566
Army Medical Library, 142
Aronson, Gerald J. , 1567
Aronson, Marvin L. , 278, 1568, 1569
Arthur, Gavin, 279
Aschaffenberg, Helga, 1127
Ashbrook, James B. , 1128
Asprey, Robert, 5
Athanasiou, Robert, 1569a
Atiya, I. M. , 1570
Atkinson, Byron H. , 2687
Atkinson, Ronald, 280
Atwell, Lee, 2775
Auchinloss, Douglas, 281
Auerbach, Stuart, 596
Austin, Sean H. , 233, 234
Ayer, A. J. , 141, 726

B

Baab, O. J. , 282

298

Bacon, Catherine L., 283
Bailey, D. S., 6, 7, 284, 285, 1129
Bak, R. C., 1571, 1572
Baker, Blanche, 16
Bakwin, Harry, 1573, 1574
Bakwin, Ruth, 1574
Baldwin, James, 727, 2971, 2972
Ball, R. B., 2246
Balogh, J. K., 2650
Banay, R. S., 1575
Bannon, Ann, 2776
Barahal, Hyman S. 1576-78
Barber, Bernard, 286
Barker, A. J., 1579
Barker, J., 1553
Barker, J. C., 1635, 2133
Barker, J. G., 1580
Barnes, J., 1581, 1582
Barnette, W. L., 1583
Barnouw, Victor, 287
Barr, James, 2973, 2974, 3101
Barr, M. L., 1584
Barr, R. H., 1585
Barth, Karl, 288
Bartholomew, A. A., 1586
Barton, George A., 289
Bassani, Giorgio, 2975
Bassin, Alexander, 2477
Baudry, Andre, 2777
Bauer, Julius, 1587
Baumeyer, F., 1588
Baxbaum, R. E., 1130
Beach, Frank A., 46, 290, 376, 1589, 1590
Beals, Ralph L., 2651
Beam, Lura, 349
Beardemphl, William, 2778, 2779
Beardmore, Edward, 2652
Beauvoir, Simone de, 291
Becher, A. L., 1591
Beck, Aaron T., 2414
Becker, Howard S., 729, 730

Becker, Raymond de, 8
Beecher, John, 731
Beggs, K. S., 234a
Bell, D. S., 1592
Benda, C. E., 1593
Bendel, R., 1594
Bender, Lauretta, 1595-97
Bene, Eva, 1598, 1599
Benedict, Ruth, 1600, 1601
Benjamin, Harry, 292, 1602-05, 2780
Bennet, E. A., 1606, 1607
Bennett, J. C., 1131
Bensing, Robert C., 1257, 1258
Benson, R. O. D., 9
Bentler, P. M., 1608
Benton, Arthur L., 1609
Berg, Charles, 10, 11, 293, 1610
Bergler, Edmund, 12, 13, 294-96, 732, 1132, 1133, 1612-23, 2653, 2654
Bergman, Harry, 597
Bergmann, M. S., 1624
Berkman, Ted, 733
Berlandt, Konstantin, 598
Berne, Eric, 297
Bernstein, I. C., 1625
Bernstein, R., 1895
Bess, Donovan, 599
Beukenkamp, Cornelius, 1626
Bickel, Alexander, 734
Bieber, Irving, 14, 300, 301, 600, 1044, 1627, 1628
Bieber, Toby, 1629
Bien, Ernest, 1630
Bills, Norman, 235
Bird, David, 603
Bird, H. W., 2206
Bird, M. S., 1631
Bishop, Bob, 2782
Bishop, Donald, 2783
Bishop, M. P., 2151
Biskind, Gerson R., 2074
Black, J., 603a

Blackman, Nathan, 302, 1633, 1634
Blaine, Graham B. Jr., 303
Blake, Rober, 15
Blakemore, C. B., 1635, 1636, 2133
Blau, Abram, 1595
Blechman, Burt, 2976
Bloch, Herbert A., 304, 1637
Bloch, Iwan, 305
Bloch, S. K., 2442
Block, Jack, 1709
Bluestone, Harvey, 1638
Blumenthal, Ralph, 604
Bollmeier, L. N., 1639
Bone, Robert A., 735
Bonime, Walter, 1640
Bontecou, Eleanor, 2655
Borstelman, L. J., 1642, 2100
Bose, G., 1643
Boss, Medard, 306
Botwinick, J., 1644
Bowling, R. W., 2656
Bowman, Karl M., 307, 1259, 1260, 1645-47, 2657, 2658
Boyd, D. A. Jr., 2570
Boyd, Malcolm, 308
Bozarth, Rene, 1135
Braaten, Leif J., 1648
Bradbury, Andrew, 2785
Bradford, Jean, 2154
Bradley, John, 2786, 2787
Bradley, John B., 2241
Bradshaw, W. V., 1649
Brady, J. P., 1650, 2143
Braff, Erwin H., 1651
Bragman, Louis J., 309, 1652
Braine, J., 737
Bramanti, R. M., 1653
Brancale, Ralph, 310, 1654
Branson, Helen P., 16, 2788
Breazeale, E. L., 1916
Breger, Louis, 1655

Breward, Ian, 738
Brien, Alan, 740, 741
Brierley, J. R., 2659
Brill, A. A., 311, 1656-60
British Medical Association, 143, 2008
Britten, F. H., 313
Broderick, Carlfred B., 2660
Brodwin, Leonora J., 2661
Brody, E. B., 1663
Brody, M. W., 1664
Bromberg, Walter, 312, 1665-68, 1859
Bromley, Dorothy D., 313
Bronstein, P., 2090
Broster, L. R., 1669
Brown, Daniel G., 314, 1670-75, 2662, 2663
Brown, Fred, 315
Brown, J. H., 1676
Brown, Julia, 2664
Brown, P., 2421, 2422
Brown, P. T., 1677, 1678, 2551
Brown, W. Paterson, 316
Brussel, J. A., 1679
Bryan, Douglas, 1680
Bryan, John, 605
Bryce, Dean T., 228, 1136
Buckley, Michael J., 17
Buckley, Tom, 742
Buckley, William F. Jr., 606, 743, 744
Buki, Rudolph A., 1681, 1682
Bunzel, Peter, 745
Burgess, Anthony, 2977
Burgess, Ernest W., 317
Burke, Tom, 746
Burns, John H., 3102
Burrow, Trigant, 1683
Burtchaell, James, 1684
Burton, Arthur, 1685
Burton, Richard F., 318
Butts, William M., 1686
Bychowski, Gustav, 319, 1687-91

300

Byrne, Thomas R. Jr.,
1261

C

Cabeen, C. W., 1692, 1693
Cain, James, 2978
Calder, W., 2665
Caldwell, Alexander B.,
1694
Call, Harold L., 954, 2789,
2790
Cambridge Department of
Criminal Science, 320
Cameron, Bruce, 2979
Cameron, Norman, 321
Campbell, George E., 1262
Campbell, John D., 1918
Canavan, Francis, 1138
Cantor, Donald J., 749,
1263
Cantor, Gilbert M., 322
Caplan, J., 2237
Caporale, Domenico, 1264
Cappon, Daniel, 18
Caprio, Frank S., 19, 323-
26, 471, 750
Caron, Yves, 1265
Carpenter, C. R., 1695
Carpenter, Edward, 20
Carr, Arthur C., 1696,
2233, 2360
Carroll, Jerry, 607
Carroll, Paul, 751
Carson, Laura E., 2666
Carstairs, G. Morris, 327,
1697, 1698
Casey, R. P., 1139
Cason, Hulsey, 1700
Cassity, John H., 1701
Castell, D., 2422, 2251,
2252
Castelnuovo-Tedesco, P.,
1702
Cattell, R. S., 1704
Catterall, R. D., 1705
Cautela, J. R., 1706
Cavan, Sherri, 2667

Cavanagh, John, 21, 1141,
1266, 1707, 1708
Chang, Judy, 1709
Chapman, A. H., 1710
Chapman, Diana, 1711
Chappell, D., 1267
Chataway, Christopher, 754
Chatterji, N. N., 1712, 1713
Chayefsky, Paddy, 3085
Chesser, Eustace, 22, 328,
1714
Chester, Alfred, 756
Chideckel, Maurice, 23
Chikes, Thibor, 1142
Childs, Marquis, 608
Chornyak, John, 2441
Christensen, Cornelia V.,
384
Churchill, Wainwright, 24,
970
Clark, D. F., 1715
Clark, F. A. Jr., 2560,
2561
Clarke, R. V. G., 1716, 2083
Cleckley, Hervey, 25
Clifford, W., 1269
Clines, Francis X., 613
Coady, Matthew, 760
Coates, Stephen, 761, 1717
Coburn, Vincent, 1270
Cocteau, Jean, 4
Cody, Bart, 2793
Cohen, Elias S., 1271
Cohen, M. M., 1718
Cole, William G., 329
Coleman, J. C., 1692, 1693
Coleman, Lonnie, 2980
Collins, Carol, 615
Collins, Michael, 2794
Colton, James, 2981, 2982
Comfort, Alex, 1719
Conn, J. H., 1722
Connell, Sydney, 1638
Connery, J. R., 1145
Conrad, Earl, 507
Conway, C. G., 1635, 2133
Conwell, Chic, 330
Cooke, R. A., 1723

301

Coon, Earl O., 1724
Cooney, William, 616
Cooper, W. L., 1725
Coopersmith, Lewis J., 2795
Coppen, A. J., 1726, 1727
Coriolan, John, 2983
Coriot, Isador H., 1728
Cormier, Bruno M., 331
Cornsweet, A. C., 1729
Cory, Donald W., 26-29,
86, 332-35, 1730, 1731,
2668, 2797, 3103
Cotter, J., 1146
Coulton, James, 2984
Council on Religion and the
Homosexual, 146-51
Courage, James A., 2985
Coward, Noel, 3086
Craft, Michael, 1733
Craig, Alfred, 2798
Crane, H. W., 336, 1734
Crane, Lionel, 617
Crawford, Kenneth, 763
Creadick, R. N., 1735
Crespi, Leo P., 337
Crisp, Quentin, 30
Croft-Cooke, Rupert, 31, 32
Cromey, Robert W., 1148
Crompton, Louis, 152
Crooke, A. C., 1737
Cross, Harold H. U., 338
Cross, Rupert, 1276
Crowley, Mart, 3087
Crowley, R. M., 1738
Crowther, R. H., 2799,
2800
Crumpler, Wm. B., 1276a
Culbert, Mike, 619
Cullen, Tom, 768
Cupp, M. E., 1739, 2258
Curran, Charles, 770
Curran, Desmond, 1740-42
Curtler, Martin S., 771
Custis, Douglass L., 1277
Cutler, Marvin, 33
Cutler, S. Oley, 1278
Cutter, Fred, 1743

D

Dahl-Iversen, E., 1945
Daly, Claude D., 1744
Daniel, Marc, 2801, 2802
Daniel, S., 1745
Dank, B. M., 235a
Darke, Roy A., 1746, 1747
Darling, C. Douglas, 1648
Dart, John, 620, 621
Dashon, Paul G., 236
Davenport, William, 339
David, Henry P., 237,
1748
David, Lester, 772
David, W. A., 2669
Davidoff, L., 1575
Davids, Anthony, 1749, 2154
Davidson, Bill, 773
Davidson, David, 34
Davidson, Janice R., 1279
Davidson, Michael, 34a
Davies-Jones, C. W. S.,
1750
Davis, Alan J., 774
Davis, Charles A., 2096
Davis, Katherine B., 340
Davis, Maxine, 341
Dean, Dawson F., 238
Dean, Michael, 1280
Dean, P., 239
Dean, Robert B., 240,
1751, 1752, 2803
Dean, Roger, 153
DeCook, P., 1978
DeForrest, Michael, 2986
Defrain, John, 622
Delaney, Shelagh, 3088
Delay, Jean, 342
DeLuca, Joseph N., 1753,
1754
Demaria, L. A. de, 1755
DeMartino, M. F., 1756
DeMay, John A., 1281
DeMonchy, Rene, 1757,
2248
DeMott, Benjamin, 343
Dempsey, William, 1149, 1150

Freeman, David I., 2821, 2822
Freeman, Hal E., 1840
Freeman, Ira H., 632
Freeman, Thomas, 1841
Freeman, William, 377
Frei, W., 1842
Freud, Anna, 1843-45
Freud, Sigmund, 42, 378, 379, 379a, 1846
Freund, Kurt, 380, 1847-53, 2500
Frey, Egon C., 1854
Freyhan, F. A., 1855
Friberg, Richard R., 243, 1856
Friedman, Joel, 1857
Friedman, Paul, 381
Friedman, Ruth M., 2823
Friedman, Sanford, 2997
Frisbie, Louise V., 2675
Fritts, Roger M., 1302
Fritze, Herbert P., 160
Fromm, Erika O., 1858
Frosch, Jack, 1859
Fry, C. C., 161
Fugate, James B., 2824, 3090
Fuller, Norman, 162
Furlong, Monica, 633, 806

G

Gaard, David, 3091
Gadpaille, Warren J., 1860
Gagnon, John H., 383, 548, 1160, 2676, 2743, 2744
Gailey, Leah, 2825
Galbraith, Hugh M., 1977
Gallo, Jon J., 1303
Garde, Noel I., 43, 163
Gardner, G. E., 1861
Gardner, J. M., 1861a
Garland, Rodney, 2998
Garma, Angel, 383, 1862
Garner, Shelley, 2999
Gassel, Sylvia, 1857
Gaver, K. D., 2596

Gayle, S. Jr., 2561
Gaylin, Willard M., 1161, 1863, 2303, 2304
Gebhard, Paul, 384, 439, 441, 808
Geddes, Donald P., 385
Geil, George A., 1747, 1864, 1865
Geis, Gilbert, 304
Genet, Jean, 3000-03
Genne, William H., 64
Gentele, H., 1868
George, Eliot, 3004
Gerassi, John, 44
Gerber, Israel J., 45
Gershman, Harry, 1628, 1869-72
Gervis, Stephanie, 634
Giannell, A. S., 1873
Gibbens, T. C. N., 810, 1874, 2433
Gibbins, R. J., 1875
Gibbons, Don C., 2731
Gide, Andre, 46
Giedt, F. Harold, 386
Giese, Hans, 1876
Gigeroff, A. K., 46a, 2677
Gilbert, Carol, 811
Gilbert, George, 635
Gilbert, G. M., 2678
Gilbert, S. F., 1877
Gilby, Thomas, 1162
Gillespie, W. H., 387, 1878, 1879
Gilliatt, Penelope, 812
Gilmour, Ian, 813
Gingerick, William, 3005
Ginsberg, Kenneth N., 1880
Ginsberg, M., 2679
Ginsberg, Morris, 388
Gioscia, Nicolai, 1881
Gittings, Barbara B., 389
Glass, Albert J., 579
Glass, S. J., 1882-84, 2630
Glassman, S. M., 1991
Glauber, I. P., 1885
Gleason, Robert, 400, 1163
Glick, Burton S., 1886

Guze, S. B. , 1928a

H

Hacker, Helen M. , 1929, 2686, 2686a
Hadden, Samuel B. , 822, 1930-36
Hader, M. , 1937
Hadfield, J. A. , 1938, 1939
Hager, Philip, 641
Hagmeier, George, 400
Hagopian, John V. , 1940
Hahn, Milton E. , 2687
Hailsham, Viscount, 401
Haines, William H. , 1941-43
Hall, Radclyffe, 3009
Hall, Wendall, 823
Halleck, Seymour L. , 402, 403, 1944
Hamann, Deryl F. , 1264
Hamberger, C. , 1945
Hamill, Pete, 642
Hamilton, Donald M. , 1946
Hamilton, Gilbert, 172, 404, 1947
Hamilton, W. G. , 2835
Hammelmann, H. A. , 405, 1213
Hammer, Emanuel F. , 1948, 1949
Hammer, Max, 1950, 1951
Hampson, Joan G. , 407
Hampson, John L. , 406, 407
Hanauer, Joan, 824
Hannon, Michael, 2835
Hannum, T. E. 2242
Hansard, 408, 409
Hansen, Joseph, 2836, 2837, 3009a
Hansen, Terry, 643
Hanson, Doris, 50
Harding, Carl B. , 173, 2838
Harding, G. F. , 1991
Hardwick, Elizabeth, 825

Harkness, Bruce, 2688
Harms, Ernest, 1952
Harper, Fowler W. , 1314
Harper, James, 51
Harper, Robert A. , 410
Harris, Frank, 51
Harris, Louis, 644
Harris, Robert N. Jr. , 1315
Harris, Sara, 411
Harris, Sidney J. , 645, 646
Harrison, S. I. , 1953
Hart, H. L. A. , 826, 1316
Hartman, A. A. , 1954
Hartman, Bernard J. , 1955
Hartogs, Renatus, 1956
Hartsock, Mildred E. , 2689
Hartung, Philip T. , 1169, 1170
Hartweg, Norman, 2690
Hartwick, Alexander, 412
Harvey, John F. , 413, 1171-77, 1957, 1958
Harvey, Reginald, 3010
Haselkorn, Harry, 246, 1959
Haskell, Francis, 827
Hastings, Donald W. , 414, 1960
Hastings, March, 3011
Hatterer, Lawrence, 51a, 828
Hauge, L. , 2423
Haupt, Thomas D. , 1961, 2547
Hauser, Richard, 52, 829, 2839
Havemann, Ernest, 830
Hayes, Frank, 2271
Hayes, M. F. , 1729
Hayward, Sumner C. , 1962
Hearn, Wallace, 3012
Hebert, Dick, 647
Hecht, H. , 1963
Heersema, Philip H. , 1964
Hefner, Hugh, 831, 1317
Hegeler, Inge and Sten, 415
Heibrunn, G. , 1965
Heinrich, J. F. , 2442

307

I

Ikin, A. Graham,   552
Irwin, Theodore,   861
Isherwood, Christopher,
    3024, 3025
Ison, T. G. ,   1329
Ive, F. A. ,   2037
Ivy, A. C. ,   2038

J

Jackson, C. Colin,   2039-41
Jackson, Charles,   3026
Jackson, Don,   2850
Jackson, Ed,   2851
Jackson, Neville,   3027
Jackson, R. J. ,   2587
Jacob, J. S. ,   2206
Jacobi, Jolande,   2042
Jacobs, Harold,   1330
James, Anatole,   2043
James, Anthony,   61
James, Basil,   2044-47
James, Nicholas,   2852
James, Robert E. ,   2048
James, T. E. ,   429
Janis, Lee,   2058
Janus Society of America,
    178
Jason, Philip,   2853
Jefferiss, F. J. G. ,   2049-51
Jellinek, E. Morton,   1647
Jenkins, Bess,   655
Jenkins, Marion,   2052
Jenkins, Roy,   863
Jennings, Dale,   2854
Jens, R. ,   2053
Jepson, N. A. ,   2697
Jersild, Jens,   62, 63
Jimenez, D. ,   2349
Joelson, M. ,   1749, 2054
Johnson, A. M. ,   2055, 2107,
    2160
Johnson, L. G. ,   1913
Johnson, Ronald P. ,   1331
Johnson, R. W.   1883
Johnson, Roy,   2330

Jolles, I. ,   2056
Jonas, C. H. ,   2057
Jones, A. J. ,   2058
Jones, E. ,   2059
Jones, Ernest,   2060
Jones, Harold J. ,   430
Jones, H. Kimball,   64
Jones, Richard T. ,   1332
Jones, William K. ,   1333
Jourdan, Eric,   3028
Jowitt, Earl,   2061
Joyce, Marion,   865
Jung, Carl G. ,   431
Justinian,   144
Juzwiak, Marijo,   2062

K

Kahn, Eugene,   2063
Kahn, Samuel,   65
Kallett, H. I. ,   2205
Kallman, Franz J. ,   432,
    2064, 2065
Kameny, Franklin E. ,   433,
    867, 965, 970, 1188b,
    2855-58
Kane, John J. ,   180, 1189
Kanee, Eugene A. ,   2066
Kapche, R. ,   2141
Kaplan, Donald M. ,   2698
Kaplan, Eugene A. ,   2067
Kardiner, Abram,   434
Karlson, Eric,   66
Karon, Bertram P. ,   2068
Karpman, Benjamin,   435,
    1334-37, 1977, 2069-73
Kasanin, Jacob,   2074
Kassebaum, Gene G. ,   2763
Kates, Elizabeth M. ,   2075
Katz, Sidney,   181, 868, 869
Kauffmann, Stanley,   656,
    657, 870, 871
Kaufman, M. R. ,   2076
Kaye, Harvey E. ,   2077
Kayy, W. H. ,   67
Keene, Howard,   3028a
Keiser, Sylvan,   2078
Kelly, E. Lowell,   437

Lamb, Paul L. , 1342
Lambert, Carl, 2125
Lambert, R. D. , 1986
Landers, Ann, 455
Landes, Ruth, 2126
Landis, Carney, 456
Landis, J. T. , 2127
Landsman, Arthur A. , 2128
Lang, Theo, 2129
Langsley, D. G. , 2130
Lapp, J. C. , 2704
Larere, Charles, 457
Larsen, Anthony A. , 2131
Laszlo, Carl, 2132
Lathbury, Vincent T. , 880
Laubscher, B. J. F. , 458
Lavin, N. I. , 1635, 2133
Lawton, Shailer L. , 459
Layard, John, 2136
Laycock, Samuel R. , 460, 2137
Learoyd, C. G. , 2138
Leavitt, Jack, 884
Lee, Donald, 885
Legg, W. Dorr, 2870-72
Legman, Gershon, 172, 461
Leitch, A. , 1967, 2139
Leitsch, Richard, 1197, 2873, 2874
LeMoal, Paul, 462
Lenn, Ernest, 661
Lerner, Harry V. , 1343
LeRoy, John P. , 29, 2875
Leslie, Robert, 70
Levin, Harry, 2705
Levin, Meyer, 3031
Levin, S. M. , 2141
Levine, Jacob, 2142
Levinson, Lew, 3032
Levitt, E. E. , 1650, 2143
Levy, Sidney, 463
Lewinsky, Hilde, 2144, 2145
Lewinsohn, Richard, 464
Lewis, Anthony, 662
Lewis, G. M. Jr. , 2146
Leznoff, Maurice, 2706, 2707

Licht, Hans, 465
Lichtenstein, Perry 2147
Liddicoat, Renee, 251, 2148, 2708, 2709
Lieberman, Daniel, 2149, 2365
Liebman, Samuel, 2150
Liechti, R. A. , 2201
Lief, Harold I. , 485, 2151
Limoges, Therese, 2363
Lind, Earl, 71
Lindner, Robert M. , 466-68, 886, 2152
Lindop, Audrey E. , 3033
Lindzey, Gardner, 2153-55
Lion, Ernest G. , 2063
Lipkowitz, M. H. , 2156
Lipton, H. R. , 2157
Lissner, Will, 663
Lister, John, 2158
Litin, E. M. , 2160
Litkey, L. J. , 2161
Litman, Robert E. , 2162
Little, Jay, 3034, 3035
Littlejohn, Larry R. , 965
Liverant, Shephard, 1655
Lloyd, Charles W. , 469
Lloyd, Randy, 2876
Lockhart, William B. , 1344, 1345
Lockwood, Tom, 3036
Lodin, A. , 1868
Loeffler, D. L. , 251a
Loeser, Lewis H. , 2164
Loewenstein, R. , 2165
Logan, John, 2877
Lolli, Giorgio, 2166
London, Louis S. , 470, 471, 2167, 2168
Lorand, Alexander S. , 2169
Lorand, Sandor, 472, 2170
Los Angeles Police Department, 185
Lowag, Leonard A. , 74
Lowery, D. , 1198
Lowrey, Lawson G. , 473, 1346
Lubin, A. , 2172

Lucas, Donald S., 185, 2878
Lugar, Robert L., 2533
Lundberg, E., 2173
Lurie, Louis A., 2174, 2175
Lyman, Stanford M., 2737
Lynch, Norman B., 1287
Lynn, David B., 2663

M

MacCormick, Austin H., 2710
MacCullough, M. J., 1812-14, 2176-78
MacDonald, F. G., 2179
MacDonald, John M., 2180
MacDonald, John W., 2181
MacDonald, M. W., 2182
Machover, K., 2183
Machover, S., 1644, 2183
MacInnes, Colin, 890
MacKenzie, Compton, 3037
MacKenzie, D. F., 2184
MacKinnon, J., 2184a
Mackwood, J. C., 1347, 1607, 2186
Maclay, D. T., 2185
MacNamara, Donald, 2187
MacVicar, Jean A., 252
Maddocks, Lewis I., 474, 1199
Magee, Bryan, 72, 891
Mailer, Norman, 2879
Mainord, Florence R., 2188
Major, Ralph H. Jr., 893
Makis, Sal, 2880
Malin, Irving, 1200
Malloy, M., 2172
Manchester, William, 475
Mandel, Paul, 3038
Mangus, A. R., 2711
Mann, Thomas, 3039
Mannheim, Hermann, 1348, 1607, 2194
Manosevitz, Martin, 2640
Mantegazza, Paolo, 476

Many, M., 1827
Marcus, Frank, 3094
Margin, James D., 2881
Marine, Gene, 897
Marino, A. W. M. Jr., 2195
Marison, R. C., 2196
Markillie, Ronald, 477
Marks, B., 2197
Marks, I. M., 2198
Marlowe, Kenneth, 73, 74
Marmell, M., 2199
Marmor, Judd, 75, 478
Marney, Carlyle, 1201
Marone, Silvio, 2200
Marrou, H. I., 479
Marsh, J. T., 2201
Martello, Leo L., 2882
Martensen-Larsen, O., 2202
Martin, Agnes, 2203, 2204
Martin, Clyde E., 439-41
Martin, Del, 2883, 2884
Martin, E. G., 2205
Martin, Harold, 76
Martin, J. D., 1349a
Martin, John B., 480
Martin, Kenneth, 3040
Martin, Kingsley, 898
Martin, Marcel, 2885
Martin, Thomas, 2886
Marty, P., 1804
Mason, S. C., 2206
Masor, N., 481
Masserman, Jules H., 2207
Massett, Lawrence, 2208
Masters, R. E. L., 77, 292, 482-84
Matarazzo, J. D., 2596
Mather, N. J. deV., 2209
Mathes, Irma, 253
Mathis, Charles V., 899
Mathis, J. K., 1553, 1579
Mattachine Society of Washington, 186, 187
Matthews, Arthur G., 78
Maude, John, 2210
Maugham, Robin, 3042
Maves, Paul B., 1202, 1203

Monsarrat, Nicholas, 3046
Monsour, Karen J., 2253
Moody, Howard, 1229
Moore, J. E., 496
Moore, K. R., 2254
Moore, R. A., 2255
Moore, S., 1914
Moore, Thomas V., 2256
Moorehouse, Geoffrey, 667
Moos, Malcolm C., 1766
Moran, J. Terry, 1356
Moran, P. A. P., 1535, 1536
Morgan, D. I., 2434
Morgenstern, Joseph, 911
Morgenthau, Hans J., 2714
Morony, J. H., 1704
Morris, Desmond, 2257
Morrow, J. E., 2258
Morse, Benjamin, 82, 83, 497
Morson, B. C., 2259
Mosher, D. L., 2292
Motz, Anton, 1357
Mueller, Gerhard O. W., 498, 2715
Muftic, M. K., 1570
Mulcock, Donald, 2260
Mulligan, Francis M., 1261
Mullins, Claud, 2716
Munroe, R. L., 2716a
Murdoch, G. P., 489
Murphy, Arthur A., 1358
Murphy, Dennis, 3047
Murphy, F. E., 2394
Murray, G. B., 2261
Murray, Henry A., 2262
Musaph, H., 2263
Musiker, H. R., 255
Myers, C. Kilmer, 1212
Myerson, Abraham, 2264-68, 2274

N

Nacht, S., 2269
Nagler, S. H., 2270
Naiman, J., 2270a
Napley, David, 1359

Nash, John, 2271
Nathan, Ruth, 668
National Capital Area Civil Liberties Union, 190
National Educational Television, 191
Nedoma, Karel, 2272, 2357
Needham, Merrill A., 2717
Neser, W. B., 2273
Neufeld, I. L., 1894
Neustadt, Rudolph, 2264-68, 2274
Neustatter, W. Lindesay, 500, 1360-62, 2275-76a
New York Academy of Medicine, 2277
New Zealand Homosexual Law Reform Society, 192
Newman, Bernard, 2886
Newton, Kenneth P., 2526
Nice, R. W., 2718
Nichols, Beverley, 922
Nichols, Dennison W., 2894
Nicol, C. S., 2280
Nicolay, R. C., 1954
Nielson, Nils, 2281
Niemoller, A. F., 923
Nikelly, Arthur, 2593
Nitsche, C. J., 2282
Nobile, Philip, 1213
Norman, Herbert J., 2283
Norman, Jacob P., 2284
Normanton, Helena, 1364
Norton, H., 193
Nouwen, H., 669
Novey, R., 2285
Nunberg, Herman, 2286, 2287
Nydes, Jule, 2288

O

Oberndorf, C. P., 2289
O'Brien, Justin, 2719
O'Connor, P. J., 2290
Odenwald, Robert P., 501, 569, 1216
Oerton, R. T., 1365, 1366

Ploscowe, Morris, 509, 510, 980, 1223, 1372-74
Plumeau, F., 2183
Plummer, Douglas, 86
Podolsky, E., 2331
Poe, John S., 2332
Polak, Clark P., 2908-11
Politzer, Jerome F., 1224
Pollens, Bertram, 511
Pollack, C. B. R., 2334
Polozker, I. L., 2335
Pomeroy, Wardell B., 384, 439-41, 512-14
Popkess, Athelstan, 2336
Porter, H. K., 256a
Pottenger, F. M. Jr., 2337
Potter, LaForest, 87
Powers, C. A., 1553, 1579
Praetorius, Numa, 2338, 2339
Prentiss, Marlin, 2912
Prideaux, Tom, 983
Primost, Norman, 2340
Prince, C. V., 2341
Prince, G. Stewart, 2342
Prince, Morton, 2343
Pritchard, Michael J., 257, 2344, 2345
Proferes, James J., 3112
Prosin, Suzanne, 2913
Prothro, E. Terry, 2229
Proust, Marcel, 515, 3054
Purdy, James, 3055
Purpon, I., 2349
Puxon, Margaret, 1377
Puzzo, F. S., 2183

Q

Query, W. T., 2254
Quill, Zachary, 88

R

Raad, Gerry, 3095a
Rabinovitch, Ralph, 1378
Rabinowitz, S., 2356
Rabinowitz, William, 1748

Raboch, Jan, 2357
Rachman, S., 2358
Rado, Sandor, 516, 1226, 2359
Radzinowicz, Leon, 320
Rainer, J. D., 2233, 2360
Raizen, Kenneth H., 2725
Ramp, James H., 3113
Ramsey, Glenn V., 517, 2361
Ramsey, R. W., 2362
Rancourt, Rejane, 2363
Randell, J. B., 2364
Randolph, Peter, 3114
Rank, I. P., 2268
Rapaport, Walter, 2365
Rappaport, E. A., 2366
Rashman, S., 2367
Rasmussen, E. Wulff, 2368
Raudebaugh, Charles, 679
Raul, K. B., 3056, 3057
Raven, Simon, 992-94, 3058
Raybin, James B., 2370
Read, C. S., 2371
Rebow, Milton, 3059
Rechy, John, 3060, 3061, 3061a
Rees, J. R., 2372, 2373
Rees, J. Tudor, 89, 518
Reese, D. C., 1710
Reeves, Ambrose, 2726
Regardie, Francis I., 2374
Regelson, Rosalyn, 680
Reid, R. D., 2915
Reider, Norman, 2375
Reinhardt, James M., 1379, 2727
Reiss, Albert J., 1380, 2728
Reitzell, Jeanne M., 258, 2376
Renault, Mary, 3062-64
Renshaw, Vernon, 1381
Reuben, D. R., 518a
Reynolds, Winston, 2917, 2918
Rhymes, Douglas, 519, 1229

St. John-Stevas, Norman, 534
Salkeld, Pablo, 1016
Salzman, Leon, 535-37, 2410, 2411
Samuels, A. S., 2412
Sanders, Jacob, 538
Sanford, David, 1018
Sangowicz, Jadwiga M., 331
Sapirstein, Milton R., 1019, 1020
Sappenfield, B. R., 2413
Sartre, Jean Paul, 97
Saul, Leon J., 2414
Savelle, H. J., 2415
Saville, Eve, 2734
Sawyer, G. I. M., 2313, 2416, 2527
Schaffer, Dora, 2078
Schaffner, Bertram, 2695
Schamberg, I. L., 2417
Schechner, Richard, 2735
Scheinfeld, Amram, 539
Scherber, John, 2516
Schickel, Richard, 1024, 1025
Schilder, Paul, 1668, 2418, 2419
Schlegel, Richard L., 2922
Schmideberg, Melitta, 2420
Schmidt, E., 2421-23, 2550-52
Schmitthoff, C. M., 1387
Schneck, Jerome M., 2424-26
Schneiders, A., 2736
Schockley, Francis M., 2427
Schofield, Michael, 98, 829, 2428
Schonning, L., 2423
Schott, Webster, 684
Schreiber, Flora R., 1026, 2429
Schrenk-Notzing, Albert, 99
Schufeldt, R. W., 2430
Schumach, Murray, 685, 686

Schur, Edwin M., 540, 2717
Schwartz, Louis B., 1388, 1389
Schwartz, M. N., 2130
Schwartz, Richard D., 351
Schwarz, Hedwig, 2431
Schwerin, E., 2081
Schwinn, Tom L., 1393
Scott, Edward M., 2432
Scott, Marvin B., 2737
Scott, Peter D., 541, 2433, 2738
Scott, T. R., 2434
Sechrist, Lee, 2435
Secor, Neale A., 542
Segal, M. M., 2436
Segard, C. P., 2437
Seiden, Melvin, 2740
Seidenberg, R., 2438
Seifried, Stanley F., 2516
Selby, Hubert J., 3115
Selby, James, 3069
Selling, Lowell S., 543, 2439
Seltzer, A. L., 1980
Selzer, M. L., 2255
Serban, George, 2440
Severinghaus, E. L., 2441
Seward, G. H., 2442
Sewell, Mark L., 2923
Shackleton, Edward R., 200
Shannon, William V., 1235
Sharpley, Anne, 688, 689
Shaskan, Donald, 2455
Shaver, Philip, 1569a
Shaw, George Bernard, 1032
Shaw, Herbert, 2925
Shearer, M., 2456
Sheed, Wilfrid, 1033, 1236
Sheedy, Charles, 1392
Sheppe, William M., 2457
Sherman, Irene C., 2458
Sherman, Mandel, 2458
Sherrill, Robert G., 1034
Sherwin, Robert V., 544, 2459, 2460, 2741
Shields, James, 545, 1981

Shils, Edward, 2742
Shinn, Roger L., 546, 1237
Shlien, J. M., 1980
Shneidman, Edwin S., 547, 2461, 2462
Shugar, G., 2141
Sidel, Victor W., 1037
Siegal, Lewis J., 2463
Siegel, Benjamin A., 2149
Silber, A., 2464
Silver, George A., 1038
Silver, Henry, 2926
Silverberg, William V., 2465
Silverman, Daniel, 2466
Silverstein, Shel, 1039
Simms, Hector, 2927
Simon, C., 201
Simon, Robert I., 2467
Simon, William, 548, 1160, 2676, 2743, 2744
Simons, R. C., 2309
Simonsen, D. G., 2337
Sines, Jacob O., 549
Singer, M., 2468
Sinistrari, Ludovico, 100
Sipprelle, Carl N., 2469
Sjostedt, Elsie M., 2470
Skipper, J. K., Jr., 2711a
Slater, Don, 2930-33
Slater, Eliot, 545, 550, 2471-73
Slater, Patrick, 2473
Slavson, S. R., 2474
Slochower, Harry, 2475
Slough, M. C., 1393
Slovenko, Ralph, 551, 1394-96
Smail, R. C., 1043
Smalldon, John L., 2476
Smart, Mollie S., 1044
Smith, A. E., 2934
Smith, Alexander B., 2477
Smith, A. P., 2478
Smith, B. L., 1238
Smith, Charles E., 1397, 2479, 2480
Smith, Colin, 1048

Smith, Durand, 2482
Smith, E. Parkinson, 552
Smith, Favor R., 1302
Smith, Grove B., 2483
Smith, Julie, 691
Smith, Leon J., 1908
Smitt, Jarl W., 2484
Socarides, Charles W., 101, 553, 2485-89
Society for Individual Rights, 202-05
Soddy, Kenneth, 2491, 2492
Solyom, L., 2493
Sommers, Montagu, 100
Sonnenschein, Donald, 2494, 2745
Sontag, L. W., 1399
Sontag, Susan, 1050
Speckman, James, 692
Spence, James R., 1400
Spencer, J. C., 2747
Spencer, S. J. G., 260, 2495
Spevack, Norman R., 2938
Speyer, N., 2496
Spicer, Bart, 3070
Spiegel, Leo A., 2497
Spier, Leslie, 2747
Sprague, George S., 2498
Sprague, W. D., 102, 554
Sprince, Marjorie P., 2499
Srnec, J., 2500
Stafford-Clark, David, 1401, 2501, 2502
Stanley-Jones, D., 1607, 2503-08
Star, Jack, 1055, 1056
Starr, J. P., 2939
Stearn, Jess, 103, 104
Stebbins, Phillip E., 1403
Steinberg, J., 2309
Steiner, Lee R., 2940
Steiner, Lucius B., 105
Stekel, Hilda, 2509
Stekel, Wilhelm, 106, 107, 555, 556, 2510
Stephens, Barbara, 2941

319

Timm, Oreon K., 2553
Tinney, J. S., 1242
Tobin, William J., 112
Tolor, Alexander, 1775
Tong, J. E., 2554
Towne, Alfred, 1076
Treese, Robert L., 206
Trentacoste, Palma, 700
Trentzsch, Philip, 1977
Trese, Leo J., 1244
Trethowan, W. H., 1592
Trexler, Edgar R., 1245
Trice, E. R., 2196, 2559-61
Trilling, Diana, 1079
Trilling, Lionel, 1080
Trimbos, C. J., 2758
Tripp, C. A., 1246, 2947
Trosman, H., 2613
Tufo, G. F., 2562
Turnell, John, 3075
Turner, R. E., 2244-46, 2563, 2677, 2759

U

Ubell, Earl, 701
Ujhely, Valentine A., 2565
Ullerstam, Lars, 566
Ullman, Paul S., 2760
United Church of Christ, 207
United Presbyterian Church in U. S. A., 208
U. S. Congress, 209-17
U. S. Executive Departments, 218-25b
Usill, Harley V., 89
Utley, Thomas E., 226

V

Vacek, Albert E., 1408a
Vallance, M., 2219
Vanden Bergh, R. L., 2566
Van den Haag, Ernest, 227, 567, 568, 2949
Vander Veldt, James H., 569

Vann, Gerald, 1247, 1248
Van Velzen, V., 2362
Vedder, Clyde B., 113
Velikovsky, I., 2567
Verden, P., 2215
Vidal, Gore, 1088, 1089, 3076-78, 3096, 3116
Vilhotti, Anthony J., 2569, 2761
Vincent, Ben W., 1249
Vines, H. W. C., 1669
Voltaire, 570

W

Wacker, Denise, 702, 703
Wade, Carlson, 114, 115
Waggoner, R. W., 2570, 2762
Wagner, Edwin W., 2571
Wahl, Charles W., 124, 572
Wahl, Loren, 3079
Wainwright, Loudon, 1091
Walbran, B., 2409
Waldhorn, H. W., 2572
Walker, Edward L., 2573
Walker, Gerald, 3079a
Walker, Kenneth, 22, 573-75, 2574
Walker, W. H., 2575
Walman, Hal, 704
Walters, O. S., 2576
Walters, R. H., 1875
Waltrip, Bob, 2953, 2954
Wand, J. W. C., 1092
Wang, Christine, 2251
Ward, David A., 2763
Ward, Jack L., 2577
Waring, Paul, 228
Warkentin, John, 2307
Warner, Rex, 1093
Wasserman, Sidney, 2578, 2764
Watson, Angus, 1096
Watson, C. G., 2579
Wattron, John R., 2580
Watts, Alan, 1097

Woetzel, Robert K., 1112
Wohl, R. R., 2613
Wolbarst, A. L., 2614
Wolf, Ruth, 1113
Wolfe, Burton H., 1114
Wolfenden, John, 127, 1115, 2615
Wolff, Herman K., 133
Wolfgang, Michael S., 588
Wolfson, William, 2619
Wollheim, Richard, 1117
Wolman, Benjamin B., 2620
Wolowitz, Howard M., 264, 2621
Wolpe, Joseph, 2511
Wood, D. Z., 2434
Wood, Frank C. Jr., 2960, 2961
Wood, G., 2241
Wood, Robert W., 128, 2962-64
Woodward, L. T., 589, 590
Woodward, Mary, 2769
Wootton, Barbara, 1119
Worchel, P., 2114
Worthy, Ken, 129-31
Wortis, Joseph, 591, 2622-24
Wray, David P., 2965
Wright, Clifford A., 1882, 2625-30
Wright, James C., 1912
Wright, M. E., 1783
Wrong, Dennis H., 1120
Wulff, Moshe, 2631
Wyden, Peter and Barbara, 132, 713

Y

Yaker, Henri M., 2770
Yalom, Irvin D., 2632
Yamahiro, R. S., 2633
Yankowski, John S., 133
Yarnell, Helen, 2534
Yolles, Stanley F., 132
Young, W. C., 2635

Yourcenar, Marguerite, 3083

Z

Zamansky, Harold S., 2155, 2636, 2637
Zane, Maitland, 714
Zarrilli, C. L., 592
Zeff, Leo J., 2966
Zeichner, Abraham M., 2638
Zierhoffer, Marion, 2518
Zion, Sidney E., 715
Zlotlow, M., 2639
Zoghby, Guy A., 1423
Zucker, Robert A., 2640
Zuckerman, Stanley B., 2641
Zuger, B., 2642